NICK NICKELS'
CANOE
CANADA

to daddy
happy 60th birthday

love
jane & neil

Sept. 17, 1978

VNR **Van Nostrand Reinhold Ltd.** *Toronto*
New York, Cincinnati, London, Melbourne

ISBN   0 442 29930 3
Library of Congress Number 75 43066

Design by Brant Cowie/Artplus
Printed and bound in Canada by the Bryant
Press Ltd.

Cover photograph by Bruce Litteljohn

Photographs

Grateful acknowledgement is made to the following for permission to reproduce the photo-
graphs on the pages indicated:

British Columbia Government   192
Canada Government Travel Bureau   75, 188
Canadian Government Office of Tourism   viii, 185
Canadian Government Surveys and Mapping
Branch   244
Nancy Fairly   131, 140
Government of the Yukon Territory Tourism
and Information Branch   219, 222
Information Canada Phototheque   174, 229, 233
Information Canada Phototheque: photo by
Ted Grant   90
Michael Keating   124
Bruce Litteljohn   13
Manitoba Government Travel   141
Emmy Nakai   59
National Capital Commission   71
Newfoundland and Labrador Department of
Tourism and Phil Smith   2, 11
Nova Scotia Communications and Information
Centre   17
Office du film du Quebec   42
Ontario Ministry of Industry and Tourism   151
Parks Canada,   22, 35, 51, 109, 177, 205, 214
Prudham's Studio Ltd., courtesy of Mike Oude-
mans   28
The Public Archives of Canada   31, 114, 153,
   197, 217
Saskatchewan Government   158, 165, 172
Kirk Wipper   39, 55

The author   255, 257, 260, 262, 269, 270, 271

76 77 78 79 80 81 82 83 8 7 6 5 4 3 2 1

CONTENTS

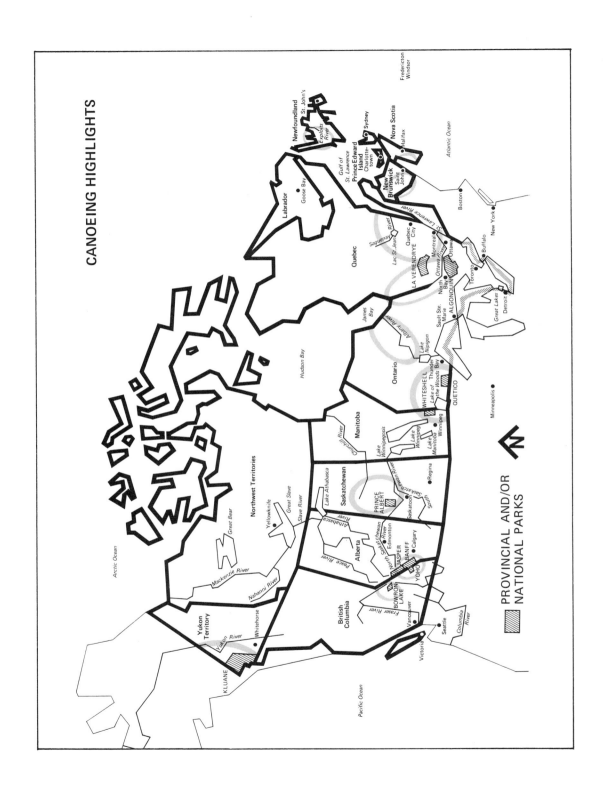

CANOEING HIGHLIGHTS

PROVINCIAL AND/OR NATIONAL PARKS

PREFACE

Canoe Canada really began about fifty-five years ago when I embarked on my first canoe trip. Almost continuously since then I've been collecting information about canoeing in Canada. Since 1971 I have written and privately published much material about canoe routes in Canada. My collection of private letters from the readers of these small books shows that canoeists want information on all aspects of the sport — for all areas of the country. I hope that this new book will finally fill that need by collecting in one place all the information I have been able to amass. It will answer such vague questions as: "Where can I go canoeing for two weeks?"; or, such specific ones as: "When does the blackfly season finish in Ontario?", or, "Is there air charter support for canoeists in Manitoba?"

The prime purpose of the book is to provide detailed information on over 600 canoe routes and alternative routes from coast to coast. As there are far too many of these for one man to paddle, even in several active lifetimes, I must express my appreciation to many friends and colleagues who have made their own personal observations available to me. To make this guide as reliable and up-to-date as possible, I have also consulted the many publications of the federal and provincial governments, as well as any aerial reconnaissance reports available, to glean the most useful bits of information from everywhere. Of course, the amount of information varies with each route. As a general rule, the most popular routes are described in the greatest detail. At the very least, however, enough information is always provided for each route to enable the canoe-tripper to begin planning a safe, enjoyable journey.

This guide has been organized to help the reader find all the information he needs quickly and easily. As far as is possible, everything has been broken down into logical, compact units. For each province or territory there is a chapter that begins with a general description of the physical characteristics of the region, giving the reader a broad picture of the canoeing opportunities in that province. A short history of the province, as well as information on climate and fishing, all help you to decide if you would like to visit in that province.

The canoe routes within each province are also grouped — usually by drainage basins. Maps have been provided to show these major divisions and to identify a few important lakes, rivers, and other places that can be useful as access points or for orientation purposes. Thus, it is easy for anyone, whether familiar with an area or not, to pinpoint a spot that will suit his canoeing needs.

Data Blocks Once you have located the particular area you wish to canoe in, you can quickly obtain basic information for all routes in the area by skimming through the data blocks at the beginning of the route descriptions. These blocks give such information as the name of the river, the length of the route, the estimated length of time it takes to paddle, access points, the number of portages, and most importantly, the names and numbers of the relevant topographical maps.

Maps The maps listed in this book are of three basic types: the Federal Topographic Series published by the Map Office in Ottawa; provincial topographic maps published by the individual provinces; and special maps published by municipalities, provincial parks, forestry districts, etc. If a map is not in the Federal Topographic Series, I have indicated this in the listing. For example, maps published by the Government of Ontario have the notation (Ont.) after the map number.

Maps are the most important part of your advance planning. In order to get a clear picture of the river that you will be travelling you must study the appropriate maps well in advance. It is important to order all of the maps listed because most of the routes extend over more than one. The "How to Read a Topographical Map" chapter on p. 243 tells you how to read, order, and understand a topographical map. A good set of maps, along with the basic information this book provides, will enable you to plan your trip thoroughly before you ever leave home.

Route Descriptions Following the data blocks, in most cases, is more detailed information on the route — lakes encountered, portages, start and finish points, diversions, camping sites and alternate routes. I would like to emphasize that the routes have not been graded according to water difficulties. I feel that it is impossible to predict the behaviour of a natural force such as a river, governed as it is by the climate and the vagaries of the seasons. Careful planning and personal investigation should provide the standards by which routes are graded.

Outfitters and Air Charter Companies To aid you further in planning, I have listed various map sources, outfitters, and air charter companies at the end of each chapter. I must warn you that, as canoe-tripping becomes more and more popular, you should book well in advance for package canoe trips and air charters.

Tips on Canoe Camping The last section of the book provides a summary of my own personal suggestions and practices in the following areas: The choice of gear and how to use it properly; the study of water and weather; bugs and what to do about them; how to use topographic maps effectively; ground signalling for survival; the care of equipment when it is not in use — in short, as much useful, practical information as I have been able to gather during my years as a guide and teacher.

NEWFOUNDLAND & LABRADOR

The Province of Newfoundland and Labrador comprises the island proper (43,359 square miles) and Labrador on the mainland (112,826 square miles). The total area of the province makes it the seventh largest in land mass size in the nation. The two land areas are separated by the Strait of Belle Isle, nine and a half miles wide at its narrowest point.

The deeply indented coastline of the island of Newfoundland is low and rocky, rising up to an inland plateau. The highest elevation is in the Great Northern Peninsula, where one peak in the Long Range Mountains reaches a height of 2,651 feet. Rivers running to the sea are short compared to mainland rivers. The Exploits River, for example, is 153 miles long and contains a drop of 140 feet at Grand Falls. The Gander River is the next longest (102 miles).

Newfoundland has forty-five provincial parks, fourteen provincial park reserves, and two national parks, Gros Morne (650 square miles) and Terra Nova (153 square miles). The Trans-Canada Highway (575 miles in Newfoundland) joins Port-aux-Basques in the southwest to the capital city, St. John's, on the Avalon Peninsula in the southeast, as well as such other large communities **en route** as Corner Brook, Grand Falls and Gander. The province's only railway, the Canadian National, parallels the highway. Some paved and many gravel highways reach out in all directions to coastal communities, even to St. Anthony and the nearby Viking landfall, l'Anse-aux-Meadows, at the northernmost tip of the island.

While the fisheries are the leading employer in Newfoundland, they account for only ten percent of the provincial wealth. Two pulp and paper plants — Corner Brook's is the largest integrated mill in the world — produce more than 585,000 tons a year. A low-grade iron mine and a copper-lead-zinc property are not producing at the present time.

Mainland Labrador is about three times the size of the island. It is chiefly a rock plateau rising gradually from the sea. It levels off at 2,000 feet and then drops away to the west and north amid rolling hills. Consequently most of the rivers drain into the Atlantic Ocean or the Gulf of St. Lawrence.

Spectacular mountain ranges stretch along Labrador's Atlantic Coast from the midway point to its northern tip. Starting at midway are the Kiglapait Mountains, which give way to the Kaumajet Range, with two 3,500 foot peaks, and the most northerly range, the Torngat Mountains, with seven massive peaks soaring to their highest point at 5,500 feet. All of the mountains rise abruptly out of the sea. A much lower range, the Mealy Mountains, runs about 150 miles east-west along the south shore of Lake Melville.

The Lake Melville valley extends 300 miles inland from the sea and drains southern Labrador via the Churchill, Goose, Beaver and Naskaupi Rivers. The harnessing of Churchill Falls for hydro power has flooded hundreds of square miles of lakes on the plateau, often making even recent maps out of date.

Labrador has iron ore fields producing very high-grade ore near the Quebec boundary. Wabush and Labrador City are the chief operating centres in this area.

Facing page. A fishing camp in Gros Morne National Park on Newfoundland's west coast. The park includes the most spectacular of the Long Range Mountains of the Great Northern Peninsula. Along its rugged coast are fine beaches and shifting sand dunes. Tucked away in dense inland forests, mountain streams and lakes provide good freshwater fishing, especially for trout and salmon.

Some 200 miles of the Quebec North Shore and Labrador Railway, running north-south between the Quebec towns of Sept-Iles and Schefferville, lie within Labrador. There are two gravel roads: a fifty mile stub running northwest from the Menehik railway siding, and a 150 mile road from Churchill Falls to the Lake Melville basin. In addition to the inland communities already mentioned, there is Goose Bay, a continental air hub, and the nearby communities of Happy Valley and North West River.

Draped in the shadows of rugged cliffs overhanging Western Brook Pond, this lone canoeist finds complete solitude. Western Brook Pond is located in Newfoundland's Gros Morne National Park.

Climate

The climate of the province can be described in two ranges, coastal-maritime and inland-maritime, to match both the island and the mainland, although the latter must be further sub-divided as indicated by the following climatic tables:

Newfoundland	Mean Temperature In Fahrenheit (Celsius)				Rainfall In Mean Inches (Millimetres)	
	Min		Max			
Southern (St. John's)						
June	42.9	(6.1)	60.9	(16.1)	2.59	(65.8)
July	51.5	(10.8)	68.7	(20.4)	2.43	(61.7)
August	53.1	(11.7)	68.7	(20.4)	4.45	(113.0)
Central (Grand Falls)						
June	42.9	(6.1)	64.1	(17.8)	3.06	(77.7)
July	52.5	(11.4)	72.9	(22.7)	3.27	(83.1)
August	51.8	(11.0)	70.8	(21.6)	3.95	(100.3)
Northern (St. Anthony)						
June	38.5	(3.6)	54.2	(12.3)	2.92	(74.2)
July	47.0	(8.3)	63.1	(17.3)	2.71	(68.8)
August	48.7	(9.3)	62.8	(17.1)	3.42	(86.9)

Labrador	Mean Temperature in Fahrenheit (Celsius)				Rainfall In Mean Inches (Millimetres)	
	Min		Max			
Central-Coastal (Cartwright)						
June	37.4	(3.0)	65.5	(18.6)	2.97	(75.4)
July	44.9	(7.2)	65.4	(18.6)	3.33	(84.6)
August	45.0	(7.2)	63.0	(17.2)	3.33	(84.6)
Continental-Inland (Churchill Falls)						
June	38.6	(3.7)	55.6	(13.1)	3.42	(86.9)
July	46.8	(8.2)	66.0	(18.9)	3.65	(92.7)
August	46.9	(8.3)	63.5	(17.5)	3.15	(80.0)
Northern (Fort Chimo, Que.)						
June	35.3	(1.8)	53.9	(12.2)	1.83	(46.5)
July	42.4	(5.8)	62.5	(16.9)	2.02	(51.3)
August	42.3	(5.7)	59.2	(15.1)	2.31	(58.7)

Fishing

The fishing season for all species comes within the summer canoeing season. The bag limits for the various species are as follows:

Salmon	4 per day
Speckled Trout	24 per day or the number of trout totalling 10 pounds in weight, plus one trout, whichever is the lesser
Lake Trout	4 per day
Northern Pike	24 per day
Artic Char	4 per day

Salmon fishing licenses for single nonresidents cost $20.00 for two weeks or $30.00 for the season. Family licenses for two weeks cost $30.00.

No person is permitted to fish for salmon in inland waters unless he holds a salmon fishing license. For the salmon rivers affected write:

Federal Department of the Environment,
Building 302
Box 5667
Pleasantville
St. John's, Newfoundland.

Nonresidents fishing for salmon in the waters of Newfoundland and Labrador must be accompanied by licensed guides — one guide for each two sportsmen.

Non resident (single) speckled trout fishing licenses cost $5.00 per season. Non resident (family) licenses cost $7.50 per season.

The above regulations came into effect in 1974. Canoeists should check in advance of visiting Newfoundland and Labrador to ensure that changes have not been made.

History

As the island of Newfoundland is closer to the Old World than any other part of North America, it was discovered by Europeans at a very early date.

First came the Vikings out of Iceland settling briefly on the island's northern tip in about the year 1000 **A.D.** It is believed that fishermen from southwestern Europe were harvesting the Grand Banks fishery prior to 1400. Documented dates of the expeditions of European explorers begin with John Cabot, for England, in 1497. He was followed by Gaspar and Miguel Corte Real, Fagundes and Gomez for Portugal, and, in 1534, Jacques Cartier for France.

Sir Humphrey Gilbert proclaimed British sovereignty over the island in 1583, making it the first English colony and the beginning of the British Empire. The first English settlement was created in 1610 on Conception Bay, but further expansion of settlement was discouraged by pirate raids and by England's reluctance to draw foreign attention to the fabulous Grand Banks fishing grounds.

A period of little development lasted for about 250 years, but it is during this time that there occurred one of the saddest episodes in Newfoundland's history. The Beothuks, the Indians native to the island, were ruthlessly hunted down and exterminated by the settlers and their Micmac allies brought to the colony from Nova Scotia for this express purpose in the mid 1770's. The last Beothuk died in a St. John's hospital in 1829. Today there are no Indians on the island of Newfoundland as a result of this infamous example of genocide.

Proclaimed a self-governing colony in 1855, financial problems, made worse by the depression, forced Newfoundland to relinquish self-government to a commission under the British Crown in 1934. In 1949 Newfoundland joined Canada as the tenth province.

The coast of mainland Labrador has had a rich history as well. The territory's early inhabitants were the Montagnais and Naskapi peoples. The former favored the heavy, spruce woodlands of the St. Lawrence shore and the inland Churchill river basin, while the latter preferred the high, open tundra of the north. To this day these remain the territories of the two tribes, which now total about 3,000 people. Eskimos from Ungava Bay and Hudson Strait infiltrated the upper half of the Atlantic coastal region, as evidenced by the profusion of settlements, bays, inlets, islands and rivers with names of Eskimo origin.

Vikings are believed to have coasted along the shores of Labrador in 986 **A.D.**, and described it in their sagas, naming it Helluland. Early Venetian, Portuguese and English explorers later skirted the coast, while French and English fishermen and whalers occasionally set foot on land.

French-Canadian seigneurs from Quebec were the first settlers, in 1703, on the coast of the Strait of Belle Isle. Acadians from the Magdalen Islands came to the same region in about 1857. In 1824, the Hudson's Bay Company established its first post trading into Labrador at Fort Chimo, Quebec, and eight more posts by 1857. Moravian missionary-traders also established themselves on the coast, as did the traders from France, the Revillion Frères. During the War of 1812, nearly all coastal communities were plundered by American privateers.

A brief history of Newfoundland would not be complete without mention of its role as a suitable geographic base for some great scientific accomplishments: the first landfall of the Atlantic cable from Europe (1858); the first wireless signals received from Europe by Marconi (1901); the first successful west to east transatlantic flight by Alcock and Brown (1919).

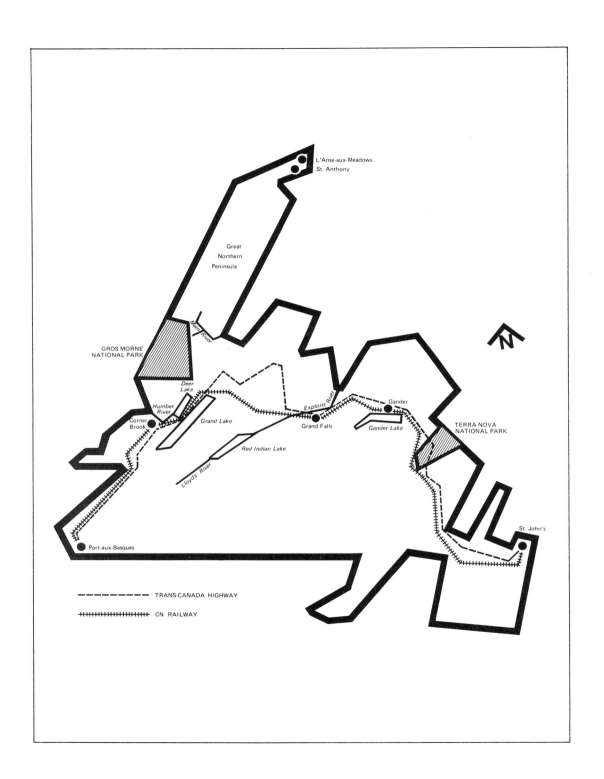

L'Anse-aux-Meadows
St. Anthony

Great
Northern
Peninsula

Main River

GROS MORNE
NATIONAL PARK

Deer
Lake

Humber
River

Corner
Brook

Grand Lake

Exploits River

Gander

Grand Falls

Gander Lake

TERRA NOVA
NATIONAL PARK

Red Indian Lake

Lloyds River

St. John's

Port-aux-Basques

- - - - - - - - - - TRANS-CANADA HIGHWAY

++++++++++++++++ CN RAILWAY

Newfoundland Routes

The Provincial Parks Service, Department of Economic Development of Newfoundland, is acutely aware that many of its fine canoeable waterways are not being developed as quickly as it would like. The department has received assistance from the federal Department of Indian and Northern Affairs in having certain waterways surveyed by teams of expert wilderness canoeists, both on the island and in mainland Labrador. These routes are noted below as having been identified by the Wild Rivers Survey.

1 HUMBER RIVER

Length   110 miles (177 km)
Approx trip time   13 - 18 days
Access   By charter floatplane from Deer Lake
Maps   Red Indian Lake 12A
Sandy Lake 12H
Gros Morne 12H/12E
Silver Mountain 12H/11W and E
Cormack 12H/6W and E
Deer Lake 12H/3W
Corner Brook 12A/13W and E
Pasadena 12H/4E

The Humber River is situated in western Newfoundland, mostly above 49° N latitude, between 57° W and 58° W longitude, flowing southwest from its source.

Segment 1 Start at Osmond's Pond and paddle through Osmond's Pond East, Upper Lake and Angus Lake to Burnt Hill Pond.
Segment 2   Burnt Hill Pond to Birchy Basin
Segment 3   Birchy Basin to Sir Richard Squires Memorial Park and campsite on Highway 2, then to Deer Lake and Deer Lake town
Segment 4   Deer Lake to Boom Siding and then to Corner Brook town. *Finish.*
    Segments 3 and 4 are subject to log drives and may be obstructed. Segments 1 and 2 are very rugged and isolated. Canoeists attempting them should be skilled and physically fit and should plan their trip carefully.

2 LLOYDS—EXPLOITS RIVERS

Length   124 miles (200 km)
Approx trip time   10 - 15 days
Access   By charter floatplane from Deer Lake
Maps   King George IV Lake 12A/4W
Puddle Pond 12A/5E and W
Victoria Lake 12A/6W
Star Lake 12A/11E and W
Lake Ambrose 12A/10W and E
Buchans 12A/15E
Badger 12A/16E and W
Grand Falls 12D/13
Red Indian Lake 12A
Gander 12D

This route covers Newfoundland's most important river system. The Lloyds River and the Victoria River (unnavigable due to dam construction) are the main branches of the Exploits River. Their headwaters rise in southwest Newfoundland and they empty into the sea at the Bay of Exploits. Canoeing ends at the town of Grand Falls.

Segment 1 Start at King George IV Lake. Paddle NE to Lloyds River, which parallels Annieopsquotch Mountain range, to Lloyds Lake.
Segment 2   Lloyds Lake to Lloyds River, and then to Red Indian Lake.
Segment 3   Red Indian Lake (pulp wood obstructions and heavily-littered shorelines) to Exploits (River) Dam
Segment 4   Exploits River to town of Badger (Highway 50 and Trans-Canada intersection), and then to 2 miles (3km) above the town of Grand Falls. *Finish*
    The Wild Rivers Survey crew found the maps to be frequently unreliable, with rapids and falls often not shown.
    This route is very rugged and for experienced canoeists only.

3 MAIN RIVER

Length   33.5 miles (54 km)
Approx trip time   5 - 8 days
Access   By charter floatplane from Deer Lake
Maps   Sandy Lake 12H

Main River 12H/14W and E
Silver Mountain 12H/11E
Jackson's Arm 12H/15W

The Main River, in the Great Northern Peninsula of Newfoundland, rises east of the Long Range Mountains, and flows east and southeast to the coast at Sop's Arm (provincial park site and settlement).

Start at Four Ponds Lake. From there the Main River drops about 1,225 feet in elevation to tide level at the coast.

The Wild Rivers Survey crew divided the route into five segments: (1) Four Ponds Lake; (2) Upper River; (3) Big Steady; (4) Rapid River; (5) Deep Valley.

Finish at Sop's Arm Provincial Park camp-site, Highway 77,

This route is noted for spectacular scenery and salmon spawning waters. Fishing is subject to Canada Department of Fisheries regulations. Canoeist must have considerable white water experience.

 # Labrador Routes

The Provincial Parks Service, Department of Economic Development of Newfoundland, is acutely aware that many of its fine canoeable waterways are not being developed as quickly as it would like. The department has received assistance from the federal Department of Indian and Northern Affairs in having certain waterways surveyed by teams of expert wilderness canoeists, both on the island and in mainland Labrador. These routes are noted below as having been identified by the Wild Rivers Survey.

In Labrador, during the fire season, each two non-resident travellers are required by law to hold a forest travel permit and to be accompanied by a licensed guide.

4 PETIT MECATINA RIVER

Length 190 miles (306 km)
Access By charter floatplane from Wabush, Labrador
Maps Lac Brulé 13D
Minipi Lake 13C
Natashquan River 12N
St. Augustin 12D
Harrington Harbour 12J

The Petit Mecatina River originates in southwest Labrador, flows southeast 240 miles, crosses the Labrador-Quebec interprovincial boundary and empties into the Gulf of St. Lawrence.

Start on the Petit Mecatina River at a point about 15 miles (24 km) above Cape

Mystery, paddle downstream through Lac Fourmont, Lac Donquan and Lac Le Breton, to *finish* at the St. Lawrence River.

Canoeists should make aerial charter reconnaisance of the canyon portion of river, about 48 miles (77 km) from the river mouth, before attempting this route. A very dangerous segment necessitates a 15 mile portage around the canyon.

The upper portion of the Petit Mecatina River is unattractive. The extremely dangerous canyon sector is for very expert canoeists only.

The description of this route is derived from an aerial reconnaisance report of the 1972 Wild Rivers Survey.

5 NASKAUPI RIVER

Access By charter land vehicle from Goose Bay
Map Kasheshibaw Lake 13L

This once great river, originating on the Labrador Plateau and emptying into Hamilton Inlet at Grand Lake, has "lost all resemblance to its original character". Man-made dykes and reservoirs have been created for the great Churchill Falls power development.

Start at Orma Lake Dyke, paddle downstream on Naskaupi River through Caribou Lake, Wuchusk Lake, Seal Lake and Naskaupi Lake, passing the mouth of the Red Wine River to *finish* at Grand Lake at North West River settlement.

This route is for intermediate canoeists.

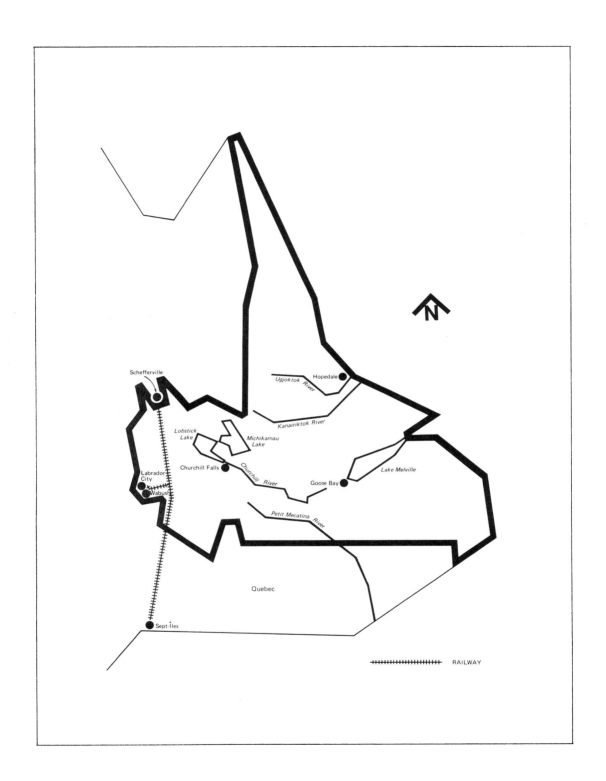

Schefferville

Ugjoktok River

Hopedale

Kanairiktok River

Lobstick
Lake

Michikamau
Lake

Churchill Falls

Labrador
City

Churchill River

Wabush

Goose Bay

Lake Melville

Petit Mecatina River

Quebec

Sept-Îles

N

╫╫╫╫╫╫╫╫╫╫╫╫ RAILWAY

The description of this route is derived from an aerial reconnaisance report of the 1972 Wild Rivers Survey.

6 GOOSE RIVER

Length About 85 miles (137 km)
Access By charter floatplane from Goose Bay
Maps Winokapau Lake 13E
Goose Bay 13F

The river headwaters originate at the small lakes on Hamilton Uplands, about 85 miles west of the village of Goose Bay. Goose River flows east 100 miles through the Hamilton and Mecatina Plateaux to Goose Bay on Lake Melville.

Start on Goose River, portaging around Goose Falls and then on to *finish* at the settlement of Goose Bay.

This route is for experienced white water canoeists only. It involves much line hauling and rugged portaging.

The description of this route is derived from an aerial reconnaisance report of the 1972 Wild Rivers Survey.

7 UGJOKTOK RIVER

Length About 113 miles (182 km)
Approx trip time 9 days
Access By charter floatplane from Goose Bay or Schefferville
Maps Mistastin Lake 13M
Hopedale 13N

Ugjoktok River, lying above 55° N latitude between W 60° and W 63° longitude, flows east from the Labrador-Quebec boundary to Ugjoktok Bay on the east coast of Labrador.

Fly by floatplane charter east from Schefferville, Quebec, to *start* at a point on the river 26 miles (42 km) below the lake site of Border Beacon (NS2942). Paddle downstream 58 miles to the mouth of the Harp River; take a sidetrip 8 miles to Harp Lake and return 8 miles to the main river. Paddle east 45 miles, passing the mouth of the Shapio River to Ugjoktok Bay on the coast and *finish* at or near Hopedale community. To reach Hopedale, you will paddle about 30 miles along a tidal inlet.

Fly by prearranged charter floatplane to the Goose Bay airport to connect with scheduled airline flights.

8 KANAIRIKTOK RIVER

Length 125 miles (201 km)
Access By charter floatplane from Schefferville
Maps Kasheshibaw Lake 13/L
Snegamook Lake 13/K
Hopedale 13/N

Fly by charter floatplane east from Schefferville to *start* at Shipiskan Lake. Paddle downstream through Snegamook Lake and *finish* at Kanairiktok Bay on the east coast of Labrador.

Fly out by prearranged charter floatplane to the Goose Bay airport to connect with scheduled airline flights.

Kanairiktok River is recommended for novice canoeists.

 Map Sources

Canada Mapping Office, 615 Booth Street, Ottawa, Ontario, is the chief supplier of topographical maps. These maps are also available from the following agents in Newfoundland:

J.W. Randall Limited
Box 757 West Street
Corner Brook, Newfoundland

Grand Falls Sport Shop Limited
Box 254
Grand Falls, Newfoundland

Crown Lands Division
Department of Mines, Agriculture & Resources
Confederation Building
St. John's, Newfoundland

Facing page. The rockiness of Newfoundland's lake and mountain areas is evident from this view of Western Brook Pond. The rugged barrenness of these lakes seems at once remote and intimate—an atmosphere quite unlike anything found elsewhere in the Atlantic Provinces.

For a provincial road map and any lure literature write:

Newfoundland & Labrador
Tourist Development Office
Confederation Building
St. John's, Newfoundland

 Outfitters

Goose Bay Outfitters
Box 171
Happy Valley, Labrador

 Air Charter Services

Canoeists requiring airlift service should write well in advance to the following companies based in Newfoundland and Labrador:

Newfoundland & Labrador
Air Transport Limited
Box 3
Corner Brook, Newfoundland
709/686-2521

Gander Aviation Limited
Box 250
Gander, Newfoundland
709/256-3421

Laurentian Air Service Limited
Box 818
R.R. 5
Ottawa, Ontario. K1G 3N3
613/521-4871
serving Labrador and Northern Quebec

Labrador Airways Limited
Box 219
Goose Bay, Labrador
709/896-2646

To further help canoe trip planners the federal Ministry of Transport lists the following floatplane bases in Newfoundland and Labrador:

Newfoundland Baie Verte, Catalina Harbour, Pinchgut Lake, Roddickton, Stephenville, St. John's, and South Brook

Labrador Cartwright, Churchill Falls, Hopedale, Makkovik, and Red Bay

Facing page. Prince Edward Island offers an ideal setting for the canoeist who enjoys a variety of summer activities. The island boasts Canada's finest white sand beaches and the warmest ocean waters north of Florida. But inland, within walking distance of the beach, there are dense thickets of coniferous forest, good freshwater fishing and a wide range of camping facilities.

PRINCE EDWARD ISLAND

Prince Edward Island, Canada's smallest province, is only 120 miles long and an average of twenty-five miles across (2,184 square miles). It has fourteen outlying islands and is itself smaller than Anticosti Island, Quebec, in the Gulf of St. Lawrence. The Northumberland Strait, which separates the island from the mainland, ranges from nine to twenty-five miles in width.

The coastlines are irregular and sharply indented by bays and inlets, while the land is generally quite level. Its rich, red soil is particularly suitable for mixed farming. Charlottetown is the provincial capital, inhabited by about 25,000 out of a total provincial population of 125,000.

Prince Edward Island has several short rivers, most of them tidal. The longest is navigable for only eighteen miles. It is a province with extensive sand beaches, prompting the tourism department to boast that for bathing, the Gulf Stream-warmed waters are "next to Florida's."

Two fleets of ferries provide the island with frequent service connecting to the mainland: from Cape Tormentine, New Brunswick, to Borden, Prince Edward Island, and from Caribou, Nova Scotia, to Wood Islands, Prince Edward Island.

 Climate

The climate is modified-maritime. The following table is for centrally located Charlottetown:

Prince Edward Island	Mean Temperature In Fahrenheit (Celsius)				Rainfall In Mean Inches (Millimetres)	
	Min		Max			
June	48.7	(9.3)	66.0	(18.9)	3.27	(83.1)
July	57.0	(13.9)	73.3	(22.9)	2.88	(73.2)
August	56.4	(13.6)	71.9	(22.2)	3.64	(92.5)

 History

Jacques Cartier discovered Prince Edward Island in 1534. Originally it was a French colonial fishing concession and settlement was negligible. The British took over the island in 1763. Six years later it was separated from Nova Scotia and made into an independent colony.

Originally laid out in lots and granted to people in England with a claim to Crown patronage, the land was eventually bought from the absentee owners by the colony and then resold to the tenant farmers.

A meeting in Charlottetown in 1864 of representatives from all the colonies of British North America led to Canadian Confederation in 1867. The island did not itself officially become a part of Canada until 1873.

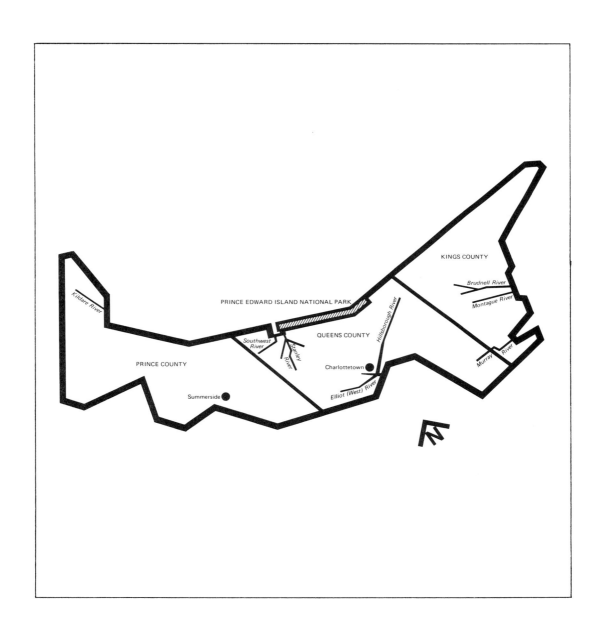

KINGS COUNTY

Brudnell River

Montague River

PRINCE EDWARD ISLAND NATIONAL PARK

Kildare River

QUEENS COUNTY

Southwest River

Stanley River

Hillsborough River

PRINCE COUNTY

Charlottetown

Elliot (West) River

Murray River

Summerside

Prince Edward Island Routes

As there are no marinas and no outfitters in the province, canoeists must supply their own canoes.

Canoeists must be sure to study and abide by the tide tables.

Dividing the province into three counties, the tourism department of Prince Edward Island lists the following rivers for canoeing, none longer than eighteen miles:

Prince County

9 KILDARE RIVER
Approx trip time 1 day
Access By Highways 2 and 153
Map Tignish 21 I/16 W and E

Queens County

10 STANLEY RIVER
Approx trip time 1 day
Access By Highways 2,6 and 8
Map Summerside 11 L/5 W and E

11 SOUTHWEST RIVER
Approx trip time 1 day
Access By Highways 6, 20, 234
Map Summerside 11 L/5 W and E

12 ELLIOTT (WEST) RIVER
Approx trip time 1 day
Access By Highways 19, 1 and 9
Map Summerside 11/L5 W and E

13 HILLSBOROUGH RIVER
Approx trip time 1 day
Access By Highways 2 and 21
Map Mount Stewart 11 L/7 W and E

Kings County

14 MONTAGUE AND BRUDNELL RIVERS
Access By Highways 4 and 3
Map Montague 11 L/2

15 MURRAY RIVER
Approx trip time 1 day
Access By Highways 315 and 202
Map Montague 11 L/2

 Map Sources

Canada Mapping Office, 615 Booth Street, Ottawa, Ontario, is the chief supplier of topographical maps. Within the province, maps may be purchased at the Prince Edward Island Tourist Information Centre, Box 940, Charlottetown, P.E.I. All maps are of a scale 1:50,000 and cost fifty cents per half sheet.

For a provincial road map and any lure literature write:

Travel Bureau
Department of Tourist Development
Box 904
Charlottetown, P.E.I.

 Outfitters

There is no list of outfitters available for Prince Edward Island.

 Air Charter Services

Canoeists have no need for such services in Prince Edward Island.

NOVA SCOTIA

Nova Scotia, Canada's second smallest province (21,425 square miles), is 380 miles long and ranges from 50 to 100 miles across, stretching lengthwise from northeast to southwest along the Atlantic coast. Cape Breton Island, at the province's northern end, comprises one-fifth of the land area.

The southern shores and Cape Breton are bold, rugged and indented, rising to equally rugged, rolling interiors. Shorelines facing the Bay of Fundy and Northumberland Strait have fertile plains and river valleys.

Of special interest on Cape Breton are the Cape Breton Highlands National Park (367 square miles) and the large, sheltered saltwater Bras d'Or Lakes. The mainland boasts Lake Rossignol and many lesser small lake chains. Some 300 short rivers and streams flow north and south to the ocean from the central spine of the province, none of them longer than fifty miles. Many of them have been developed into excellent canoe routes. Located near Lake Rossignol is the Kejimkujik National Park (147.2 square miles). The small Louisbourg National Historic Park is found on Cape Breton.

The main industries of Nova Scotia include: vast undersea coal mines in the region of Sydney; ocean fisheries, which are the second most productive in the nation; pulp and newsprint mills; agriculture, which uses about seventeen percent of the land area; steel making; and tourism.

 ## Climate

Nova Scotia's climate is maritime. An examination of Environment Canada's summer temperature and precipitation reports shows little change from one geographic centre to another.

Nova Scotia	Mean Temperature In Fahrenheit (Celsius)				Rainfall In Mean Inches (Millimetres)	
	Min		Max			
Central (Halifax)						
June	49.5	(9.7)	66.5	(19.2)	3.30	(83.8)
July	56.6	(13.7)	73.3	(22.9)	3.66	(93.0)
August	57.7	(14.3)	72.9	(22.7)	3.73	(94.7)

Previous page. The Medway River, not far from Kejumkujik National Park, is an area of interest to the canoeist and is known for the excellence of its salmon fishing. Nova Scotia's most remarkable wilderness area is found in Cape Breton Highlands National Park, where the Bras d'Or lakes offer a canoeist's paradise deep within forested highlands.

Fishing

The Nova Scotia freshwater fishing regulations are probably the most complex in Canada. The Department of Tourism, Box 130, Halifax, Nova Scotia, issues a free freshwater fishing guide which should be studied carefully before leaving for that province.

There are seven different species of freshwater game fish. Different bag limits apply to each. Dates for early and summer runs also vary for each species of fish.

It is required that all non-resident fishermen hire a guide. No more than three fishermen to one guide is permitted. Fishing license fees are $3.00 for residents and $15.00 for non-residents.

 History

"New Scotland", as it was once known, has had a rich, almost 500 year history as a maritime region. In an era when ships were a dominant mode of transportation for exploration and conquest, Nova Scotia was at the centre of discoveries and development by both the French and English, and of the battles between them.

It is possible that the Vikings were the first to sight and even briefly settle the shores of Nova Scotia in about 1000 **A.D.** However, the first documented sighting was made in 1497, by John Cabot, for England. Cabot was followed in 1524 by Giovanni de Verrazano for Portugal and ten years later by Jacques Cartier for France. Cartier's great successor, Samuel de Champlain, established his first settlement in 1605 at Port Royal on the Bay of Fundy shore. The settlement was later captured by the English from New England in 1690.

The French began construction of Fort Louisbourg on eastern Isle Madame (Cape Breton Island) in 1713. Originally intended to guard the entrace to the Gulf of St. Lawrence and France's vast inland fur empire, it was captured and destroyed by the English in 1758. Today it is being restored to its original awesome grandeur by the National Parks of Canada.

In 1749 the English founded Halifax, on one of North America's greatest sheltered harbours, and at the same time expelled the last of the French settlers, the Acadians, from Grand Pré on Minas Basin. The first Scottish settlers arrived and named the land "New Scotland" in 1773.

Nova Scotia is one of the original four partners in Confederation. The province's history is not without its share of tragedies. Halifax Harbour was nearly totally destroyed during World War I when a ship in the crowded roadstead collided with a munitions ship, resulting in great loss of life and property damage. More than any other province, Nova Scotia cherishes its Scottish heritage, especially in Cape Breton, where the Gaelic language and customs are preserved.

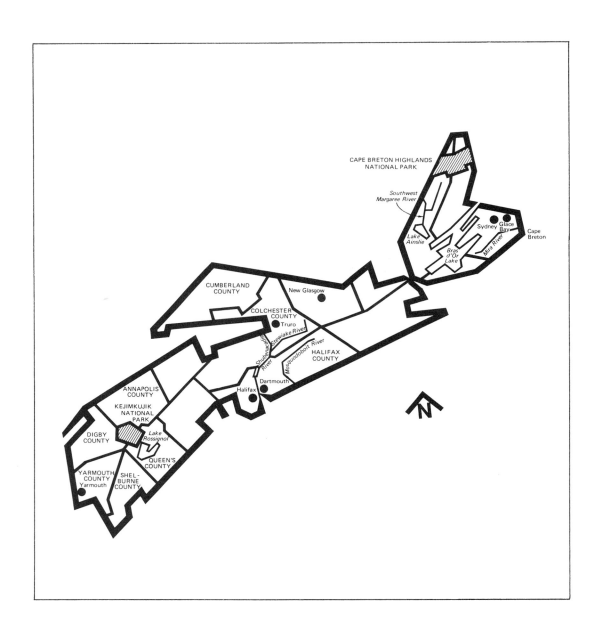

Nova Scotia Routes

Kejimkujik National Park

Kejimkujik (pronounced ke-jim-koo-jik) National Park is situated in the southwestern part of the province where Digby, Annapolis and Queens Counties meet. It is a fine wilderness, camping, canoeing and hiking complex.

Peskowesk Lake, Mersey River, Little River and West River are the four principal bodies of water for canoeing in the park. These offer a total of seven different routes. A park map showing these routes is available from the Parks Service, Department of Indian Affairs and Northern Development, Ottawa, Ontario.

16 KEJIMKUJIK LAKE — PESKOWESK LAKE

Start at Jacques Landing on Kejimkukik Lake, portage to North Cranberry Lake, Puzzle Lake, Coblielle Lake and Peskowesk Lake.

17 KEJIMKUJIK LAKE — MOUNTAIN LAKE — PESKOWESK LAKE

Start from Jacques Landing on Kejimkujik Lake, portage to Mountain Lake and Peskowesk Lake.

18 PESKOWESK LAKE — LOWER SILVER LAKE — PESKOWESK LAKE

Start from portage ends on the two previous routes, paddle into Peskowesk Lake, portage to Hichemakaar Lake, Lower Silver Lake and Back Lake, to *finish* at Peskowesk Lake.

19 PESKOWESK LAKE — BEAVERSKIN LAKE — PESKAWA LAKE

As in the previous routes, *start* from either portage end, paddle into Peskowesk Lake, paddle west, portage to Beaverskin Lake, to Peskawa Lake and Peskowesk Lake. Return.

20 KEJIMKUJIK LAKE — LOON LAKE

Branch south off Kejimkujik Lake and portage to George Lake on Mersey River. *Finish* at Loon Lake on the park boundary. Return or continue on the river.

21 BIG DAM LAKE — JEREMY BAY

Start at Big Dam Lake, portage to Little River, Frozen Ocean Lake, Little River and Central Lake, back to Little River and Jeremy Bay on Kejimkujik Lake. Return.

22 KEJIMKUJIK LAKE — LUXION BROOK

Paddle west on Kejimkujik Lake down the West River to *finish* at about the forks of Luxion Brook. Return.

Cape Breton

23 LAKE AINSLIE — MARGAREE FORKS

Approx trip time 3 hours
Access By unpaved road off Highway 19
Maps Lake Ainslie 11K/3E
Margaree 11K/6E

Start at Scotsville and *finish* at Margaree Forks, Highway 19 crossing.

24 MIRA RIVER

Length 30 miles (48 km)
Approx trip time 3 days
Access By unpaved road off Highway 22
Maps Mira 11F/16W and E
Sydney 11K/1 E
Glace Bay 11 J/4 W

Start at Mira Lake and *finish* at the mouth of the Mira River.

Kejimkujik National Park was created in 1969 to protect Indian pictographs from vandalism. Some of Nova Scotia's finest inland countryside is found within the park. Wildlife inhabiting the park includes black bear, deer, red fox, lynx, otter, beaver, 200 varieties of birds and a greater variety of amphibians and reptiles than can be found anywhere else in eastern Canada.

25 MIRA — SALMON RIVERS

Access By unpaved road off Highway 22
Maps See Mira River above

Start at Mira Lake and take a round trip.

26 PORTREE BRIDGE — MARGAREE FORKS

Approx trip time 6 hours
Access By unpaved road off Highway 19
Maps Margaree 11K/6E
St. Ann's 11K/7 W

Start at Portree. *Finish* at Doyle Bridge near Margaree Forks.

27 SOUTHWEST MARGAREE RIVER

Length 26 miles (42 km)
Approx trip time 2 days
Access By unpaved road off Highway 19
Maps See Portree Bridge above.

Start at Scotsville, go through Lake Ainslie, and *finish* at Margaree Harbour.

Cumberland County

28 LA PLANCH RIVER

Length 15 miles (24 km)
Approx trip time 2 days
Access Inquire at Amherst
Maps Amherst 21H/16E

Start at the north side town of Amherst and go to Round Lake. Return by the same route.

29 PARRSBORO — HANCOCK BROOK

Access By Highway 2
Maps Parrsboro 21H/8W
River Hebert 21H/9W

Start at the town of Parrsboro and *finish* where River Hebert crosses Highway 2.

Colchester County

30 STEWIAKE RIVER
Length 30 miles (48 km)
Approx trip time 2 days
Access Highway 289
Maps Schubenacadie 11E/3 W and E
Upper Mosquodoboit 11E/2W

Start at Upper Stewiake and *finish* at the Stewiake Municipal Park.

31 MOSQUODOBOIT RIVER
Length 60 miles (97 km)
Approx trip time 3 days
Access By Highway 357
Maps See Stewiake River above

Start at the Cariboo Road at Upper Mosquodoboit and *finish* at Meagher's Grant (a bridge at the sawmill).

Halifax County

32 BANOOK LAKE -- SHUBENACADIE
Length 45 miles (72 km)
Approx trip time 2 days
Access Inquire at Dartmouth
Maps Halifax 11D/12E
Uniake 11D/13E
Musquodoboit 11D/14W
Shubenacadie 11E/13W

Start at Banook Lake and *finish* at the Shubenacadie bridge on Highway 2.

33 DARTMOUTH — MAITLAND
Length 62 miles (100 km)
Approx trip time 4 days
Access Inquire at Dartmouth
Maps Truro 11E/6W
Shubenacadie 11E/3W
Musquodoboit 11D/14W
Uniake 11D/13E
Halifax 11D/12E

Start at Banook Lake and *finish* at Maitland.

Annapolis County

34 ANNAPOLIS RIVER — AUBURN — ANNAPOLIS ROYAL
Length 20 miles (32 km)
Approx trip time 2 days
Access By Highway 1
Maps Berwick 21A/2W
Gaspereau Lake 21A/16W
Bridgetown 21A/14E and W

Start at the bridge west of Auburn and *finish* at the Dunromin Campsite.

Digby and Yarmouth Counties

35 LAKE JOLLY — SISSIBOO RIVER
Length 25 miles (40 km)
Approx trip time 3 days
Access Inquire at Bear River
Maps Weymouth 21A/5E and W

Start at Lake Jolly at the end of road from Bear River. *Finish* at the Nova Scotia Power Commission Road crossing of Sissiboo River.

36 SISSIBOO RIVER — WEYMOUTH
Length 20 miles (32 km)
Approx trip time 4 days
Access Inquire at Weymouth
Map Weymouth 21A/5W

Start at Hackmatack Lake and *finish* at Weymouth Bridge, Highway 1.

37 TUSKET RIVER (east branch)
Length 12 miles (19 km)
Approx trip time 1—2 days
Access Inquire at Tusket
Map Wentworth Lake 21A/4E

Start at the east branch of the Tusket River and *finish* at the Kemptville Bridge.

38 LAKE JOLLY — TUSKET RIVER
Length 50 miles (80 km)
Approx trip time 7 days
Access Inquire at Weymouth
Maps Weymouth 21A/5E
Wentworth Lake 21A/4E

Start at the secondary road of Lake Jolly and *finish* at the east branch of the Tusket River.

39 NEW TUSKET — KEMPTVILLE
Length 15 miles (24 km)
Approx trip time 2 days
Access Off Highway 340 — inquire at Tusket

Maps See Lake Jolly — Tusket River above

Start east of New Tusket and *finish* at North Kemptville.

Shelburne County

40 BARRINGTON RIVER
Length 20 miles (32 km)
Access Inquire at Barrington, Highway 3
Map Pubnico 20P/12E

Start at Fairweather on Great Pubnico Lake and *finish* at Barrington.

41 BEAVER DAM LAKE — ROUND BAY
Length 8 miles (13 km)
Approx trip time 2 days
Access Inquire at Shelburne, Highway 3
Map Lockeport 20P/11W

Start at Beaverdam Lake, 10 miles (16 km) west of Shelburne, Highway 3. *Finish* 10 miles (16 km) south of Highway 3 at Birchtown.

42 CLYDE RIVER
Length 15 miles (24 km)
Approx trip time 2 days
Access Inquire at Clyde River, Highway 3
Maps Lake Rossignol 21A/3W
Tusket 20P/13E
Lockeport 20P/11W

Start at Black Lake and *finish* one mile below Clyde River.

43 ROSEWAY RIVER
Length 20 miles (32 km)
Approx trip time 2 days
Access Inquire at Shelburne, Highway 3
Maps Lake Rossignol 21A/3W
Shelburne 20P/14W

Start at Indian Fields and *finish* at Carlyle Bowers.

44 SKUDIAK LAKE — JUNCTION LAKE
Length 20 miles (32 km)
Approx trip time 3 days
Access Inquire at Sable River, Highway 3
Map Lake Rossignol 21A/3W

Start at Skudiak Lake and head north to *finish* at the end of Junction Lake.

45 SKUDIAK LAKE — ROSEWAY RIVER
Length 10 miles (16 km)
Approx trip time 1 day
Access Inquire at Sable River, Highway 3
Map Lake Rossignol 21A/3W

Start at Skudiak Lake and *finish* at the Upset Falls Bridge.

Queen's County

46 BIG DAM LAKE — LAKE ROSSIGNOL
Length 20 miles (47 km)
Approx trip time 3 days
Access Inquire at Maitland Bridge, Highway 8
Maps Kejimkujik Lake 21A/6 E and W

Start at Low Landing on the north side of Big Dam Lake and *finish* at Loon Lake Falls.

47 LAKE ROSSIGNOL
Access Inquire at Caledonia, Highway 8
Maps Lake Rossignol 21A/3E
Kejimkujik Lake 21A/6E

Start at Indian Gardens, Low Landing, Lake Rossignol. *Finish* at the landing on the road to Caledonia.

48 LAKE ROSSIGNOL — BROAD RIVER
Length 22 miles (35 km)
Approx trip time 4 days
Access Inquire at Summerville Centre, Highway 3

Maps Fort Mouton 20P/15W
Liverpool 21A/2W
Lake Rossignol 21A/3E

Start at the Nova Scotia Power Commission
dam and *finish* at Devil's Elbow

49 LAKE ROSSIGNOL — HIGHWAY 3
Length 32 miles (51 km)
Approx trip time 4 days
Access Inquire at Middlefield, Highway 8
Map Liverpool 21A/2W

Start at Lake Rossignol. Go down the Mersey
River to *finish* 15 miles (24 km) west of
Liverpool.

50 EIGHTEEN MILE BROOK — INDIAN GARDENS
Length 20 miles (32 km)
Approx trip time 2 days
Access Inquire at Middlefield, Highway 8
Maps Bridgewater 21A/7W
Liverpool 21A/2W

51 EIGHTEEN MILE BROOK — GREENFIELD
Length 8 miles (13 km)
Approx trip time 1 day
Access Inquire at Middlefield, Highway 8
Map Bridgewater 21A/7W

Start at Eighteen Mile Brook and Highway 8
crossing. *Finish* at Greenfield.

52 CAMERON'S LANDING — GREENFIELD
Length 9 miles (14 km)
Approx trip time 1 day
Access Inquire at Middlefield, Highway 8
Map Bridgewater 21A/7W

Start at Cameron Lake and *finish* at
Greenfield.

53 PLEASANT RIVER — CAMERONS LANDING
Length 17 miles (27 km)
Approx trip time 2 days
Access By Highway 208
Map Bridgewater 21A/7

Start at Pleasant River and *finish* at
Camerons Landing.

54 CALEDONIA — CAMERON LAKE
Length 9 miles (14 km)
Approx trip time 1 day
Access Inquire at Pleasant River, Highway 208
Maps Kejimkujik Lake 21A/6E
Bridgewater 21A/7W

Start at Medway River and *finish* at
Cameron Lake.

55 PLEASANT RIVER — GREENFIELD
Length 19 miles (31 km)
Approx trip time 2 days
Access Inquire Pleasant River, Highway 208
Map Bridgewater 21A/7W

Start at Pleasant River and *finish* at Greenfield.

56 GREENFIELD — MILL VILLAGE
Length 15 miles (24 km)
Approx trip time 1 day
Access Inquire at Greenfield, off Highway 8
Map Liverpool 21A/2 W and E

Start at Medway River and *finish* at Mill Village,
Highway 3

57 LOW LANDING — FIRST LAKE
Length 11 miles (18 km)
Approx trip time 2 days
Access Inquire at Caledonia, Highway 8
Maps Kejimkujik Lake 21A/6E
Bridgewater 21A/7W

Start at Low Landing, Lake Rossignol, and
finish at Second Christopher Lake.

58 LOW LANDING — FIRST LAKE (VIA APPLE TREE AND BIG ROCKY LAKES)
Length 14 miles (23 km)
Approx trip time 2 days
Access Inquire at Caledonia, Highway 8
Maps Kejimkujik Lake 21A/6E
Bridgewater 21A/7W

Start at Low Landing and *finish* at Second
Christopher Lake.

59 EIGHT MILE LAKE — MEDWAY RIVER
Length 6 miles (10 km)
Approx trip time 1—2 days

Access Inquire at Mill Village, Highway 3
Map Liverpool 21A/2W

Start at Eight Mile Lake and *finish* Medway River below Globe Falls.

60 TEN MILE LAKE — MERSEY RIVER
Length 8 miles (13 km)
Approx trip time 1 day
Access Inquire at Milton or Middlefield, Highway 8
Map Liverpool 21A/2W

Start at the Provincial Picnic Park Highway 8 and *finish* at the No. 4 Nova Scotia Power Commission dam, five miles above Milton.

61 JORDAN RIVER
Length 23 miles (37 km)
Approx trip time 3 days
Access Inquire at Jordan Falls, Highways 3—103
Maps Lake Rossignol 21A/3W
Lockeport 20 P/11

Start at Silver Lake and *finish* at Jordan Falls.

Guysborough and Pictou Counties

62 CAMERON SETTLEMENT — ISLAND LAKE
Length 18 miles (29 km)
Approx trip time 3 days

Access Inquire at Caledonia.
Maps Lochaber 11E/8W
Liscomb 11E/1W and E

Start at Cameron settlement and *finish* at Island Lake.

63 CROOKED BROOK — ISLAND LAKE
Length 10 miles (16 km)
Approx trip time 2 days
Access Inquire at Caledonia
Map Liscomb 11E/1W

Start at the head of Rocky Lake and *finish* at the end of Island Lake.

64 ROCKY LAKE — NEW CHESTER ROAD
Length 12 miles (19 km)
Approx trip time 3 days
Access Inquire at Caledonia.
Map Liscomb 11E/1W and E

Start at Rocky Lake and *finish* at South Arm Lake.

65 ROCKY LAKE — SOUTH ARM LAKE
Length 20 miles (32 km)
Approx trip time 4 days
Access Inquire at Caledonia.
Map Liscomb 11E/1W and E

Start at Rocky Lake and *finish* at South Arm Lake.

 Map Sources

Canada Mapping Office, 615 Booth Street, Ottawa, Ontario is the chief supplier of topographical maps. Maps for the province are also available from the following dealers in Nova Scotia:

Dunlap Bros. & Co. Ltd.
Box 369
Amherst, N.S.

Maritime Resource Management Services
Box 310
Amherst, N.S.

Annapolis Home Hardware Ltd.
Annapolis Royal, N.S.

Bridgetown Hardware
Bridgetown, N.S.

L. St. Clair Baird Ltd.
54 Webster St.
Kentville, N.S.

G.W. Sampson
Sales & Service
Kingston, N.S.

Liscomb Lodge
Liscomb Mills, N.S.

Corbett's Gun & Tackle
45 Union St.
Liverpool, N.S.

Le Have Stationers Ltd.
587 King St.
Bridgewater, N.S.

Mr. Aubrey S. Evans
Chester, N.S.

Information Canada Bookshop
1683 Barrington St.
Halifax, N.S. 76945

Nova Scotia Dept. of Mines
P.O. Box 999
Stellarton, N.S.

R.H. Davis & Co. Ltd.
Main Street
Yarmouth, N.S.

Nova Recreation Development Co. Ltd.
P.O. Box 455
Yarmouth, N.S.

Nova Scotia Communications &
    Information Centre
Hollis Bldg., P.O. Box 2206
Sackville St. & Bedford Row
Halifax, N.S.

Smith Industries North
    America Limited
Kelvin Hughes Division
5140 Prince St.
Halifax, N.S.

The Trail Shop Co-operative Ltd.
6260 Quinpool Rd.
Halifax, N.S. 90491

C. & G. MacLeod
361 Charlotte St.
Sydney, N.S.

The College Bookshop
Xavier College
P.O. Box 193
Sydney, N.S.

Wilcox Brothers Hardware
Windsor, N.S.

South Shore Sales & Service Ltd.
Box 700 Lunenburg
Lunenburg Co., N.S.

Middleton's Hardware Store Ltd.
P.O. Box 159
Middleton, N.S.

Herald Stationers Ltd.
302 Commercial St.
North Sydney, N.S. 41898

Mr. John A. MacLellan
Bonnie Doon Motels
Pleasant Bay, N.S.

Clare Real Estate Ltd.
Box 61
Saulnierville, N.S.

Robertson's Hardware Ltd.
Box 370
Shelburne, N.S.

For a provincial road map and any further canoe route information write:

Travel Bureau
Department of Tourism
5670 Spring Garden Road
Halifax, N.S.

 Outfitters

There are no government listings for outfitters in Nova Scotia.

 Air Charter Services

Due to the shortness of Nova Scotia canoe routes — none longer than sixty miles — it is very doubtful that canoeists would ever plan airlift assistance. There are no charter floatplane operators listed by the Ministry of Transport for the province but the following floatplane bases are listed by the department: Digby; Shearwater; Shubenacadie; Sydney.

NEW BRUNSWICK

New Brunswick is Canada's eighth largest province (28,354 square miles). Roughly rectangular in shape, it is situated on the rolling plateau of the Acadian Highlands. The terrain is generally rocky, supporting prolific forest growth and, except in the Saint John River valley, is mostly unsuitable for agriculture.

There are many rivers in New Brunswick. The main ones are the Saint John (400 miles long), St. Croix, Petitcodiac, Miramichi, Nepisiguit and Restigouche Rivers. The Atlantic coast is indented by three deep bays: Baie de Chaleur, which is also partly in Quebec; the Bay of Fundy, which boasts tides of sixty feet (the highest in the world) and is partly in Nova Scotia; and Miramichi Bay.

Mines in the Bathurst region produce silver, copper, zinc and lead. New Brunswick's ocean fisheries rank third in Canada's east coast fishing economy, and the province has eight pulp and paper mills. Mixed farming in the agricultural upper valley of the Saint John River is dominated by potato growing, of which some ten million bushels a year are produced.

 ## Climate

Because it is situated in the track of prevailing westerly winds, New Brunswick is strongly exposed to continental weather. But throughout the year this influence is tempered on the Atlantic coast by the Gulf of St. Lawrence. Both snow and rainfall are heavy there.

The different summer weather patterns for the province are accurately suggested by a division into three geographical regions as follows:

South Maritime (Saint John)	Mean Temperature In Fahrenheit (Celsius) Min		Max		Rainfall In Mean Inches (Millimetres)	
June	46.6	(8.1)	66.6	(19.2)	3.60	(91.4)
July	52.7	(11.5)	72.8	(22.7)	3.06	(77.7)
August	53.0	(11.7)	72.9	(22.7)	4.31	(109.5)
Central Inland (Fredericton)						
June	49.2	(9.6)	72.6	(22.6)	3.12	(79.3)
July	55.1	(12.8)	78.0	(25.6)	3.47	(88.1)
August	53.0	(11.7)	75.8	(24.3)	3.45	(87.6)
North Inland-Maritime (Campbellton)						
June	49.1	(9.5)	69.4	(20.8)	3.50	(88.9)
July	55.9	(13.3)	76.0	(24.4)	3.83	(97.3)
August	53.5	(11.9)	73.6	(23.1)	3.44	(87.4)

Canoeists battling rapids on the St. Croix River. Along this river, which forms the international boundary between New Brunswick and the state of Maine, lies an island of the same name where as early as 1604 a post was established by Samuel de Champlain.

Fishing

The 1975 angling regulations, limits and licenses are determined by both the federal and provincial governments, and as a result are unusually complicated. Visiting canoeists should write to the Fish and Wildlife Branch, Ministry of Natural Resources, Fredericton, New Brunswick, for a free summary. Canoeists must be careful not to fish where private or freehold salmon fishing rights prohibit fishing by outsiders. The general pattern for non-residents is as follows:

Species	Waters	Daily Bag Limits	Nonresident Licenses		Any fish but Salmon	
			Season	7 day	Single & Family	
Atlantic Salmon	All waters are open for salmon fishing	2	75.00	35.00		
Spring Salmon	All waters are open for salmon fishing (The Restigouche River system, with the exception of Upsalquitch River, is closed for salmon fishing.)	1	75.00	35.00		
Trout	Nictor Lake, Little Nictor Lake, Bathurst Lake, California Lake, South Oromocto and Arnold Lakes	10			25.00	10.00
	The rest of the province	15	75.00	35.00		
Landlocked Salmon	International waters	5				
	The rest of the Province	10	75.00	35.00		
Togue	The entire Province	5	75.00	35.00	25.00	10.00
Black Bass	The entire Province	15	75.00	35.00	25.00	10.00
Striped Bass Pickerel, Perch and all other species of coarse fish	The entire Province	no limit	75.00	35.00	25.00	10.00

History

European explorers first sighted the shores of New Brunswick in 1521 when the Portuguese navigator Giovanni da Verrazano skirted its Atlantic coast. Jacques Cartier, the French explorer, made the first landfall on the Baie de Chaleur in 1534. Samuel de Champlain landed on the shore of the Bay of Fundy in 1604. The first mainland settlement was attempted by the French in 1610.

The British assaulted that and other settlements by sea in 1758-1760 and founded a British community at Saint John in 1762. Following the American Revolutionary War, the earliest of 12,000 British patriots from New England started to settle in the Saint John River valley. New Brunswick, previously part of one colony with Nova Scotia became a separate colony in 1784. It was an original partner in Confederation in 1867. In 1874 it was linked to Quebec City and Halifax by the Intercolonial Railway.

Fredericton, the capital, has a population of about 25,000. Saint John, with about 50,000 people, is the largest city, followed by Moncton.

Once upon a time
only men did the paddling!

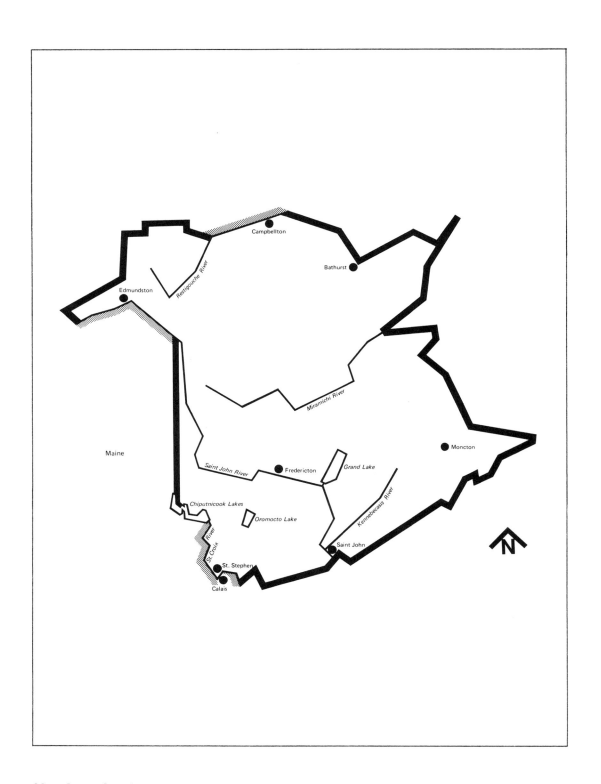

New Brunswick Routes

New Brunswick is earnestly trying, and succeeding, in updating and modifying many early, often conflicting, reports on its canoe routes.

Obviously, the province wants to promote canoeing on the one hand while protecting local salmon fishermen and guides on the other. Canoe club president Tedd Weyman says canoeing in New Brunswick is a means of transportation rather than a sport in its own right. Canoes provide easy access to salmon fishing pools. "One sees more poling than paddling on our rivers, except for the four main canoeing rivers," Weyman says, "especially during summer draw-down and evaporation."

A free chart, *N.B. Canoeing-Canotage* from Tourism, New Brunswick, makes planning reference easier. It is also advisable for the responsible canoe tripper to obtain ahead of time a "Fishing Guide" folder for the river of his choice. It will clearly show restricted fishing areas. Write to Fish and Wildlife Branch, Department of Natural Resources, Fredericton, New Brunswick. The cost is one dollar each.

The province can be divided into nine drainage basins. Some contain several tributaries while others are only single rivers:
(1) Saint John River — Upper, Middle and Lower Saint John River; St. Francis River; Tobique River; Keswick River, Portobello Creek; Oromocto River; Salmon River; Canaan (Washademoak) River; Nerepis River and Kennebecasis River
(2) St. Croix River — Eel River, St. Croix Headwaters, St. Crois River and Little Digdequash (North Brook) River
(3) Miramichi River — Main Southwest Miramichi River and Cains River
(4) Restigouche River — Restigouche River; Kedgwick River; Upsalquitch and Northwest Upsalquitch Rivers
(5) Nepisiguit River
(6) Pokemouche River
(7) Tracadie River

(8) Kouchibouguac River
(9) Richibucto River

Saint John River Drainage Basin

66 UPPER SAINT JOHN RIVER
Length 42 miles (68 km)
Access Inquire at Edmundston, Highway 2 — US 1
Maps Lac Baker 21N/7E
Connors 21N/2W and E
Edmundston 21N/8W

Start at the mouth of the St. Francis River and *finish* at Edmundston city.

67 MIDDLE SAINT JOHN RIVER
Length 74 miles (119 km)
Access Inquire at Beechwood, Highway 2
Maps Florenceville 21J/15E
Woodstock 21J/4E
Millville 21J/3W
Canterbury 21G/14W and E
Fredericton 21G/15W and E

Start at the village of Beechwood and *finish* at the Mactaquac Provincial Park.

68 LOWER SAINT JOHN RIVER
Length 109 miles (175 km)
Access By Mactaquac, Highway 105
Maps Fredericton 21G/15W and E
Grand Lake 21G/16W and E
Hampstead 21G/9E
Saint John 21G/8E

Start at Mactaquac Dam and *finish* at the city of Saint John.

69 ST. FRANCIS RIVER
Length 20 miles (32 km)
Access Inquire at Edmundston, Highway 2 — US 1

Maps   Estcourt 21N/6E
Little Black River 21N/3E
Connors 21N/2W

Start at Beau Lake, Quebec, and *finish* at the Saint John River.

70   TOBIQUE RIVER (NICTAU LAKE TO TOBIQUE NARROWS)

Length   85 miles (137 km)
Access   Inquire at Tobique Narrows, Highway 108
Maps   Nepisiguit Lake 21O/7W
Aroostock 21J/13E
Sisson 21O/6E
Riley Brook 21O/3W
Plaster Rock 21J/14E

Start at Nictau Lake and *finish* at Tobique Narrows.

71   KESWICK RIVER

Length   12 miles (19 km)
Access   Inquire at Zealand Station, Highway 104
Maps   Burtt's Corner 21J/2W
Fredericton 21G/15W

Start at the village of Zealand and *finish* at the Saint John River.

72   PORTOBELLO CREEK

Length   30 round trip miles (48 km)
Access   Inquire at Zealand Station
Maps   Fredericton 21G/15E
Grand Lake 21G/16W

Start at Church Road in the village of Maugerville and *finish* at Lakeville Corner.

73   OROMOCTO RIVER

Length   24 miles (39 km)
Access   Inquire at Hoyt, Highway 101
Maps   Fredericton 21G/15E
Fredericton Junction 21G/10E
Grand Lake 21G/16W

Start at the settlement of West Milk (Hoyt) and *finish* at Oromocto.

74   SALMON RIVER

Length   20 miles (32 km)
Access   Chipman, Highway 10
Maps   Harcourt 21I/6W
Chipman 21I/4W

Start at Chipman Village on the Red Bank Creek and *finish* at Little Forks

75   CANAAN RIVER

Length   36 miles (58 km)
Access   Inquire at Canaan Forks, Highway 112
Maps   Codys 21H/13W and E
Chipman 21I/14E
Grand Lake 21G/16E
Hampstead 21G/9E

Start at Canaan Forks, go through Washademoak Lake and *finish* at the Saint John River.

76   NEREPIS RIVER

Length   13 miles (21 km)
Access   By Welsford, Highway 101
Map   Saint John 21G/8W and E

Start at the village of Welsford and *finish* at the CNR bridge at Lingley.

77   KENNEBECASIS RIVER

Length   92 miles (148 km)
Access   By Penobsquis off Highway 2
Maps   Petitcodiac 21H/14W
Sussex 21H/12W and E
Loch Lomond 21H/5W
Saint John 21G/8E

Start at the village of Penobsquis. *Finish* at either Hampton or the city of Saint John.

St. Croix River Drainage Basin

78   ST. CROIX RIVER (HEADWATERS)

Length   41 miles (66 km)
Access   Inquire at St. Stephen, Highway 1 and US 1
Maps   Fosterville 21G/13W and E
Forest City 21G/12 W and E
McAdam 21G/11 W

Start at North Lake Provincial Park and *finish* at the village of St. Croix.

As early as 1887 and 1890, volumes by Dean Sage, an American sportsman, and Arthur Peters Silver, a Nova Scotian, praised the wonderful canoeing, fishing and camping found along the Restigouche and Miramichi Rivers. Today, New Brunswick's waterways continue to draw great numbers of canoeists and sportsmen from outside the province.

79 ST. CROIX RIVER
Length   41 miles (66 km)
Access   St. Croix, Highway 4
Maps   McAdam 21G/11 W
Rolling Dam 21G/6 W
St. Stephen 21G/3 W & E

Start at the village of St. Croix and *finish* at the town of Grand Falls.

80 EEL RIVER
Length   18 miles (29 km)
Access   Inquire at Eel River Crossing, off Highway 280
Maps   Fosterville 21G/13E
Woodstock 21J/4E

Start at Eel River and *finish* at the village of Benton.

81 LITTLE DIGDEQUASH RIVER
Length   13 miles (21 km)
Access   Inquire at Digdequash, Highway 1 and 27
Map   McAdam 21G/11W

Start at the Georgia Pacific Road (between Third and Fifth Lakes) and *finish* at the Spednic Lake Provincial Park.

Miramichi Drainage Basin

82 MIRAMICHI RIVER (MAIN SOUTHWEST PART)
Length   80 miles (129 km)
Access   By Boiestown, Highway 8
Maps   Doaktown 21J/9E
Blackville 21I/12W and E
Newcastle 21I/13W and E

Start at the village of Boiestown and *finish* at Enclosure Provincial Park.

83 CAINS RIVER

Length 48 miles (77 km)
Access Inquire at Nashwaak Bridge, Highways 8 and 107
Maps Boiestown 21J/8W and E
Salmon River Road 21I/5W
Blackville 21 I/12W and E

Start at Bantalor, paddle to the mouth of the Cains River and *finish* at the village of Howard.

Restigouche River Drainage Basin

84 RESTIGOUCHE RIVER

Length 93 miles (150 km)
Access By Ste.-Anne-De-Madawaska, Highway 2
Maps Grandmaison 21N/9E
Grand River 21O/5W and E
Gounamitz 21O/12W and E
Kedgwick 21O/11W
Menneval 21O/14W and E
Campbellton 21O/15W

Start at Cedar Brook and *finish* at Christopher at the city of Campbellton.

85 KEDGWICK RIVER

Length 46 miles (74 km)
Access By Ste.-Anne-de-Madawaska, Highway 2
Maps States Brook 21 O/13W and E
Gounamitz 21O/12E
Kedgwick 21O/11W

Start at Gin Creek and *finish* at the Restigouche River.

86 UPSALQUITCH RIVER

Length 52 miles (84 km)
Access By Ste.-Anne-de-Madawaska, Highway 2
Maps Kedgwick 21O/11E
Upsalquitch Forks 21O/10W and E
Campbellton 21O/15W

Start at Twenty-five Mile Brook and *finish* at the village of Robinsonville

Nepisiguit River Drainage Basin

87 NEPISIGUIT RIVER

Length 69 miles (111 km)
Access By Ste.-Anne-de-Madawaska, Highway 2
Maps Nepisiguit Falls 21P/5W and E
Bathurst 21P/12E

Start at Ste.-Anne-de-Madawaska and *finish* at Baie de Chaleur.

Pokemouche River Drainage Basin

88 POKEMOUCHE RIVER

Length 29 miles (47 km)
Access Inquire at St. George, Highway 350
Maps Burnsville 21P/11E
Tracadie 21P/10W

Start at Spruce Brook and *finish* at the village of Inkerman.

Tracadie River Drainage Basin

89 TRACADIE RIVER

Length 32 miles (51 km)
Access Inquire at Tracadie, Highway 11
Maps Burnsville 21P/11E
Tabusintac River 21P/6E
Wishart Point 21P/7E

Start at a point near the village of Bois Gagnon and *finish* at Val Comeau, also a village.

Kouchibouguac River Drainage Basin

90 KOUCHIBOUGUAC RIVER

Length 9 miles (14 km)
Access Inquire at Kouchibouguac National Park, Highway 11
Maps Kouchibouguac 21I/14E
Point Sapin 21I/15W

Start at the village of Kouchibouguac and *finish* at Logiccroft, also a village.

Richibucto River Drainage Basin

91 RICHIBUCTO RIVER

Length   34 miles (55 km)
Access   Inquire at Bass River, Highway 116
Maps   Rogersville 21I/11E
Richibucto 21I/10W

Start at Smith's Corner and *finish* at Jardine
Provincial Park.

 Map Sources

Canada Mapping Office, 615 Booth Street, Ottawa, Ontario, is the chief supplier of topographical maps. Maps for the province are also available from the following dealers in New Brunswick.

W.J. Kent & Co. Ltd.
150 Main Street
Bathurst, N.B.

Omer Renault Hardware
36 Roseberry St.
Campbellton, N.B.

McDonald Hardware & Fuels Ltd.
Duke St. at Cunard
Chatham, N.B.

Morneault Ltd.
26 St. Francis St.
Edmundston, N.B.

King Sports Ltd.
297 Mountain Road
Moncton, N.B.

Frank Fales & Sons Ltd.
61 Dock Street
Saint John, N.B.

Pauls Bowling Alley
St. Leonard, N.B.

S. Smith & Sons (Canada) Ltd.
Kelvin & Hughes Division
72 Germain St.
Saint John N.B.

Bookmark Ltd.
K-Mart Plaza
Moncton, N.B.

Roy's Sporting Goods
Water St.
Saint Andrews, N.B.

For a provincial road map and more detailed canoe route information write:

Promotion and Development Branch
Department of Tourism
Box 1030
Fredericton, N.B.

When requesting detailed canoe route information ask for: the proper route maps; national, provincial and local highway numbers pertinent to access and take-out points; permits and licences required; outfitters' and guides' names and addresses relevant to selected routes. Write to

Parks Branch
Department of Natural Resources
Room 575, Centennial Building
Fredericton, N.B.

Outfitters

While New Brunswick is one of the nation's largest builders and exporters of pleasure canoes and lists important routes on more than twenty-five rivers, its tourism literature states that "canoes are rarely offered for rent . . . and then only by sporting outfitters." These companies are primarily interested in equipping major fishing expeditions rather than small groups of canoeists.

Air Charter Services

The Ministry of Transport does not list any air charter services for New Brunswick. However, it does list the following floatplane bases: Saint John, St. Leonard, Andover, Campbellton, Chipman, Fredericton and Woodstock.

It is quite likely that charter air carriers in the neighbouring provinces of Quebec and possibly Newfoundland would provide airlift services upon request and prior arrangement.

QUÉBEC

Québec is the largest province in the nation (594,860 square miles), of which a significant proportion (71,000 square miles) is inland fresh water. The province is bounded on the north by Hudson Strait and Ungava Bay, on the west by Hudson Bay and James Bay, on the east by Labrador, and on the south by New Brunswick, Maine, New Hampshire, Vermont, New York and Ontario.

Québec is divided into three geographic regions: Precambrian, Appalachian and the St. Lawrence River lowlands. The Precambrian Shield covers ninety percent of Québec, a vast and desolate expanse of granitic knobs and upland plateaus coursed by rivers, lakes, muskegs and swamps. High in its north-central highland lies the source of eighteen major rivers that flow out in four different directions.

Québec's chief rivers are: the St. Lawrence, Ottawa, Koksoak, Eastmain, George, Saguenay, Nottaway, Rupert, St. Maurice, Manicouagan, Outardes, Whale, Harricanaw, Bersimis (Betsiamites) and Richelieu.

Its largest lakes are Mistassini, St. John, Clearwater, Minto, Bienville, d'Iberville, Payne and Nichicun. Lake Timiskaming and Lake Abitibi are two large lakes on the border with Ontario.

The Appalachian region in the southeast is a continuation of the mountains of New England. The Shickshock Range in the Gaspé at one point reaches 4,100 feet, the highest elevation in the province. The St. Lawrence lowlands spread out on both sides of the St. Lawrence River as well as spilling into the Ottawa River valley. This is the richest agricultural region but occupies only four percent of the total land area.

The forests of Québec support a level of sawmill production that is second only to that of British Columbia. The province also produces forty-five percent of Canada's pulp and paper. It shares with Labrador vast, rich iron ore deposits and has five aluminum smelter plants which produce one-third of the aluminum ingot output in the world. Asbestos, gold, copper and zinc account for further segments of the mining economy.

Québec's rivers produce one-half the hydro electric power in Canada, although it is said that only half of its potential has been developed. The James Bay hydro development is expected to harness 6,000,000 horsepower by the 1980s.

The St. Lawrence River transportation systems and facilities handle two-thirds of Canada's foreign trade.

 ## Climate

The summer climate of Québec varies from the warm, humid temperatures of the St. Lawrence valley lowlands, through the more moderate climate of the central plateau highlands, to the coolness of the northern areas. There are no truly accurate temperature records kept for those regions on the arctic Hudson Strait and Ungava Bay, as the closest northern settlement is Schefferville on the north-central plateau.

Previous page. Quebec's rivers can sometimes provide a turbulent and demanding adventure. Canoeing can bring total involvement, whether it be amidst the rush of rapids or while pausing to admire magnificent wilderness.

Québec	Mean Temperature In Fahrenheit (Celsius)				Rainfall In Mean Inches (Millimetres)	
	Min		*Max*			
Southern (Montreal)						
June	55.8	(13.2)	74.8	(23.8)	3.27	(83.1)
July	60.8	(16.0)	79.4	(26.3)	3.35	(85.1)
August	58.4	(14.7)	77.2	(25.1)	3.41	(86.6)
West Central (Mistassini)						
June	44.8	(7.1)	65.7	(18.7)	3.34	(84.8)
July	51.1	(10.6)	70.7	(21.5)	3.93	(99.8)
August	49.4	(9.7)	67.1	(19.5)	4.22	(107.2)
North Central (Schefferville)						
June	37.9	(3.3)	56.6	(13.7)	2.86	(72.6)
July	45.9	(7.7)	63.3	(17.4)	3.49	(88.7)
August	43.7	(6.5)	59.1	(15.1)	3.79	(96.3)
Permafrost begins in the vicinity of Great Whale River.						

 Fishing

·Canada's largest province also offers the most diverse range of sport fish species and fishing zones.

The species are smallmouth bass, maskinonge, pike, walleye, lake sturgeon; brook, sea, Quebec red, lake, splake, brown, rainbow and cutthroat trout; ouananiche (landlocked Atlantic salmon).

Some species have different open seasons in each of the different areas, but in general it seems that the canoeist, if properly licensed, may fish for most species from June 15 to Labor Day.

There are nineteen provincial parks and reserves, some differing from others in species and open seasons. In order to get the clearest possible picture of the Quebec sport fishing scene, the canoeist should write well in advance for detailed information from:

Department of Tourism, Fish and Game,
Place de la Capitale,
150 St Cyrille Blvd. East, 15th Floor,
Québec, P.Q.

The 1975 angling fees were as follows:

residents under 65 years $3.25
residents over 65 years $ .50
nonresident, season $25.50
nonresident, 3 day $10.50
dependent of nonresident license holder
(wife and each child under 18 years) $4.25

La Verendrye Provincial Park is one of Quebec's finest and most popular canoeing areas and the largest fishing and game preserve in the province (5,000 square miles). The park contains well over 100 species of birds and 50 of mammals. Northern and walleyed pike, and speckled, gray and red trout are only the most popular of the many fish to be found in the park's 4,000 odd lakes.

 **History**

European discovery and exploration of Québec began with Jacques Cartier. In 1534, he made a landfall on the Baie de Chaleur and claimed the Gaspé region for France. The following year, his ships explored the Gulf of St. Lawrence, the St. Lawrence River and visited the Indian villages of Stadacona (now Quebec City) and Hochelaga (Montreal).

Samuel de Champlain first reached Québec in 1603 and began a settlement there in 1608. The arrival of Louis Hébert and his family in 1617 symbolizes the first real colonization. In 1642, Montréal was founded by Sieur de Maisonneuve. It was intended to be a centre for missionary work among the Indians but quickly became a fur trading centre as well.

Determined to keep the lucrative fur trade, the French attempted to drive the rival English fur traders from James Bay and Hudson Bay. By capturing ships and forts of the Hudson's Bay Company from Rupert House to York Factory over the years 1688-97, they almost succeeded. With the Treaty of Utrecht, signed in 1713, France gave back to Britain the two bays, the traders of New France withdrew from them and the Hudsons's Bay Company resumed trading through its coastal forts.

In 1759, Québec fell to the English and four years later, by the Treaty of Paris, the English were granted the royal colony of New France. In 1791, the old province of Québec was divided into Lower Canada (now Québec) and Upper Canada (now Ontario). In 1837, the French of Lower Canada showed their preference for the British form of law and order by rejecting a small band of radicals led by Louis Joseph Papineau. In 1867 Lower Canada and Upper Canada joined New Brunswick, Nova Scotia, and Upper Canada in Confederation. Since then it has been known by the historic name, Québec.

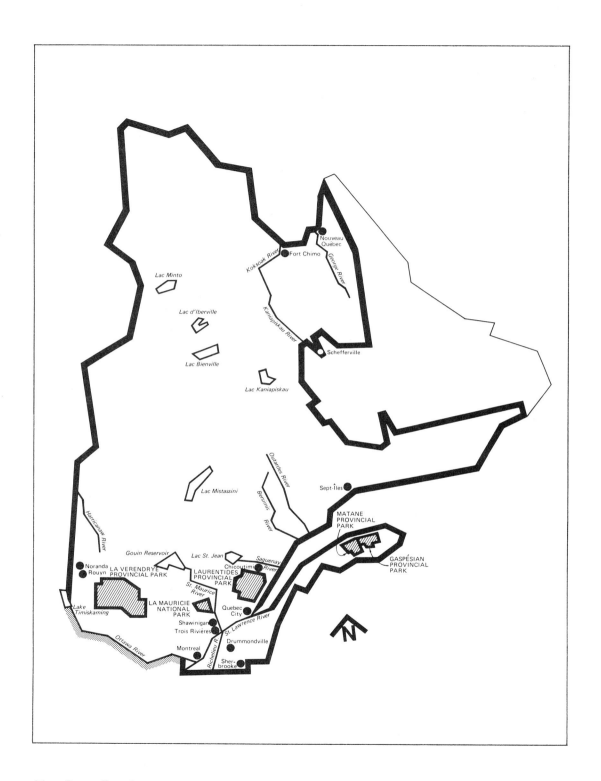

Lac Minto

Lac d'Iberville

Lac Bienville

Lac Kaniapiskau

Nouveau Québec

Koksoak River

Fort Chimo

George River

Kaniapiskau River

Schefferville

Lac Mistassini

Outardes River

Bersimis River

Sept-Îles

MATANE PROVINCIAL PARK

Harricanaw River

Gouin Reservoir

Lac St. Jean

Saguenay River

Chicoutimi

GASPÉSIAN PROVINCIAL PARK

Noranda
Rouyn

LA VERENDRYE PROVINCIAL PARK

LAURENTIDES PROVINCIAL PARK

St. Maurice River

Lake Timiskaming

LA MAURICIE NATIONAL PARK

Quebec City

St. Lawrence River

Shawinigan

Trois Rivières

Ottawa River

Montreal

Richelieu R.

Drummondville

Sher-brooke

N

Québec Routes

Quebec's canoe route system is complex. The province's waterways flow in the four primary directions. It is helpful to classify the routes within eight principal drainage basins. These are: Chaleur Bay; Gaspe; St. Maurice River; Saguenay River; North Shore-Labrador; James Bay south; Hudson Strait-Ungava Bay; Ottawa R.

The drainage basin boundaries are somewhat arbitrary. These boundaries are based on topographical maps, but even hydrographers are unable to determine exact boundaries. The water table of Lake Kaniapiskau illustrates the problem: rivers drain away from the lake in all four primary directions.

Within these drainage basins are eight provincial parks and one national park. It seems to be Quebec government policy to keep canoeing within parks boundaries as much as possible and it has succeeded in laying out and controlling well-defined routes.

Other controlled routes in Quebec flow down some dozen "**timber limit rivers**". This means that they flow through Crown lands granted by the government to pulp, paper and lumber companies for the cutting and driving of pulp and timber — sometimes for hundreds of miles — to main transportation points or mills. Since some companies use sections or full lengths of their rivers, only they can allocate sections for public use. Users will, therefore, have to arrange for travel permits with the custodian companies, whose names are given with the appropriate routes.

The addresses of these companies are as follows:

James MacLaren Company Ltd.
Forestry Engineering Department
Buckingham, P.Q. J8L 2X3

Canadian International Paper Co. Ltd.
Forestry Engineering Department
Sun Life Building
Dominion Square
Montreal, P.Q. H3B 2X1

Consolidated-Bathurst Ltée
Forestry Engineering Department
Box 69
800 Boul. Dorchester W.
Montreal 101, P.Q.

The Price Company Ltd.
Box 63
Chicoutimi, P.Q. G7H 5B6

New Brunswick International Paper Company
Woodland Division
Dalhousie, New Brunswick E0K 1B0

La Compagnie Donohue Ltée.
Forestry Engineering Department
Claremont, P.Q. G0T 1C0

Quebec North Shore Paper Co.
Forestry Engineering Department
Baie Comeau, P.Q. G4Z 1K6

Domtar Ltd.
Forestry Engineering Department
2950 Boul. Sir Wilfred Laurier
Quebec, P.Q. G1V 2M4

Paradis & Fils Ltée.
Box 1120
Senneterre, P.Q.

A third group of rivers in Quebec is situated within the James Bay south drainage basin. Hydro Quebec has closed these rivers to canoe travel while building the world's largest hydro-electric power development in the region.

If canoe trip planners keep these complexities in mind, they should have no difficulty in choosing and enjoying some of the finest canoeing rivers in Canada.

Finally, included in their proper drainage basins are canoe routes supplied to me by hardy individuals who have written up trip logs which are used here with their permission.

Ottawa River Drainage Basin

92   RIVIERE DU LIEVRE
Timber company   James MacLaren Company Ltd.
Maps   These maps are to a scale of 1:125,000

Ottawa 31G
Mont Laurier 31J
Kempt Lake 31O
Buckingham 31G/NW
Maniwaki 31J/SW

Mont Laurier 31J/NW
Petawaga 31O/SW
Kempt Lake 31O/SE
Parent 31O/NE

This river runs from north to south, discharging near Masson on the Ottawa River. It is open to use by canoe campers but subject to restrictions imposed by the timber company.

93 GATINEAU RIVER

Timber company Canadian International Paper Co. Ltd.

94 OPAWICA RIVER

Timber company Canadian International Paper Co. Ltd.

St. Maurice River Drainage Basin

95 ST. MAURICE RIVER

Timber company Canadian International Paper Co. Ltd.

96 BASTICAN RIVER

Timber company Consolidated-Bathurst Ltée
Maps Trois Rivières 31I
La Tuque 31P

The company doesn't drive this river.

97 MATTAWIN RIVER

Timber company Consolidated-Bathurst Ltée.
Maps Trois Rivières 31I

The company drives the river during the summer from Toro Reservoir to St. Maurice

98 VERMILLION RIVER

Timber company Consolidated-Bathurst Ltée.
Map LaTuque 31P

The river is clear of driving operations

99 METABETCHOUAN RIVER

Timber company Consolidated-Bathurst Ltée.
Maps Baie St. Paul 21M
LaTuque 31P

No more driving takes place on the river.

100 JACQUES CARTIER RIVER

Timber company Domtar Ltd.

101 MONTMORENCY RIVER

Timber company La Compagnie Donohue Ltée.
Maps Lac Jacques Cartier 21M/11E
Lac Sautaurski 21M/6E

102 METABETCHOUAN RIVER, KISKISSINK SECTION OF LAURENTIDES PROVINCIAL PARK

Access By Highway 54, to Camp Montagnais, a compulsory departure point. No canoes for rent.
Maps Free canoe routes map

The Metabetchouan River is good for canoeing from about mid-July to mid-August only, due to pulp driving on some parts of the river. For further information write:

Parks Branch
Reservations Office
Department Tourism, Fish and Game
Box 8888
Quebec, P.Q.
The maximum length of stay is five days.

103 PERIBONCA RIVER

Length 250 miles (402 km)
Access Northwest of Lake St. Jean Highway 167
Timber companies Price Company and Consolidated-Bathurst Ltée.
Maps Chicoutimi 22D
Pipmuacan Reservoir 22E

This pulp driving river is located in Chibougamou Provincial Park. It flows north-south into Lac St. Jean at the town of Peribonca. The last 100 miles is not navigable. Above that point there would seem to be about 150 miles of excellent canoeing waters starting northward near Lake Peribonca.

104 TRENCHE RIVER

Timber company Consolidated-Bathurst Ltée.
Maps La Tuque 31P
Roberval 32A

Driving operations take place on the river during the summer from a little above Lake Trenche to the St. Maurice River. There are two dams on the Trenche.

Saguenay River Drainage Basin

105 MALBAIE RIVER
Timber company La Companie Donohue Ltée.
Maps St. Urbain 21M/10
Lac des Martres 21M/15
Lac au Plongeon 21M/16
La Malbaie 21M/9E

The river is driven during the whole year and is not always open.

106 CHICOUTIMI RIVER
Timber company La Compangie Donohue Ltée.
Map Lac Jacques Cartier 21M/11E

107 MISTASSINI RIVER
Timber company Domtar Ltd.

108 SHIPSHAW RIVER
Timber company Price Company

The river is approximately 75 miles long, flowing north to south from Lac Pipmuakan to discharge at Kénogami. The lower 55 miles, however, is for pulp driving and not navigable. Above this point and in the region of Lac Pipmuakan, which spreads easterly, are possibly excellent canoeing regions. Arrange all pre-planning with the company.

Maps covering the permissible canoeing sections are available. Access to jump-off would appear to be by air charter with companies based at Chicoutimi or Roberval.

Gaspé Drainage Basin

109 ST. JEAN RIVER
Timber company La Compagnie Donohue Ltée.
Maps L'Anse St. Jean 22D/1E
Ferland 22D/2E

North Shore—Labrador Drainage Basin

The following rivers are situated on the north shore of the St. Lawrence River and flow from north to south.

110 FRANQUELIN RIVER
Timber company Quebec North Shore Paper Co.
Maps Godbout 22E/SW
Rivière Godbout 22E/12W

This river is open to canoeing but has many obstacles, falls and rapids.

111 PISTUACANIS RIVER
Timber company Quebec North Shore Paper Company
Maps Rivière Godbout 22E/12W
LacMiquelon 22F/9E
LacAmariton 22F/16E

You may canoe this river if you join a fishing club.

112 ST. NICHOLAS RIVER
Timber company Quebec North Shore Paper Company
Maps Godbout 22E/SW

113 GODBOUT RIVER
Timber company Quebec North Shore Paper Company
Maps Godbout 22E/SE
Rivière Godbout 22E/12W

114 MANICOUAGAN RIVER
Timber company Quebec North Shore Paper Company

There is wood driving and rafting along the full length of the river. As well, there are four hydro dams.

115 BERSIMIS (BETSIAMITES) RIVER
Length 150 miles (241 km)
Access By Highway 138
Timber company Price Co.

The river flows from northwest to southeast, rising most likely in Lac des Prairie and discharging into the St. Lawrence River, north shore, at the village of Bersimis. The lower 50 miles is not navigable and is used for driving pulp by Anglo-Canadian pulp and paper mills.

Large scale federal maps for the upper portion of this river are available when definite routes are determined. It seems possible above the jump-off point to turn west and enter Lac Pipmuakan waters and come down the company's Shipshaw River to *finish* where designated on that river. Alternate access is by driving east to Baie Comeau or Hauterive to arrange a flight with air charter companies based there.

116 MOISIE RIVER
Length 310 miles (499 km)
Approx trip time 18 days

Access   Quebec North Shore and Labrador Railway to Labrador City

Start at Wabush Lake, Labrador. Paddle through Long Lake, a chain of unnamed lakes, to a height of land, down Carheil Lake, Carheil River and Pekans River, to the Moisie River. Pass the junctions of River Doree and the Nipissis River to *finish* at a new highway bridge across Moisie River. There is chartered ground transport to Sept Iles.

W.A. Richardson has reported: "Overall, trip very interesting . . . gorges very scenic and not the problem anticipated. The river is very fast and has few large drops. In August most rapids 'chute-able' with care and scouting by *experienced* canoeists."

Should be attempted only by the most experienced whitewater experts.

From individual trip reports (printed with permission): W.A. Richardson, Stewart T. Coffin, Henry Franklin.

117   NATASHQUAN RIVER

Length   180 miles (290 km)
Approx trip time   8-14 days
Access   Goose Bay/Happy Valley, Labrador
Maps   Maps found to contain inaccuracies. Refer to Edition 1 ASE, Series A501
Lac Brulé 13D
Lac de Morhiban 12M
Natashquan 12N
Musquaro 12K

Natashquan River, one of the major systems draining southern Labrador, flows about four-fifths its length, 220 miles, in Québec to tidewater at Point-Parent village on the north shore of the St. Lawrence River.

There is a 2,000 foot drop in elevation from the headwaters to the mouth. The last 35 miles to the mouth of the river is controlled by a private salmon fishing club. An aerial survey of the upper Natashquan River showed that the river there was not suitable for canoeing. The river is a former major Indian travel route.

Take a charter floatplane from Goose Bay/ Happy Valley, Labrador (120 air miles-193 km) to start at a point 11 miles (18 km) below the forks of Masquamanaga and Natashquan Rivers. The survey crew divided the route into sections as follows:

Segment 1   Natashquan River to the forks of East Natashquan River.

Segment 2   East Natashquan forks to mileage 33 from forks.

Segment 3   Mileage 33 to multi-rapids section.
Segment 4   Long Steady Section.
Segment 5   To the mouth of the Natashquan River and *finish* at the village of Pointe-Parent. Ride by charter vehicle to the village of Natashquan. Weekly air or coastal steamer service from here to Sept Iles city is available.

Reports on this route indicate that it is rugged, possesses little beauty, and contains many rapids and shallows.

Baie de Chaleur Drainage Basin

118   MATAPEDIA RIVER

Access   By Highway 6 (Mont Joli-Matapedia)
Timber company   New Brunswick International Paper Co.
Maps   Matane 22B

The river rises east of Lac Matapedia in the Matane region, which is south of the St. Lawrence River in Eastern Quebec/New Brunswick. The company advises that pulp is driven on the river.

119   NOUVELLE RIVER

Timber company   New Brunswick International Paper Co.

120   CASCAPEDIA RIVER

Timber company   New Brunswick International Paper Co.

Hudson Strait — Ungava Bay Drainage Basin

121   GEORGE RIVER

Length   340 miles (547 km)
Approx trip time   15 days
Access   Charter float plane from Schefferville
Maps   These maps are to a scale of 1:500,000. Although inaccurate in some markings, they are generally sufficient.
Dyke Lake 23NE
Indian House 24SE
George River 24 NE

The George River flows north through Quebec from headwaters in the Labrador-Quebec "right-angle corner", which lies between the longitude of 64° and 66° west and the latitude of 55° and 59° north.

The river drops 1400 feet in elevation from the headwaters at Cabot Lake to tidewater at Ungava Bay. The river starts with a gradual descent which becomes steeper between higher, steeper and narrower valleys and then flattens out near the estuary at Ungava Bay.

Take a charter floatplane from Scheffer-ville, flying east to *start* at Cabot Lake. Paddle downstream on the George River through connecting Lac Lacasse, Resolution Lake, Advance Lake, passing the drainage tributary of Whitegull Lake, Thousand Island Expansion (of river) and the mouth of Rivière de Pas to Indian House Lake.

Paddle the length of Indian House Lake (50-60 miles), join the George River inlet and *finish* on the river at Port Nouveau, Quebec.

Radio from here to Schefferville for charter floatplane pick-up.

S.T. Coffin reports: "For very experienced canoeists; much lining down rapids, some very rugged portaging. Along lower river some tourist fishing outcamps and lodges on leased portions of the George River. The above trip made in August during drought water conditions."

From individual trip reports (printed with permission): Bob Davis, Stewart T. Coffin

122 RIVIÈRE DE PAS
Length 390 miles (628 km)
Access From Schefferville, Quebec
Maps These maps are to a scale of 1:500,000
Although inaccurate in some markings, generally sufficient
Dyke Lake 23NE
Indian House 24SE
George River 24NE

Rivière du Pas is an alternate starting point for the George River trip, and joins the George River.

The *start* is easily accessible from Scheffer-ville, Quebec, 12 miles (19 km) by charter truck to Iron Arm.

Paddle across Attikamagen Lake (requires critical navigation due to a maze of islands and channels). Portage over a height of land into Snowshoe Lake; paddle through Secalar,

Frederickson, Doublet, McNeill, Blenac, Girard, La Porte, Dillon, Talon, and James Lakes. Continue 80 miles down Rivière de Pas (said to be full shallow rapids and hazardous at low water) to its junction with the George River.

For the remainder of the route, see the previous George River route.

From individual trip reports (printed with permission): Bob Davis, Stewart T. Coffin

123 KANIAPISCAU AND KOKSOAK RIVERS
Length 600 miles (965 km)
Approx trip time 29 days
Access From Labrador City by Charter floatplane

The Kaniapiscau River with its many tributaries constitutes a major drainage system for the central Ungava region. Fifty miles (80 km) above Fort Chimo, the Kaniapiscau is joined by the Larch River flowing in from the south-west and the main stream becomes the Koksoak River.

Take a charter floatplane from Labrador City 45 miles (72 km) southwest to *start* at Lac Sevestre. Paddle to the outlet of the lake to Lac Gensart, Lac Grosse Roche, Lac Goupil, Lac Opiscotee, Lac Lapointe, Lac Nouveau, Lac Tournon, Lac Kaniapiscau, Lac Delorme, Upper George and past the mouth of the Iron River.

Continue past the Lower George, Eaton Canyon, Cambrian Lake, Swamp Bay River and Manitou Gorge to join the Koksoak River at its intersection with the Larch River and *finish* on the Koksoak at Fort Chimo.

S.T. Coffin reports: "Entire route is very dangerous, each lake joined by many miles of rapids, impassible falls, much portaging. Trip should not be considered except by very expert canoemen and, by them, only after much research and study of previous reports. Governmental travel permits for this route may be difficult, if not impossible, to obtain."

From individual trip reports (printed with permission): Stewart T. Coffin and Bob Davis.

James Bay South Drainage Basin

124 MISTASSINI PROVINCIAL PARK

Length 100 miles (161 km)
Access 330 miles (531 km) north of Quebec, on Highway 167
Maps Free canoe route maps from Parks Branch.

The canoeing season is from about June 1 to September 15. There is compulsory registration at park gate office. No canoes are for rent in the park, but they may be rented at the town of Chibougamau, 15 miles (24 km) from the park gate.

For information and maps write:

Parks Branch, Reservations Office,
Department of Tourism, Fish and Game,
748 Marcotte Blvd.,
Roberval, P.Q.

Laurentides Provincial Park

125 RIVIÈRE MÉGISCANE (ABITIBI REGION)

Access Town of Senneterre, Quebec Highways 45 and 58; Canadian National Railway, east of Senneterre to jump-off at Forsythe
Timber company Paradis & Fils Ltée.
Map Senneterre 32C

Together with its many connecting tributaries and lakes a limits area of about 1,500 square miles is encompassed. It seems to offer adequate canoeing country, but canoeing is at the sole discretion of the company.

126 WASWANIPI RIVER

Timber company Domtar Ltd.

This river is located in Laurentides Provincial Park. Many other excellent planned canoe routes are laid out within the park. They are maintained and controlled by Quebec Provincial Parks. South of this park area the land is privately owned. As well, a restricted section flows through the Canadian Forces research camp at Valcartier. Aside from the park routes, all planning should be done through Domtar.

La Vérendrye Provincial Park

127 LA VÉRENDRYE RIVER

Access Canoe base office is at Le Domaine on Lac des Loups, 36 miles (58 km) south of the park gate on Highway 58, 220 miles (354 km) northwest of Montreal.
Maps An excellent white print map at a scale of about 3 miles to 1 inch or a federal 1:50,000 scale map are both available at the canoe base.

Located in the Ottawa River drainage basin, this canoeing network is 1,300 miles long. Six hundred miles are marked to indicate campsites and portages. The park is situated northwest of Hull and Ottawa on Highway 58.

Canoeing is good from approximately mid-May to mid-September. One hundred canoes are available for hire but trippers are advised to bring their own canoes and equipment. For advance information write:

Canoe-Camping Section
Le Domaine
La Vérendrye Provincial Park
Gatineau County, P.Q. J0W 1T0

La Mauricie National Park

La Mauricie National Park, located in the St. Maurice River drainage basin, is open for canoeing from June to September. The park is 210 square miles in area and is situated to the west of the St. Maurice River on Highway 19, 7 miles (11 km) north of Grand'Mère, 17 miles (27 km) from Shawinigan and 35 miles (51 km) from Trois Rivières.

In spring the St. Maurice River presents dangers to canoeists. Swollen by snow-melt, the river flows very quickly carrying with it thousands of floating logs of the spring log drive.

Five distinct canoe routes have been laid out. Excellent free maps are available from the Superintendent of the park at P.O. Box 758, Shawinigan, P.Q.

128 METABEROUTIN

Length 13 miles (21 km)
Portages 3 (2.72 miles in total)

129 LAURENTIAN
Length 30 miles (48 km)
Portages 4 (5.09 miles in total)

130 ATIKAMEG
Length 68 miles (109 km)
Portages 10 (9.77 miles in total)

131 LAC À LA PÊCHE – DES CINQ
Length 22 miles (35 km)
Portages 16 (9.98 miles in total)

132 LAC À LA PÊCHE-BERUBE
Length 8 miles (13 km)
Portages 6 (.72 miles in total)

Avoid the lower stretches of the Mattawin
River. This river is narrow and filled with falls
and rapids from Lac des Cinq portage to its
mouth at the St. Maurice River. It is not
navigable by canoe.

James Bay Development

The James Bay Development Corporation has
stopped all tourist travel for an undetermined
period in the region of its multi-billion dollar
hydroelectric project. The project covers an
area equal to the combined land masses of New
York, Maine, Massachusetts, New Hampshire,
Vermont, Connecticut, Rhode Island, Maryland
and Hawaii (about 133,377 square miles, or
about the size of England). When fully developed a few years hence, the project may well
produce more than 15 million kilowatts of
power — more than from any other such project ever undertaken in the world.

Seven rivers, their tributaries and connecting lakes chains will be affected and changed
beyond recognition: Nottaway, Broadback,
Rupert, Eastmain, La Grande, Great Whale and
Kaniapiscau River. This situation presents
problems to wilderness canoeists who are already
familiar with some of the rivers or those who
have planned trips, for the Government of
Quebec officially discourages canoeing in the
area.

*Scaling the heights above the Clearwater River,
these two men have just completed the toughest
leg of a difficult portage.*

Map Sources

Canada Mapping Office, 615 Booth Street, Ottawa, Ontario, is the chief supplier of topographical maps. Maps for the province are available from the following map dealers in Quebec:

Jules Lefrancois
Articles de Sport
C.P. 548
Ville St. Gabriel
Cté. Berthier, P.Q.

Le Domaine de la Passe
C.P. 279
St. Michel des Saints
Cté. Berthier, P.Q.

Paquet Sporting Goods
432-1st Ave.
Ville St. Georges Est,
Beauce-Est, P.Q.

L'Ami du Sport Enr.
620 Boul. Labelle
Blainville, P.Q.

Mitchs Sporting Goods
490 Main St.
Buckingham, P.Q.

Pierre Duguay
110 St-Alphonse
Cap-de-la-Madelaine, P.Q.

Pierre Duguay
526-15e Rue Sud
Charney, P.Q.

Jos-Savage
c/o Jos-Sport-Enrg.
349-3ième Rue
Chibougamau, P.Q.

Marius Pomerleau
534-1'er rue
Chibougamau, P.Q.

Comptoir d'Information et de Diffusion
   Cartographique
930 Est Jacques Cartier
Chicoutimi, P.Q.

Camp Kapitachowane
Kapitachowane, P.Q.
Via Senneterre, P.Q.

Jacques Darche Inc.
Katevale, P.Q. J0B 1W0

Mr. Bertrand Maltais
C.P. 84
Chicoutimi-Nord, P.Q.

Le Centre d'Etude Géo-Cartographique
263 Lafontaine
C.P. 301
Chicoutimi, P.Q. G7H 4T6

Dolbeau Air Service Inc.
586 Blvd. Walberg
Dolbeau, P.Q.

Gemme Le Sport
584 Principale
Farnham, P.Q. J2N 1K9

Tabagie Michel Ltée.
399 Main St.
Gatineau, P.Q.

Lafreniere-Ethier Enr.
Sport Shop
Gracefield, P.Q.

Authier & Frère Inc.
261 Rue Principale
Granby, P.Q.

L.P.I. Photo Enr.
Grande Rivière (Gaspé Est), P.Q.

Paul Gendron Sports
888 Puyjalon
Hauterive, P.Q.

Royaume du Sport Enr.
2088 Ste. Hélène
Jacques Cartier, P.Q.

De Beaudry Sport Inc.
740 St. Antoine
Joliette, P.Q.

Lithographie Jean Belanger
1525 Boul. Gaboury, C.P. 33
Mont Joli, P.Q. G5H 3K8

A. Chalifoux Ltd.
301, de la Madone
Mont Laurier, P.Q.

Kipawa Air Services Ltd.
Kipawa, P.Q.

J.A. Larocque
Nominigue
Lac Bourget, P.Q.

Megantic Sporting Goods Reg'd
5441 Frontenac
Lac Megantic, P.Q.

Mr. Réjean Lafrenière
General Store
Lac Ste. Marie, P.Q.

Dorvals Camp-on Kipawa Lake
Laniel, P.Q.

Paul Tremblay
C.P. 822
La Sarre, P.Q.

J.O. Lejeune Ltée.
C.P. 188
Latuque, P.Q.

Nelson Andrews Gun Shop
Lennoxville, P.Q.

Hudon & Vigneux Inc.
471 Main St. West,
Magog, P.Q.

J.O. Hubert Ltd.
P.O. Box 820
Maniwaki, P.Q.

J.H. Poirier & Fils
139 Main St.
Maniwaki, P.Q.

Librairie Sauvageau Enr.
591 Cinquième Rue
Shawinigan, P.Q.

Skinner & Nadeau Co.
82 N. Wellington St.
Sherbrooke, P.Q.

Société Canadienne D'Ecologie
St. Faustin
C.P. 90
Cté. Terrebonne, P.Q.

J.E. Beauséjour Inc.
4559 Rue Papineau
Montreal 178, P.Q.

Cartex Incorporated
1029 Bleury St.
Montreal 128, P.Q.

Quebec Wild Life Federation
6424 St. Denis
Montreal, P.Q.

Select Press Ltd.
1555 Louvain St. W.
Montreal 355, P.Q.

Sir George Williams University
Bookstore
2085 Bishop St.
Montreal 25, P.Q.

Smith Ind.
716 Golf Rd.
Nuns Island
Montreal, P.Q.

Marc Brunelle
C.P. 10
Parent, Cté. Lavioletee, P.Q.

Librarie Garneau Corp. Ltd.
47-49 Rue Buade
Quebec 4, P.Q.

Sandford's Parent Lake Lodge
P.O. Box 554
Senneterre, P.Q.

Beaulieu Sport
408 Place du Marche
St Jerome, P.Q.

Librairie Poirier Enr.
1505 Rue Royale
Trois Rivières, P.Q. G9A 4J9

J. Leo Gagnon, Stationery
867-3rd Ave.
Val D'Or, P.Q.

W. Golinski
Angliers
Temiscaminque, P.Q.

Wakefield Sports
Station Building
Wakefield, P.Q.

For a provincial road map and provincial parks canoe routes maps, write:

Tourism Branch
Department of Tourism, Fish & Game
Place de la Capitale
150 St. Cyrille
15th Floor
Quebec, P.Q.

For marked road route maps write:

Imperial Oil Ltd.
2 Place Ville-Marie
Montreal, P.Q.

Supertest-B.P. Canada
1245 Sherbrooke St. W.
Montreal, P.Q.

Texaco Canada Ltd.
1425 de la Montagne
Montreal, P.Q.

 Outfitters

An independent canoeing group, which has tried to compile a list of outfitters, finds that there are few such services in the province. Many firms list package rates to remote fishing camps where accommodation is provided. Therefore, in the opinion of the survey group, it is safe to assume that such tripper services in Quebec should not be counted on by canoeists.

 Air Charter Services

When making plans for a trip, canoeists requiring air services may contact the following commercial carriers:

Air Brazeau Inc.
Rouyn Airport
Rouyn, P.Q. J9X 5B7

Air Roberval Ltée
Aeroport
Roberval, P.Q.

Brochu Air
3700 Boul. St. Joseph E.
Montreal, P.Q.

Dolbeau Air Services Inc.
10305 Papineau
Montreal 359, P.Q.

Fecteau Air Transport Ltd.
Box 368
Amos, P.Q.

Gagnon Air Service Ltd.
Box 341
Chicoutimi-Nord, P.Q.

Kipawa Air Service Inc.
Kipawa, P.Q.

La Sarre Air Services Ltd.
Box 638
La Sarre, P.Q.

Laurentian Air Services
Box 818
R.R. 5
Ottawa, Ont. K1G 3N3

Nordair Ltd.
Hangar 5
Montreal International Airport
Montreal, P.Q.

Northern Wings Ltd.
Dept. 2012
Sept-Iles Airport
Sept-Iles, P.Q.

Northwestern Airways Inc.
Box 244
Noranda, P.Q.

Quebecair Ltée.
Box 490
Montreal International Airport
Montreal, P.Q.

St. Felicien Air Services Ltée.
C.P. 910
St. Felicien, P.Q.

In addition to these companies and their home bases, the Ministry of Transport lists the following floatplane bases in the event that some of them may fit into airlift plans:

Alma, Blanc Sablon, Clapham Lake, Cranston Lake, Drummondville, Eastmain, Estcourt, Fort George, Fort Rupert, Gaspé, Grindstone, Harrington Harbour, Harve St. Pierre, Inoucdjouac, Lac des Ecorces, Lac-du-Cerf, Lac Duchamp, Lac Kaiagamac, Lac St. Augustin, Lac St. Louis, Laniel, Matagami, Mingan, Natashquan, Nouveau-Comptoir, Oskelaneo, Port Nouveau-Quebec, Poste-de-la-Baleine, Povungnituk, Rapids Lake, Ste. Agathe-des-Monts, Senneterre, Shipshaw, St. Jovite, Tête-à-la-Baleine, Val D'Or, Ivujivik, Lac-à-la-Tortue and Fort Chimo.

ONTARIO

Ontario is Canada's most centrally located province. It is second in size to Quebec (412,582 square miles), stretching 1,000 miles from west to east and 1,050 miles from south to north. Its southernmost point — Point Pelee — lies in the same latitude as northern California (41° 41'); its northern latitudes are subarctic. The southern boundary of Ontario stretches along the St. Lawrence River, Lake Ontario, Lake Erie, Lake Huron, Lake Superior and Lake of the Woods. Some 680 miles of its 750 mile northern boundary lies on the coastal tidewater lowlands of Hudson Bay, the remainder on James Bay. It is bordered on the west by Manitoba and on the east by Quebec, with which it shares the shorelines of Lake Timiskaming, Lake Abitibi and the Ottawa River.

Ontario has two distinct geographical regions: the north and south. The north, consisting of 360,000 square miles, is chiefly on the Precambrian Shield and the fringe of the Hudson Bay-James Bay lowlands. Within it, near the Quebec boundary is the twenty million acre agricultural Clay Belt.

The southern region of Ontario is a wedge, partially covered by the Shield, with the remainder forming the rich agricultural lands of the northern Great Lakes and St. Lawrence River lowlands. The regional dividing line corresponds to the French and Mattawa Rivers. The height of land above Lake Superior divides the flow of rivers to the Arctic (Hudson Bay-James Bay) and to the Atlantic (Great Lakes-St. Lawrence River). The highest point of land, near Sault Ste. Marie, is only 2,183 feet above sea level.

In addition to the Great Lakes, the larger lakes in Ontario include: Nipigon (1,870 square miles); Lake of the Woods (953), Lac Seul (539), Nipissing (350), Abitibi (313), Simcoe (283) and Rainy Lake (291).

The larger Ontario rivers are: Albany, Severn, Attawapiskat, Ottawa, Abitibi, Winisk, Mattagami, Missinaibi, Ekwan, English, Fawn, Groundhog, Kapiskan, Kapuskasing, Little Current, Otoskwin, Sachigo, St. Lawrence and Seine.

Ontario's population of almost eight million people makes it the most heavily populated province. Most of the population is located in Southern Ontario, and the region of Metropolitan Toronto, the provincial capital, alone accounts for about three million. The nation's capital, Ottawa, is also in Ontario. The province is the most highly industrialized and urbanized, with the greatest number of occupied farms. Yet it is also the largest fur producer in the nation.

Sixty per cent of the nation's minerals — nickel, uranium, copper, gold, iron and salt — come from Ontario. As seventy-five percent of the province is covered by forests, the pulp and paper industry is the third largest in the country. Output from the various sources of hydro, thermal and nuclear power is enormous.

Three of Ontario's 121 provincial parks cover great areas: Polar Bear (9,300 square miles); Algonquin (2,910 square miles) and Quetico (1,750 square miles). Algonquin and Quetico attract the greatest number of vacationing canoeists in North America.

Previous page. The canoeist can choose from an enormous number of canoeing possibilities in Ontario. These can range from the pleasures of paddling along the placid waters of the Rideau Canal to the challenges and excitement of more turbulent rivers - sometimes with prospects not unlike the daunting portage encountered by this group.

Climate

Ontario's climate is continental with a tempering influence in the region of the lower Great Lakes. The north has short, hot summers; temperatures in the central region vary widely, situated as it is in the path of one of the major storm tracks of the continent. The climate of the southern portion of the province is mostly moderate. Ontario basically offers a range of three climatic regions to canoeists: south-central, central (Precambrian shield) and northern (Hudson Bay lowlands). The following summer temperatures and rainfall are tabled by the federal data control centre of Environment Canada:

Ontario	Mean temperatures In Fahrenheit (Celsius)				Rainfall In mean inches (Millimetres)	
	Min		Max			
Southern-central (Peterborough)						
June	53.3	(11.8)	74.3	(23.5)	2.98	(75.7)
July	57.4	(14.1)	78.5	(25.8)	2.53	(64.3)
August	55.6	(13.1)	77.1	(25.1)	2.71	(68.8)
Central-shield (Geraldton)						
June	42.4	(5.8)	68.0	(20.0)	3.12	(79.3)
July	48.4	(9.1)	73.7	(23.2)	3.04	(77.2)
August	45.7	(7.6)	69.9	(21.1)	3.63	(92.2)
Northern-Hudson Bay lowlands (Trout Lake)						
June	42.7	(5.9)	62.7	(17.1)	2.63	(66.8)
July	51.6	(10.9)	69.8	(21.0)	3.74	(95.0)
August	49.6	(9.8)	66.3	(19.1)	3.40	(86.4)

Fishing

Ontario is the province with perhaps the greatest number of recently introduced sport fish species, jurisdictional divisions and varying fishing seasons. This is as a result of its huge concentrated population pressures, its influx of tourists from several states to the south and its sprawling geographic range.

The fish species are pike, walleye, sauger, perch, blue pickerel, maskinonge, large and smallmouth bass, brook, brown, rainbow, lake and splake trout, Atlantic and Pacific salmon, whitefish, and sturgeon.

Crowded fishing conditions for canoeists are not a problem but sometimes complicated regulations are. Canoeists should apply early for the Ontario fishing folder from the Ministry of Natural Resources, Queen's Park, Toronto, or from any of the district offices scattered conveniently across the province.

The most recent angling fees are:

Ontario residents   free
nonresidents of Ontario $4.00
nonresidents of Canada (seasonal) $10.75
nonresidents of Canada (3 day) $6.00

 History

Very soon after Samuel de Champlain founded Quebec in 1609, the French were pushing through Ontario waterways by canoe. In 1615 Champlain explored the Georgian Bay region and wintered there. Twenty-four years later the French established, in Ontario, the first European settlement in inland North America.

This settlement, Ste. Marie, was the centre of a Jesuit mission to some twenty Huron Indian villages, said to be the largest congregation of Indians in North America. The Hurons, encouraged by the French, acted as middlemen in the fur trade, taking furs brought from farther west and trading them in Montreal and Quebec. The principal enemies of the Hurons were the Iroquois of northern New York State, who were allies of the English and Dutch fur traders of the Hudson River valley. To break the Huron monopoly on western fur and direct it southward, the Iroquois ravaged the Huron settlements and put to death by torture the French missionaries. The mission of Ste. Marie has been rebuilt in recent years on the River Wye near Midland and is an impressive showplace of both historic and religious interest. Adjacent to Ste. Marie is a nature preserve open to the public.

The English, meanwhile, headed by explorer Henry Hudson, had by 1610 entered Hudson Bay. In 1670 the English formed the Hudson's Bay Company, building a number of forts or storehouse "factories" in Ontario. Within the following six years these were built at Moose Factory, Fort Albany, Charlton Island and Henly House — 100 miles upstream on the Albany River and the first English inland trading post. The company built other posts on the Quebec and Manitoba shores during the same era.

Canada became an English colony in 1763 (the Treaty of Paris), but settlement was slow in Ontario and in the earliest years after the British conquest most of the activity was still related to the fur trade. The traders of Montreal used the Ottawa-French-English Rivers route as they pushed westward into Manitoba and beyond. Other English traders on the James Bay shore pushed inland up the Albany River to the English River and westward. Only after the American Revolution did serious settlement begin. In 1791 the area now known as Ontario was broken off from the old Province of Quebec to become the Province of Upper Canada. Various American invasions during the War of 1812-1814 were repulsed by the new settlers. Their preference for British parliamentary and legal systems was confirmed in 1837 when a feeble republican rebellion was soundly defeated.

Quetico Provincial Park is a place that retains its wilderness character and suggestions of a colourful past. Mysterious Indian petroglyphs (above), etched into the rock, speak of the earliest men to travel the area's waterways, and memories of the fur traders abound along its rivers, which formed part of the main route between the western plain and the trading centres in the east.

Ontario was the strongest proponent of Confederation in 1867 and was one of the four original provinces to join in forming the Dominion of Canada in that year.

Ontario's canoe route system is the most extensive in the country and as a result is very complex. For convenient reference, Ontario's canoe routes have been grouped below under the following headings: Ontario Canals, Southern Ontario Routes; Northern Ontario Routes. The east-west line of the Nipissing, French and Mattawa Rivers divides the province into its northern and southern regions. Each region can then be divided into drainage basins as follows:

Northern Ontario Lake Huron; Moose River; Albany River; Attawapiskat River; Winisk River; Severn River; Winnipeg River; Lake of the Woods; Lake Superior.

Southern Ontario Lake Huron; Ottawa River; Lake Ontario; Lake Erie. In some of the drainage basins the water table lakes (whose waters flow out in more than one direction) further complicate flow patterns. Two prime examples are: the Trent-Severn Canal System that flows to both Lake Ontario and Lake Huron, from Balsam Lake; the Rideau Canal System that flows north to the Ottawa River and south to Lake Ontario, from Chaffey's Lock. Even in Algonquin Provincial Park — said to be the busiest canoe tripping waterway in North America — some rivers flow north into the Ottawa River and other rivers southeast, also into the Ottawa River, with both debouchments miles apart.

Again, as in Quebec, drainage basin boundaries have been plotted as carefully as possible, but because of the complicated topographical conditions they may be at times disputable.

 # Southern Ontario Routes

Ontario Canals

133 RIDEAU CANAL

The distance from Lake Ontario to the Ottawa River following the Rideau canal route is about 125 miles. There are forty-seven locks and each normally takes ten to fifteen minutes to pass through. The total length of artificial canal channel is only about twelve miles; the remainder of the main route passes through improved lake and river channels. The speed limit in artificial canal channels is 6 miles per hour (10 km/h) or as posted. It should be emphasized that the speed limit on Dow's Lake in Ottawa is 6 mph (10 km/h) and this is rigidly enforced.

The Rideau Canal was built by the Royal Engineers in the years 1826-1832 to provide 5 feet (1.5m) draught. The Tay Branch was built in the years 1831-1834 by a private company to provide 4 feet (1.2 m) draught. Control of the Rideau Canal has now been transferred to the Department of Indian Affairs and Northern Development, Parks Branch.

During the navigation season, Rideau Canal charts may be purchased by counter sale only, from the lockmaster at Ottawa Lock Station, the lockmaster at Smiths Falls Detached Lock Station, the lockmaster at Kingston Mills Lock Station, the Canal Superintendent at Smiths Falls or from the Rideau Canal office, 370 Sparks Street Ottawa, Ontario.

They can be purchased by counter sale or mail order from the Chart Distribution Office, Canadian Hydrographic Service, 615 Booth St., Ottawa, Ontario.

Boat campers on the Rideau Canal are permitted to use waterway reserve lands for camping purposes when on a trip through the system. Boat campers are permitted to stay one or two nights at a lock station but must apply to the lockmaster for permission to camp. The lockmaster will issue a permit and campers must comply with its provisions and any other directions of the lockmaster.

Miles
From
Ottawa Structure, Locality and Landmarks

(Mean level for the Ottawa River is 135 feet
above sea level)

0.00 Ottawa Locks, 1 to 8 in flight (at the
Ottawa River near the city centre)
0.22 Confederation Square (concrete arch
and steel bridge)
0.40 Mackenzie King (concrete, fixed-span
bridge)
0.54 Laurier Ave (steel, arch bridge)
1.50 Fixed bridge
1.56 Bridge 1, Pretoria Ave (vertical lift)
2.81 Bank St. (concrete, arch bridge)
3.42 Bronson Ave. (concrete, fixed-span
bridge)
3.72 Dow's Lake Canadian Pacific Railway
swing bridge
4.17 Hartwell Locks 9 & 10 in flight
5.10 Fixed Bridge
5.23 Hogs Back Locks 11 & 12 in flight
5.25 Bridge 4, Hogs Back (swing) — canal
enters Rideau River
7.43 Canadian National Railways / high-
level bridge
9.25 Lock 13, Black Rapids
14.25 Long Island Locks 14 & 16 in flight
14.33 Bridge 5, Long Island over lock 16
(swing)
16.03 Manotick high level fixed bridge
23.00 Fixed Bridge
23.33 Public Wharf

DIVERSION South Rideau to Kemptville
(navigable by shallow draught vessels only)
30.48 Channel to Kemptville
33.38 Kemptville Wharf

31.93 Becketts high-level, fixed bridge
38.93 Lock 17, Burritts Rapids
39.43 Bridge 9, Burritts Rapids (swing)
41.83 Flight Lock 18 (Nicholsons)
42.09 Flight Lock 19 (Nicholsons)
42.10 Bridge 10, over lock 19 (Nicholsons,
swing)
42.50 Lock 20, Clowes
44.30 Merrickville Canadian Pacific Railway
high level bridge
44.65 Flight Lock 21 (Merrickville)
44.71 Flight Lock 22 (Merrickville)
44.81 Flight Lock 23 (Merrickville)

44.81 Bridge 11, over lock 23 (Merrickville
swing)
52.81 Lock 24 (Kilmarnock)
52.82 Bridge 13, over lock 24 (Kilmarnock,
swing)
56.22 Lock 25, Edmonds
57.72 Canadian Pacific Railway high-level
bridge (Smith Falls)
57.72 Old Slys Locks 26 & 27 in flight
57.77 Bridge 15 (Old Slys, swing)
58.52 Locks 28, 29 & 30 in flight
(Smith Falls)
58.58 Bridge 17, Beckwith Street (channel
width reduced to 28 ft., swing)
58.86 Bridge 19, Abbott Street (swing)
58.88 Detached lock 31 (Smiths Falls)
58.98 Canadian National Railways
bascule bridge
60.98 Lock 32, Poonamalie
61.58 Entrance to Lower Rideau Lake

DIVERSION Tay Canal to Perth (6.12 miles)
65.10 Diversion to Tay Branch
65.80 Canal entrance, Beveridge Bay
(Rideau Lake)
66.00 Lock 33 (Beveridges)
66.09 Fixed bridge
66.32 Lock 34 (Beveridges)
71.52 Fixed Bridge, public wharf (Craig
Street, Perth)
71.77 Fixed bridge, Beckwith Street (Perth)
71.86 Fixed bridge, Drummond Street (Perth)
71.92 Basin Wharf (Perth)
71.96 Fixed bridge, Gore Street, *end of canal
to Perth*

67.02 Bridge 26, Rideau Ferry (swing)

DIVERSION Channel to Portland Wharf on
South Shore Big Rideau Lake
72.42 Diversion to Portland
78.90 Portland Public Wharf

80.02 Lock 35 (The Narrows)
80.02 Bridge 27 The Narrows (swing)
80.08 Entrance to Upper Rideau Lake
For Upper Rideau Lake the summit level is
408.01 feet above sea level

DIVERSION Channel to Westport Wharf on
West Shore Upper Rideau Lake
80.08 Diversion to Westport
85.33 Westport Public Wharf

84.43 Newboro high level, fixed bridge
84.74 Lock 36, Newboro

89.74	Canadian National Railways high-level bridge
90.00	Lock 37 (Chaffey's) The lock from which the waterway flows north to Ottawa River and south to Lake Ontario.)
90.00	Bridge 30, Chaffey's (swing)
92.15	Lock 38, Davis
96.45	Lock 39 (Jones Falls)
96.48	Jones Falls basin
96.59	Locks 40 to 42 in flight (Jones Falls)
96.63	Bridge 33, over lock 41 (Jones Falls, swing)

DIVERSION Channel to Morton Dam on Morton Creek

99.38	Diversion to Morton
101.00	Morton dam, no public wharf

DIVERSION Channel to Seeleys Bay, village & wharf

100.88	Diversion to Seeleys Bay
101.53	Seeleys Bay Public Wharf

103.08	Bridge 36, Brass Point (swing)
107.28	Locks 43 & 44 in flight, Upper Brewers
107.58	Fixed bridge
109.06	Bridge 39, over entrance to Lock 45 (lower Brewers, swing)
109.06	Lock 45, Washburn (Lower Brewers)
118.81	Lock 46 (Kingston Mills)
118.81	Bridge 41, Kingston Mills over lock 46 (swing)
118.83	Kingston Mills basin
118.91	Locks 47 to 49 in flight (Kingston Mills)
118.93	Canadian National Railways high-level bridge over locks 47 & 48
119.56	fixed bridge (Highway 401)
123.53	Kingston — Lasalle Causeway Bascule Bridge

Mean level for Lake Ontario is 245.9 feet above sea level

Canoeists on Canals: Of all pleasure craft, only the canoe is exempt from lockage fees imposed in 1975 on the Rideau and Trent-Severn Canals. However, each canoe must display a registration number, obtained free from any Canada Customs office. Otherwise, it may have to be carried around the lock site.

134 TRENT-SEVERN WATERWAY
The distance from Lake Ontario to Georgian Bay, following the Trent Canal route, is about 240 miles and there are 43 locks and 1 marine railway. The passage through each lock normally takes 15 to 20 minutes. The total length of the artifical canal channels is about 33 miles and the remainder of the main route (207 miles) is through improved lake and river channels.

An ancient river, the Algonquin River, followed much the same route as the Trent portion of the waterway. This river was the outlet of Lake Algonquin which then covered Lakes Superior, Michigan and Huron as well as areas extending southeastward across Lake Simcoe and Balsam Lake to Fenelon Falls. From here the Algonquin River followed the Kawartha Lakes to Stony Lake and reached Rice Lake through the Indian and Otonabee Rivers. Rice Lake was then an arm of a huge lake (called Lake Iroquois), which in those times covered the present Lake Ontario and a large area of adjacent territory.

The main route of the waterway also follows the historic Iroquois Trail, the pathway followed by the Iroquois in their deadly descents on the Huron tribesmen. It was the route followed by Champlain when he discovered Lake Ontario while on a retaliatory raid with the Hurons in 1618. By the same warpath the Iroquois returned thirty years later to annihilate the Hurons and the flourishing missions of the Jesuits amongst them.

The canal was begun in a small way in 1833 with the construction of a few locks on the Trent and Otonabee Rivers, and on the Kawartha Lakes, in order to connect the small pioneer settlements along their banks and shores. In addition to performing this vital service, these early locks and dams, supplemented by an extensive system of log slides, contributed for many years to the flourishing lumber trade of the district.

In order to avoid the series of rapids at and above Peterborough, an artifical channel, four miles long, has been cut through the eastern limits of the city. This waterway connects with the river again at Nassau. Located within this section is the world's highest hydraulic lift lock, number 21. Two large chambers, 140 feet long and 33 feet wide, are balanced on two huge plungers working in deep presswells in such a manner that when one chamber is up and opening into the upper reach of the canal the other is down and opening into the lower reach.

The two chambers are so arranged that the depth of water in the descending chamber is greater than that in the ascending chamber. It is this greater depth and, consequently, greater weight of water in the descending chamber which causes the lock to operate.

After the gates at the ends of the chambers and at the ends of the adjoining reaches have been closed, the simple opening of a valve between the two presswells allows the water to flow freely between them, permitting the lighter ascending chamber to be lifted on its plunger by the heavier descending chamber. In this way the lift of sixty-five feet may be accomplished by a vessel in about seven minutes. A second hydraulic lift lock with a lift of forty-six feet is located at Kirkfield (mileage 169.36).

Since early in 1972, control of the Trent-Severn Canal system has been transferred from the Department of Transport to the Department of Indian Affairs and Northern Development, Parks Branch. Charts may be ordered from, and are for sale at, the Trent Canal Office, Parks Canada, Armour Road, Peterborough, Ontario.

Boat campers on the Trent-Severn Canal are permitted to use waterway reserve lands for camping purposes when on a trip through the system. Boat campers are permitted to stay one or two nights at a lock station but must apply to the lock-master for permission to camp. The lockmaster will issue a permit and campers must comply with its provisions and other directions from the lockmaster.

Miles
from
Trenton Structure, Locality and Landmarks

Lake Ontario—mean level is 245.9 feet above sea level

0.00	Entrance to Bay of Quinte, Bridge 1 (Dundas Street, Trenton; highway swing)
0.32	Fixed bridge
0.36	Bridge 2 (Canadian National Railways, swing)
0.86	Bridge 3 (Canadian Pacific Railway, high level)
1.74	Bridge 4 (Canadian National Railways, high level)
1.78	Lock 1, Trenton
2.24	Bridge 4A (high level highway)
2.41	Lock 2, Trenton
3.67	Bridge 5, Glen Miller (highway, swing)
3.85	Lock 3, Glen Miller
5.15	Lock 4 (Township of Sidney)
6.38	Lock 5 (Township of Sidney)
7.26	Lock 6, Frankford
7.56	Bridge 6, Frankford (highway, swing)
8.01	Emergency dam
13.82	Lock 7, Glen Ross
13.85	Bridge 7, Glen Ross (highway, swing)
13.96	Bridge 8 (Canadian National Railways, swing)
25.26	Lock 8 (Township of Seymour)
26.41	Lock 9 (Township of Seymour)
27.99	Lock 10 (Township of Seymour)
29.68	Locks 11 & 12 in flight, Ranney Falls
29.75	Bridge 11 (highway, swing)
30.69	Bridge 12 (Canadian National Railways, bascule)
30.77	Bridge 13 (Canadian National Railways, high level)
31.13	Bridge 14, Campbellford (highway, bascule)
32.17	Lock 13 (Township of Seymour)
33.70	Lock 14 (Township of Seymour)
33.72	Emergency dam
36.16	Lock 15, Healy's Falls
36.18	Bridge 15 (highway, swing)
36.51	Locks 16 & 17 in flight, Healy's Falls
37.14	Fixed bridge
43.38	Bridge 17, Trent Bridge (highway, swing)
51.13	Lock 18, Hastings
51.16	Bridge 18 (highway, swing)
51.95	Bridge 19 (Canadian National Railways, swing)
57.00	Entrance to Rice Lake
69.00	Mouth of Otonabee River
76.53	Bridge 20, Bensfort (highway, swing)
80.35	Bridge 21, Wallace Point (highway, swing)
87.34	Fixed bridge
88.74	Lock 19, Peterborough
88.83	Bridge 22 (highway, swing)
88.94	Bridge 23 (Canadian National Railways, swing)
89.51	Lock 20 Peterborough
89.61	Bridge 24, Maria Street (swing)
89.72	Bridge 25 (Canadian Pacific Railway, swing)
90.10	Lock 21, Peterborough (hydraulic Lift)
90.58	Bridge 26, Norwood Road (high level)
91.01	Bridge 27, Warsaw Road (highway, swing)

91.03	Guard Gate
93.25	Guard gate, Nassau
93.33	Bridge 28 (Canadian National Railways, swing)
93.38	Bridge 29, Nassau (highway swing)
94.25	Lock 22 (Township of Douro)
94.84	Lock 23 (Township of Douro)
96.38	Lock 24, (Township of Douro)
97.29	Lock 25 (Township of Douro)
98.72	Lock 26, Lakefield
99.00	Bridge 30, Lakefield (high level)
99.04	Guard Gate, Lakefield
104.38	Bridge 31, Young's Point (high level)
104.47	Lock 27, Young's Point
104.49	Guard Gate, Young's Point
112.92	Fixed Bridge
112.96	Lock 26, Burleigh Falls
114.75	Lock 30, Lovesick
120.66	Lock 31, Buckhorn
120.66	Bridge 33, Buckhorn (highway, swing)

DIVERSION Chemong Lake

132.68	Bridge 61, Bridgenorth (Chemong Lake, rock causeway with steel swing span)

130.17	Bridge 34, Gannon's Narrows (high-level)
138.17	Bridge 35, Bobcaygeon (swing)
138.21	Lock 32, Bobcaygeon
138.23	Guard Gate
148.00	Sturgeon Point

DIVERSION Sturgeon Lake to Port Perry

156.19	Fixed bridge
156.31	Bridge 66, Lindsay Street (fixed)
156.35	Lock, Lindsay
157.20	Bridge, 67 (Canadian National Railways, high-level)
157.87	Bridge 68, Ops (highway, fixed-span)
157.95	Bridge 68A, (Lindsay bypass highway, fixed-span)
183.00	Port Perry

153.61	Lock 34, Fenelon Falls
153.61	Fixed Bridge
153.98	Bridge 37 (Canadian National Railways, swing)
157.17	Lock 35, Rosedale
157.98	Fixed Bridge
158.10	Entrance to Balsam Lake

Balsam Lake — summit level is 841.0 feet (256 m) above sea level

163.91	Guard gate, Balsam Lake*

165.24	Bridge 39, Victoria Road (highway, swing)
166.82	Bridge 40, Portage Road (high-level)
167.88	Guard gate
169.26	Guard gate, Kirkfield
169.36	Lock 36, Kirkfield, (hydraulic lift)
172.98	Bridge 42, (high-level arch)
175.23	Bridge 43, Bolsover (highway, swing)
176.85	Bridge 44, Boundary Road (highway, swing)
177.04	Lock 37 (Township of Thorah)
178.05	Lock 38 (Township of Mara)
179.07	Bridge 46 (Kane's Highway, swing)
179.63	Lock 39 (Township of Thorah)
180.09	Lock 40 (Township of Thorah)
180.74	Lock 41 (Township of Thorah)
180.79	Bridge 47, Gamebridge (high-level)
181.70	Bridge 48 (Canadian National Railways, high-level)
182.15	Bridge 50, Lakeshore Road (highway, swing)
182.20	Entrance to Lake Simcoe

Warning Do *not* cross Lake Simcoe by canoe. It is reknowned for its unpredictability and is too dangerous for crossing by canoe. Lake Simcoe-level is 718.3 feet (218.9 m) above sea level

197.57	Fixed bridge
197.66	Bridge 52, Atherley Narrows (Canadian National Railways, swing)
208.27	Bridge 54, Muskoka Road (high level)
209.14	Bridge 55 (Canadian National Railways, Washago swing)
209.87	Guard (Couchiching)
209.89	Lock 42 (Couchiching)
209.90	Bridge 56 (Couchiching, highway high-level)
212.73	Bridge 57, Hamlet (highway, swing)
222.40	Bridge 58, Ragged Rapids (Canadian National Railway, high-level)
224.45	Lock 43, Swift Rapids
228.07	Bridge 59, Severn Falls (Canadian Pacific Railway high-level)
232.45	Big Chute (marine railway)
240.55	Lock, Port Severn
240.55	Bridge 60 Port Severn (highway swing)
240.56	Entrance to Georgian Bay

(Lake Huron — mean level, 580.6 feet (176.9 m) above sea level)

* Balsam Lake is the water table lake from which the waterway flows northwest to Lake Huron and east to Lake Ontario.

The following Lindsay Forest District canoe routes join the main stream of the Trent-Severn Waterway:

(1) Crowe River route D — joins at Crowe Bay below Healy Falls
(2) Indian River route H — joins on north shore Rice Lake
(3) Deer Bay Creek (Eel's Creek Route) joins at Deer Bay, Buckhorn Lake
(4) Mississauga River route A — joins at lower Buckhorn Lake
(5) Burnt River route A — joins at Cameron Lake
(6) Gull River route A — joins at Balsam Lake

With these possible additions to routes in mind, combinations of loop tours in various directions are numerous.

Canoeists on canals: Of all pleasure craft, only the canoe is exempt from lockage fees imposed in 1975 on the Rideau and Trent-Severn Canals. However, each canoe must display a registration number, obtained free from any Canada Customs office. Otherwise, it may have to be carried around the lock site.

Ottawa River Drainage Basin

135 MISSISSIPPI — BON ECHO — CLARENDON LAKE LOOP

Length 66 miles (106 km)
Approx trip time 4 days
Access By Highway 41
Maps Kaladar 31C/11
Mazinaw Lake 31C/14
Portages 10 (Write the District Forester for a free comprehensive sketch-map folder)

In the Tweed Forest District camp and eat only at designated campsites and picnic spots. Provisions can be obtained only at the one store along the route, in Ardock. All drinking water should be boiled. Any important species of fish in the area are indicated on a free map available from the District Forester. This will be useful for canoe routes information as well.

Be sure to keep near the shores of the large lakes and *use the portages.*

This 66 mile canoe route along the Upper Mississippi River to Crotch Lake and including the Clarendon Lake westward return loop is the first stage in the development of a canoe route system which, in the next two or three

years, will link Mazinaw Lake with the Ottawa River by means of the Mississippi River.

Day 1
Start at Bon Echo Provincial Park (Mazinaw Lake) boat landing and go to campsite A on Kashwakamak Lake (14 miles). At the south end of Lake Mazinaw, carry 100 yards over a dam. Before entering Marble Lake there is a 10 foot float through the portage over a large block of marble. Portage 200 yards around the rapids between Marble and Georgia Lakes. Portage 100 yards to bypass the rapids between Georgia and Kashwakamak Lakes.

Day 2
Start at campsite A and continue to campsite B on Cross Lake (14 miles). Portage around a dam at the end of Kashwakamak Lake and then carry 200 yards around a log jam. There is a lot of white water in this section and the inexperienced canoeist is advised to take the trail along the south shore. Portage 150 yards around a dam at the end of Fawn Lake. Portage 880 yards past several rapids.

Day 3
Start at campsite B and continue to campsite C on Clarendon Lake (19 miles). Portage 35 yards around a beaver dam and rough water to the next portage, 100 yards around a dam.

Day 4
Start from Campsite C and go to Bon Echo (19 miles). Portage 550 yards around beaver dams and a dry creek bed to Shoepack Lake. Portage 440 yards from Shoepack to *finish* on Kashwakamak Lake.

136 BON ECHO PROVINCIAL PARK (MAZINAW LAKE, KISHKEBUS, SHABOMEKA LOOP)

Length 13 miles (21 km)
Approx trip time 1 day
Access By Highway 41
Maps Write the District Forester for a free sketch map. There are no rapids. Mazinaw Lake 31C/14

137 YORK AND MADAWASKA RIVERS

Length 40 miles (64 km)
Approx trip time 15 hours
Access Off Highway 648
Maps Wilberforce 31E/1E
Whitney 31E/8E and W

Portages 15 (average of 1,230 yards)

Start at any point on Elephant Lake (wherever access is available). Paddle to the end of the lake, bearing west into the mouth of the York River. Paddle 5.1 miles to the rapids. Portage 480 yards to the left, put in at a small pond, paddle to the right side and portage 570 yards around High Falls, coming out at High Falls Pond. It's a good campsite. Paddle west across High Falls Pond for 0.6 miles and portage 400 yards to the York River. Follow for 1/2 mile to Gutt Rapids.

Portage 200 yards on the right of the rapids and paddle 3/4 of a mile up the York to another 200 yard portage around a dam. Paddle 3/4 of a mile into Byers lake. There is a campsite on a point about half way up the lake. Paddle 3-1/2 miles north and west to Branch Lake, and then across it to the junction of the York and North York Rivers. Follow the right branch (North York) to a portage on the left, where the river narrows. Portage 2,800 yards to Little Billings Lake.

Paddle north to a 40 yard portage into Billings Lake (campsite here) and then one mile to the north end of Billings Lake. There is a system of old logging roads which provide 3,200 yards of easy walking to Billings River. Paddle north on the river for 3 miles through Little Branch Lake to a campsite. Portage west of the mouth of the stream, then north-northwest along an old roadbed for 2,200 yards, enter a long pond, paddle its length — 1/2 mile — and portage 1,300 yards to Little Hay Lake. Paddle across Little Hay Lake 0.6 miles to midway along the north side to Hay Creek.

Portage west of the creek for 70 yards, paddle 1/2 mile down the creek and lift out at the second beaver dam. Portage 1,150 yards to Hay Lake, across a causeway of logs and paddle 0.4 miles northeast to the cribbing of an old floating bridge. Lift out on the north side of the bridge, where there is a campsite, and portage 1,000 yards to Cauliflower Lake along an old road. Paddle west along the shoreline to the outlet of Cauliflower Creek and follow this for approximately 3 miles. Portage for 1,760 yards northwest to the Madawaska River, where you can paddle north for 4 miles into Clydegale Lake, and through Rock Lake, Galeairy Lake, Otter Creek and back to *finish* on Hay Lake. This circuit is about 25 miles

Lake Ontario Drainage Basin

138 LONG LAKE TO BUCKHORN VILLAGE
Length   30 miles (48 km)
Approx trip time   10 hours
Access   Off Highway 28
Maps   Burleigh Falls 31D/9E and W
Gooderham 31D/16W
Portages   22 (average length of 140 yards)

Start at Long Lake landing (public access point) and paddle west on Long Lake 3-1/2 miles through narrows between Loucks and Long Lakes when the water is high. When it's low, portage to the left for 130 yards. Travel north on Loucks Lake 1/2 mile to portage 88 to 155 yards, depending on the water depth.

Paddle north along the east shore of Cox Lake to its northwest corner. Portage 1,050 yards to the east shore of Cold Lake and paddle along the west shore of Cold Lake for 7 miles. Continue north on Cold Lake and along the west shore of Gold Lake. Paddle west through narrows to Mississaugua Lake and south on the lake to dam at the start of the Mississaugua River.

Portage 50 yards around the west side of the dam, a public access point. Paddle 1-1/10 miles downstream to the rapids. Portage 175 yards around the west side of the rapids. There is a campsite on the east shore of the last rapids. Paddle 1/2 mile to portage. Carry 44 yards on the west side of the rapids. Paddle 1-1/2 miles to the log jam. Portage 45 yards over flat rock on the west side to a campsite. Paddle 1/2 mile to portage. Carry 44 yards west of the rapids. Paddle 1-1/2 miles to a log jam. Portage 66 yards over flat rock on the east side to a campsite.

Prepare to paddle a series of short hops. Paddle 110 yards to portage at the south end of the island. Portage 88 yards to the west side. Paddle 220 yards. Portage 176 yards around the east end of an old rock dam. Paddle 110 yards. Portage 66 yards south and west of the rapids. Paddle 220 yards. Portage 440 yards south on the west side of the rapids. Paddle 1-1/2 miles to a series of 3 rapids. Walk, float the canoe through the first two rapids, 44 and 22 yards, respectively. Portage 240 yards to the east side of the third rapids. Paddle 1/2 mile. Portage 144 yards around a small rapids. Paddle 1/2 mile. Portage 88 yards over a rock ridge around rapids to a campsite. Paddle 1/10 mile and through rapids for 1/2 mile.

Paddle through a second set of rapids, paddle 3/10 mile to the third rapids and paddle through. Paddle 1/2 mile to a dam. Portage 200 yards around the west side. Paddle 1/2 mile to a stretch of fast water; paddle through or walk around. Paddle 100 yards to another stretch of fast water and paddle through. Paddle 1/2 mile. Portage 10 yards over a rock on the west side. Paddle 1 mile to Highway 36. *Finish.*

You have entered the mainstream Trent-Severn Waterway (see canal description).

139   LONG LAKE TO SUCKER LAKE

Length   20 miles (32 km)

Approx trip time   7 hours

Access   Off Highway 28

Portages   5 (average length of 290 yards)

Maps   See Long Lake to Buckhorn Village route (Route 138)

Start at Long Lake landing. Paddle west through Long and Loucks Lakes and north on Cox Lake through Lakes Cold, Gold, Cavendish and Beaver. Continue west through narrows where they widen into Catchacoma Lake, swinging north to the mouth of Bottle Creek. Paddle up the creek to a dam. Portage around the dam and paddle east to Bottle Lake and north along the east shore to the mouth of the stream. Portage on the south shore of the stream for 200 yards into Sucker Lake. Return via the same route to Catchacoma Lake.

You may return the way you came to Gold Lake or paddle south on Catchacoma Lake into Mississaugua Lake, back to Gold, or on to the mouth of the Mississaugua River.

140   LONG LAKE LOOP (LAKES LOUCKS, COX, COLD, GOLD, ANSTRUTHER, WOLF, CRAB AND POPLAR. RETURN.)

Length   25 miles (40 km)

Approx trip time   10 hours

Access   By Highway 28

Maps   See Long Lake to Buckhorn Village route (Route 138)

Portages   15 (average length of 370 yards)

Start at Long Lake landing. As in previous route, paddle to Gold Lake, then along the shore of the second large bay (2-1/2 miles from the portage at Cold Lake). Portage over 150 yards to north Anstruther Creek and launch

in the creek. Paddle 3/4 mile. Carry 66 yards on the north side of the dam into Anstruther Lake. Paddle along the south shore of Anstruther Lake for 2-3/10 miles. Portage 670 yards into Wolf Lake. If you bear northwest for 1-3/10 miles on Wolf Lake you come to a public access point, a car landing on the Anstruther Lake road, off Highway 28.

Paddle south on Wolf Lake for 1/4 mile. Portage 150 yards between Wolf and Crab Lakes. Paddle south and west on Crab Lake for .8 miles. At the stream exit carry 170 yards to an open stretch of stream. Paddle along the stream 1/4 mile. Carry 600 yards along the north side of the stream. Paddle .6 miles through a marshy area to portage on the north side. Portage 330 yards. Paddle 1/2 mile through a marsh and stream (you will probably have to pull the canoe over five or six beaver dams here).

Enter Poplar Lake and paddle 1 mile to the stream exit. Carry 930 yards on the north shore of the creek. Launch in a small pond and paddle its length. Portage 600 yards into Cox Lake. Return to *finish* where you began at Long Lake.

141   ANSTRUTHER LAKE LOOP

Length   17 miles (27 km)

Approx trip time   7 hours

Access   By Highway 28

Maps   See Long Lake to Buckhorn village route (Route 138)

Portages   9 (average length of 420 yards)

Start at the public access point, Anstruther Lake. Paddle north 4 miles along the east shore of Anstruther Lake. Portage 180 yards into Rathbun Lake.

Paddle northeast for 1/2 mile to the mouth of Anstruther Creek. Carry 370 yards along the creek. Paddle 1.1 miles through a marshy area. Carry 930 yards into Copper Lake. Paddle 1-1/2 miles to the northwest bay of Copper Lake. Portage 33 yards into the marsh area. Paddle 1/2 mile. Portage 80 yards. Paddle 1 mile. Portage 100 yards into Serpentine Lake. Paddle east 1-1/2 miles to the end. Portage 660 yards into Anderson Lake. Paddle 1-1/2 miles and along a creek into Copper Lake. Paddle southeast 1 mile to portage into Anstruther Creek. Return to *finish* at Anstruther Lake landing starting point.

An alternate route for these lakes is to begin at Anstruther Lake but continue into Rathbun Lake. Paddle north 1.1 miles. Portage 170 yards into North Rathbun Lake. Paddle 1.1 miles to north shore. Portage 1760 yards to Serpentine Lake. Paddle *either* east 2 miles to the end of the lake to continue into Anderson and Copper Lakes, *or* east 1 mile to the south end of Serpentine Lake and into Copper Lake. From either choice paddle back through Copper Lake, Anstruther Creek and Rathbun Lakes as described above.

142 LONG LAKE AND COX LAKE LOOP

Length   10 miles (16 km)
Approx trip time   4 hours
Access   By Highway 28
Maps   See Long Lake to Buckhorn village route.
(Route 138)
Portages   5 (average of 560 yards)

Start at Long Lake landing. Paddle to Loucks Lake to its southwest corner and .2 miles into a creek. Portage 130 yards into Compass Lake. Paddle south 1 mile. Portage 200 yards along the stream and take the right ford of the portage. Paddle 1/2 mile up the creek. Cross a small dam into Cherry Lake. Paddle north 1-1/2 miles to the north shore of Triangle Lake. Carry 1670 yards to Cox Lake.

An alternate route is to take the left fork of the portage at the foot of Compass Lake. Portage 270 yards into Stoplog Lake. Paddle south 3/4 of a mile. Portage 100 yards due west into Turtle Lake. Paddle 3/4 of a mile to the north bay. Portage 130 yards into Cherry Lake. Paddle beyond as above. (This change adds 1 mile and 2 portages to the above route; the longest portage is 1670 yards and the average length is 560 yards.)

143 LONG LAKE — DEER BAY CREEK — BUCKHORN

Access   By Highway 28
Deer Bay Creek is navigable by canoe at high water in spring and early summer. It passes through private land much of the way. Canoeists should ask permission from land-owners to use this route.

Follow the previous canoe route to Stoplog Lake. Paddle south 1.8 miles to the source of Deer Bay Creek. Paddle 6-1/2 miles to where the creek crosses Highway 36 and 9 miles beyond to Buckhorn Lake. You are in the mainstream of the Trent-Severn Waterway.

144 EEL'S CREEK

Length   23-1/2 miles (37.8 km)
Approx trip time   8 hours
Access   By Highway 28
Maps   See Long Lake to Buckhorn village route (Route 138)
Portages   19 (average length of 140 yards)
Start downstream on a creek in Apsley village where it crosses the south bypass. Launch below the bridge. Paddle south 1 mile to the bridge. Carry 60 yards on the right across the highway. Paddle 2 miles to the old dam. Carry 90 yards to the right. Paddle 5-1/2 miles. Carry 170 yards on the right along a road around the rapids. Paddle 1/8 mile. Carry 40 yards to the right around the rapids. Paddle 1/2 mile. Portage 200 yards on the right. Paddle 2-1/4 miles. Portage 60 yards on the right. Paddle the length of the pond, passing the river exit to a portage of 770 yards (this bypasses a 1/2 mile gorge).

Paddle south 1/2 mile through some fast navigable water, then 1/4 mile which requires that the canoe be floated through for three short distances. Portage 40 yards on the left. Paddle 1/4 mile. Pull through or paddle 10 yards through rapids. Paddle 1/8 mile. Portage 150 yards on the right. Paddle 1/8 mile. Portage 130 yards on the left. Walk 1/4 mile through shallow rough rapids pulling the canoe. Paddle 1/4 mile. Portage 200 yards on the right. Paddle 1/4 mile. Lift out on the right, at the Department of Highways roadside park, Highway 28, before the highway bridge.

Carry around the bridge and down the left river bank for 440 yards, to bypass rapids. Paddle 3-1/4 miles. Portage 20 yards on the left. Paddle 2 miles. Portage 20 yards on the left. Paddle 1/2 mile. Portage 60 yards on the right. Paddle 1 mile to High Falls. Portage around the falls 180 yards to the left.

DIVERSION   At the northeast corner of the falls a portage is the beginning of a 3.3 mile marked, hiking trail to the site of the Peterborough petroglyphs (rock carvings).

Paddle 1/4 of a mile along the right side of a small lake. Paddle or drift through some fast water. Paddle 1 mile and Portage 20 yards on the left. Paddle 1/8 mile, then portage 3 yards over the right. Paddle 1/2 mile through the creek exit to Stoney Lake. Finish, for the creek route, but you can paddle several miles east, south and west.

It is a heavily populated area. Watch for many power boats. You are in the mainstream of the Trent-Severn Waterway.

An alternate route is from near Haultain highway portage to carry from Eel's Creek to Deer Bay Creek. One-quarter mile above Haultain portage, on a 3-1/4 mile stretch,

enter the stream to the right and paddle 1/2 mile to Big Cedar Lake (the creek is shallow with several beaver dams to pull over). Paddle 2-1/4 miles across Big Cedar. Portage 200 yards across a swampy area. Paddle 1/8 mile to Coon Lake and up the creek to a beaver dam. Portage 440 yards to Deer Bay Creek. From this point you can paddle north 1.8 miles to Stoplog Lake as described in the alternate route in Route 142 or paddle south on Deer Bay Creek as described in Route 143.

Camping and Stopping Spots on the Eel's Creek Route

Camp	Stop only	Location	Distance in miles from start	Remarks
X		fifth portage and the river is 1/8 mile before it on both sides	9-3/8 to 9-1/2	Crown Game Preserve
X		all around small pond and along the 770 yard portage and 1-1/2 miles below portage to the shallow rapids, walk through	11-7/8 to 14	Crown Game Preserve left side, ordinary Crown Land and cottage lots on right
	X	Picnic area where the river crosses Highway 28	14-5/8	Department of Highways of Ontario Park
X		5/8 miles before and 3/8 miles after the first rapids past Highway 28 (Haultain), both sides of river.		1-1/8 miles past Haultain Crown Game Preserve left side of river, ordinary Crown land on right.
X		3/8 miles above High Falls and 1/8 mile below High Falls on small lake	21-1/8 to 21-3/4	Crown Game Preserve on left, ordinary Crown land on right. Hiking Trail at High Falls

Burnt River System

The following routes, located on the Burnt, Drag and Irondale Rivers, include only the simpler routes. Other more strenuous ones are possible from these main routes. Most of the land bordering these routes is privately owned, and canoeists should be careful not to trespass, and to ask permission from landowners before using their lands for camping. Areas of Crown

Land where camping is allowed are listed on the last page of this section.

145   DRAG AND BURNT RIVERS

Length   59 miles (95 km)
Approx trip time   20 hours
Access   By Highways 530 and 121
Maps   Haliburton 31E/2E
Minden 31D/15E
Fenelon Falls 31D/10E and W
Portages   15 (average length of 142 yards)

Start at the Haliburton town dock, paddle 2-1/2 miles through Head Lake, Grass Lake and into Kashagawigamog Lake. Paddle along the shore of this lake for 7-1/2 miles to the bridge at Ingoldsby. Paddle along the shore of Canning Lake 2 miles to the dam. Portage left of the dam for 90 yards, paddle south for 1/4 miles: portage 40 yards on the left of the bridge and paddle 1/4 mile through a shallow, wide stream, walking through 3 very shallow spots. Paddle 7/8 of a mile and through a series of small portages and walk-throughs for 1/4 mile. Continue to paddle for 1-1/4 miles, passing Gelert to a 440 yard portage around rapids.

Portage to the right just before the railway bridge. Due to fast, shallow waters, this section should be travelled downstream only. Paddle 6 miles down river to a 10 yard portage or step-over. Paddle 3 miles, passing the entrance of the Irondale River. Lift out on the left on an old railway bed and carry for 260 yards around 3 spectacular falls of 20, 10 and 22 feet, respectively.

Paddle 4-1/8 miles down the river to Kinmount. Portage on the left at the dam and over the rocks for 70 yards. Paddle 1/4 mile and lift over the rocks on the right for 20 yards. Paddle south 1-1/8 miles and portage 420 yards on the right of the rapids. Paddle 2-3/8 miles and portage 40 yards on the right. Paddle 3-3/8 miles and portage around an old bridge for 60 yards on the left. Paddle 3/4 of a mile and portage on the left for 440 yards. Paddle 1/2 mile and portage on the left 200 yards.

Paddle south on the river for 15-3/4 miles to Rosedale. From here it is 4-1/2 miles across Balsam Lake to Balsam Lake Provincial Park.

146 IRONDALE RIVER (GOODERHAM TO THE BURNT RIVER)

Length 23 miles (37 km)
Approx trip time 8 hours
Access By Highways 503 and 507
Maps Gooderham 31D/16W
　　　　Minden 31D/15E
Portages 10 (average length of 149 yards)

Start at Gooderham Park. Paddle downstream 7/8 of a mile to a rapids which can be floated or carried on the railway bed to the left for 60 yards. Paddle 3/8 of a mile to a 40 yard portage along the railway bed around a rapids. Paddle 2-1/2 miles and portage 590 yards on the railway bed around a rapids and falls to an old bridge. Paddle 3/8 of a mile and portage for 50 yards at an old bridge. Paddle 1-3/4 miles, walking through two shallow spots in the first 1/4 mile and portage 40 yards on the right on the railway bed.

Paddle 1/2 mile and portage 50 yards. Paddle 1/4 mile and portage 60 yards. Paddle 3/8 of a mile and portage 40 yards. Paddle 1/4 mile, then portage 460 yards around Devils Gap Dam on the right. Paddle 13-1/4 miles to a 100 yard carry on the left around a rapids. Paddle 2 miles to join with Burnt River and Route 145.

Rideau Canal, Ottawa.

Camping and Stopping Spots on the Haliburton and Irondale River Routes

Camp	Stop only	Location	Distance in miles from start	Remarks
Route 145				
X		On either side of the river at the bend where the stream enters	32-3/4	2-5/8 miles from Kinmount
X		North 1-1/2 miles from the second bridge past the last stop and south 3/4 of a mile from this bridge to the first rapids and portage. East side only.	36-1/8 to 38-3/8	Anywhere along the east side of this 2-1/4 mile stretch
X		Right side of the river for 1-1/2 mile from Goose Lake in the area where Burnt River divides into the Otonabee River and Cameron Lake.	51-3/4 to 53-1/2	
X		North Bay of Balsam Lake	59	Balsam Lake Provincial Park
Route 146				
	X	Right side of the river where the river crosses Highway 121	19-1/2	Department of Highways of Ontario picnic spot. There is a falls and rapids here which require portage.

No camping spots are available on the Irondale River route.

Gull River System

The following routes, on or adjacent to the Gull River, are only the main routes. Many deviations and side routes are possible. Much of the land through which these routes pass is under private ownership, and hence camping spots are in short supply. The areas of Crown Land where you can camp are listed on the last page of this section. If you wish to camp elsewhere, you should seek permission of the land owners. Most of the lakes and portions of the rivers on these routes have many summer cottages on them.

147 GULL RIVER (BALSAM LAKE TO BOSHKUNG LAKE)

Length 41 miles (66 km)
Approx trip time 14 hours
Access By Highway 46

Maps Fenelon Falls 31D/10W and E
Minden 31D/15W and E
Haliburton 31E/2E
Portages 8 (average length of 244 yards)

Start at Balsam Lake Provincial Park, paddle southeast 2 miles to Indian Point; circle the point, paddle north 4-1/2 miles to Coboconk; portage on the right of the dam for 44 yards; paddle up the Gull river 6-7/8 miles through Silver and Shadow Lakes to Norland. Portage 150 yards on the right, taking out on a flat rock below a picturesque falls. Paddle 1/2 mile up the Gull river to a rapids, lifting over the rocks on the right for 10 yards; paddle upstream 1-1/8 miles to Elliot's Falls.

Portage on the left, at the base of the old power house, or on the right at the bottom of the falls for 80 yards. Paddle north 4-1/2 miles into Moore Lake and 1-1/4 miles to Moore's Falls. Portage 80 yards between the dams and paddle the west shore of Gull Lake for 6-5/8 miles to Gull River. Paddle up the river 5-3/8 miles to a 660 yard portage, starting on the west of the highway bridge, following the road past the dam.

Paddle 2-1/4 miles to the rapids and then portage 880 yards on the west, following the road. Paddle the west shore of Horseshoe Lake 2-1/2 miles to the narrows between Horseshoe and Mountain Lakes. Paddle north on Mountain Lake 3/4 of a mile to the base of Twelve Mile Lake. Portage 50 yards on the east of the dam, crossing the highway. Paddle 2-7/8 miles up the west side of Twelve Mile Lake to Little Boshkung Lake. Paddle across Little Boshkung 1-1/8 miles into Boshkung Lake.

148 BOSHKUNG, KUSHOG, KENNISIS, EAGLE LAKES LOOP

Length 53-5/8 miles (87 km)
Approx trip time 18 hours
Access By Highway 35
Maps Haliburton 31E/2E and W
Wilberforce 31E/1W
Portages 17 (average length of 572 yards)

Start in Boshkung Lake where Route 147 leaves off. Paddle 2 miles northwest to the mouth of the river and portage 970 yards on the north side. Paddle west and north on Lake Kushog for 6-1/8 miles to Ox Narrows; paddle 2-1/8 miles to St. Nora Lake; paddle northeast 1-3/4 miles on St. Nora Lake and then portage on the west of the Boshkung River mouth. Put in at the beaver pond. Paddle 1/8 of a mile and carry from the top of the pond 220 yards to Sherborne Lake. Paddle 2-3/4 miles along Sherborne Lake, then portage 990 yards to Big Hawk Lake.

Paddle east and north 2-7/8 miles across the top of Big Hawk Lake and along the Kennisis River; portage 220 yards around the Nunikani dam. Paddle 1-5/8 miles to the northeast end of Nunikani Lake and 3/4 of a mile on Kennisis River; portage 530 yards around Red Pine Dam. Paddle 3 miles across Red Pine Lake and along the Kennisis River; portage 20 yards around the Kennisis Dam. Paddle east across Kennisis Lake for 3-1/2 miles. Portage 1400 yards (past an active sawmill) to Little Redstone Lake.

Paddle 2-1/4 miles into Redstone Lake and south on Redstone for 4-1/4 miles; portage 1850 yards from the dam by the road to a small lake. Paddle 5/8 of a mile across this lake and then 3/4 of a mile down the East Redstone River, making 3 small portages of 100 yards each. Portage 60 yards at the bridge into Eagle Lake; paddle 1-5/8 miles to the Eagle Dam. The river is low at this point, and it is usually better to portage by road 1980 yards to the first bridge crossing the river. Paddle 1-1/4 miles to Cranberry Lake and then 1-3/4 miles, the length of Cranberry Lake. Portage 290 yards on the north of the rapids and an old wooden bridge.

Paddle 1/2 mile to Pine Lake and 1 mile across the lake. Paddle 5/8 of a mile along the Gull River and 1-1/8 miles across Green Lake. Paddle 1-1/8 miles along the Gull River and 2 miles across Maple Lake. Portage 260 yards between Maple and Beech Lakes. Paddle 1-1/2 miles across Beech Lake and portage 220 yards on the north side of the river. Paddle 1/2 mile along Gull River into Boshkung Lake and paddle south 1-5/8 miles to *finish* at the starting point.

149 KENNISIS LAKE TO RAVEN LAKE

Length 27-1/2 miles (44 km)
Approx trip time 10 hours
Access North of Highway 530
Maps Haliburton 31E/2E and W
Wilberforce 31E/1E and W
Portages 12 (average length of 884 yards)

Start at Kennisis Dam via previous route. Paddle east and north 3-1/2 miles across Kennisis Lake to the Kelly Lake outlet; paddle across Kelly Lake for 1 mile north and portage 260 yards into Johnson Lake. Paddle 1 mile across Johnson Lake and portage beside the creek for 2200 yards to the southwest end of Havelock Lake. Paddle 1 mile along the south shore at Havelock Lake and portage 2640 yards into a pond. Paddle across the pond 1/4 mile and portage 170 yards into Stocking Lake. Paddle 1-1/4 miles to the end of the lake and portage 100 yards into Slipper Lake. Paddle 3/8 of a mile to a point midway on the northwest shore.

Portage 1000 yards to Kawagama Lake. Paddle west into Minden Bay and south a total of 7 miles and portage 260 yards into Herb Lake. Paddle 2-1/4 miles to the southwest corner of Ernest Lake. Portage 220 yards. Paddle 1/8 of a mile across a pond; portage 60 yards and then paddle 1 mile southwest on Gun Lake. Portage 480 yards into Raven Lake.

From here one can return by way of the same route or can paddle south 1-5/8 miles down a long narrow bay and portage 44 yards to a gravel road. Follow the road to the right for 1230 yards and portage 180 yards to Plastic Lake. Paddle 1/4 mile across Plastic Lake, taking out at a landing on the south end.

Portage down the gravel road 880 yards and then follow a cottage road for 880 yards to the north shore of St. Nora Lake and back to the previous route.

150   EAGLE LAKE TO HALIBURTON LAKE

Length   10-1/2 miles (17 km)
Approx trip time   3 hours
Access   Highway 519
Maps   Wilberforce 31E/1W
Portages   2 (average length of 130 yards)

Start at Eagle Lake from previous route. Paddle east 1 mile into Moose Lake and then north 2-1/2 miles into the Gull River. Portage around a bridge for 40 yards on the left. Paddle 1-1/2 miles and portage 220 yards on the left into Oblong Lake. Paddle 1 mile across Oblong Lake and into Haliburton Lake. Paddle north 4-1/2 miles to the top of Haliburton Lake. Return via the same route to Eagle Lake.

Camping and Stopping Spots on the Gull River Routes

Camp	Stop only	Location	Distance in miles from start	Remarks
Route 147				
X		North bay of Balsam Lake	0	Balsam Lake Provincial Park
	X	Right side of Gull River just before dam and falls	13-1/2	Norland public access point
	X	Left side of Gull River just past dam	15-1/8	Elliot Falls public access point
X		Right side of Gull River	16-1/8	
X		East shore of east bay of Moore Lake	19-3/8	
X		West shore of Gull Lake	23-5/8	
	X	North end of Minden	32-3/8	Rotary Park 8-5/8 miles to end of Route 147
Route 148				
	X	Across the dam at Kushog Lake	2-1/2	Public access point 11-1/8 miles from last stop on Route 14
X		East shore of Kushog Lake	5-1/4 to 7	
X		East shore of Kushog Lake Ox Narrows	9 to 10-1/4	
X		Peninsula on right between Kushog and St. Nora Lakes	10-3/4	
X		Most of east and north shores of St. Nora Lake, and most of Sherborne Lake		

Camp	Stop only	Location	Distance in miles from start	Remarks
X		North bay of Big Hawk Lake	18 to 19	
X		All of Nunikani Lake and most of Red Pine Lake, particularly south shore	to 24-1/2	No further crown areas for camping or stopping on the 29-1/8 miles of this route
Route 149				
X		Bottom half of Herb Lake	23-1/4	23-1/2 miles from last stop on Route 148. Camping is allowed most places along the 3-1/4 miles from Herb Lakes to Route 148.
X		All of Gun Lake, all of narrow bay of Raven Lake, all of Plastic Lake, most of St. Nora Lake shore.		

Route 150 — No Crown Land available for camping or stopping.

The Kawartha Lakes region is typical of popular canoeing and summer resort areas found throughout Southern Ontario. In contrast to the rugged wilderness of Northern Ontario, the Southern region of the province has a gentle face and tends to be much more highly developed. The Kawartha Lakes have been a popular vacation centre from very early days.

Crowe River System

As well as the portages, there are several shallow water walk-throughs and lift-overs, totalling 2-1/2 miles. Many log jams are located in the first sections of this system.

It passes through a great deal of privately owned land, and therefore, canoeists should be careful not to trespass. The areas of crown land where camping overnight is allowed are listed at the end of the canoe route description.

As the summer progresses and water levels drop, this route becomes increasingly difficult, with more areas of shallow rapids appearing. The portion from Chandos Lake to Tangamong Lake is best as a downstream route only, except in the very early spring when water levels are quite high.

151 CHANDOS LAKE TO HEALY'S FALLS

Length 67-1/2 (109 km)
Approx trip time 30 hours
Access By Highway 620
Maps Campbellford 31C/5W and E
Bannockburn 31C/12W and E
Coe Hill 31C/13W
Portages 13 (average length of 263 yards)

Start at the north end of Chandos Lake where Highway 620 crosses the Crowe river exit. Paddle down the river 4-1/2 miles; walk through a rapids for 40 yards. Paddle 3-5/8 miles, pass beneath a bridge and continue for 8 miles, (several small log jams). Paddle 1-1/8 miles, walk 1/2 mile through a series of shallow spots. Portage on the right for 200 yards around a gorge and a falls. Walk 1/2 mile through shallow spots. Paddle 1/4 mile and walk 3/4 of a mile through shallow spots. Paddle 1/4 mile and walk through a shallow area for 100 yards. Paddle 1-1/2 miles to Tangamong Lake.

Paddle south and then east 1-7/8 miles; portage 60 yards on the south side of the north channel into Whetstone Lake. Paddle 2-1/2 miles.

Portage 300 yards on the right around a set of rapids. Paddle 1/2 mile and then 1/4 mile, stepping over three short rapids. Paddle 1/2 mile and walk through a shallow rapids. Paddle 1/4 mile and portage 300 yards on the left around a series of rapids with two waterfalls. Paddle 1-1/8 miles into Mud Turtle Lake and 1-3/4 miles to the outlet of Crowe River.

Portage 280 yards on the right around a rapids and a falls. Paddle 3/4 of a mile to a small lift-over and then 1/4 mile to a shallow rapids you can walk through.

Paddle 1/2 mile, walking through shallow stretches. Paddle 1/2 mile and walk through a small rapids. Paddle 5/8 of a mile. Portage on the left 90 yards. Paddle 1/4 mile and then portage on the left 180 yards. Paddle 1/4 mile, then carry on the left for 330 yards around a rapids and 15 foot falls. Paddle 1/2 mile and step over a small rock area. Paddle 3/4 of a mile into Cordova Lake. Paddle 2 miles down to the south end of the lake. Portage on a road to the left for 1100 yards around a series of rapids and shallow spots. Paddle 2 miles into Belmont Lake, south 1-5/8 miles into Crowe River Bay and 1 mile to a rapids.

Portage 80 yards on the right. Paddle 1 mile. Portage 130 yards on the right of a rapids. Paddle 1-1/2 miles into Crowe Lake. Paddle south and then northeast 4-1/2 miles through Crowe Lake to the Crowe River. Paddle down the Crowe River 2 miles. Portage 20 yards on the right of the dam at Marmora. Paddle 6-5/8 miles down the river to Allan Mills. Paddle 5-3/4 miles past Crowe Bridge into the Trent Canal System and up to Healey's Falls.

Camping and Stopping Spots on the Crowe River System

Camp	Stop only	Location	Distance in miles from start	Remarks
X		.2 miles on either side of the river	.8	
X		.8 miles on either side of the river	16 miles	
X		1 mile on either side of the river	20.2 miles	
X		East shore of Tangamong Lake from the first stream, for .8 miles	22.4 miles	
X		Either side of the river for 1 mile	26 miles	
X		Two small spots on the south side of the bend in the river	28 miles	
X		East of the river for .2 miles before the stream entrance	35.4 miles	
X		West of the river for .4 miles after the stream entrance	35.6 miles	
X		.4 miles on the north side of the bend in the river	36.2 miles	
X		4 islands 2/3 of the way down Cordova Lake	38.6 miles	
	X	Bottom of Cordova Lake at a long portage	39.4 miles	Crown fish hatchery. Portage bypasses one mile of rough rapids.
X		North River Bay of Belmont Lake	45.2 miles	Both sides of the river to the dam and 1/4 mile north of the river on the west shore of North River Bay.
X		Four islands at the south-west end of Crowe Lake	50.4 miles	
X		part of northwest shore of Crowe Lake	52.8 miles	

152 INDIAN RIVER (STONEY LAKE TO RICE LAKE)

Length 26 (42 km) (155 foot drop in elevation between Stoney and Rice Lakes)

Approx trip time 2 days

Access County road east off Highway 28, north of Lakefield

Maps Peterborough 31D/8E
Rice Lake 31D/1

This route has been in the process of being surveyed by the Otanabee Region Conservation Authority since 1965. It could be a spin-off for canoeists who have completed the following: Route 143 at Buckhorn Lake outlet of Deer Bay Creek; Route 138, Mississauga River outlet, Lower Buckhorn Lake; Route 144 at Stoney Lake outlet of Eel's Creek. They would simply paddle to Gilchrist Bay, midway on the south shore of Stoney Lake. Otherwise Indian River is easily accessible by numerous Peterborough County and Township roads and by Highway 7 East. The route is recommended for downstream travel.

Lift around the concrete control dam over a rock shelf at the right of the dam to *start* downstream. Paddle downstream under an iron bridge, 100 yards. Lift around a driftwood jam on the left bank. (The private Gilchrist Park campsite is on the left bank from the dam to the jam).

Paddle under a concrete highway bridge 1/4 mile into (White) Dummer Lake. Paddle south 2 miles. Take two very shallow rapids over a limestone bottom into Little Joe Lake (pond); float through 3/4 of a mile. There are long, very shallow rapids for 4,000 feet. Float through. The river deepens for 600 feet. Take another 1,000 foot shallows into the third rapids, 3,800 feet long. Float through. Paddle 1,000 feet through Payne's Pond. Lift over Payne's Dam. Paddle with caution through two shallows. Float through. Lift over a rock dam.

Paddle to the nearby Warsaw Caves Park and campsite. Indian River disappears here for a drop of 15 feet and reappears. Portage over the rock banks of the highwater river falls bypass and float in the still river water below. Paddle 3 miles to the Warsaw village dam. Lift over the dam. Paddle in shallows for about 1 mile. The river deepens. Paddle 5 miles to Cruikshank Dam. (There are shallows 1,000 feet long about midway along this stretch; float through). There are shallow rapids for 2-1/2 miles. Paddle with caution or float.

The river deepens for about one mile and then becomes shallow for one mile. The river deepens for 1-1/2 miles to Hope (sawmill) Dam. Lift over. Float through the shallows for 1/4 mile. Enter deeper water for 3/4 of a mile to Lang (stone gristmill) Dam. Pass Century Pioneer Village on the left bank. Lift over the dam.

There are shallows and rapids for 2-1/2 miles. Float through. A Canadian National Railways bridge crosses about halfway on this segment and then an abandoned dam in the last third of this segment. Paddle 2 miles (Keene village is on the right bank) through a wide estuary of the Indian River into Rice Lake. Paddle 1-1/2 miles southwest on the lake to Serpent Mounds Provincial Park and campsite. *Finish.*

At the park canoeists join boat traffic in the mainstream of the Trent-Severn Waterway, east and west.

Of special note is a comprehensive route map folder issued in October of 1973. It may be had for the asking from the Ontanabee Region Conservation Authority, 727 Lansdowne Street West, Peterborough, Ontario.

153 MOIRA RIVER-KAYAK TRIP
Length 17 miles (27 km)
Approx trip time 1 day
Access Off highway 37
Maps Tweed 31C/6W
Belleville 31C/3W
Start at bridge 3 miles (5 km) south of Tweed town to *finish* at Belleville city.

Georgian Bay — Muskoka Drainage Basin

154 MOON RIVER
Length 24 miles (39 km)
Approx trip time 2 days
Access Off highway 612
Maps This map is to a scale of 1:125,000
Muskoka 31E/SW
Portages 12

Travel west on a gravel road, approximately 3 miles (5 km) north of Moon River, to reach the access point on the north side of Moon River at an old Dept. of Lands and Forests fire tower. *Start* by paddling downstream to Curtain Chute and the first portage on the South shore.

Portage 220 yards over a knoll to the base of Curtain Chute. Approximately 2 miles further, the river divides into two channels, with two long narrow islands separating the north and south channels. Paddle down the south channel to the rapids running between the two long narrow islands and turn south passing these rapids to portage on the southeast corner of the second island immediately above a falls and rapids.

Portage 88 yards along the north shore, over a gentle rise to the launching site. Just above the site is a steep trail. Travel with caution. Paddle northwest down the river to portage 66 yards along the south shore, bypassing a 4 foot drop in water level. The river now turns southwest and passes through a narrows forming a small eddy above Moon Falls.

Portage 484 yards on the north side along a rocky trail around Moon Falls. From Moon Falls and Moon Rapids, paddle west across Moon Basin and enter Moon River Bay. Turn north to portage at the northeast corner of Moon River Bay directly west of Healey Creek. Continue to portage along 1,100 yards of well-used wagon trail along the north side of Healy Creek. A shuttle service at the Healey Lake end of the portage can usually be hired to transport canoes and equipment across the trail. On the south shore of Healey Lake, a short distance east of this trail is an overnight campsite.

Paddle east from the campsite following the south shore of Healey Lake to enter Kapikog Bay. Paddle southeast across Kapikog Bay to portage on the east side of Kapikog Creek, carrying for 110 yeards over a rock knoll around Kapikog Lake Dam. Paddle south down the creek and across Kapikog Lake to portage near the southwest corner of the Lake for 22 yards along the east bank of the creek to a beaver pond. Paddle across the beaver pond on the south shore to portage to an unnamed lake. Portage 15 yards, bypassing a beaver dam. Paddle south across the unnamed lake to portage 45 yards over a smooth rock knoll to a beaver pond.

Paddle east and then south through the beaver pond to portage on the south shore. Floating vegetation in the south part of this beaver pond makes it necessary to hunt for a suitable channel in order to reach the next portage, a 682 yard carry over bald rock along the west side of a brushy swamp surrounding a small lake. Paddle through the short section of floating vegetation to the main waters of Eagle Lake and paddle south to a lunching site on the northern most island in Eagle Lake.

Paddle southeast down Eagle Lake to a creek at the south end of the middle bay. Paddle down the creek to portage along the northeast shore of the creek for 175 yards along the top of a small rock ridge ending at the northwest end of Buckhorn Lake. Paddle southeast down Buckhorn Lake to portage at the southeast end of the lake for 1,232 yards along a well-used trail and road to the Moon River and access point. This portage may be shortened to a 330 yard carry by driving the vehicles to a small parking area 330 yards from Buckhorn Lake.

155 SOUTH BRANCH MUSKOKA RIVER

Length 26 miles (42 km)
Approx trip time 2 day
Access By highway 118
Maps Bracebridge 31E/3 E and W
Gravenhurst 31D/14E and W
Portages 11 (from 50 to 880 yards)

In August, 1826, Lieutenant Briscoe of the Royal Engineers, travelling from the Severn River to the Ottawa River, via the Muskoka River, became the first white man to cross through the heart of what was to become Muskoka. In 1837, famed explorer David Thomson was sent out to map a water route between Lake Huron and the Ottawa River. That year he paddled up the South Branch of the Muskoka River

The total length of all portages is 2,575 yards or 1.46 miles. The number of campsites is limited. Most of the area is privately owned. Approximately 1 1/2 miles below the second portage, the islands in the river and the adjacent shoreline are Crown Land. The next portage also crosses Crown Land. Camping is allowed on these areas. Provisions can be obtained at the general store in Baysville or Fraserburg.

Leave Baysville to paddle downstream on the South Branch of the Muskoka River to portage and bypass Fair Falls. Approximately 1/4 mile below the falls, the river becomes narrow and the channel is on the left. During low water, in midsummer, it may be possible to "rope" the canoe through the shallows.

Portage 45 yards on the right side. Approximately 1 1/2 miles below this portage, the river splits, forming two islands. Either channel may be used. Both islands and the shoreline opposite the islands are Crown Land. Camping is allowed here.

Portage 100 yards on the left side. This portage bypasses the very scenic Cooks Falls. One-quarter mile above and below this falls is Crown Land where camping is permitted.

Portage 175 yards on the right side and later another 75 yards on the right side. Two miles downstream from this portage, known as Slater's Falls, is the village of Fraserburg. A grocery store and public telephone are available there.

Portage 250 yards on the left side. This area is known as May Chutes. Watch for poison ivy. Portage again for 50 yards on the left side.

This falls is shown on the map as Croziers Falls (the local name is Island Rapids). Then portage 300 yards on the right side just above the bridge, following a gravel road that bypasses two sets of rapids. This is the last portage before the Mathiasville Dam. Since the erection of this dam, the rapids shown on the map as Rocky Rapids have disappeared. This dam produces hydro-electric power for Orillia.

Portage 450 yards on the left side of the dam (the portage follows the road). Portage 75 yards on the right side over quite rocky ground, bypassing Tretheway Falls. Then portage 880 yards on the left side around Hanna Chutes and South Falls. Follow a gravel road to the paved township road, turn right for 150 yards and follow the gravel road, passing under a highway bridge and down the hill to the power house.

Three miles downstream from this portage, the South and North Branches of the Muskoka River join at Bracebridge. Approximately 1/2 mile up the river to the right can be found the Bracebridge Municipal Park. An overnight camp-site is available for a fee. There are no portages between Bracebridge and Lake Muskoka, approximately 3 1/2 miles downstream. Power boats abound on this stretch of the river.

Smoked Pickerel River System

156 SMOKED PICKEREL (MAIN LOOP)

Length 49 miles (79 km)
Approx trip time 5 days
Access By Highway 69
Maps Muskoka 31E/SW (Ont.)
Parry Sound 41H/SE (Ont.)

For best access, turn west off Highway 69 onto James Bay junction road, 3 miles (4.8 km) south of Parry Sound. Leave Parry Sound, paddle south under the Parry Island swing bridge, and follow the east shore of Five Mile Narrows to a small bay known as Squirrel's Cove. At the southwest corner of the cove is the Canoe Lake Portage picnic site and a portage (no. 1) of 330 yards over a steep hill ending at a small dock on the northwest end of Canoe Lake. Paddle east across Canoe Lake to the northeast corner to the next portage (no. 2), a short carry over a rocky knoll. Paddle east down the length of Jack's Lake to the narrow neck of land separating Jack Lake and McCoy Lake and

portage (no. 3) 30 yards over a narrow neck of land which descends sharply to McCoy Lake.

Paddle south across McCoy Lake and then east to portage (no. 4) 110 yards to the north end of Three Legged Lake. Paddle south down the north leg of Three Legged Lake onto the east leg and begin to portage (no. 5) at the public access point following the township road, portage 550 yards to Scott's Lake. Paddle east across Scott's Lake to the next portage (no. 6) at the east tip of the lake, where a small creek flows into Otter Lake.

Follow the edge of the creek and portage 750 yards. It can be dangerous, so care should be taken. Paddle east across the mouth of an island dotted bay and east down the Long Arm of Otter Lake to portage (no. 7), 900 yards along the south shore of the Long Arm near the end of the bay.

Paddle southeast across Portage Lake to the next portage (no. 8) which begins where the township road touches the lake. Continue along the township road to Blackstone Lake for 45 yards. Care must be taken on this portage during the summer — road traffic may be busy.

Paddle south to the end of Blackstone Lake to the river that joins Blackstone Lake to Crane Lake. Turn south on the river into the first bay on Crane Lake to next portage (no. 9) 45 yards over fairly rough ground at the south end of bay. Birch Lake is higher in elevation than Crane Lake and you will be packing uphill. Paddle Birch Lake along the south shore to the west corner of the lake to the next portage (no. 10) of 1,650 yards to Healey Lake.

Paddle southwest out of the north bay of Healey Lake and swing west through a narrow channel between a long island and the north shore. At the west end of the long narrow island paddle southwest again, passing south of two small islands to the dam and the next portage (no. 11) of 1,310 yards over a good trail at the west end of Healey Lake. A tractor and wagon can usually be hired to shuttle canoes, boats and equipment across this portage. Paddle northwest across Moon River Bay to Moon Island Picnic Site on the southeast tip of Moon Island. Paddle north following the east shore of Moon Island.

At the north end of Miron Island, paddle west between Crooked Island and Pennsylvania Island. The Pilgrim's Rest Picnic Site is located on the north end of Winnet Island. To bypass the rough waters of Georgian Bay around the

Sans Souci area, turn north at Pennsylvania Island and paddle to the mainland shore where a bay runs to the west. Paddle west up the bay through a very narrow gorge to the west end of a 220 yard portage (no. 12) to Gooseneck Bay of Spider or Cowper Bay. Paddle northeast along the southeast shore of Gooseneck Bay to an overnight campsite. Out of Gooseneck Bay paddle west through Spider Bay, then north and northeast along the mainland of Cowper Township to the Devil's Elbow Picnic Site.

From Devil's Elbow, paddle east and then northeast through Seven Mile Narrows, past McLaren Island, across Five Mile Bay, through Squaw Channel and back to Parry Sound.

157 SMOKED PICKEREL (FIRST ALTER-NATE ROUTE)

Length 41 miles
Approx trip time 3 days
Access By Highway 69
Maps Muskoka 31E/SW (Ont.)
Parry Sound 41H/SE (Ont.)

The first alternate route follows the main route from Parry Sound to Otter Lake. Then paddle south for approximately 3/4 of a mile to portage (no. 13) at the southeast shore of the lake directly behind the last two islands in the bay. Portage 45 yards to reach the end of a small bay on the north shore of Salmon Lake.

Paddle south on Salmon Lake to portage (no. 14) 440 yards across a good trail at the southeast corner of the lake. Paddle southeast down Clear Lake and through the creek that leads to Crane Lake. Continue south on Crane Lake past the bay which leads to Stonehouse Lake, then turn west down the long narrow bay to Crane Lake Dam. Portage (no. 15) 88 yards, beginning at the north side of the dam and ending at a small pool below the rapids. Paddle a short distance to portage on a low bank on the west shore. Now portage (no. 16) 45 yards over rolling terrain. A short distance downstream on the east shore is a portage (no. 17) of 45 yards along the east shore over fairly flat ground to bypass shallow rapids. A short paddle takes you to the next portage (no. 18), which passes through an old clearing on the east shore.

The previous four portages may be avoided by using one long 880 yard carry from the south side of Crane Lake Dam along a road which passes through an old clearing to terminate at the last portage (ie no. 18). This portage is

recommended during periods of low water.

Paddle downstream through a marshy section of land to portage (no. 19) 20 yards through a narrow gut to the base of the falls. Paddle downstream to Little Blackstone Lake and the overnight campsite on the south shore, a short distance east of the river outlet.

Portage (no. 20) immediately north of the outlet of the Blackstone River southwest to a small bay on Blackstone Harbour.

Paddle south down Blackstone Harbour and west through the straits leading to Woods Bay. Continue west to Moon Island and turn north following the east shore of the island. Upon rounding Miron Island paddle southwest and then north through the channel between Vanderdasson Island and the mainland. Paddle to the north end of the bay to portage (no. 21) at the north side of an old farm, continuing northeast for 790 yards to the southwest leg of Spider Lake.

Paddle north to the north end of Spider Lake; portage (no. 22) 550 yards, passing a hunt camp and ending at the southeast end of Canoe Lake. Paddle northwest on Canoe Lake to the original portage to Five Mile Bay. Paddle north up Five Mile Bay, through Squaw Channel under the Parry Island swing bridge and return to Parry Sound.

This route may be shortened to 32 miles (51 km) or 3 days by beginning at the Three Legged Lake access point to the fifth portage. Follow the first alternate route to Spider Lake, then turn east near the north end of the lake and south to portage (no. 23) 394 yards over a good wagon road that ends at Button's Resort on Three Legged Lake. From Button's Resort it is only a 1-1/2 mile paddle back to the Three Legged Lake access point.

158 SMOKED PICKEREL (SECOND ALTERNATE ROUTE)

Length 31 miles
Approx trip time 3 days
Access By Highway 69
Maps Muskoka 31E/SW (Ont.)
Parry Sound 41H/SE (Ont.)

The second alternate route is a three day canoe trip combining part of the main loop and part of the first alternate route. There are two possible access points for this route: for the first, Three Legged Lake public access point, turn west off Highway 69 onto James Bay

Junction Road, 3 miles (4.8 km) south of Parry Sound; for the second, Crane Lake public access point, turn west off Highway 69 onto the Blackstone-Crane Lake Road at Horseshoe Lake, approximately 10 miles (16 km) south of Parry Sound.

Using the Crane Lake access point, paddle west across Crane Lake to the junction of the north arm. Paddle up the north arm, through the channel and to the northwest end of Clear Lake. Complete portage 14 and travel north across Salmon Lake to portage 13. Continue, north and then paddle down the long east arm following the main route to Lakes Portage, Blackstone, Crane, Birch and Healey, and Moon River Bay.

Follow the east shore of Woods Bay to Blackstone Harbour. From Blackstone Harbour backtrack on the first alternate route to Little Blackstone Lake, Blackstone River, Crane Lake and back to the Crane Lake access point.

For a more complete description of lakes and portages see the applicable sections of the main loop and the first alternate route.

159 SMOKED PICKEREL (THIRD ALTERNATE ROUTE)

Length 18 miles (29 km)
Approx trip time 2 days
Access By Highway 69

The third alternate route is also a combination of the main route and the first alternate route. *Start* at the Crane Lake access point and paddle west to the junction of the north arm of Crane Lake. Continue up the north arm, across Clear Lake and over portage 14. Paddle north on Salmon Lake and complete portage 13. Paddle north on Otter Lake and then east down the Long Arm. Cross portage 7 to Portage Lake. Paddle across Portage Lake, complete portage 8 and continue to the south end of Blackstone Lake. Paddle down the river to Crane Lake and on back to the access point.

For a more complete description of the lakes and portages see the appropriate sections on the main route and the first alternate route.

160 SMOKED PICKEREL (FOURTH ALTERNATE ROUTE)

Length 20 miles (32 km)
Approx trip time 2 days
Access By Highway 69

The fourth alternate route starts from the Crane Lake access point. Paddle west across Crane Lake and down the west arm to the Crane Lake Dam and portage 15. Paddle down the Blackstone River and do portages 16, 17, 18 and 19 to Little Blackstone Lake. Paddle across Little Blackstone Lake and do portage 20 to Blackstone Harbour. Paddle out to Woods Bay and then turn south following the east shore to Moon River Bay.

Do portage 11 to Healey Lake and paddle northeast to portage 10. Do portage 10, paddle Birch Lake and do portage 9 to the south end of Crane Lake. Paddle west and then northeast, completing the loop to the public access location. This route may also be entered by the Healy Lake access point.

For a more complete description of the lakes and portages see the appropriate sections of the main loop and the first alternate route.

161 SMOKED PICKEREL (FIFTH ALTERNATE ROUTE)

Length 17 miles (27 km)
Approx trip time 2 days
Access By Highway

The fifth and final in this series of alternate routes *starts* at Parry Sound. Paddle down to South Channel, following the main route in reverse to Spider Bay. Paddle northeast up Spider Bay to where the Spider River flows into the bay. Paddle upstream, locate portage (no. 24) to Spider Lake. Portage 180 yards along the north bank. Paddle to the northeast corner of Spider Lake and locate portage 22. Do portage 22, paddle Canoe Lake, do the first portage to Five Mile Narrows. Return to *finish* at Parry Sound.

For a more complete description of the lakes and portages see the appropriate section of the main route and the first alternate route.

162 PICKEREL AND KEY RIVERS

Access By Highway 69
Maps Byng Inlet 41H/NE (Ont.)
　　　　　Sudbury 41I/SE (Ont.)

The waters of the Pickerel and Key Rivers were for centuries the highways of early Indian travellers as well as more recently for the voyageurs. The two major access points, Gurd Lake and Pakeshkag Lake are both within

Grundy Lake Provincial Park, which is approximately 50 miles (80 km) north of Parry Sound. Provisions may be purchased at the Grundy Trading Post at the corner of Highway 69 and Pakesley Road (which leads to Grundy Park). Nautical charts for the Georgian Bay portion of the route are available at the Chamber of Commerce Office in Parry Sound.

If you are beginning at the Gurd Lake access, paddle east on Gurd Lake until reaching the southeast corner and entering a narrow channel which runs along the east end of the lake between a narrow neck of brush and the shore. Once in the channel, follow the east end of the lake to portage at the northeast corner. Portage 300 yards over fairly smooth rock to the southwest corner of Beaver Lake. Paddle across Beaver Lake to portage 110 yards over rock ridges to a small beaver pond. Cross the beaver pond to portage from the northeast shore of the beaver pond to the southwest corner of Pakeshkag Lake and then another 132 yards over bald rock to a good launching site.

If desired, the first three portages may be eliminated by using the Pakeshkag Lake access location. Paddle northeast to the end of Pakeshkag Lake and take a short lift around a small eddy at either side of the falls. Cross the eddy and paddle down the river which empties from the east corner. Paddle down the river for a short distance to portage across the Canadian Pacific Railway and follow the east side of the river for 200 yards to an unnamed lake or widening of the river. Follow the Pakeshkag River to Pickerel River. Paddle west on the Pickerel River and pass under the Canadian Pacific Railway trestle and past Highway 69. Approximately 3 miles down the river from Highway 69 is the first overnight campsite, on the south shore.

Downstream 3-1/2 miles on the north shore east of the Canadian National Railways trestle is a small store where additional supplies may be purchased. Approximately 1 mile below the Canadian National Railways trestle, Pickerel River divides into two branches. Follow the south branch to portage 45 yards over a dry section of rock outcrop. Paddle along the east shore for approximately 110 yards to a small narrows. It may be necessary to lift the canoe over the rocks if the water level is extremely low. Once through the narrows turn south and paddle through another narrow channel which

also may require lifting over the rocks.

Upon entering Georgian Bay at the mouth of the Pickerel River, paddle east to the second overnight campsite. Paddle east and then south following the east shore. Enter Key Harbour on the north bank of Key River, which has a small store where supplies may be purchased. Paddle east on the Key River past the Highway 69 bridge and Hurds Marina to the Canadian National Railways trestle at Ludgate.

When passing under the Canadian National Railways trestle, a short stretch of swift water is sometimes encountered during the spring runoff. Paddle northwest for approximately 1/2 mile to portage 175 yards around a rapids to Portage Lake. Paddle northwest on Portage Lake to portage 440 yards to Pakesley Road, directly opposite the Grundy Park entrance. It is approximately 1-1/2 miles back to the Gurd Lake access point. It is impossible to navigate a canoe up the creek leading to Gut Lake. It is necessary to walk back to the Gurd Lake access point to reach your vehicle.

163 WOLF AND PICKEREL RIVER

Length 38 miles (61 km)
Approx trip time One week
Access Off Highway 522
Maps Detailed township maps plotting the route can be obtained from the Ministry of Natural Resources, Port Loring, Ont.; 50¢ each.
Byng Inlet 41H/NE (Ont.)
North Bay 41L/SW (Ont.)

There is one portage of 500 feet around Pine Lake Dam and rapids. The trail is wide and in excellent condition. Good drinking water is available from a spring located near the dam just south of the trail. Numerous undeveloped campsites are available along the route. Canoe rentals are limited in the area. Arrangements for canoes should be made in advance. Supplies and other equipment can be obtained locally.

The Wolf and Pickerel River canoe route starts at a public access point located near the bridge, crossing the Wolf River on the township road, 4 miles (6 km) north of Loring. The route ends at the government dock on Waquimakog Lake at Port Loring. To reach Loring, turn west off Highway 11 at Trout Creek, which is 25 miles (40 km) south of North Bay, and proceed down Highway 522 for approximately 40 miles (64 km).

It is necessary to make arrangements for transportation back to your starting point from Port Loring, a distance of five miles.

Magnetawan River System

The Magnetawan River and associated canoe routes pass through some of the most picturesque parts of the Parry Sound Forest District. They are rich in the history of the early logging days when the virgin White Pine was cut off the areas and driven downstream to the mill and railway at Ardbeg, or westward to the mill of Graves and Bigwood and the shipping port of Byng Inlet. Evidence of these earlier days can still be seen today as you pass along the route of the old river drivers.

Provisions may be purchased at Parry Sound, Dunchurch or Whitestone, if you are using the Wahwashkesh access. Parry Sound or Pointe au Baril are good bases to the Harris Lake access. The only marinas where rental canoes are available are at Parry Sound.

164 MAGANETAWAN (MAIN ROUTE)

Length 47 miles (76 km)
Approx trip time 5 days
Access By Highway 69
Wahwashkesh public access point or
Harris Lake access point
Maps Byng Inlet 41H/NE (Ont.)

The Wahwashkesh public access point is reached by following Highway 69 north from Parry Sound to Highway 124; take Highway 124 northeast to Dunchurch and Highway 520; take Highway 520 north and then west to the Wahwashkesh Lake access road, to Wahwashkesh Lodge and the public access point.

Leave Wahwashkesh access point, paddle east, north and then northwest through a cluster of islands at the northwest corner of Wahwashkesh Lake and the outlet of the Magnetawan River. Paddle west following the north shore to portage at the west end of Deep Bay.

To bypass Wahwashkesh Dam and a series of rapids, begin at the northwest end of Deep Bay and portage 1,320 yards along a good trail to a rough, rocky launching site directly below the Canal Rapids. Paddle downstream a short distance around a bend to Grave Rapids to portage on the south shore on a rocky landing that is dangerous during high water. Portage 440 yards over rocky terrain to a good smooth rock launching area. Paddle the length of Trout

Lake, to the west end and through a short area of swifter water which leads back into the Magnetewan River. Paddle west to the overnight campsite on the south shore near the junction of the North and South Magnetewan Rivers. From the campsite, paddle west downstream for approximately 2-1/2 miles to portage on the north shore, 26 yards above the Mountain Chute across a flat, sandy landing. Portage for 350 yards over hilly terrain to a rocky launching area. Paddle west, keeping north of a long narrow point which extends east up the river. Pass the small Carve Island.

Approximately 1/4 mile west of Carve Island is Stovepipe Rapids. The swift water can either be run or the canoe can be lined along the north side. Paddle the channel west to the larger part of Little Island Lake, turn southwest to East Bay and enter the southwest arm of the lake. Paddle to portage on the west shore above a rapids.

Portage 40 yards over a rocky point from a flat broken rock landing area to a rock launching site. Paddle west, through the lower Three Snye rapids to portage 330 yards from a sandy flat on the south shore to a good rocky launching area over rolling terrain. Paddle downstream to Sellers Rapids to portage on the south shore for 40 yards over rolling terrain from a smooth rock landing to a rock ledge launching site. Approximately 200 yards below the Sellers is McDonald's Chute. Care must be taken while locating the next portage on the south shore. The falls are very difficult to see.

There is a good landing of smooth rock with a 40 yard carry over rolling rocky terrain to a smooth rock launching site. Paddle downstream with care; there are 100 yards of fast moving water coming to the landing of the next portage on the south shore only 100 feet above the falls. Cross the Canadian National Railways in a 3,500 yard carry over fairly flat rocky terrain to a rough launching site. Paddle across the river to portage on the north shore.

Portage 40 yards around Farm Rapids over rolling terrain, from a flat sandy landing to another flat, sandy launching site. These rapids can be navigated by experienced canoeists. Paddle west from Farm Rapids past the old clearing to a widening in the river known as Miner Lake. On the north shore is the second overnight campsite. Portage next on the south shore in a small bay across from the campsite.

Portage 3,500 yards over rolling terrain to

the South Magnetawan River and a flat rock launching site above South Magnetawan Dam. Paddle east to the inlet of Harris Lake, on the south shore approximately one mile up the river. As you enter Harris Lake, passing through a narrows, turn west and cross the north part of Harris Lake to Harris Lake Marina.

Harris Lake access point is reached by following Highway 69 north from Parry Sound approximately 35 miles (56 km) to the Harris Lake access road and then along the road to the public launching area.

Immediately south of the marina is a narrow bay which runs west, ending at Harris Lake Dam and the public access point. This access point may be used as alternate access to this route.

Paddle from Harris Lake Marina southeast down the south bay to a southern extremity and portage to Paddy Gordon Lake for 585 yards over a good trail to the north end of Paddy Gordon Lake. Paddle southeast down the north arm of Paddy Gordon Lake to a small bay near the southeast end of the lake and portage 88 yards over a fairly level trail which drops sharply to Kelly Lake. Paddle southeast down Kelly Lake to Kelly Creek, which can be navigated its length to Naiscoot Lake, except for a couple of beaver dams. Lift the canoe and gear over to reach the lower levels. At the mouth of Kelly Creek, on Naiscoot Lake, is an overnight campsite.

Paddle east for approximately 6 miles and enter the narrows, cross Little Wilson Lake through the gorge leading to Big Wilson and to the portage on the north shore, a short distance east of the gorge.

Portage 1,100 yards to Secret Lake. The first 440 yards is uphill. Portions of the last 660 yards may be wet during the early season. Paddle north up Secret Lake to portage just west of the stream flowing out of the lake.

Portage 330 yards over a rocky ridge to Miskokway Lake. The latter part of the trail falls quite sharply to Miskokway Lake. Paddle east across Miskokway through the narrows in the centre to the east end. Paddle a short distance up the creek flowing into the lake to portage 1,760 yards to the west end of Bolger Lake, passing by a hunt camp and underneath the hydro line. Paddle east across Bolger Lake, staying fairly close to the south shore of the lake to the overnight campsite on the east end of Bolger Lake and the south side of the creek

flowing into Kashegaba Lake.

Paddle down the river to portage at the southeast corner of Kashegaba Lake for 1,100 yards along an old abandoned railway bed to Snake Lake. Paddle down Snake Lake to the southeast end and through a short narrows into Maple Lake. Follow the north shore of Maple Lake to a narrow creek flowing through a marshy area to Duck Lake. Paddle through the marsh to the northeast corner of Duck Lake to portage 440 yards following an old abandoned railway which runs along the north side of the creek to Wahwashkesh Lake. Paddle east over Wahwashkesh Lake, east to Ritter's Narrows and to Indian Narrows, then on to the Wahwashkesh access point.

165 MAGNETAWAN (FIRST ALTERNATE ROUTE - KASHEGABA)

Length 17 miles (27 km)
Approx trip time 2 days
Access By Highway 520

After travelling the main loop from Wahwashkesh access point to the end of portage 2 at Graves Rapids, paddle west following the south shore for 3/4 of a mile to Kashe Creek to Magnetawan River. Paddle south up the creek for a short distance to portage to Kashegaba Creek. Start at a muddy landing and portage 110 yards to a smooth flat rock launching site. Paddle upstream a short distance to portage on the west bank of the stream.

Portage 50 yards along a flat marshy area from a marshy landing to a launching area of flat rock. Paddle south for a short distance to portage on the west bank of the creek. Portage 10 yards over flat rock from a good landing to an equally good launching site. Paddle upstream and across the east end of White Lake and up Kashe Creek to portage on the west side of the creek for 90 yards over rolling terrain from a sand flat landing to a sand flat launching site.

The next portage to Kashegaba is on the north shore of the creek below Kashe Dam. Portage 50 yards around Kashe Dam over rocky and rolling terrain to a good sandy launching site above the dam. Paddle south across Kashe Lake to the overnight campsite on the west shore a short distance south of the dam. From the Kashe campsite, paddle south across the lake to the southeast end of Portage Bay and follow the main loop back to the Wahwashkesh access point.

166 MAGNETAWAN RIVER (SECOND ALTERNATE ROUTE)
Length 39 miles (63 km)
Approx trip time 4 days
Access By Highway 520

Paddle from the Wahwashkesh access point and across Trout Lake to the overnight campsite. From the campsite paddle south and down the South Branch of Magnetawan River, continuing south and west for approximately 3 1/2 miles to portage 330 yards over a good trail which ends at a pool below the falls. Care must be taken while crossing the pool. The current can be very strong during periods of high water. Pass under the Canadian National Railway trestle further down river, continue southwest across the main channel of the river and paddle into Big or Fool's Bay to portage at the southeast end of Big Bay.

It is a very difficult portage due to the extremely steep cliff which rises from Big Bay. After the initial portage, the 175 yard trail levels out and ends at a low, flat launching area. Paddle to the south end of Clear Lake to a portage on the east shore, 330 yards over fairly level terrain from a good landing to an equally good launching site on the See See Lake.

Paddle over See See Lake, which is horseshoe shaped, to the southeast end to portage 135 yards from a gentle, sloping rock, passing over fairly rough terrain to end at a rough launching site below a narrow gut leading to Lone Tree Lake. Paddle southwest down Lone Tree Lake to its south end and a series of two small beaver ponds which require a short lift to lower the canoe to the next level. Paddle west down the creek, across a small unnamed lake to portage on the north bank of the creek adjacent to a beaver dam.

Portage 220 yards along the right side of the creek to a good launching site immediately below the rapids. Paddle across Rock Lake and down a narrow bay which runs west from the main portion of the lake near the southwest corner. On the north shore near the west end of the bay portage 460 yards over fairly flat terrain and *finish* at the Naiscoot Lake overnight campsite. Join the main loop and return to the Wahwashkesh access point.

167 BLACK LAKE
Length 14 miles (23 km)
Approx trip time 2 days
Access By Highway 35
Maps Haliburton 31E/SE (Ont.)

There are three suggested campsites along this route. Provisions are to be had at Dorset, although only limited canoe rental services are available.

It is advisable to bring both canoe and camping equipment. Public access is at Shoe Lake west of Highway 35 along a township road, 4 miles (6 km) south of Dorset. Parking space is limited. Unload equipment at this location, drive car directly across Highway 35, and walk back to starting point of the route.

Portage from the southwest end of Shoe Lake to Blue Chalk (or Clear) Lake and follow an old logging road for 1,300 yards, portage 150 yards, crossing a private cottage road at the midway point of the portage. Portage from Red Chalk Lake to Skeleton Lake. The beginning of this portage is a gradual uphill climb but declines steeply near Skelton Lake. Portage 720 yards over reasonably flat ground from Skeleton Lake to Upper Pairo Lake.

From Upper Pairo Lake to Lower Pairo Lake portage 200 yards and then from Lower Pairo Lake to the Black River portage 1,700 yards. It leads to the remains of an old logging camp near the river bank, 1/4 mile downstream from Black Lake. Portage 880 yards from the east end of Black Lake to the Lower Marsh on the Black River. In places follow the old Lands and Forests ground circuit telephone line. Portage 370 yards to connect the Lower Marsh on the Black River to the Upper Marsh. Portage along the north side of the Black River from the Upper Marsh to Wren Lake for 240 yards around an old logging dam (present control dam). From Wren Lake to Raven Lake portage 100 yards around the control dam on Raven Lake. Paddle north and then northeast on Raven Lake back to the access point and parking lot.

168 BLACK RIVER
Length 90 miles (145 km)
Approx trip time 6 days
Access By Highway 35
Maps Haliburton 31E/2W and E
　　　　 Gravenhurst 31D/14E
　　　　 Orillia 31D/11

The portion of the Black River herein described is from Little Wren Lake, Ontario Highway 35 to Washago village, Highway 69. Drive to the access point at Little Wren Lake, 5 miles (8 km) south of Dorset village, Highway 35.

Start, paddling chiefly on the Black River along most of its route, passing the hamlets of Black Lake, VanKoughnet and Cooper's Falls. Pass the junction of Head River and join the Severn River to *finish* at the village of Washago on Highway 69.

Numerous access points along the route enable the canoeist to start and finish at will. Beyond the hamlet of Vankoughnet, the Black River can only be travelled during spring high water.

169 MUSKOKA RIVER

Length 55 miles (88 km)
Approx trip time 4 days
Access By Highway 69
Maps Lake Joseph 31E/4E and W
Penetanguishene 31D/13E
Portages 13

This segment of the Muskoka River is a loop route from the village of Bala and back. *Start* at the river access point 4 miles below the village at the Ontario Hydro dam. Paddle across Stump Lake, portage around the Big Eddy Dam, take right channel to Gray Lake and 20 foot falls. Continue through Flat Rock Lake, Go Home Lake, portage at Three Rock Chute and follow the river outlet into Georgian Bay, Lake Huron.

Paddle the bay waters in shelter of the islands, but use caution. Then paddle 8 miles across open water using *extreme caution*. Proceed to navigation markers at the outlet of Go Home River, Go Home Bay.

Paddle upstream to Go Home Lake, the Flat Rock rapids and Muskoka River to *finish* at Bala village.

Kayak Routes

A number of Ontario rivers seem to be especially popular with kayakers. This information comes from a pamphlet issued to members of Ontario Voyageurs Kayak Club. Detailed route descriptions and sketch maps are available in a recent publication which can be purchased from the club for $2.00.

170 MAITLAND RIVER

Length 145 miles (233 km)
Approx trip time 2-3 days
Access By Highways 4 and 86
Maps Wingham 40P/14W
Goderich 40P/12E
Lucknow 40P/13E

Start at Riverside Park, continue past Wingham to *finish* at Goderich.

171 BIGHEAD RIVER

Length 7 miles (11 km)
Approx trip time 1 day
Access Off Highway 10
Map Owen Sound 41A/10E

Start on the Bighead River, continue past Oxmead to *finish* at Meaford.

172 BEAVER RIVER

Length 7 miles (11 km)
Approx trip time 1 day
Access Off Highway 10, inquire at Thornbury
Maps Nottawasaga 41A/9W
Collingwood 41A/8W
Markdale 41A/7E

Start at Heathercote and *finish* at Thornbury.

173 SOUTH SAUGEEN RIVER

Length 15 miles (24 km)
Approx trip time 1 day
Access By Highway 89
Maps Durham 41A/2 W
Palmerston 40P/15 W
Walkerton 41A/3 W

2-1/2 miles west of Mount Forest, downstream.

174 UPPER SAUGEEN RIVER

Length 18 miles (29 km)
Approx trip time 1 day
Access By Highway 6
Maps Durham 41A/2 W
Walkerton 41A/3 E

Start at Durham and *finish* at the bridge past Hanover.

175 UPPER MADAWASKA RIVER

Length 20 miles (32 km)

Approx trip time 2 days
Access By Highway 60
Maps Opeongo Lake 31E/9 E
Whitney 31E/8 E
Round Lake 31F/12 W

Start at Whitney village and *finish* at Madawaska village.

176 MADAWASKA RIVER

Length 140 miles (225 km), shorter distances below
Access By Highway 60 in Algonquin Park
Maps Opeongo Lake   31E/9 E
Whitney   31E/8 E
Round Lake   31F/12 W
Barrys Bay   31F/5 W and E
Brudenell   31F/6 W and E
Denbigh   31F/3 W and E

All the above maps pertain to river references only as far as the village of Griffith.

The Madawaska River rises in Algonquin Park and empties into the Ottawa River at Arnprior. Experienced kayakers find many sections of it very challenging; only the calmer stretches should be attempted by novices.

On Highway 60 in the park put in to *Start* at Mew Lake landing. Portage around two control dams on this 20 mile stretch to Whitney. The stretch from Whitney to Madawaska village, 17 miles long, presents a series of rapids for the expert. Water is quiet to Bark Lake. From the hydro dam to Lake Kamaniskeg is a very rough section (the MKC whitewater school is located here).

Now proceed through quiet water again by lake and river through the village of Combermere, then on through the village of Palmer Rapids and 9 miles beyond to Little Rapids.

From Little Rapids proceed 17 miles to the village of Griffith. Grades 2-6 rapids make the river suitable for experts only. Then a series of hydro control dams have resulted in many quiet water sections and portages, a few rapids as far as the outlets at Arnprior to *finish*.

In view of the fact that the Madawaska River has both quiet and boisterous sections, road maps should be studied to find the road access points most suitable to the skills of the canoeist.

Algonquin Park Routes

Situated on the southern quadrant of the Precambrian Shield, between Georgian Bay and the Ottawa River, a 2,910 square mile area makes Algonquin Provincial Park Ontario's largest. A large area of the park may be reached only by canoe or on foot. In order to provide access and certain facilities, some development has been necessary, particularly along Highway 60.

The early Laurentian Indians, some 6,000 years ago, made no pottery and used only stone tools and weapons. They were driven out by stronger Algonkian people, small bands of family groups whose wanderings were governed by their needs and the dictates of the seasons.

Early European explorers did not enter the park area but bypassed it on the Ottawa River to the north, as did the fur traders who established trading posts along the river.

The fur trade eventually gave way to the logging of white pine for square timber. In the early 1800's, cutting within the present day park accounted for a large portion of the pine logging industry. It filled many shiploads of square timber to sustain the shipbuilding industry of Great Britain. The park is rich in tales of the camboose logging camps and the river drives of that era.

The protection of the park watershed became essential. The area is high-domed in the centre and rivers flow off the highlands in all directions. Most of the park is occupied by the Petawawa watershed but parts of the Bonnechere, Madawaska, Oxtongue and Amable du Fond watersheds have their sources in the park. It is a canoe-camper's paradise. In 1971 more than 51,000 interior camping permits were issued to canoeists. Their numbers tend to increase by about ten percent per year.

The most recent park entry fee is $1.50. The daily camping fee is $2.00. A sixteen day fee for canoe-campers is $20.00 and a license for nonresident anglers is $8.50 per year. Access is by Highway 60, which runs across the park.

Mention should also be made of Canada's first (1973) whitewater school on the Madawaska River. Besides being recognized as running a very highly rated kayaking course, the school's rubber rafting fun trips are being enjoyed by hundreds on two sections of the river: three mile Bells Rapids between Bark and Kamaniskeg Lakes and a 12 mile, all day run downstream from Palmer's Rapids.

Write for details and a brochure to:

Hermann & Christa Kerckhoff
Madawaska Kanu Camp
2 Tuna Court
Don Mills, Ontario

During July and August write them at:

Box 68
Combermere, Ontario.

Access is by the county road off Highway 60 (inquire at Barrys Bay) or by the county road off Highway 62 (inquire at Combermere).

Maps dealing with Algonquin Park routes can be obtained from the Ontario Map office.
Algonquin 31E/NE (Ont.)

Canada Topographic Series maps to cover this area are:
Algonquin 31E/10E and W
Opeongo Lake 31E/9E and W

177 CANOE LAKE TO CEDAR LAKE AND RETURN

Length 80 miles (129 km)

Start at the public dock at the south end of Canoe Lake. Paddle to the northeast bay and portage 175 yards along the old road on the west side of the stream to Joe Lake. Paddle north one mile, then follow the east arm of Joe Lake and enter Little Joe Lake. Paddle to the north tip of Little Joe Lake to a small stream and then upstream to portage about 600 yards to Baby Joe Lake.

Paddle to a 200 yard portage leading to Burnt Island Lake; paddle through Burnt Island Lake to a portage about midway along its northeast shore for about 900 yards to the southwest bay of Little Otterslide Lake. Paddle to the most northern narrows of Little Otterslide Lake, which leads into the southwest bay of Otterslide Lake.

Paddle north through the west bay of Otterslide Lake to a portage; paddle north over a series of further portages and small unnamed lakes and streams to Big Trout Lake. (These portages follow the small streams joining

Otterslide and Big Trout Lakes. The distances are affected by the water levels during the summer).

There are 6 portages in all, varying in length from about 180 to 600 yards, a combined distance of about one mile. Paddle through Big Trout Lake to a portage at its most northerly bay for 330 yards to Longer Lake. Paddle through Longer Lake to a short portage which leads into Portal Lake.

Paddle to the northeast bay of Portal Lake and portage 180 yards into Perley Lake. Paddle through Perley Lake into the Petawawa River which flows into Catfish Lake. (There are 3 portages on this position of the Petawawa River, the Cedar, Snowshoe and Catfish Rapids, a combined distance of about 1200 yards).

Paddle through Catfish Lake to the northeast bay and a portage of 200 yards into Narrowbag Lake. Paddle to a further portage of 2600 yards to Stack's Rapids on the Petawawa River. There is one short portage before reaching the widening of the river, followed by 200 yard portage around a rapids.

Follow the Petawawa River to a portage around the dam; paddle to Cedar Lake. Return by backtracking over the route to Canoe Lake.

Extra supplies may be purchased at Brent on Cedar Lake.

178 CANOE, CEDAR, RADIANT, LAVIEILLE, OPEONGO, JOE LAKE LOOP

Length 125 miles (201 km)

Follow Route 177 from Canoe to Cedar Lake. Paddle southeast through Cedar Lake to an outlet on the southeast shore leading into the stream. Portage for over 1050 yards at the dam and across several small connecting lakes to portage around rapids. (From the foot of Cedar Lake downstream, extreme care should be taken to avoid being drawn into the current at the head of all rapids.); Portage 200 yards, then 925 yards leading in the northwest arm of Radiant Lake; cross Radiant and enter Petawawa River. Follow the river and a series of portages to Kildeer Lake (there are several portages along this stretch of Petawawa River, from 150 to 800 yards, a combined distance one mile).

Portage 800 yards from the south shore of Kildeer Lake to Crow River. Follow the Crow

Traversing deadfalls in Algonquin Park, these canoeists need a deft touch and a sure sense of balance. The park is Ontario's most popular canoeing area— a vast semi-wilderness within a few hours drive of the major urban centres.

River upstream to the east arm of Lake Lavieille (there are many portages along the latter half of Crow River, a combined distance two miles). Paddle west across Lake Lavieille, through Crow Bay into Crow River; follow the Crow River upstream to Big Crow Lake (eight portage on the river, varying up to 1,300 yards).

Paddle across Lakes Big Crow and Little Crow, enter Crow River, reaching Proulx Lake to portage on the southwest bay. Portage 1200 yards (a segment follows the logging road to a small lake, either cross it or portage along the east shore) and then carry 180 yards to the north arm of Opeongo Lake. Cross the north arm to a portage on the northwest bay. Portage 2400 yards to Happy Isle Lake and cross the lake to portage on the southwest bay. Portage 1000 yards to Shiner Lake and then 2000 yards to a small lake. Portage again for 600 yards to the northeast arm of Otterslide Lake and return to Canoe Lake over Route 177.

179 CANOE, CEDAR, NORTH TEA, NIPISSING RIVER, JOE LAKE LOOP
Length 175 miles (282 km)

Follow Route 177 from Canoe Lake to Cedar Lake. Paddle northwest through Cedar, Little Cedar, Aura Lee, Laurel and Little Cauchon Lakes to the northwest end of Cauchon. Portage 475 yards into Mink Lake (three short portages around the rapids before entering Little Cauchon). Paddle northwest through Mink Lake and portage 1700 yards into Kioshkokwi Lake. Cross the lake to the extreme southwest arm and follow Amable du Fond River to Wilkes (Manitou) Lake (three portages around the rapids, a combined distance one mile on this stretch of river).

Paddle through Wilkes Lake to the south bay and portage 600 yards into North Tea Lake. Paddle west, south and east to the east end of the southeast bay of North Tea. Portage 260 yards, then 50 yards and then 150 yards passing through two small unnamed lakes into the west bay of Biggar Lake. Paddle east one mile to the mouth of Loughrin Creek and then up the creek. Paddle 1800 yards and 600 yards to Loughrin Lake.

Paddle south through the lake to the southwest arm and portage 350 yards into Nod Lake. Then portage 1600 yards over a height of land

to Nipissing River. Paddle east along the river downstream to Cedar Lake (involves many portages around dams and rapids on Nipissing River). Return from Cedar Lake to Canoe Lake by Route 177.

Supplies are available at Brent and Kiosk.

180 CANOE, BIG TROUT, HAPPY ISLE, JOE LAKE LOOP
Length 40 miles (64 km)

Follow Route 177 from Canoe Lake to Big Trout Lake; paddle northeast through Big Trout, turn east, round the peninsula into a deep bay and then paddle east upstream one mile to portage 2100 yards to Merchant Lake. Paddle to the south shore of the lake to portage 375 yards into Happy Isle Lake. Follow Route 178 from Happy Isle Lake to Canoe Lake.

181 CANOE, MCINTOSH, BIG TROUT, BURNT ISLAND, JOE LAKE LOOP
Length 45 miles (72 km)

Follow Route 177 to Joe Lake. Paddle north following the west shore of Joe Lake through the channel leading into Tepee Lake; follow the east shore of Tepee Lake north through the channel leading into Littledoe Lake. Paddle north through the channel to Tom Thomson Lake and paddle northwest through Tom Thomson Lake to a portage on its northwest bay of about 2100 yards, leading into Ink Lake. Paddle the stream north out of Ink Lake and enter McIntosh Lake.

Paddle northeast through McIntosh Lake to a portage which starts in the vicinity of the entrance of McIntosh Creek. Portage about 575 yards to a point on the McIntosh Creek. Follow the creek a short distance to a portage of about 850 yards to a widening in McIntosh Creek.

Paddle downstream into Grassy Bay of Trout Lake and then east and north through White Lake to the narrows leading into Big Trout Lake. Paddle through the narrows and then south to a portage located on the south tip of Big Trout Lake. Backtrack Route 177 from Big Trout Lake to Canoe Lake.

182 CANOE LAKE — MCINTOSH LAKE
Length 80 miles (129 km)

Follow Route 181 from Canoe Lake to McIntosh Lake. Paddle to the northwest bay of McIntosh Lake to portage about 500 yards into Timberwolf Lake. Paddle across Timberwolf Lake, entering the long narrow arm at its northeast side to portage 100 yards into a small unnamed lake. Portage around a rapids into Misty Lake. Paddle north across Misty Lake to a portage of 600 yards on the north central arm into a small unnamed lake then paddle west to a portage of about 350 yards to Shah Lake. Paddle north across Shah Lake to a portage of about 1100 yards north into the Tim River.

Paddle east and downstream to the entrance of the Tim River into Shippagew Lake and portage 1200 yards about midway on the Tim River. Paddle across Shippagew Lake to a portage on the northeast bay and portage about 1700 yards into Longer Lake. Paddle south through Longer Lake.

Backtrack Route 177 from Longer to Canoe Lake.

183 CANOE, BUTT, LONGER, BURNT ISLAND, JOE LAKE LOOP
Length 60 miles (96 km)

Follow Routes 181 and 182 from Canoe Lake to Misty Lake. Paddle to west bay of Misty Lake and portage about 1100 yards into Little Misty Lake. Paddle west and enter the Petawawa River. Paddle upstream to a portage of about 450 yards into the most easterly arm of Daisy Lake. Paddle west about one mile to a portage adjacent to the stream connecting Daisy Lake and Butt Lake and portage about 1600 yards into Butt Lake.

An alternative route goes from the Petawawa River (upstream from Little Misty Lake) to portage south via two short carries to Moccasin Lake, then east via a 190 yard portage to Juan Lake. Portage 480 yards to Jubilee Lake; then 700 yards to Sawyer Lake and 350 yards to Rain Lake. Paddle west to the north shore of Rain Lake. Portage 1400 yards to Casey Lake and cross Casey to portage about 1200 yards to Daisy Lake and return to the main route via a 1600 yard portage to Butt Lake.

Paddle northeast to portage on the east bay of Butt Lake. Portage 500 yards into Little Trout Lake. Paddle east through the lake and over a short portage to Queer Lake to another portage of 2100 yards east into Tim River. Paddle east downstream, following Route 182

to Longer Lake. Backtrack Route 177 from Longer Lake to Canoe Lake.

184 RADIANT LAKE TO NORTH RIVER LAKE AND RETURN
Length 60 miles (96 km)

Start at Radiant Lake, adjacent to the Canadian National Railways. Access to Radiant Lake is possible by rail or by canoe from the Petawawa River. (This route is usually considered as a side trip from Route 178.)

Paddle north from Radiant Lake and enter the North River. Then paddle east through Shoal Lake to Clamshell Lake, enter the North River from Clamshell Lake, and paddle upstream.

Portage around a rapids and paddle north into North Depot Lake to its most northerly bay. Again enter the river which leads into Allan Lake. Paddle north through Allan Lake for about one mile to the entrance of North River into Allan Lake on the west shore. Paddle west and upstream and portage three times — lengths of 720, 200 and 80 yards — into North River Lake. Return over the same course to Radiant Lake.

185 ROCK, WELCOME, LOUISA LAKES
Length 30 miles (48 km)

Start at the public dock of Madawaska River at the north end of Rock Lake. Paddle south on the river to Rock Lake and then to the southwest tip of Rock Lake. Portage 400 yards into Pen Lake. Paddle south to portage on the south shore Pen at Galipo River. Paddle upstream and portage 1800 yards into Welcome Lake. Paddle west and north into Harry Lake, lift over the bridge. Paddle to the southwest tip of Harry Lake and lift over the bridge. Paddle upstream to Rence Lake. Paddle up the creek of the north shore of Rence to portage 450 yards to Frank Lake.

Paddle north to the northwest shore of Florence Lake to portage 1800 yards to Lake Louisa (a section of the portage follows a lumber road) and paddle to the east end of Louisa Lake to portage. Portage 3000 yards to Rock Lake. The portage jogs south along a lumber road near Lake Louisa. Paddle north to the starting point.

186 SMOKE LAKE, BIG PORCUPINE, LAWRENCE LAKE LOOP

Length 30 miles (48 km)

Start on the north bay of Smoke Lake, adjacent to Highway 60 at a public dock; paddle to a portage around a dam at the most southerly bay of Smoke Lake. Portage about 200 yards into Ragged Lake and paddle around the east side of the large island to a portage in the most southerly tip of Ragged Lake. Portage about 900 yards into the north arm of Big Porcupine Lake. Paddle southwest, then east and again south to a portage about midway on the east shore of Big Porcupine Lake. Portage for about 200 yards to the most westerly arm of Bonnechere Lake and then north to the tip of the northeast bay of Bonnechere Lake to a portage of about 650 yards to the second Bonnechere Lake.

Paddle to a portage around a rapids leading into the third Bonnechere Lake. Paddle northeast to the narrows leading to a portage of about 550 yards into Lawrence Lake. Paddle northeast through the narrows and portage 75 yards into Harness Lake. Paddle north through Harness Lake to the portage adjacent to the most northern tip of Harness Lake and portage about 1100 yards into the small creek leading into Head Lake. Paddle through Head Lake to a portage on the northwest shore. (*Do not* follow the creek leading out of Head Lake).

Portage about 1700 yards into Cache Lake. Paddle north and west through the narrow channel leading into Tanamakoon Lake. Paddle to a portage on the south shore of the west arm of Tanamakoon Lake and portage about 150 yards around a dam and enter a small unnamed lake. Paddle to a portage leading into Little Island Lake and portage for about 280 yards.

Paddle to the most westerly bay of Little Island Lake and portage about 250 yards to Kootchie Lake. Paddle to a portage of about 900 yards leading into Smoke Lake and then continue north to *finish* at the starting point.

187 OPEONGO, CROW, LAVIEILLE, DICKSON LAKE LOOP

Length 50 miles (80 km)

Start at a public dock at Sproule Bay, Opeongo Lake and paddle to the north arm of the lake to

portage 180 yards to a small lake. Cross the small lake or portage along the east shore for 1,200 yards from the small lake to Proulx Lake (a segment follows a logging road). Paddle northeast across Proulx and then northwest to enter Crow River and follow it to Little Crow Lake. Enter the narrows running east into Big Crow Lake and paddle east across the lake. Again enter Crow River and paddle downstream to Lake Lavieille (eight portages on this section of river, varying up to 1,300 yards). Water levels have a bearing on the length of portages.

Paddle east and then south to the southeast tip of Lavieille. Portage 100 yards into Dickson Lake and then paddle 3 miles to Bonfield Lake. Paddle west across Bonfield to portage 280 yards to Wright Lake. Paddle southwest to portage 600 yards to the south arm of Opeongo Lake to the starting point.

188 OPEONGO, BOOTH, VICTORIA LAKES AND RETURN

Length 50 miles (80 km)

This route is not recommended for novices.

Start at the public dock of Sproule Bay, Opeongo Lake and paddle to the dam at the outlet of Annie Bay. Carry 100 yards to Opeongo River and paddle to Tip-up (Tattler) Lake.

Portage 880 yards along the river to Booth Lake and paddle to the east end of the lake to a portage. Portage 50 yards to Kitty Lake and paddle to end of the lake to portage 20 yards. Then paddle along the river to Farm Lake, east to Crotch Lake to Shall Lake to Victoria Lake, making portages totalling 1/2 mile. Return to Sproule Bay along the same route.

An alternate route is to follow Route 189 from Crotch to Dickson Lake and Route 11 from Dickson Lake to Sproule Bay.

189 CROTCH, WEST BONNECHERE, DICKSON, ROUND ISLAND, BOOTH LAKE LOOP

Length 35 miles (56 km)

Start at the public landing at Crotch Lake. (Crotch Lake is accessible by Victoria Lake road which runs north from Highway 60 in the town of Madawaska). Paddle to the north end of Crotch Lake to portage 1,000 yards along the road to Shirley Lake. Paddle to the east shore of Shirley Lake to portage 600 yards to Ryan Lake. Paddle to the northeast tip of Ryan Lake and portage 375 yards into a small, unnamed lake. Paddle to portage 925 yards to Mudville Lake. Paddle south to the east shore of Shrew Lake to portage 1,800 yards to West Bonnechere Lake.

Paddle to the northwest shore of West Bonnechere Lake to portage 550 yards into Hidden Lake. Paddle to the northwest tip of Hidden Lake and portage 1,300 yards into Fairy Lake. Paddle to the northwest shore of Animoosh Lake and portage 1,200 yards into Cisco Bay of Dickson Lake.

Paddle northwest through Cisco Bay into narrows; paddle southwest through narrows to portage on the south shore of Dickson Lake for 4,500 yards to Round Island Lake. (This portage must be followed carefully as it crosses and follows lumber roads). Paddle to portage on the west shore of the southeast bay of Round Island Lake for 700 yards into Mountain Lake. Paddle across Mountain Lake and portage 650 yards into Marshy Lake. Paddle to portage 850 yards into Presto Lake. Paddle across Presto Lake to portage 525 yards into Chipmunk Lake. Paddle southwest through Chipmunk Lake to portage 450 yards into a small unnamed lake and then for 800 yards more into Booth Lake. Follow Route 188 from Booth Lake to the starting point of this route at Crotch Lake.

190 LAKE TRAVERSE, PETAWAWA RIVER TO MONTGOMERY LAKE
Length 30 miles (48 km)

Start at the public landing on the southwest corner of Lake Traverse. The lake is accessible by the Lake Traverse Road and the Canadian National Railway from Pembroke. Paddle northeast across Lake Traverse and enter Petawawa River. Follow the river and connecting lakes to Montgomery Lake, the terminal point of the route (connecting lakes are widenings of the river). Many sections of fast water and rapids must be bypassed by portaging. Some may be run by experienced canoeists but novices must use portages.

The portages are as follows: Lake Traverse Dam, 50 yards; Little Thompson Rapids, 330 yards; Grillade Rapids, 176 yards; next rapids, 130 yards; Crooked Chute, 2,600 yards; Rollway Rapids, 725 yards; Natch Rapids, 132 yards; Schooner Rapids to Coveo Lake, 4,270 yards; Coveo to Whitson Lake, 5,280 yards (in two portages); Whitson Lake to Petawawa River, 100 yards and the final portage is 3 miles below Whitson Lake.

From this point paddle to Montgomery Lake, the end of the route. There is a cabin and telephone at the Montgomery Lake Bridge. Phone here for arrangements for truck car transportation to Pembroke, 30 miles (48 km) away.

191 SMOKE, BIG PORCUPINE, LAKE LOUISA LOOP
Length 35 miles (56 km)

Follow Route 186 from Smoke Lake to Big Porcupine. Paddle south through the lake to its southwest tip and portage 325 yards into Little Coon Lake. Paddle to the south tip of Little Coon to portage 900 yards into Whatnot Lake. Cross the north shore of Whatnot to portage on the east shore 500 yards to McGarvey Lake. Then continue east across the lake to portage 800 yards to Lemon Lake and then 200 yards to North Grace Lake. Paddle east to portage on the most easterly bay, North Grace, and portage 1,200 yards, crossing a lumber road into Lake Louisa.

Portage 650 yards into Rod and Gun Lake and then again at the north tip; portage 350 yards into Lawrence Lake. Paddle northwest, then west and then northeast to narrows leading to Harness Lake. Follow Route 186 from Lawrence to Smoke Lake.

Little Coon, McGarvey and Lemon Lakes do not offer good overnight campsites.

 Map Sources (Southern Ontario)

The map numbers with (Ont.) after them are published by the Provincial Government of Ontario and are available from:

Ministry of Natural Resources,
Administrative Services Branch,
Whitney Block,
Queen's Park,
Toronto, Ontario.

Steens Cigar Store
Box 33
Aylmer, Ont.

Bancroft Sport Centre
Box 818
Bancroft, Ont.

McGees Sports & Gifts
Box 729
Bancroft, Ont.

General Manager
Barrie Chamber of Commerce
Wilson Bldg.
Fred Grant Street , Barrie, Ont.

Mr. C.J. Murray
Barry's Bay, Ont.

James Text Ltd.
183-185 Front St.
Belleville, Ont.

Bobcaygeon Chamber of Commerce
Bobcaygeon, Ont.

Currells Books & Records
32 Manitoba St.
Bracebridge, Ont.

Stedman's Bookstore Ltd.
154 Colborne St.
Brantford, Ont.

Martins Stationery
P.O. Box 310
Brighton, Ont.

Scientific Hobbies
1000 Islands Mall
Brockville, Ont.

Ship'n Shore
St. Lawrence Engine Co. Ltd.
Brockville, Ont.

Dept. of The Environment
Canada Centre for Inland Waters
867 Lakeshore Rd.
P.O. Box 5050
Burlington, Ont.

Robert O. Elstone, Stationery
3009 New St.
Burlington, Ont. L7R 1K3

Black Donald Tent & Trailer
R.R. #3
Calabogie, Ont. K0J 1H0

Geo. W. Eades Ltd.
Bridge St.
Box 821
Carleton Place, Ont.

Mr. R.C. Taylor
Tennyson General Store
R.R. #2
Carleton Place, Ont.

Kelly's Marina
Chaffey's Lock, Ont.

The Opinicon Ltd.
Chaffey's Lock, Ont.

Robert J. Lucier
Rayans Campsite
R.R. #1
Chalk River, Ont.

Elwood Epps
Box 338
Clinton, Ont.

Mr. J. Savigny
Realtor
Cloyne, Ont.

Saunders
P.O. Box 103
Collingwood, Ont.

Kyte's Ltd.
217 Pitt St.
Cornwall, Ont.

Mr. M. Hanes
Hanes Grocery & Gulf Service
Dacre, Ont.

G. Longhurst
General Store
Dalton, Ont.

The Delta Market
Delta, Ont.

Mr. R.O. Clark
Clark's Sporting Goods
Deep River, Ont.

Ryans Campsite
R.R. #1
Deep River, Ont.

Grand & Toy Limited
33 Green Belt Drive
Don Mills, Ont.

Clayton General Store & Marina
Dorset, Ont.

Robinsons General Store
Dorset, Ont.

Dept. of Transportation & Communication
Records Services Sec.
East Bldg.
Downsview, Ont.

The Art Service Reg'd.
152 Queen St.
Dunnville, Ont.

Algonquin Outfitters
R.R. #1
Dwight, Ont.

Fenelon Falls Chamber of Commerce
Fenelon Falls, Ont.

Mr. F.G. Ryan
Frontier Gun & Sport
8 Canboro Rd.
Fonthill, Ont.

Bennetts Hardware Ltd.
Gananoque, Ont.

Donevans Hardware Ltd.
Gananoque, Ont.

The Book Shop
39 Main St. South
Georgetown, Ont.

Mrs. Joyce Babcock
R.R. #2
Godfrey, Ont.

MacDuffs Texaco Services
Gooderham, Ont.

Rollies Sport & Cycle
Grand Bend, Ont.

Kennedy's Bookstore
125 Upper Wyndham St.
Guelph, Ont.

Wayne B. Wood
The Municipality of Dysart et al
Maple Ave.
Haliburton, Ont.

Silver Valley General Store
R.R. #1
Haliburton, Ont. K0M 1S0

The Bookcellar
144 James St.
Hamilton, Ont.

Cloke & Son
Box 2035, M.P.O.
Hamilton, Ont.

Temagami Sportsmen Service Ltd.
Suite 302
50 King St. E.
Hamilton, Ont.

Huntsville Pharmacy
Box 670
Huntsville, Ont.

Lipka's Rexall Drug
Box 1060
Huntsville, Ont.

Muskoka Boat Tours
R.R. #2
Huntsville, Ont.

Muskoka Sports Centre
P.O. Box 2280
Huntsville, Ont.

The Bookcase
Box 1500
Huntsville, Ont.

The Now Shop
47 Main Street East
P.O. Box 2227
Huntsville, Ont. P0A 1K0

Kincardine Public Utility Commission
P.O. Box 579
Kincardine, Ont.

R.W. Alford & Co.
121 Princess St.
Kingston, Ont.

The Port Hole
Kingston Shopping Centre
Kingston, Ont. K7L 1H2

The Provident Bookstore
117 King Street West
Kitchener, Ont.

C.G. Crackuell
P.O. Box 172
Lanark, Ont.

Nick Nickels
Box 479
Lakefield, Ont. K0L 2H0

Mr. Robert Holmes Ltd.
240 Dundas St.
London, Ont.

Oxford Book Shop Ltd.
742 Richmond St.
London, Ont. N6A 1L6

Mr. C.W. Shaw
Black Rapids
Lyndhurst, Ont.

Parkside Servicentre
Ben Barbarys
Hwy 7 Silver Lake
Maberly, Ont.

Minnow Haven Gas Bar
R.R. #1
Mactier, Ont. P0C 1H0

Rays Sport Shop
Madoc, Ont.

Leo's Sport Shop
28 McGill St.
Marmora, Ont.

Slaters Store
McArthur's Mills, Ont.

Voyageur Canoe Co.
Millbrook, Ont.

H.E. Alrutz
R.R. #1
Minden, Ont.

Manager
Niagara Falls Chamber of Commerce
1433 Victoria Ave.
Niagara Falls, Ont.

The Three Bears
1705 River Rd.
Niagara Falls, Ont.

Manager
Ellwood Epps Orillia Ltd.
R.R. #3
Orillia, Ont.

Can. Owners & Pilots Assoc.
77 Metcalfe St., Rm. 401
Ottawa, Ont.

Canadian Transportation Commission
275 Slater St.
Ottawa, Ont.
Attn. Ray Cramful, Rm 534

Information Canada Bookstore
171 Slater St.
Ottawa, Ont.
Attn. Mr. Houle

The Fishing Hole
125 Holland Ave.
Ottawa, Ont.

Eldred's Canoe Sales
354-26th St. W.
Owen Sound, Ont.

Secretary-Manager
Parry Sound Chamber of Commerce
2 Louisa St.
Parry Sound, Ont.

Pembroke Air Services Ltd.
R.R. #6
Pembroke, Ont.

Mr. Grant Bailey
Bailey's Sport Centre
159 Pembroke St. W.
Pembroke, Ont.

District Manager
Min. of Natural Resources
Box 220, Riverside Drive
Pembroke, Ont. K8A 6X4

Mr. Arnold Carson
P.O. Box 800
Perth, Ont.

James Bros. Hardware Ltd.
Perth, Ont.

Trent University Bookstore
Charlotte St.
Peterborough, Ont.

Petrolia Public Utilities Commission
Box 640
Petrolia, Ont.

McPhail Hardware Ltd.
168 Raglan St.
Renfrew, Ont.

Manleys
142 Lochiel St.
Sarnia, Ont.

Grays Sport Centre
Hardware-Electrical Appliances
Seeley's Bay, Ont.

Sharbot Lake Marina Ltd.
Sharbot Lake, Ont.
Beatties Desk & File
14 Queen St.
St. Catharines, Ont.

Peninsula Press Ltd.
Box 334
339 Ontario St.
St. Catherines, Ont.

Strathroy Public Utilities Commission
137 Frank St.
Strathroy, Ont.

Lakeview Marine & Sports
R.R. #1
Tecumseh, Ont.

Pockeles Sport Shop
10 Queen St. N.
Tilbury, Ont.

Mariner Texaco Service
Jack Salen
Box 9
Tobermory, Ont.

H.M. Dignam Corp. Ltd.
85 Bloor St. E.
Toronto 5, Ont.

Eddie Bauer
22 Bloor St. W.
Toronto, Ont.

Dora Hood Bookroom
34 Ross St.
Toronto 28, Ont.

Information Canada Bookstore
221 Yonge St.
Toronto, Ont. M5B 1N4

Marlborough's Stationary Shop
2346 Bloor St. W.
Toronto 9, Ont.

Ministry of Natural Resources
Map Distribution Office
Parliament Bldg.,
Whitney Bl., Rm 640
Toronto, Ont. M7A 1W4

Oscars Sport Shop
1201 Bloor St. W.
Toronto 4, Ont.

Tarling Map Mounting Ltd.
105 Church St.
Toronto, Ont. M5C 2G3

University of Toronto,
Bookstore
St. George Campus
Toronto 5, Ont.

Wellington Bookstore
P.O. Box 415
Adelaide St.
Toronto, Ont.

York University Bookstore
2275 Bayview Ave.
Toronto 12, Ont.

Darlings Stationery
24 Dundas St. West
Trenton, Ont.

Guy Hughes Ltd.
Box 241
Tweed, Ont. K0K 3J0

Mr. J.D.M. Phillips
Cartographic Services
4081 Kennedy Road
Unionville, Ont. L3K 2E5

Shaws Hardware
339 James St.
Wallaceburg, Ont.

Schendel Stationery Ltd.
120 King St. S.
Waterloo, Ont.

University of Waterloo
Bookstore
Waterloo, Ont.

Mr. Joe Miller
Sporting Goods
563 King St.
Welland, Ont.

Brennan's Sporting Goods & Gifts
Box 69
Westport, Ont. K9G 1X0

Mr. V. Gibson
Westport, Ont.

Mr. R.J. Merkley
Westport, Ont.

Mr. Fritz Sorensen
Bear Trail Lodge
Whitney P.O., Ont.

Canada Post Office
Postal Service Centre "C"
Fairview Mall Shopping Centre
Willowdale, Ont.

R.A. Clarke — Land Surveyors
640 Victoria Ave.
Windsor 12, Ont.

The Bookstore
Windsor Public Library
850 Ouelette Ave.
Windsor, Ont. N9A 4M9

Wally's Baits
3195 Sandwich St. W.
Windsor 10, Ont.

The Wingham Advance Times
P.O. Box 390
Wingham, Ont.

Mr. A.M. MacKenzie
Professional Engineer
528 Adelaide St.
Woodstock, Ont.

For a provincial road map and lure
literature on canoe routes write:

Ministry of Tourism & Information
Queen's Park
Toronto, Ontario

For marked road maps write:

Sun Oil Ltd.
85 Bloor St.
Toronto, Ont.

Petrofina (Canada) Ltd.
1910 Yonge St.
Toronto, Ont.

Shell Canada
505 University Ave
Toronto, Ont.

Gulf Oil Canada
800 Bay St.
Toronto, Ont.

District Offices of the Ontario Ministry of Natural Resources (Southern Ontario)

The following is a list of ministry offices throughout Southern Ontario. By contacting the office closest to your area of interest, you may obtain other up-to-date information.

Algonquin Region

Parry Sound District
4 Miller Street
Parry Sound, Ont.
P2A 1S8

Bracebridge District
P.O. Box 1138
Bracebridge, Ont.
P0B 1C0

Algonquin Park District
Whitney, Ont.
K0J 2M0

Minden District
Minden, Ont.
K0M 2K0

Bancroft District
Box 500
Bancroft, Ont.
K0L 1C0

Pembroke District
Riverside Drive
P.O. Box 220
Pembroke, Ont.
K8A 6X4

Eastern Region

Ottawa District
P.O. Box 434, R.R. #6
Ottawa, Ont.
K1G 3N4

Cornwall District
Box 1749
40 Fifth Street
Cornwall, Ont.
K6H 5V7

Napanee District
Napanee, Ont.
K0K 2R0

Brockville District
Brockville, Ont.

Tweed District
Metcalf Street
Tweed, Ont.
K0K 3J0

Lanark District
P.O. Box 239
Lanark, Ont.
K0G 1K0

Central Region

Lindsay District
322 Kent Street West
Lindsay, Ont.
K9V 2Z9

Maple District
Maple, Ont.
L0J 1E0

Huronia District
Midhurst, Ont.
L0L 1X0

Cambridge District
Beaverdale Rd, R.R. #1
Cambridge, Ont.
N3C 2V3

Niagara District
Highway 20
P.O. Box 1070
Fonthill, Ont.
L0S 1E0

Southwestern Region

Simcoe District
5 Queensway West
Simcoe, Ont.
N3Y 2M7

Aylmer District
353 Talbot Street West
Box 940
Aylmer West, Ont.
N5H 2S8

Chatham District
Kent Co. Municipal Bldg.
435 Grand Ave. W.,
Box 1168
Chatham, Ont.
N7M 5L8

Wingham District
Highway 4 South
P.O. Box 490
Wingham, Ont.
N0G 2W0

Owen Sound District
611 Ninth Avenue East
Owen Sound, Ont.
N4K 3E4

Outfitters (Southern Ontario)

	canoe rental only	partial outfitting	complete outfitting	packaged canoe trips
Niagara District				
Serendipity Sailing 649 Niagara Blvd. Fort Erie, Ont.	X			
Lakes & Trees Campground Vineland, Ont.	X			
Campbell's Marine Jordan, Ont.	X			
Bar-B-Q Restaurant Dunnville, Ont.	X			
Whelan Marine & Guns Welland, Ont.	X			
Huronia District				
D. Howell R.R. #1 Waubaushene, Ont.	X			
Harris Boat Livery 697 Atherly Road Orillia, Ont.	X			
Edenvale Garage R.R. #1 Minesing, Ont.	X			
Hugh P. MacMillan Northwest Company R.R. #1 Rockwood, Ont. N0B 2K0				X
Metro Toronto				
Algonquin Waterways Wilderness Trips 271 Danforth Ave. Toronto, Ont. M4K 1N2				X
Madawaska Kanu Camp Hermann & Christa Kerckhoff 2 Tuna Court Don Mills, Ont. (July & August) Box 68, Combermere, Ont.				X

	canoe rental only	partial outfitting	complete outfitting	packaged canoe trips
South Central				
Windermere Camp D.N. Hodgetts Lakefield College School Lakefield, Ont.			X	
Bancroft Sport & Marine 198 Hastings N. Bancroft, Ont.	X			
Long Lake Lodge Apsley (Long Lake), Ont.	X			
Happy Navajo Campground Apsley, Ont.	X			
Davis Marina Paudash Lake, Ont.		X		
Driftwood Marina & Snack Bar R.R. #3 Bancroft, Ont.	X			
Gary's Outboard Power Products 262 Hastings N. Bancroft, Ont.	X			
Tweed District				
Smarts' Marina R.R. #1 Cloyne, Ont.		X		
Bon Echo Villa R.R. #1 Cloyne, Ont.	X			
Owen Sound District				
The Compleat Angler 967-26th Street W. Owen Sound, Ont.			X	
Eldred's Canoe Sales 354-26th Street W. Owen Sound, Ont.			X	
Parry Sound District				
Lilli Kup Kamp P.O. Box 33 Katrine, Ont.	X			
River View Canoe Rentals P.O. Box 83 Burks Falls, Ont.		X		

	canoe rental only	partial outfitting	complete outfitting	packaged canoe trips
Grundy Lake Supply Post R.R. #1 Lost Channel Rd. Britt, Ont.		X		
Pine Grove Camp Port Loring, Ont.			X	
Buchanan's Garage & Marine Port Loring, Ont.	X			

Georgian Bay District

	canoe rental only	partial outfitting	complete outfitting	packaged canoe trips
Killbear Marina R.R. #1 Nobel, Ont.	X			
Dillon Cove Marina R.R. #1 Nobel, Ont.	X			
Bert Reekie R.R. #1 Nobel, Ont.	X			
Killbear Boat Rental, Ponderosa Morris Burden R.R. #1 Nobel, Ont.			X	
Bayfield Lodge Pointe au Baril, Ont.	X			
Albert Desmasdon's Point au Baril, Ont.	X			
Rogerson's Enterprises Ltd. Port Loring, Ont.		X		
Richardson's Rentals 51 Great North Road Parry Sound, Ont.	X			
Ruggles Sales & Service 113 Bowes St. Parry Sound, Ont.	X			
Bios Adventure Ed Robinson Loring, Ont.			X	

Algonquin Park District

	canoe rental only	partial outfitting	complete outfitting	packaged canoe trips
Bartlett Lodge 2 Avalon Blvd. Scarborough, Ont.			X	

	canoe rental only	partial outfitting	complete outfitting	packaged canoe trips
Portage Store Algonquin Park, Ont.			X	
Kish-Kaduk Lodge Brent, Ont.			X	
Killarney Lodge Algonquin Park, Ont.		X		
Opeongo Outfitting Store Whitney, Ont.			X	
Algonquin Outfitters R.R. #1 Dwight, Ont.			X	
Northern Wilderness Outfitters 726 Willow Ave. Milton, Ont.			X	
Baymore Marina R.R. #1 Dwight, Ont.			X	
Rainbow Lodge Whitney, Ont.	X			
Bear Trail Lodge Whitney, Ont.	X			
Wilderness Tours Box 661, Pembroke, Ont. OR Edward G. Coleman 1286 Washington St., Indiana, Pa 15701			X	

Winisk

Severn River

Attawapiskat

Attawapiskat River

Attawapiskat
Lake

Otoskwin River

Albany River

Moosonee

Moose
River

Missinaibi River

PAKWASH PROVINCIAL PARK

Lac Seul

Sioux Lookout

Lake Nipigon

Kapus-
kasing

Groundhog River

Mattagami River

Cochrane

Lake
Abitibi

Kenora

English River

Geraldton

Kirkland
Lake

Lake of
the Woods

Timmins

Rainy Lake

Seine River

Atikokan

Thunder
Bay

Lake Superior

Lake
Temagami

North
Bay

Lake Nipissing

QUETICO PROVINCIAL PARK

Sudbury

Mattawa R.

Ottawa River

KILLARNEY
PROVINCIAL
PARK

ALGONQUIN
PROVINCIAL PARK

Sault Ste. Marie

Lake Huron

Northern Ontario Routes

Ottawa River Drainage Basin

192 OTTAWA RIVER (UPPER OTTAWA, PEMBROKE TO LAKE TIMISKAMING)

Length 100 miles (161 km)
Approx trip time 5 days
Access By Highway 17
Maps Fort Coulonge 31F/NE
Golden Lake 31F/NW
Deep River 31K/SW
Mattawa 31L/SE
Lac Beauchene 31L/NE
Tomiko 31L/NW
Haileybury 31M/SW
New Liskeard 31M/NW
These maps are all to a scale of 1:125,000

193 MATTAWA WILD RIVER PARK (TROUT LAKE TO MATTAWA)

Length 25 miles (40 km)
Approx trip time 4 days
Access By Highway 17
Maps Write district forester for a free map booklet.

To *start* the trip, paddle east from the west end of Trout Lake to the Lands and Forests Chief Ranger Headquarters, North Bay District, to the campsite at Camp Island or continue further to the sandy bluff at the east end of the dam. Either is a good campsite. Paddle east to the end of Turtle Lake to Portage de la Mauvaise Musique. Portage to Robichaud Lake. Paddle to the portage marker at Portage Pin de Musique and portage 250 feet to Talon Lake.

Paddle to Grasswell's Point and Portage de Talon, a short, steep carry bypassing a 40 foot waterfall in two cascades between 100 foot walls. Paddle through the gorge to Pimisi Bay north to Décharge des Perches. If the water is low, portage, but if deep enough, ride or track the canoe. From Décharge des Perches, it is only a short distance downstream, between steep banks to Portage de la Cave, a gloomy ravine.

At Portage Parasseux, portage around a 30 foot waterfall. Paddle downstream, between granite cliffs.

To the left is a large, shallow cave, La Porte de l'Enfer (the gate of Hell). There is turbulent dark water at the base of the cliffs. Past La Porte de L'Enfer, the canyon stretches for 1/4 of a mile before the banks become level enough for a campsite.

There are two sets of rapids in the next short section of the trip. The first, Les Epingles, is tricky, but not dangerous for an experienced canoeist. The second, Portage des Roches, is located at the end of Bouillon Lake; it contains many large rocks which may necessitate a portage. Run two more riffles before reaching the mouth of the Amable de Fond River. Here, at Samuel de Champlain Provincial Park, you may finish the trip or travel 10 miles downstream to the village of Mattawa.

The only portage in the 10 miles is at Hurdman's Dam at the end of Chant Plain Lake. From Hurdman's Dam paddle a short distance to Explorer's Point where the Mattawa joins the Ottawa River.

Supplies may be purchased at North Bay, Rutherglen and Mattawa.

194 ENGLEHART RIVER TO LAKE TIMISKAMING

Length 75 miles (121 km)
Approx trip time 5 days
Access By Highway 66
Maps Elk Lake 41P/NE
New Liskeard 31M/NW
These maps are to a scale of 1:125,000

Start at Highway 66 and Englehart River (20 miles (32 km) west of Kirkland Lake) passing through Lakes Kushog, Kinogami and Robillard to *finish* at Blanche River.

195 LARDER LAKE TO ENGLEHART

Length 40 miles (64 km)
Approx trip time 3 days

Access By Highways 59 and 624
Maps Rouyn — Larder Lake 320/SW
New Liskeard 31M/NW
These maps are to a scale of 1:125,000

Start at either Raven and Wendigo Lakes on
Larder and Blanche Rivers respectively. Trip
could extend from Englehart down Blanche
River to Lake Timiskaming, 30 miles.

196 MISEMA RIVER AND HOWARD LAKE

Length 24 miles (39 km)
Approx trip time 2 days
Access By secondary road from Highway 66
or Kirkland Lake road to Esker Lakes
Provincial Park.
Map Rouyn — Larder Lake 32D/SW
This map is to a scale of 1:125,000

Start either by secondary road from Highway
66 to Beaverhouse Lake, or by Kirkland Lake
access road to Esker Lakes Provincial Park.
Paddle Misema River through a chain of lakes
to Howard Lake on the height of land (Arctic
watershed).

197 ESKER LAKES PROVINCIAL PARK

Length 6 miles (10 km)
Access From Kirkland Lake
Map Rouyn — Larder Lake 32D/SW
These maps are to a scale of 1:125,000

Pass through 22 small lakes within the park.

198 LAKE TEMAGAMI LOOP

Length 45 miles (72 km)
Approx trip time 4 days
Access By Highway 11
Maps Maple Mountain 41P/SE
Haileybury 31M/SW
Capreol 41 I/NE
Tomiko 31L/NW
These maps are to a scale of 1:125,000

Start at Temagami, Highway 11. From a
Hudson's Bay Company Post on Bear Island,
paddle south into the south arm of Lake
Temagami. Pass through Outlet Bay, Lakes
Cross, Wakasina, Driftwood and Iceland then
along the Tetapaga River.

199 TEMAGAMI, KOKOKO, GULL, CROSS LAKES

Length 80 miles (129 km)
Approx trip time 12 days
Access By Highway 11
Maps See Lake Temagami

Paddle around Lake Temagami and through a
series of short loops connecting the arms of the
lake. Start at Temagami and paddle for 8 miles
on the north side of the Northeast Arm and
portage to Hay Bay. Paddle through Lakes
Command, McLaren and Spawning, Spawning
Bay, Kokoko Bay, Kokoko Lake and finish at
Lake Temagami.

200 TEMAGAMI TO LAKE WANAPITEI

Length 70 miles (113 km)
Approx trip time 5 days
Access By Highway 11
Maps See Lake Temagami

This route runs from the Ottawa to the Lake
Huron watershed. *Start* at Temagami, Highway
11, to Manitou Lake bypassing Bear Island
through Lakes Gull, Skunk and Turtleshell to
Manitou Lake.
Paddle from Manitou Lake to Lake Wanapitei through Sturgeon River, Lakes Wawiash-
kashi, Murray Lake, Maskinonge, Rice, Mata-
gamasi and Wanapitei, to Skead on Highway 541.
An alternate route is to pass through Obabika
Inlet, Lakes Obabika and Emerald on through
Lakes Diamond, Wakimika, Obabika and Emerald to Lake Manitou.

201 TEMAGAMI — FLORENCE LAKE

Length 130 miles (209 km)
Approx trip time 12 days
Access By Highway 11
Maps Maple Mountain 41P/SE
Capreol 41 I/NE
These maps are to a scale of 1:125,000

Start at Bear Island, Lake Temagami. Paddle
to the northwest arm of the lake through
Obabika Inlet and lake to Wawiagama Lake and
Obabika River. Paddle south and west across
Obabika Lake through Wawiagama Lake, then
south on Obabika River until it joins Sturgeon
River. Paddle north on the Sturgeon to Yorston
River and north to Linger Lake. Portage Sea-
gram Lake and paddle through Mudchannel
Lake, Bluesucker Lake, Florence Lake and
Duff Lake to the South Lady Evelyn River.

Paddle north to the junction of the South Lady Evelyn and Lady Evelyn Rivers. Paddle Lady Evelyn east through Lakes Macpherson and Katherine. East of Katherine Lake turn south into the south channel of Lady Evelyn River. Paddle to Diamond Lake, through Sharp Rock Inlet and into Lake Temagami.

An *alternate route* is to leave Lake Temagami by Obabika Inlet and paddle north via Sharp Rock Inlet, Lakes Diamond and Wakimika to *finish* at Obabika Lake. (See the description of Wakimika Route.)

Another *alternate route* is to start from Katherine Lake and paddle the North Channel of Lady Evelyn River. (See details of North Channel).

A third *alternate route* is to *start* from Sucker Gut Lake and paddle 16 miles north into Lady Evelyn Lake and portage 20 yards into Diamond Lake. There is a good campsite along the route. (From Diamond Lake the route is described in the Lake Temagami route.)

202 MOWAT LANDING TO ELK LAKE LOOP

Length 160 miles (257 km)
Approx trip time 10 days
Access By Highway 11
Maps Elk Lake 41P/NE
Maple Mountain 41P/SE
Haileybury 31M/SW
New Liskeard 31M/NW
These maps are to a scale of 1:125,000

Start at Mowat Landing and paddle southwest on the Lady Evelyn River to the east end of Lady Evelyn Lake. Continue west through Obisaga Narrows to the North Lady Evelyn River, south through Katherine Lake and north to Grays River, Grays Lake, Banks Lake, Makobe River, Elk Lake to *finish* at Mowat Landing via Elk and Mountain Lakes and Montreal River.

203 MOWAT LANDING, MENDELSSOHN, MONTREAL RIVER LOOP

Length 50 miles (80 km)
Approx trip time 5 days
Access By Highway 11
Maps See Mowat Landing to Elk Lake loop.

Start at Mowat Landing, Montreal River. Paddle south along the Lady Evelyn River and

Lake, through Obisaga Narrows, Sucker Gut Lake, Willow Creek, Hobart, Anvil, Bergeron, Greenwater, Skull and Mendelssohn Lakes, Spray Creek, Big Spring Lake and part of the Montreal River.

204 LADY EVELYN LAKE AND MONTREAL RIVER LOOP (FROM TEMAGAMI)

Length 112 miles (180 km)
Approx trip time 10 days
Access By Highway 11
Maps Maple Mountain 41P/SE
Haileybury 31M/SW
Elk Lake 41P/NE
These maps are to a scale of 1:125,000

Start at Bear Island, Lake Temagami and paddle north to Lady Evelyn Lake, Montreal River Bay, Anima-Nipissing, MacLean, Red Squirrel Lakes to *finish* at Lake Temagami.

205 SHININGWOOD BAY TO HIGHWAY 11

Length 18 miles (29 km)
Approx trip time 1 day
Access By Highway 11
Map Tomiko 31L/NW
This map is to a scale of 1:125,000

Start at Shiningwood Bay and take Lake Temagami through Denedus, Wasaksina, Greenlaw, Brophy, Waha, Ingall and Jumping Cariboo Lakes to Highway 11.

206 WHITEFISH BAY LOOP

Length 50 miles (80 km)
Approx trip time 4 days
Access By Highway 11
Maps Maple Mountain 41P/SE
Haileybury 31M/SW
These maps are to a scale of 1:125,000

Start at Whitefish Bay, Lake Temagami and continue to the Aston, Turner, Eagle, Little Eagle, Whitewater, McLean Lakes and Anima-Nipissing Rivers, Red Squirrel Lake and return.

207 WEST SHINING TREE LAKE — OKAWAKENDA LAKE — MICHIWAKENDA LAKE

Length 15 miles (24 km)
Approx trip time 2 days
Access By Highway 560

The unusual rock formations alongside this river are characteristic of the rugged, scenic nature of the Canadian Shield. The granite surface of the landscape bears the imprint of the ice ages which scored the land, leaving exposed some of the earth's oldest rock and creating literally thousands of lakes that have long delighted and challenged canoeists.

Map Gogama, 41P/NW
This map is to a scale of 1:125,000

Start at West Shiningtree Lake (Highway 560), loop through Okawakenda and Michiwakenda Lakes to *finish* 6 miles (10 km) from the starting point on Highway 560.

Killarney Provincial Park

Access to the park is by Highway 637. Write for the booklet *Canoe Routes: North Georgian Bay Recreational Reserve* for detailed information on the following ten routes.

208 GEORGE LAKE TO CARLYLE LAKE
Length 12 miles (19 km)
Maps Lake Panache 41 I/3W

Start at George Lake and pass through Lakes O.S.A., Killarney, Norway, Kakakise and Terry to finish at Carlyle Lake.

209 KILLARNEY LAKE LOOP
Length 12 miles (19 km)
Maps Lake Panache 41 I/3W

Start at George Lake and pass through Lakes Freeland, Killarney and O.S.A. to *finish* at George Lake.

210 THREENARROWS LAKE LOOP
Length 22 miles (35 km)
Maps Lake Panache 41 I/3W
Whitefish Falls 41 I/4E

Start at George Lake and pass through O.S.A. Lake, Muriel Lake, Artist Creek, Baie Fine, Threenarrows Lake, Killarney Lake and Freeland Lake to *finish* at George Lake.

211 BELL LAKE LOOP
Length 22 miles (35 km)
Maps Lake Panache 41 I/3E and W

Start at Carlyle Lake and pass through Johnnie Lake, David Lake, Balsam Lake, Bell Lake and Johnnie Lake to *finish* at Carlyle Lake.

212 TYSON LAKE LOOP
Length 26 miles (42 km)
Maps Lake Panache 41 I/3E and W

Start at Carlyle Lake and pass through Lakes Johnnie, Bell, Grey, Tyson and the Mahzenazing River to *finish* at Carlyle Lake.

An *alternative route* is to take Johnnie, David, Balsam and Bell Lakes. A side trip from Tyson Lake to Spoon Lake and Atlee Lake is also of interest.

213 LAKE PANACHE LOOP
Length 64 miles (103 km)
Maps Lake Panache 41 I/3E and W
Whitefish Falls 41 I/4E

Start at Carlyle Lake continue through Johnnie, Bell, Balsam, Harry, Panache and Bear Lakes, Whitefish River, Lang Lake, Cross Lake, Charlton Lake, Howry Creek, Murray, Howry, Fish, Great Mountain, David and Carlyle Lakes.

214 WHITEFISH RIVER LOOP
Length 70 miles (113 km)
Maps Lake Panache 41 I/3E and W
Whitefish Falls 41 I/4E

Start at George Lake and pass through Lakes Carlyle, Panache and Bear (See Lake Panache Loop route), the Whitefish River, Whitefish Falls, Iroquois Bay, Kirk Creek, Lakes Baie Fine, O.S.A., Killarney and Freeland to *finish* at George Lake.

215 WANAPITEI RIVER TO BYNG INLET
Length 85 miles (137 km)
Maps Delamere 41 I/2W and E
Key Harbour 41H/15W and E
Noganosh 41H/16W and E
Noelville 41 I/1W and E

Start at Wanapitei River and pass through Wanapitei Bay, Hartley Bay to reach Pickerel River, Dollars Lake, Kawigamog Lake, Naganosh Lake, Island Lake and Magnetawan River to *finish* at Byng Inlet. Take a side trip from Naganosh Lake to Still River Ranger Tower of 5-1/4 miles (8.5 km).

216 FRENCH RIVER TO KILLARNEY
Length 45 miles (72 km)
Maps See Wanapitei River to Byng Inlet route

Start at the French River (Chaudiere Falls) and *finish* at the Eastern Outlet (French River). An *alternative route* is to take the French River to Georgian Bay. Another *alternative route* is to take the Eastern Outlet to Killarney, 40 miles (64 km) along the shore of Georgian Bay.

217 WAHWASHKESH LAKE LOOP
Length 79 miles (127 km)
Maps Key Harbour 41H/15E
Noganosh Lake 41H/16E and W
Point au Baril 41H/9E and W
Naiscoot River 41H/10E

Start at Byng Inlet and pass through Magnetawan River, Island, Wahwashkesh, Maple, Bolger, Kashegaba and Trout Lakes, South Magnetawan Channel, Big Bay, Lone Tree Lake and Naiscoot Lake to *finish* at Charles Inlet.

Lake Huron Drainage Basin
218 NORTH BAY TO GEORGIAN BAY VIA FRENCH RIVER
Length 82 miles (132 km)
Approx trip time 5-7 days
Access By Highway 17

Maps   Nipissing 31L/4W
       Noelville 41I/1E and W
       Delamere 41I/2E and W
       This map is to a scale of 1:125,000

The trip across Lake Nipissing should be made by chartering a power boat at North Bay. *The lake is too dangerous to navigate in a canoe.* Grand Manitou Island is 4 miles out from North Bay. Goose Island is 12 miles out. Five miles beyond the southeast arm of Lake Nipissing is the head of the French River.

At Franks Bay transfer from power boat to canoe. The route leads downstream passing many islands. Satchell's Bay indents the south shore and 3 miles further is Hardy Bay, also on the south shore. The head of Okikendawt Island is reached 4 miles to the west.

The island is 7 miles long and 3 miles wide. It divides the river into two channels. The route follows the south channel for a short distance to a series of rapids called the Chaudiere Falls. Avoid rapids by turning into a bay from the west end where a 500 yard portage crosses to another bay which leads back to the river below the falls and on to Keeso's Point.

The current is swift here but the reach below offers a wide channel for the next 8 miles to Eighteen Mile Island and Commanda Island. The route leads along the south shore of Eighteen Mile Island where a series of rapids, known as the Five Mile Rapids, extends for about 4 1/2 miles.

The first of these, the Little Pine Rapids, are avoided by a portage of 50 yards on the north shore. One-half mile below, the Big Pine Rapids are bypassed by a portage of 100 yards on the north shore. A 3/4 mile run below this portage ends at the Big Parisien Rapids, which are bypassed by a portage of 200 yards on the north shore.

Below these rapids the river is level for 2 miles to the Little Parisien Rapids. Portage 50 yards on the south shore. The Crooked Rapids one mile further are bypassed by a 1/2 mile portage on the north shore.

Nine miles below Crooked Rapids a large oval rock, the Owl's Head, stands on the north shore. In the river are three small rock islands. Five miles further is Lost Child Bend. The route circles an island at this point and continues along the main channel to the Canadian Pacific Railway bridge at French River Station.

Two miles below the bridge a 15 yard portage on the south shore bypasses the dangerous Recollet Falls. About one mile below the falls a small rapids breaks the stream.

The route continues for 3 1/2 miles past Potvin's Island to a second small rapid known as the Flat Rapid. Both rapids can be run but should be reconnoitered beforehand.

Two miles further, the Canadian National Railway crosses the river and widens into Ox Lake. Cross to Wanapitei Lake. The route turns south at this point. Follow the Main Channel for 3 miles, then turn west for 1 1/2 miles to the Dalles Rapids. Here is the last portage, 400 yards on the south shore.

Take a short paddle to the village of French River. Two miles below the village the river empties into Georgian Bay.

For alternate routes ask for the proper chart.

No railway serves French River Harbor. The canoeist must retrace his route to the Canadian National Railway at Hartley Bay or Pickerel River, or, to the Canadian Pacific Railway at French River Station.

219   THOR LAKE — VERMILION RIVER

Length   150 miles (241 km)
Approx trip time   7-10 days
Access   By Thor Lake, 50 miles (80 km) north of Sudbury on the Canadian National Railways
Maps   Westree 41P/SW
       Capreol 41 I/NE
       Cartier 41 I/NW
       Espanola 41 I/SW
       These maps are to a scale of 1:125,000

Start at Thor Lake, 50 miles (80 km) north of Sudbury on the Canadian National Railways. Follow the Canadian National Railways line to Capreol and then southwest to Naughton on Highway 17.

220   BISCOTASING — SPANISH RIVER

Length   132 miles (212 km)
Approx trip time   10 days
Access   At Biscotasing on the Canadian Pacific Railway
Maps   Biscotasing 41O/SE
       Westree 41P/SW
       Cartier 41 I/NW
       Espanola 41 I/SW
       These maps are to a scale of 1:125,000

Start at Biscotasing on the Canadian Pacific Railway. Paddle downstream on the Spanish River to Espanola.

221 GOGAMA — MOLLIE RIVER — EAST SPANISH RIVER

Length 65 miles (105 km)
Approx trip time 5 days
Access At Gogama, Highway 144
Maps Gogama 41P/NW
Westree 41P/SW
These maps are to a scale of 1:125,000

May be combined with the Biscotasing — Spanish River route and the Mattagami River route, in a continuous 650 mile trip from James Bay to Lake Huron. Arrange transportation at Gogama to cross the 5 mile portage by the logging road from Dividing Lake to the Spanish River watershed.

222 GRASSY RIVER (SINCLAIR LAKE TO TIMMINS)

Length 75 miles (121 km)
Approx trip time 4 days
Access By Highway 560 from Gogama
Maps Gogama 41P/NW
Timmins 42A/SW
These maps are to a scale of 1:125,000

Start at Sinclair Lake (south and east on Highway 560 from Gogama, then 25 miles (40 km) north along a secondary road). Paddle through Sinclair Lake, Grassy River, Kapiskong and Peterlong Lakes to Mattagami River. *Finish* at Timmins.

223 NABAKWASI RIVER (NABAKWASI LAKE TO GOGAMA)

Length 22 miles (35 km)
Approx trip time 3 days
Access Off Highway 560
Maps Gogama 41P/NW
This map is to a scale of 1:125,000

Start at the south end of Nabakwasi Lake on a secondary road from Highway 560. Paddle the Nabakwasi River past the junction of Minisinakwa and Nabakwasi Rivers to Mattagami Lake. *Finish* the trip at an Indian settlement, Gogama, near the outlet of Minisinakwa River into Mattagami Lake.

224 MINISINAKWA LAKE, MOLLIE RIVER, DIVIDING LAKE, NEVILLE LAKE, MAKAMI LAKES LOOP

Length 60 miles (97 km)
Approx trip time 8 days
Access By Gogama, Highway 144
Maps Gogama 41P/NW
Ridout 41O/NE
Westree 41P/SW
These maps are to a scale of 1:125,000

Start at Gogama, circle southwest through Minisinakwa Lake, Mollie River, Mollie Lake, Dividing Lake, a chain of small connecting lakes to Neville Lake and Mesomikenda Lake. Enter Makami Lake to Gogama.

225 MISSISSAGI RIVER (BISCOTASING TO AUBREY FALLS)

Length 110 miles (177 km)
Approx trip time 7 days
Access By Canadian Pacific Railway
Maps Biscotasing 41O/SE
Bark Lake 41J/NE
Wakomata Lake 41J/NW
These maps are to a scale of 1:125,000

Start at Biscotasing Lake, 80 miles (129 km) northwest of Sudbury on the Canadian Pacific Railway. (Supplies and canoes from outfitters at Biscotasing), through Ramsey Lake, Spanish River, First Lake, Abney Lake, Bardney Creek and Lake, Sulphur, Surprise, Circle, Mississagi, Upper Green, Kasbogama, Shanguish, Mississagi River to Limit, Kettle, Upper Bark, Bark and Rocky Island.
You can leave the river where the road connects with Highway 564 to Iron Bridge or Highway 108 to Elliot Lake. You can also extend onward to Abinette River, Rocky Island Lake to Aubrey Lake and Falls. Leave the river at the access point to Highway 129.

226 MISSISSAGI RIVER (AUBREY FALLS TO LAKE HURON)

Length 90 miles (145 km)
Approx trip time 5-7 days
Access Off Highway 129
Maps Wakomata 41J/NW (Ont.)
Thessalon 41J/SW (Ont.)
Blind River 41J/SE (Ont.)
These maps are to the scale of 1:125,000

Start at Aubrey Falls, 67 miles (108 km) north of Thessalon on the Mississagi River, on through Tunnel Lake to the river again, past Iron Bridge to Mississagi Falls, to Lake Huron. Paddle east 3 miles to Blind River.

Both of the above routes are for very experienced whitewater canoeists. They include 29 portages in total.

227 AUBINADONG RIVER TO MISSISSAGI RIVER

Length 30 miles (48 km)
Approx trip time 3 days
Access By Highway 129
Maps Wenebigon Lake 41O/SW (Ont.)
Wakomata 41J/NW (Ont.)
These maps are to a scale of 1:125,000

Enter this tributary of the Mississagi River at various points along Highway 129. It is for experienced canoeists only.

228 RANGER, GONG, MEGISAN LAKES, NUSHATOGAINI RIVER LOOP

Length 69 miles (111 km)
Approx trip time 10 days
Access By forest access road from Highway 556
Maps Wakomata 41J/NW (Ont.)
Wenebigon Lake 41O/SW (Ont.)
These maps are to a scale of 1:125,000

229 RANGER, GONG, MEGISAN, GOULAIS, LODESTONE LAKES LOOP

Length 70 miles (113 km)
Approx trip time 12 days
Access By forest access road from Highway 556
Map Wakomata (Ont.) 41J/NW
This map is to the scale 1:125,000.

230 RANGER, GONG, MEGISAN, GOULAIS, SOUTH BRANCH, TUJAC LAKES LOOP

Length 70 miles (113 km)
Approx trip time 12 days
Access By forest access road from Highway 556
Maps Wakomata Lake 41J/NW
Wenebigon Lake 41O/SW
These maps are to the scale 1:125,000

231 BOLAND RIVER

Length 35 miles (56 km)

Approx trip time 4 days
Access By Highway 546
Maps Bark Lake (Ont.) 41J/NE
This map is to the scale 1:125,000

Start at Mount Lake near the end of Highway 546. *Finish* at Highway 639.

232 DUNLOP, TEN MILE, EZMA, MACE LAKES LOOP

Length 26 miles (42 km)
Approx trip time 3 - 5 days
Access By Highway 108
Maps Bark Lake 41J/NE (Ont.)
Blind River 41J/SE (Ont.)
These maps are to a scale of 1:125,000

This is a circular route through nine lakes in the Mississagi Provincial Park. *Start* and *finish* at Dunlop Lake, 8 miles (13 km) north of Elliot Lake, on Highway 108.

233 FLACK, OLYMPUS, ASTONISH, TEN MILE, DOLLYBERRY, SAMREID LAKES LOOP

Length 30 miles (48 km)
Approx trip time 4 days
Access Highway 639
Maps See Route 232

This is a circular route. *Start* and *finish* where Flack Lake meets Highway 639 in the Mississagi Provincial Park.

234 ELLIOT LAKE-DEPOT LAKE

Length 20 miles (32 km)
Approx trip time 3 days
Access By Highway 108
Maps See Route 232

Start at the town Elliot Lake and *finish* at Depot Lake on Highway 108.

235 SEMIWITE LAKE-OMPA LAKE ROUTE

Length 20 miles (32 km)
Approx trip time 3 days
Access By Highway 108
Maps See Route 232

Start at Mississagi Provincial Park and *finish* at Ompa Lake on Highway 639.

236 BATCHAWANA RIVER

Length 30 miles (48 km)

Approx trip time 4 days

Access By Algoma Central Railway to Batchawana Station

Maps Batchawana 41N/SE (Ont.)
Sault Ste. Marie 41K/NE (Ont.)
These maps are to a scale 1:125,000

Start from Sault Ste. Marie on the Algoma Central Railway to Batchawana Station (Mile 80) (km 130) (Canoe only in May or June at high water levels) to Trans Canada Highway 17, 43 miles (69 km) north of Sault Ste. Marie.

237 GOULAIS RIVER (RAGGED LAKE TO SEARCHMOUNT)

Length 40 miles (64 km)

Approx trip time 5 days

Access By Highway 552

Maps Wenebigon Lake 41O/SW (Ont.)
Wakomata Lake 41J/NW (Ont.)
Sault Ste. Marie 41K/NE (Ont.)
These maps are to a scale of 1:125,000

Start at Ragged Lake and *finish* at Searchmont. Both are accessible by the forest access road.

238 GARDEN RIVER

Length 40 miles (64 km)

Approx trip time 2 days

Access From Highway 556

Maps Wakomata Lake 41J/NW (Ont.)
Sault Ste. Marie 41K/NE (Ont.)
These maps are to a scale of 1:125,000

Start at a logging dam adjacent to the forest access road from Highway 556, 25 miles (40 km) northeast of Sault Ste. Marie and *finish* at Garden River on Highway 17. Canoeing advisable during periods of high water in May and June *ONLY.*

Moose River Drainage Basin

239 MATTAGAMI RIVER (HIGHWAY 11 TO MOOSONEE)

Length 200 miles (322 km)

Approx trip time 7-10 days

Access By Highway 11

Maps Smooth Rock 42H/SW
Kapuskasing 42G/SE
Island Falls 42H/NW
Opasatika 42G/NE
Coral Rapids 42 I/SW

Blacksmith Rapids 42 I/NW
The maps above are to a scale of 1:125,000
Smoky Falls 42J
Moosonee 42P

Enter Mattagami River system at one of three points along Highway 11: at Kapuskasing to Mattagami; from Fauquier on the Groundhog River to Mattagami; and at Smooth Rock Falls on the Mattagami River. Paddle to Missinaibi River forming Moose River, to Moosonee.

240 KAPUSKASING RIVER (ELSAS TO KAPUSKASING)

Length 70 miles (113 km)

Approx trip time 3 days

Access By Elsas on Canadian National Railways

Maps Foleyet 42B/SE
Elsas 42B/NE
Kapuskasing 42G/SE
These maps are to a scale of 1:125,000

Start at Elsas on Kapuskasing Lake. Paddle to Kapuskasing.

241 MISSINAIBI RIVER (MATTICE TO MOOSONEE)

Length 200 miles (322 km)

Approx trip time 7-10 days

Access By Highway 11

Maps Moosonee 42P
+Blacksmith Rapids 42 I/NW
Smoky Falls 42J
+Hearst 42G/NW
+Kapuskasing 42G/SE
Maps marked + are to a scale of 1:125,000

Start at Mattice, 42 miles (68 km) west of Kapuskasing on Highway 11, to Moosonee. Return to Cochrane and Highway 11 on Ontario Northland Railway. This route is for experienced canoeists only.

242 GOAT RIVER-MATTAWITCHEWAN RIVER

Length 100 miles (161 km)

Approx trip time 5-7 days

Access From Mile 88 on the Canadian National Railways

Maps Fire River 42B/NW
Hornepayne 42F/SE (Ont.)
Opasatika Lake 42G/SW
Hearst 42G/NW
These maps are to a scale of 1:125,000

Poling on the Abitibi River in 1905. Today the Abitibi region is a centre of pulp and paper production. The river itself is a major source of hydropower, serving four power developments.

Start at Minnipuka Lake at Mile 88 (142 km) on the Canadian National Railways. Paddle the Goat River down to the junction with Matta-witchewan River, to Oba at the intersection of the Algoma Central Railway and the Canadian National Railways.

243 GROUNDHOG RIVER (HIGHWAY 101 TO HIGHWAY 11)

Length 104 miles (167 km)
Approx trip time 7 days
Access By Highway 101
Maps Foleyet 41B/SE
Elsas 42B/NE
Kapuskasing 42G/SE
These maps are to a scale of 1:125,000

Start at the Groundhog River bridge, 32 miles (51 km) west of Highway 101. *Finish* at Highway 11, 17 miles (27 km) east of Kapuskasing.

244 MATTAGAMI RIVER (GOGAMA TO SMOOTH ROCK FALLS)

Length 140 miles (225 km)
Approx trip time 8 days
Access By Highway 144
Maps Timmins 42A/SW
Gogama 41P/NW
These maps are to a scale of 1:125,000

Start at Minisinakwa Lake, Gogama, on Highway 144, on to Timmins and then to *finish* at Smooth Rock Falls, Highway 11.

245 TATACHIKAPIKA LAKE TO TIMMINS, VIA THE TATACHIKAPIKA AND MATTAGAMI RIVERS

Length 60 miles (96 km)
Approx trip time 6 days
Access By Highway 101

Maps Gogama 41P/NW
Timmins 42A/SW
These maps are to a scale of 1:125,000

Start west of Timmins, Highway 101 and then take Highway 144 south to Tatachikapika Lake. Paddle the Tatachikapika River to Miskwamabi Lake and the Mattagami River. *Finish* at Timmins.

246 KAMISKOTIA RIVER (OPISHING LAKE TO TIMMINS)

Length 62 miles (100 km)
Approx trip time 5 days
Access By Highway 101
Maps Timmins 42A/SW
Ramour 42A/NW
These maps are to a scale of 1:125,000

Start at Opishing Lake, 32 miles (51 km) west of Timmins, Highway 101. Follow the Kamiskotia River to the junction with the Mattagami River to *finish* at Timmins.

247 SANDBANK LAKE TO MOOSONEE, VIA AGWASUK, KWATABOAHEGAN AND MOOSE RIVERS

Length 130 miles (209 km)
Approx trip time 8 days
Access By air from Moosonee
Maps Ghost River 420
Moosonee 42P

To reach the starting point of this difficult wilderness trip, fly west from Moosonee to Sandbank Lake, 90 air miles (145 km). Paddle the Agwasuk, Kwataboahegan, and Moose Rivers to Moosonee. Guides and aircraft are available at Moosonee.

248 PARTRIDGE RIVER TO JAMES BAY

Length 175 miles (282 km)
Access At Moosonee
Maps Moose River 42I
Moosonee 42P

This difficult trip (for big water experts), along the tidal flats of James Bay, *starts* at Moosonee. Paddle the Moose River into James Bay. Starting times depend on the tides and winds. On James Bay paddle south to Partridge River. Paddle upstream. *Finish* upstream travel

at a 20 foot waterfall. Return to Moosonee. Consult (if not hire) local guides.

249 GOWGANDA-MATACHEWAN (MAIN ROUTE)

Length 40 miles (64 km)
Approx trip time 3 days
Access By Highway 560
Maps Elk Lake 41P/NE
This map is to a scale of 1:125,000

There are three routes. *Start* near Gowganda Highway 560 and *finish* near Matachewan, Highway 66.

250 GOWGANDA - MATACHEWAN (ALTERNATE ROUTE 1)

Length 42 miles (67 km)
Approx trip time 3 days
Access By Gowganda Highway 560
Portages 8 (short ones)

Start at Wapus Creek and *finish* at Matachewan via West Montreal River, Lakes Matikemedo, Penassi and Mistinikon.

251 GOWGANDA - MATACHEWAN (ALTERNATE ROUTE 2)

Length 25 miles (40 km)
Approx trip time 2 days
Access By Highway 560
Portages 9 (totalling one mile)

Start at Burk Lake and *finish* at Matchewan via Edith, Obuskong Lakes, Montreal River and Sisseny Lake.

252 GOWGANDA - MATACHEWAN (ALTERNATE ROUTE 3)

Length 20 miles (32 km)
Approx trip time 2 days
Access By Highway 560
Portages 7 (totalling one mile)

Start at Longpoint Lake and *finish* at Montreal River via Mooseheart, Eagle, Shillington and Sydney Lakes. It is 20 miles (32 km) long and involves 7 portages, totalling one mile.

253 KORMAK TO FOLEYET, VIA THE KINOGAMA AND IVANHOE RIVERS

Length 63 miles (101 km)
Approx trip time 3 days

Access By Kormak on the Canadian Pacific
Railway
Maps Chapleau 41O/NW (Ont.)
Ridout 41O/NE (Ont.)
Foleyet 42B/SE
These maps are to a scale of 1:125,000

Start at Kormak on the Canadian Pacific Railway and travel 16 miles (26 km) by road east of Five Mile Lake Provincial Park and 12 miles (19 km) northwest of Wakami Lake Provincial Park. Paddle the Kinogama River, Ivanhoe River to Ivanhoe Lake Provincial Park. May *finish* here or continue to Foleyet on Highway 101.

254 CHAPLEAU TO ELSAS LOOP

Length 130 miles (209 km)
Approx trip time 7 - 12 days
Access By Highway 129
Maps Missinaibi Lake 42B/SW
Foleyet 42B/SE
Chapleau 41O/NW
These maps are to a scale of 1:125,000

Start at Chapleau, Highway 129, paddle the Chapleau River, Henderson, D'Arcy and Schewabik Lakes to the town of Elsas on Kapuskasing Lake. Follow the Nemegosenda River to Chapleau via Nemegosenda, Mate, Westover, Leblanc, Emerald and Borden Lakes to the starting point at Chapleau.

255 GARDINER FERRY TO MOOSONEE, VIA THE ABITIBI, ONAKAWANA AND MOOSE RIVERS

Length 210 miles (338 km)
Approx trip time 10 days
Access By Highway 579
Maps Smooth Rock 42H/SW
Island Falls 42H/NW
Coral Rapids 42I/SW (Ont.)
Blacksmith Rapids 42I/NW (Ont.)
These maps are to the scale 1:125,000
Moosonee 42P

Start at Gardiner Ferry, down the Abitibi River to Otter Rapids. Not navigable between Otter Rapids and the confluence of the Onakawana River. Take the Ontario Northland Railway from Otter Rapids to Onakawana Station or Moose River Station. Paddle on the Moose River to Moosonee.

256 SHUMKA TO MISSANABIE

Length 55 miles (88 km)
Approx trip time 3 - 5 days
Access By Shumka on the Canadian Pacific Railway
Map Missinaibi Lake 42B/SW
This map is to the scale 1:125,000

Start at Shumka on the Canadian Pacific Railway, 50 miles (80 km) northwest of Chapleau. Through a series of short streams to Bolkow Lake, cross a height of land through small lakes, including Abbey Lake and Trump Lake to Missinaibi Lake. Continue through Baltic Bay and Crooked Lake over the height of land to Dog Lake and to Missanabie on Highway 651. Several side trips are possible in Missinaibi Provincial Park.

257 MISSINAIBI RIVER (MISSANABIE TO MATTICE)

Length 147 miles (237 km)
Approx trip time 7 - 10 days
Access By Highway 651
Maps Hearst 42E/NW
Fire River 42B/NW
Opasatika Lake 42G/SW
Missinaibi Lake 42B/SW
These maps are to the scale 1:125,000

Start at Missanabie, at the junction of Highway 651 and the Canadian Pacific Railway. Paddle Dog Lake, Crooked Lake and Baltic Bay of Missinaibi Lake. Take the Missinaibi River to Mattice, on Highway 11 and the Canadian National Railway line, east of Hearst. From Mattice, you may continue along the Missinaibi River to the Moose River to Moosonee (see earlier route Mattice-Moosonee).

Lake Superior Drainage Basin

258 WHITE RIVER TO BREMNER

Length 7 miles (11 km)
Approx trip time 2 days
Access By Highway 17 and 631
Map White River 42C/NW
This map is to the scale 1:125,000

Start at the town of White River and *finish* at Bremner on Highway 17.

259 WHITE RIVER TO PAKOAWAGA LAKE
Length 7 miles (11 km)
Approx trip time 2 days
Access By Highway 17 and 631
Map White River 42C/NW
This map is to the scale 1:125,000

It is an extension of the White River to Bremner route. *Start* and *finish* at Highway 17.

260 WHITE RIVER, BREMNER RIVER, PINEI LAKE
Length 40 miles (64 km)
Approx trip time 5 days
Access By Highways 17 and 631
Maps White River 42C/NW
Pokaskwa River 42C/SW
These maps are to the scale 1:125,000

By commercial air services fly to Pinei Lake and reach Highway 17.

261 LITTLE WHITE RIVER - POKIE LAKE
Length 20 miles (32 km)
Approx trip time 3 days
Access By Highway 17
Maps White River 42C/NW
Pokaskwa River 42C/SW
These maps are to the scale 1:125,000

Start at Highway 17, 11 miles (18 km) south of White River, and on to Pokie Lake to *finish* at White River.

262 TEDDER RIVER TO WAWIGAMI LAKE
Length 22 miles (35 km)
Approx trip time 4 days
Access By Highway 17
Map White River 42C/NW
This map is to the scale 1:125,000

Start at the Tedder River bridge, Highway 17, 6-1/2 miles (10-1/2 km) east of White River, through several lakes to Wawigami Lake.

263 HAMMER LAKE, UNIVERSITY LAKE, OBATANGA LAKE
Length 18 miles (29 km)
Approx trip time 4 days
Access By Highway 17
Map White River 42C/SW
This map is to the scale 1:125,000

Start at Highway 17, 17 miles (27 km) east of White River and 5 miles (8 km) west of the entrance to Obatanga Provincial Park. Continue through Hammer Lake, University Lake and Obatanga Lake to rejoin Highway 17, 5 miles (8 km) south of the starting point.

264 KNIFE LAKE, UNIVERSITY RIVER, HAMMER LAKE
Length 24 miles (39 km)
Approx trip time 4 days
Access By Highway 17
Map White River 42C/SW
This map is to the scale 1:125,000

Start at the Fungus Creek bridge, 22 miles (35 km) east of White River on Highway 17, the northern boundary of Obatanga Provincial Park. It is an extension of the above route.

265 MICHIPICOTEN RIVER (LAKE SUPERIOR TO DOG LAKE)
Length 60 miles (97 km)
Approx trip time 3 - 5 days
Access By Highway 17
Maps Goudreau 42C/SE
Batchawana 41N/NE
These maps are to the scale 1:125,000

Start from Highway 17 to *finish* at Highway 651 on Michipicoten River.

266 SAND RIVER TO LAKE SUPERIOR PROVINCIAL PARK
Length 35 miles (56 km)
Approx trip time 6 days
Access Algoma Central Railway
Map Batchawana 41N/NE
This map is to the scale 1:125,000

Start from Sault Ste. Marie, by the Algoma Central Railway for 140 miles (225 km) to Sand Lake to *finish* at Lake Superior Provincial Park.

Lake Superior Provincial Park

267 GAMITAGAMA LAKE, OLD WOMAN LAKE, MIJINIMUNGSHING LAKE
Length 30 miles (48 km) return
Approx trip time 3 days
Access By Highway 17 - Park headquarters

Maps Lake Superior Provincial Park (scale 1"
to 1 mile)
Michipicoten 41N/NE (Ont.)
This map is to the scale 1:125,000

Start from Gamitagama Lake, 30 miles (48
km) south of Wawa, to *finish* at Mijinimungshing
Lake and the forestry dock at the northwest
corner of the lake. The dock is accessible from
Highway 17 by road. Pick up can be arranged.

268 MIJINIMUNGSHING, ALMONTE, OGAS, ANJIGAMI LAKE

Length 40 miles (64 km) round trip
Approx trip time 4 - 6 days
Access By Highway 17 - Park headquarters
Maps Lake Superior Park (scale 1" to 1 mile)
Michipicoten 41N/NE (Ont.)
This map is to the scale 1:125,000

Start from Mijinimungshing Lake in the north
part of Lake Superior Park. It is accessible by
a gravel road which leaves Highway 17 to the
east approximately 27 miles (43 km) south
of Wawa, *finish* at Anjigami Lake.

269 GAMITAGAMA, OLD WOMAN, MIJINIMUNGSHING, ALMONTE, OGAS, ANJIGAMI LAKES

Length 64 miles (103 km) round trip
Approx trip time 7 - 9 days
Access By Highway 17 (Park Headquarters)
Maps Lake Superior Park (scale 1" to 1 mile)
Michipicoten 41N/NE (Ont.)
This map is to the scale 1:125,000

Start from Gamitagama Lake to *finish* at
Anjigami Lake.

270 SAND LAKE, SAND RIVER, LAKE SUPERIOR

Length 70 return miles (113 km)
Approx trip time 5 - 7 days
Access By Highway 17 - Park headquarters
Maps Lake Superior Provincial Park Map
(scale 1" = 1 mile)
Batchawana 41N/SE (Ont.)
Michipicoten 41N/NE (Ont.)
These maps are to a scale of 1:125,000

Start from Sand Lake, adjacent to the Algoma
Central Railway, 138 miles (222 km) from
Sault Ste. Marie to Lake Superior — at a point
on Highway 17, 48 miles (77 km) east of Wawa

and 100 miles (161 km) west of Sault Ste.
Marie, Ontario.

271 RABBIT BLANKET LAKE - SURF LAKE

Length 8 miles (13 km) round trip
Approx trip time 2 days
Access By Highway 17 - Park Headquarters
Maps Lake Superior Provincial Park
(scale 1" = 1 mile)
Michipicoten 41N/NE (Ont.)
This map is to a scale of 1:125,000

From the campground on Rabbit Lake, located
approximately 21 miles (34 km) south of Wawa
adjacent to Highway 17 on the west side,
continue to Surf Lake in the interior of Lake
Superior Park, approximately 22-1/2 miles (4 km)
southwest of Rabbit Blanket Lake. Surf Lake
is not accessible either by car or train.

272 SLIEVERT LAKE - BELANGER LAKE

Length 7 miles (11 km) round trip
Approx trip time 2 days
Access By Highway 17 - Park headquarters
Maps Michipicoten 41N/NE (Ont.)
This map is to the scale 1:125,000
Lake Superior Park (scale 1" = 1 mile)

Start from Slievert Lake in the west central
portion of the park, west of Highway 17 and
north of the Gargantua Road to Belanger Lake
in the west central portion of the park and
north of Slievert Lake. Belanger Lake is not
accessible by road or railway.

273 THE CIRCLE ROUTE

Length 23 round trip miles (37 km)
Access By Highway 17 - Park headquarters

Circle route refers to the central portion of the
park and the great number of small lakes between Old Woman Lake, Highway 17 and the
Sand River.

274 DAWSON TRAIL ROUTE - KAMINISTIQUIA ROUTE

Length 76 miles (122 km)
Approx trip time 6 days
Access By Highway 11
Maps Lac des Milles Lacs 52B/NE (Ont.)
Marmion Lake 52B/NW (Ont.)
Agnes Lake 52B/SW (Ont.)
Sand Point Lake 52C/SE (Ont.)
These maps are to a scale of 1:125,000

This route was named after Simon Dawson who was commissioned to construct a wagon road from Lake Superior to Shebandowan Lake along the portages of the Voyageur Route. The road, linked by steam ferries, was intended to improve communication between Ontario and the new Red River settlement near Fort Garry (now Winnipeg). The first major use of the road was in 1870 when the 1,800 member Wolseley expedition was dispatched westward to suppress the Riel Rebellion in the Red River Colony.

Start at Shebandowan on Highway 11, pass through Lac des Mille Lacs, Lakes French, Pickerel and Sturgeon through Maligne River to Lac La Croix, in Quetico Provincial Park. *Finish* at French Lake on Highway 11 or continue 120 miles to Rainy Lake and Fort Frances.

275 KASHABOWIE LOOP
Length   20 miles (32 km)
Approx trip time   2 days
Access   By Highway 11
Map   Nipigon 52B/NE
This map is to a scale of 1:125,000

Start at Kashabowie on Highway 11, Upper Shebandowan, Greenwater River, portage to Greenwater Lake, East Bay, Loch Erne and Upper Shebandowan.

276 GULL RIVER TO LAKE NIPIGON
Length   100 miles (161 km)
Approx trip time   7 days
Access   Off Highway 800
Map   Nipigon 52H

Start at Heaven Creek at the secondary road off Highway 800 to Gull River. *Finish* at the highway crossing near Gull Bay of Lake Nipigon.

277 LAKE NIPIGON
Length   Covers 1,870 sq. miles (3,009 km²) and is the largest lake in Northern Ontario
Maps   Armstrong 52 I
Nipigon 52H

It is not recommended for canoeing and is very dangerous.

278 BLACKWATER RIVER
Length   27 miles (43 km)

Approx trip time   2 days
Access   By Highway 11
Map   Jellicoe 42E/NW
This map is to a scale of 1:125,000

Start from Jellicoe and continue to Beardmore. The route runs parallel to Highway 11.

279 STEEL LAKE AND STEEL RIVER LOOP
Length   96 miles (155 km)
Approx trip time   10 - 15 days
Access   By Highway 17
Maps   Steel Lake 42E/SE
Heron Bay 42D/NE (Ont.)
These maps are to a scale of 1:125,000

Start and *finish* at Highway 17, approximately 25 miles (40 km) west of Neys Provincial Park.

280 STEEL LAKE (STEEL RIVER TO LONGLAC)
Length   92 miles (148 km)
Approx trip time   10 - 15 days
Access   From Highway 17 east of Terrace Bay
Maps   Longlac 42E/NE
Steel Lake 42E/SE
Heron Bay 42D/NE (Ont.)
These maps are to a scale of 1:125,000

Follow the Steel Lake Circle Route (279) but continue through a chain of lakes to *finish* at Longlac on Highway 11.

281 BLACK STURGEON RIVER
Length   40 miles (64 km)
Approx trip time   3 days
Access   By Highway 17, inquire at Nipigon
Maps   Fort William 52A
Nipigon 52H

Start at the Black Sturgeon River (parallel to the Nipigon River) and continue to Lake Superior, *finish* where the river crosses Highway 17.

282 NIPIGON RIVER
Length   30 miles (48 km)
Approx trip time   4 days
Access   By Highway 585, inquire at Pine Portage
Maps   Fort William 52A
Nipigon 52H

This river drops 250 feet in 30 miles. It is for skilled canoeists only.

Lake of the Woods Drainage Basin

283 KASHABOWIE RIVER TO NORTHERN LIGHT LAKE, VIA SAGANAGA LAKE
Length 50 miles (80 km)
Approx trip time 4 days
Access By Highway 11
Maps Lac des Milles Lacs 52B/NE (Ont.)
Agnes Lake 52B/SW (Ont.)
Northern Light Lake 52B/SE (Ont.)
These maps are to a scale of 1:125,000

Start at Upper Shebandowan Lake. Paddle through Lakes Grouse, Squeers, Heart and Nelson, Nelson and Weikwabinonaw Creeks to Northern Light Lake's Trafalgar Bay. Portage to Saganaga Lake, paddle Curran Bay, Northern Light Falls and Nelson Bay to Highway 588.

284 NORTHERN LIGHT LAKE LOOP
Length 60 miles (96 km)
Approx trip time 4 days
Access By Highway 588
Map Northern Light Lake (Ont.) 52B/SE
This map is to the scale 1:125,000

Take Highway 588 to Northern Light Lake. Paddle Mowe, Plummes, Greenwood, Twinhouse, Elevation, Saganaga and Wantelto Lakes. Extend to Weikwabinonaw Lake on Weikwabinonaw River.

285 WEIKWABINONAW RIVER (MARKS LAKE TO SAGANAGA LAKE)
Length 75 miles (121 km)
Approx trip time 5 days
Access By secondary road extension of Highway 590
Maps Northern Light Lake 52B/SE (Ont.)
Agnes Lake 52B/SW (Ont.)
These maps are to a scale of 1:125,000

Take a secondary road extension of Highway 590 to Marks Lake. Paddle Weikwabinonaw Lake and River, Greenwood, Dart, Hew, Elevation and Saganaga Lakes to *finish* either at Cache Bay on Saganaga Lake or at the starting point.

286 BURCHELL LAKE TO QUETICO PARK
Length 50 miles (80 km)
Approx trip time 7 days
Access By Highway 802
Maps Lac des Milles Lacs 52B/NE (Ont.)
Northern Light Lake 52B/SE (Ont.)
Marmion Lake 52B/NW (Ont.)
Agnes Lake 52B/SW (Ont.)
These maps are to a scale of 1:125,000

Start at Burchell Lake (reached by a secondary road from Highway 802). Portage through Hernia Lake to Fountain Lake, Span Lake Creek, Snodgrass Lake, Wawiag River, Powell Creek and Mack Creek to *finish* at Mack Lake on the east edge of Quetico Provincial Park.

Quetico Provincial Park

Quetico contains 1750 square miles of forest and waterways. Access to the north side of the park is by Highway 11, Dawson Trail Campground, French Lake. Canoeists intending to pass through the boundary waters must clear Canadian Customs at one of the four outpost stations along the international boundary. See the booklet, *Canoe Routes: Quetico Provincial Park* and Map 52B - Quetico.

287 HUNTER'S ISLAND LOOP
Length 126 miles (203 km)

Start at French Lake, continue through Pickerel Lake, Sturgeon Lake, Lac La Croix, Basswood Lake, Knife Lake and Kawnipi Lake to *finish* at Russell Lake.

288 OLIFAUNT LAKE LOOP
Length 40 miles (64 km)

Start at French Lake on through Pickerel Lake to *finish* at Olifaunt Lake.

289 WALTER LAKE LOOP
Length 60 miles (97 km)

Start at French Lake, pass through Pickerel Lake, Jesse Lake, Walter Lake and Sturgeon Lake to *finish* at Olifaunt Lake.

290 McKENZIE LAKE LOOP
Length 75 miles (121 km)

Start at French Lake, pass through Lakes Pickerel, Dore, Sturgeon, Russell and Kawnipi to *finish* at McKenzie Lake.

291 QUETICO LAKE LOOP
Length 85 miles (137 km)

Start at French Lake, pass through Lakes Pickerel, Kasakokwag, Quetico and Jean to *finish* Sturgeon Lake.

292 CIRRUS, JEAN LAKE LOOP
Length 70 miles (113 km)

Start at Lerome Lake, pass through Lakes Bewag, Cirrus, Quetico, Jean, Sturgeon, Olifaunt, Pickerel and McAlpine to *finish* at Kasakokwog Lake.

293 MALIGNE, BEAVERHOUSE LAKE LOOP
Length 90 miles (145 km)

Start at Lake Nym, pass through Lakes Batchewaung, Jesse, Walter and Sturgeon, Maligne River, Lac La Croix, Namakan River, Beaverhouse Lake and Quetico to *finish* at Kasakowog Lake

294 ORIANA, QUETICO LAKE LOOP
Length 85 miles (137 km)

Start at Lake Nym, pass through Lakes Batchewaung, Jesse, Oriana, Quetico and Kasakokwog to *finish* at McAlpine Lake.

295 KAHSHAHPIWI LAKE LOOP
Length 65 miles (105 km)

Start at Basswood Lake and pass through Lakes Shade, McNiece, Kahshahpiwi, Sark, Cairn, Shelley, Kawnipi and Agnes to *finish* at Sunday Lake.

296 KAWNIPI LAKE LOOP
Length 60 miles (96 km)

Start at Lake Basswood and pass through Lakes Sunday, Agnes, Kawnipi, Saganagons Lakes, Cache Bay and Knife Lake to *finish* at Birch Lake.

297 AGNES LAKE, MALIGNE RIVER LOOP
Length 115 miles (185 km)

Start at Lake Basswood and pass through Lakes Sunday, Agnes, Kawnipi, Shelley and Russell, Maligne River and Lac La Croix to *finish* at Crooked Lake.

298 JEAN LAKE LOOP
Length 70 miles (113 km)

Start at Lac La Croix and pass through Maligne River, Lakes Sturgeon, Jean, Quetico and Beaverhouse, through Quetico River to *finish* at Threemile Lake.

299 DARKY LAKE LOOP
Length 40 miles (64 km)

Start at Lac La Croix and pass through Lakes Darky and Argo to *finish* at Crooked Lake.

300 THE MAN CHAIN LOOP
Length 45 miles (72 km)

Start at Basswood Lake and pass through Lakes Carp, Man and Saganagons by Cache Bay to *finish* at Knife Lake.

301 BRENT LAKE LOOP
Length 60 miles (96 km)

Start at Basswood and pass through Lakes Sarah, MacIntyre, Brent, Darky and Argo to *finish* at Crooked Lake.

302 VOYAGEURS' HIGHWAY (LAC LA CROIX TO RAINY LAKE)
Length 80 miles (129 km)
Approx trip time 4 days
Access Highway 11
Map International Falls 52C

Start at Fort Frances on Rainy Lake, continue to Namaken Lake and *finish* at Lac La Croix.

303 VOYAGEURS' ROUTE (GRANDE PORTAGE TO LAC LA CROIX)
Length 150 miles (241 km)
Approx trip time 8 days
Access By Ontario Highway 61 — Minnesota Highway 61
Maps Northern Light Lake 52B/SE (Ont.)
Thunder Bay 52A/SW (Ont.)
Agnes Lake 52B/SW (Ont.)
Sand Point Lake 52C/SE (Ont.)
Seine River 52C/NE (Ont.)
These maps are to a scale of 1:125,000

Follow Pigeon River from the end of Lake Superior to Lac La Croix or continue to Rainy Lake. The route marks the international boundary between Quetico Provincial Park and Superior National Forest, Minnesota, U.S.A.

304   SEINE RIVER (ATIKOKAN TO RAINY LAKE)

Length   95 miles (153 km)
Approx trip time   5 days
Access   By Highway 11
Maps   Quetico 52B
International Falls 52C

Highway 11 runs parallel to the route. *Start* at Steep Rock Lake near Atikokan and paddle along the Seine River to *finish* at Fort Frances.

305   FORT FRANCES TO VERMILION BAY, VIA PIPESTONE LAKE

Length   100 miles (161 km)
Approx trip time   10 days
Access   By Highway 11
Maps   International Falls 52C
Dryden 52F

Start at Fort Frances or Hope Portage on Rainy Lake, through Lakes Footprint, Jackfish, Loonhaunt, Pipestone, Lawrence, Rowan, Atikwa and Chancellor. *Finish* at Meridian Bay on Eagle Lake.

306   VOYAGEURS' HIGHWAY (RAINY LAKE TO THE MANITOBA BORDER, VIA THE RAINY RIVER)

Length   200 miles (322 km)
Approx trip time   14 days
Access   By Highway 11
Maps   International Falls 52C
Detailed chart No. 6201 @50¢ from Canadian Hydrographic Service, Department of Energy, Mines & Resources, 615 Booth Street, Ottawa, Ontario.

Start at Fort Frances and *finish* at the Lake of the Woods. Because of the wide expanse of water and the relatively shallow depth, cross the southern section of the lake (the Big Traverse) with extreme caution.

307   LAKE OF THE WOODS

Access   By a variety of access points in Ontario and Minnesota

Map   Kenora 52E
Detailed charts No. 6202, 6203, 6204, 6205 are available at 50¢ each from the Canadian Hydrographic Service, Department of Energy, Mines and Resources, 615 Booth Street, Ottawa, Ontario.

With 12,000 islands, Lake of the Woods provides a variety of access points and canoe trips.

308   TURTLE RIVER

Length   120 miles (193 km)
Approx trip time   7-10 days
Access   By Highway 11
Maps   Dryden 52F
International Falls 52C

Start by paddling through Swell Bay and Red Gut Bay on Rainy Lake, then along the Turtle and Wabigoon Rivers to Dinorwic Lake. *Finish* at the community of Wabigoon on Highway 17.

309   MANITOU LAKES

Length   125 miles (201 km)
Approx trip time   12 days
Access   By Highway 17
Maps   International Falls 52C
Kenora 52E
Dryden 52F

Start at Wabigoon, *finish* at Fort Frances on Rainy Lake.

310   LAKE OF THE WOODS, EAGLE LAKE LOOP

Length   115 miles (185 km)
Approx trip time   10 days
Access   By Highway 17 or Highway 71
Maps   Dryden 52F
Kenora 52E

Start at Sioux Narrows or Rushing River Provincial Park, Highway 71, or at Vermilion Bay on Highway 17. Pass through Lakes Dogtooth, Hawk, Highwind, Porcus, Winrange, Teggau, Eagle and Dryberry, and then for 45 miles among the islands in Lake of the Woods.

311   VERMILION BAY (SOUTHERN LOOP)

Length   110 miles (177 km)
Approx trip time   10 days
Access   By Highway 17 or Highway 71
Maps   Kenora 52E
Dryden 52F

This is a difficult and challenging route. *Start* at Vermilion Bay, on Highway 17, or at Sioux Narrows on Highway 71. Circle through Lakes Teggau, Dryberry, Caviar, Eliza, Rupert, Atikawa and Populus, to the Piskegomang River and Eagle Lake. Return to *finish* at Vermilion Bay.

312 VERMILION BAY TO DRYDEN

Length 60 miles (97 km)
Approx trip time 7 days
Access By Highway 17
Maps Kenora 52E
　　　　Dryden 52F

Start at Vermilion Bay and continue to Dryden through Bear Narrows and Osbourne Bay on Eagle Lake, then through Lakes Ingall, Dore and Trapp into Contact Bay on Wabigoon Lake to *finish* at Dryden.

313 KAKAGI LAKE LOOP

Length 40 miles (64 km)
Approx trip time 3 days
Access By Highway 71
Map Dryden 52F

Start at Kakagi Lake, Highway 71, and pass through Lakes Cameron, Shingwak, Isinglass, Caviar, Dogpaw, Flint and Cedartree.

Winnipeg River Drainage Basin

314 WINNIPEG RIVER (THE VOYAGEURS' ROUTE)

Access By Highway 596
Maps Kenora 52E

Start at the Winnipeg River, downstream from Kenora and continue through Whitedog Dam, Tetu Lake, Boundary Falls and Eaglenest Lake. (Manitoba Whiteshell Provincial Park). Return by Highway 596, Whitedog Falls, or by Lakes Swan, Pelicanpouch and Pickerel to *finish* at Kenora.

315 CARIBOO FALLS LOOP

Length 32 miles (51 km)
Approx trip time 2 days
Access Off Highway 596 extension
Maps Pointe du Bois 52L

Start at the Whitedog power dam, 60 miles (97 km) north of Kenora, on the Winnipeg River, and continue through Tetu Lake, English River, go past Cariboo Falls into Umfreville Lake and Whitedog Indian Reserve. To extend the route two weeks pass through Umfreville Lake, Sturgeon River, Sidney Lake and either the Oiseau or Talon Rivers to Eagle Lake. Complete the loop through the Oiseau River, Lakes Snowshoe, Wilson and Trapline through the Winding River to *finish* at Umfreville Lake.

316 BALL LAKE LOOP

Length 125 miles (201 km)
Approx trip time 14 days
Access By air charter from Kenora at the end of Highway 609
Maps Lac Seul 52K
　　　　Pointe du Bois 52L

Start at Ball Lake and continue along the English, Sturgeon and Longlegged River systems.

317 UPPER WABIGOON - ENGLISH RIVER

Length 70 miles (113 km)
Approx trip time 7 days
Access By Highway 609
Map Dryden 52F

Start at Clay Lake, Highway 609 and continue along the Wabigoon River through Ball Lake, Tide Lake and along the English River to *finish* at Ear Falls on Highway 105.

318 CEDAR RIVER

Length 70 miles (113 km)
Approx trip time 7 days
Access By Highway 609
Map Dryden 52F

Start at Highway 609 at Clay Lake and continue to Twilight Lake. The route, which crosses Highway 105 twice, may *finish* at Ear Falls or extend up Chukuni River to the town of Red Lake.

319 BLUE LAKE PROVINCIAL PARK LOOP

Length 10 miles (16 km)
Approx trip time 3 days
Access By HIghway 17, park headquarters
Map Dryden 52F

Start in the park; the loop includes Daniels

The many rivers reaching across the vast expanse of Ontario's Canadian Shield provide the experienced canoeist with ample opportunity to test out his skills. When canoeing in whitewater even the most experienced canoeist should be sure his skills match the challenge and that he uses proper safety equipment at all times.

and Cobble Lakes. *Finish* at McIntosh on the Canadian National Railways line.

320 RED LAKE, LONGLEGGED LAKE LOOP

Length 160 miles (257 km)
Approx trip time 7 - 10 days
Access By Highway 105
Maps Carroll Lake 52M
Trout Lake 52N
Pointe du Bois 52L
Lac Seul 52K

Start at Red Lake on Highway 105 and continue through Lakes Parker, Medicine Stone and Loglegged, along the Loglegged and English Rivers to Ear Falls. Complete the circle through Pakwash Lake and Chukuni River.

321 PAKWASH LAKE, RED LAKE, TROUT LAKE LOOP

Length 228 miles (367 km)
Approx trip time 15-18 days
Access By Highway 105
Maps Trout Lake 52N
Lac Seul 52K

Start at Pakwash Provincial Park and pass through a chain of lakes, Trout Lake, the Nungesser and Chukuni River to *finish* at Pakwash Lake.

322 LAC SEUL (SIOUX LOOKOUT TO RED LAKE)

Length 165 miles (266 km)
Approx trip time 7 - 10 days
Access By Highway 72
Maps Sioux Lookout 52J
Lac Seul 52K
Trout Lake 52N

Start at Sioux Lookout, continue through Lac Seul and along the Chukuni River to *finish* at Red Lake.

323 IGNACE TO WHITE OTTER LAKE

Length 22 miles (35 km)
Approx trip time 4 days
Access By Highway 17
Maps Press Lake 52E/NW (Ont.)
Gulliver River 52E/SW (Ont.)

Metronga Lake 52E/NE (Ont.)
Pakashkan Lake 52E/SE (Ont.)
These maps are to the scale 1:125,000.

Start from Agimak Lake and continue west of Igance on Highway 17. The return trip to Ignace takes either 4 days or 8 days via the Turtle and Wabigoon Rivers to Dinorwic on Highway 17.

324 ENGLISH RIVER (PRESS LAKE TO SIOUX LOOKOUT)

Length 52 miles (84 km)
Approx trip time 5 days
Access On secondary road from Highway 599
Maps Sioux Lookout 52J
Ignace 52G

Start at Press Lake (15 miles (24 km) west on the secondary road from Highway 599) and continue through Lakes Minnitaki and Abram to *finish* at Sioux Lookout, Highway 72.

325 SANDBAR LAKE, BARREL LAKE, PRESS LAKE, MAMEIGWESS LAKE

Length 85 miles (137 km)
Approx trip time 6 days
Access By Highway 599
Maps Sioux Lookout 52J
Ignace 52G

Start at Sandbar Lake Provincial Park and continue through undeveloped lakes.

326 SANDBAR LAKE, DOWNHILL LAKE, ENGLISH RIVER AND INDIAN LAKE LOOP

Length 80 miles (129 km)
Approx trip time 6 days
Access By Highway 599
Maps Ignace 52G
Sioux Lookout 52J

Start at the Sandbar Lake Provincial Park and pass through the connecting lakes to *finish* at Sandbar Lake.

327 ENGLISH RIVER, SOWDEN LAKE, BARREL LAKE AND SANDBAR LAKE

Length 125 miles (201 km)
Approx trip time 6 - 8 days
Access By Highway 17
Maps See Route 328

Start from the English River at Highway 17, paddle 90 miles to Barrel Lake and then pass through 35 miles of connecting lakes to *finish* at Sandbar Lake Provincial Park.

328 SIOUX LOOKOUT, MARCHINGTON LAKE, STURGEON RIVER

Length 100 miles (161 km)
Approx trip time 10 days
Access By Highway 72
Maps See Route 328

Start east from Sioux Lookout and pass through Marchington Lake, Sturgeon River and Sturgeon Lake to *finish* at a landing at Highway 599.

329 SIOUX LOOKOUT, MARCHINGTON RIVER LOOP

Length 120 miles (193 km)
Approx trip time 8 days
Access By Highway 72
Maps See Route 328.

Start and *finish* at Sioux Lookout.

330 VERMILION RIVER, MINISS RIVER, ROOT RIVER LOOP

Length 250 miles (402 km)
Approx trip time 14 days
Access Check Ministry of National Resources at Sioux Lookout
Maps Sioux Lookout 52J
Lake Saint Joseph 52 O

Albany River Drainage Basin

331 ALLANWATER TO ARMSTRONG STATION

Length 130 miles (209 km)
Approx trip time 14 days
Access By Canadian National Railways
Maps Armstrong 52I
Sioux Lookout 52J

Start at Allanwater on the Canadian National Railways, west of Lake Nipigon. Take the Allanwater River to pass through Brennan, Wabakimi and Cariboo Lakes. *Finish* the trip at Atmstrong, on the Canadian National Railways.

332 FLINT RIVER

Length 30 miles (48 km)
Approx trip time 3 days
Access By Highway 11
Map Taradale 42F/NW (Ont.)
This map is to the scale 1:125,000

This is a relaxed trip through a wilderness area. *Start* at Klotz Lake Provincial Park on Highway 11. *Finish* at the Canadian National Railways near Flintdale. It is possible to extend the trip into the Kenogami River to James Bay at Fort Albany.

333 WABABIMIGA, DROWNING RIVER LOOP

Length 87 miles (140 km)
Approx trip time 10 - 15 days
Access By Highway 11
Map Nakina 42L

Take Highway 584 from Highway 11 at Geraldton to Nakina on the Canadian National Railways.

334 PAGWACHUAN RIVER

Length 45 miles (72 km)
Approx trip time 4 - 6 days
Access By Klotz Lake Provincial Park
Maps Taradale 42F/NW (Ont.)
Longlac 42E/NE (Ont.)
These maps are to the scale 1:125,000

Start near Klotz Lake Provincial Park and *finish* at Highway 11.

335 BURROWS RIVER - KENOGAMI RIVER

Length 33 miles (53 km)
Approx trip time 4 days
Access By Highway 584
Maps Nakina 42L
Longlac 42E

Start at the public dock on Murky Creek, 26 miles (42 km) north of Geraldton on Highway 584, or at Alfred Lake, 6 miles (10 km) from Geraldton. *Finish* at Longlac on Highway 11.

336 GERALDTON TO LONGLAC, VIA KENOGAMISIS AND KENOGAMI RIVERS

Length 34 miles (55 km)
Approx trip time 3 days

Access   By Highway 11
Map   Longlac 42E

Start at the MacLeod Provincial Park on Highway 11 and *finish* at Longlac.

337 LIMESTONE RAPIDS TO FORT ALBANY, VIA KABINAKAGAMI, KENOGAMI AND ALBANY RIVERS

Length   250 miles (402 km)
Approx trip time   6 - 8 days
Access   By Highway 11
Maps   Hearst 42E/NW (Ont.)
Calstock 42F/NE (Ont.)
The above maps are to the scale 1:125,000
Kenogami River 42K
Kapiskau River 43B
Albany River 43A
Ogoki 42N
Ghost River 42 O

Take Highway 11, 22 miles (35 km) west of Hearst, then continue 27 miles (43 km) north on Rogers Road. *Start* at the Albany River system at Limestone Rapids on Kabinakagami River. Indian guides are available at the Calstock Indian Reserve on the Rogers Road. *Finish* at Fort Albany.

See also Sioux Lookout to Fort Albany, Routes 340 and 341.

338 OSAWIN, FOCH, NAGAGAMI AND SHEKAK RIVER

Length   130 miles (209 km)
Approx trip time   7 days
Access   By Highway 11
Maps   Taradale 42F/NW (Ont.)
Obakamiga Lake 42F/SW (Ont.)
Hornepayne 42F/SE (Ont.)
Calstock 42F/NE
These maps are to the scale 1:125,000

Start at Pagwachuan River bridge on Highway 11, 70 miles (113 km) west of Hearst. Paddle a loop through the Osawin, Foch, Nagagami and Shekak Rivers. *Finish* at the Shekak River bridge, 34 miles (55 km) west of Hearst. It is also possible to go by train from Hornepayne near Nagagamisis Provincial Park to Osawin River.

339 NAGAGAMI RIVER

Length   60 miles (97 km)
Approx trip time   3 days
Access   By Highway 631

Maps   Calstock 42F/NE (Ont.)
Hornepayne 42F/SE (Ont.)
These maps are to a scale of 1:125,000

Use Nagagamisis Provincial Park, on Highway 631, 25 miles (40 km) south of Highway 11, as a base for short trips.

340 SIOUX LOOKOUT TO FORT ALBANY

Length   650 miles (1,046 km)
Approx trip time   30 days
Access   By Highway 72
Maps   Fort Albany 43A
Kapiskau River 43B
Ghost River 43 O
Ogoki 42N
Fort Hope 42M
Miminiska Lake 52P
Lake Saint Joseph 52 O
Sioux Lookout 52J
Trout Lake 52N

Start at Sioux Lookout. Cross Lac Seul and Lake St. Joseph and go down the Albany River to Fort Albany on James Bay. Suitable for the most experienced canoeists only. There are few sources of supplies or assistance.

Arrange air transporation from Fort Albany to Ontario Northland Railway railhead at Moosonee.

341 SIOUX LOOKOUT TO FORT ALBANY (ALTERNATE ROUTE)

Length   800 miles (1,287 km)
Approx trip time   52 days

Start at Abram Lake (Sioux Lookout town), paddle through Pelican Lake, Lac Seul (42 miles long) and the community of Goldpines. Portage around the Ear Falls hydro power dam and continue along the Chukuni River to Pagwash Provincial Park (Highway 105).

Paddle northeast up the Troutlake River, through lakes Bruce, Woman and Swain. Portage to Shabumini Lake and Birch Lake. Continue east through Lakes Springpole, Kezik, North Bamaji, Blackstone, St. Joseph to Osnaburgh to join the Albany River proper.

Portage or line down the following 8 sets of rapids or falls. Assistance from the current makes it easy to cover 40 miles per day. Continue to Ogoki Post to *finish* at Fort Albany.

A very experienced tripper, Davis, paddled the extra 105 miles (169 km) down the west coast of James Bay and up Moose River to Moosonee. It took him six days. This leg is definitely *not* recommended for most canoeists.

Take a scheduled floatplane from Fort Albany to Moosonee.

From individual trip reports (printed with permission): Bob Davis.

Attawapiskat River Drainage Basin

342 ATTAWAPISKAT RIVER (LANSDOWNE HOUSE TO JAMES BAY)

Length 320 miles (515 km)
Approx trip time 7 - 10 days
Access By air 150 miles to start at Lansdowne House
Maps Kapiskau River 43B
Missisa Lake 43C
Matateto River 43F
Lansdowne House 43D

Use an experienced local guide. Arrange it through the Hudson's Bay Company at Lansdowne House or the Department of Indian Affairs and Northern Development, Geraldton, Ontario. *Start* at Lansdowne House and return by air from Attawaspiskat village at the mouth of the river.

343 SPRUCE RIVER (MENAKO LAKE TO BADESDAWA LAKE)

Length 45 miles (72 km)
Approx trip time 3 - 4 days
Access By secondary road off the end of Highway 808
Maps North Cariboo Lake 53B
Miminiska Lake 52P
Lake Saint Joseph 52 O

It is a tributary stream of Attawapiskat River. By road it's 100 miles (161 km) north of Pickle Lake on Highway 599. *Start* at the public landing on Menako Lake; continue to the junction with Otoskwin River to a road crossing at the outlet from Badesdawa Lake.

Winisk River Drainage Basin

344 WINISK RIVER (WINISK LAKE TO HUDSON BAY)

Length 250 miles (402 km)
Approx trip time 10 - 14 days
Access By air to a Village of Webiqui

Maps Lansdowne House 43D
Winiskisis Channel 43E
Matateto River 43F
Sutton Lake 43K
Winisk 43N

The Winisk River flows north out of Winisk Lake to Hudson Bay for 270 miles. On the first 100 miles of the river from Winisk Lake there are many rapids, falls and long stretches of fast water. For the next 100 miles, the river and the surrounding country change as the river drops below the level of the land. Rapids are not found here. The high clay banks and an old burn that scars the east bank for over 10 miles replace the rapids in this section.

As the river nears the Bay, there are limestone rapids between high white limestone cliffs, piles of ice-deposited gravel and islands. Finally, the village of Winisk, 4 miles inland from Hudson Bay, appears on the north bank.

It is strongly recommended that you rent canoes and the services of guides at the village of Webiqui on Winisk Lake. The Winisk is big, dangerous and extremely isolated.

The cost of moving canoes by airfreight to Winisk Lake to start the trip, together with the passenger fare makes it expensive. There are no roads anywhere near Winisk Lake and it is necessary to fly 200 miles (322 km) north to the village of Webiqui from Nakina.

Detailed information on costs is available from "Winisk River Camps", Webiqui Ontario via Nakina, or from the Department of Indian Affairs and Northern Development, Geraldton, Ontario.

The Hudson's Bay Company store at Webiqui carries a supply of groceries but many canoeists prefer to bring dried packaged goods.

Plan on at least a ten day trip from Webiqui to Winisk, allowing a couple of extra days for bad weather or for fishing. Fishing is excellent along the entire river; nonresidents must purchase a fishing licence *before* flying into Webiqui.

345 EKWAN RIVER - JAMES BAY COAST

Maps Ekwan River 43G
Matateto River 43F

The Ekwan River runs eastward into James Bay. There are no landing sites to accommodate air transport to an upstream starting point, but check this out with charter flying companies at Moosonee. Fly from Moosonee to Attawapiskat: then continue with guides, in large canoes, for the 25 mile (40 km) trip up the James Bay coastline to the mouth of the Ekwan River.

Approx trip time 10 - 14 days
Access By air charter from Big Trout Lake
Maps Clendenning River 43L
Fort Severn 43M
Ashweig River 53H
Fawn River 53I
Dickey River 53P

Severn River Drainage Basin

346 FAWN RIVER (BIG TROUT LAKE TO FORT SEVERN)
Length 250 miles (402 km)

Do *not* attempt this trip before June 15th. Arrange for guides and air transportation through the Department of Indian and Northern Affairs. Indian Bands have outpost fishing camps at points on the Fawn River.

 Map Sources

The map numbers with (Ont.) after them are published by the Provincial Government of Ontario and are available from:

Ministry of Natural Resources,
Administrative Services Branch,
Whitney Block,
Queen's Park,
Toronto, Ontario.

Canada Mapping Office, 615 Booth Street, Ottawa, Ontario, is the chief supplier of topographical maps. Maps for the province are available from the following map dealers in Northern Ontario:

Can. Quetico, Outfitters
P.O. Box 910
Atikokan, Ont.

H.R. Hamilton Ltd.
Box 566
Atikokan, Ont.

Leishman's Pharmacy
208 O'Brien St.
Atikokan, Ont.

Quetico Tackle Co.
Box 267
Atikokan, Ont.

Mr. C.V. Davidson
Pickle Lake Landing
Central Patricia, Ont.

District Forester
Ministry of Natural Resources
Cochrane, Ont.

Girard Esso Service
Box 1423
Cochrane, Ont.

Trumball's Cabins
Box 1796
Cochrane, Ont.

Mr. Les Barrett
Les Barretts Sports
Dryden, Ont.

Dryden District Chamber of Commerce
Dryden, Ont.

District Forester
Ministry of Natural Resources
Chapleau, Ont.

Harry Kwenhnert
Tamara Lodge
R.R. #1
Charlton Station, Ont.

Rose Point Lodge
Ken Flowers
P.O. Box 29
Charlton Station, Ont.

Claim Post
Box 474
Cobalt, Ont.

Mr. Douglas Pollard
Highway Bookshop
Cobalt, Ont.

Cochrane Sport & Marine
  Supply Ltd.
Cochrane, Ont.

Weavers Hardware & Sports
Box 70
Ear Falls, Ont.

Long Point Airways
Elk Lake,
Ont.

Mr. Arch MacDougall
Moosehorn Hotel
Elk Lake, Ont.

Elk Cabins
Rene Pelissier
Box 38
Elk Lake, Ont. P0J 1C0

W.O.K. Books
52 Ontario Ave.
Elliot Lake, Ont.
P5A 1Y1

Freeman Bros. Sports
P.O. Box 295
Espanola, Ont.
P0P 1C0

Michons Sport Shop
Box 1158
Espanola, Ont.

Agnew's Newstand
232 Scott St.
Fort Frances, Ont.

Gogama Sports Centre
P.O. Box 87
Gogama, Ont.

Bullocks,
Gowganda Lake Camp
Gowganda, Ont.

Gowganda Sales & Service
Gowganda, Ont.

Jim Murphys White Pine Lodge
Haileybury, Ont.

Hawk Supply Co.
Hawk Junction, Ont.

Mooseland Esso Service
P.O. Box 1329
Hearst, Ont.

Manager
Ignace Airways Ltd.
Ignace, Ont.

Kakabeka Falls Motor Hotel
Kakabeka Falls, Ont.

Guenette Enterprises
Box 370
Kapuskasing, Ont.

Howard Johnston
Mountain Chutes Camp
R.R. 2
Kenabeek, Ont.

Strains Stationery Ltd.
Kenora, Ont.

Winkler Enterprises
218 Second St. S.
Kenora, Ont.

Halverson's Bait and Tackle
1407 Highway 17 East
Kenora, Ont.

Sportsman's Inn
Killarney, Ont.

R & A Trussler Ltd.
Box 877
Kirkland Lake, Ont.

Turner's (Manitoulin) Ltd.
Little Current, Ont.

Skinner's Acre Tourist Service
Box 153
Longlac, Ont.

Lost Forest Park
R.R. 1
Magnetawan, Ont.

Marine Service Garage
Magnetawan, Ont.

Marathon Pharmacy
Box 34
Marathon, Ont.

Joan A. MacDonald
The Trapper Trading Post
Marten River, Ont.

Mr. N.G. Mennear
Timberland Lodge
Marten River, Ont.

Rock Pine Resort
Marten River, Ont.

Sturdy's Motor Service
Box 240
Massey, Ont.

Mrs. Charlotte Vautour
Box 28
Massey, Ont.

Quetico Provincial Park, to the west of Lake Superior, is one of the most scenic and popular canoeing areas in Northern Ontario. The only travel routes within the park are found along its one thousand or more lakes and waterways. Camping and backpacking are very much a part of the canoe trips taken by most visitors to the area.

Ginn-McLean Hardware Ltd.
P.O. Box 190
Matheson, Ont.

Kiss Motel & Gift Shop
Box 49
Matheson, Ont.

Sid Turcotte Park
Box 549
Mattawa, Ont.

Camp Missanabie Ltd.
Missanabie, Ont.

Sportsmen's Outfitting
Nakina, Ont.

The Wilderness Outfitters
P.O. Box 22
Nakina, Ont.

The Maple Leaf Gift Shop
P.O. Box 247
Nestor Falls, Ont.

F.S. Fosdick
150 Main St.
North Bay, Ont.

J.W. Richardson Hardware
2021 Algonquin Ave.
P.O. Box 197
North Bay, Ont.

Canadian Can—Tex
Div. of Boea Holding Ltd.
P.O. Box 451
North Bay, Ont.

Trout Lake Marine
P.O. Box 465
North Bay, Ont.

Sec.-Manager
Chamber of Commerce
401 McIntyre St. E.
North Bay, Ont.

Orillia Air Services Ltd.
R.R. #3
North Bay, Ont.

Richardson's Hardware
188 Main St. N
Box 417
North Bay, Ont.

Mr. Wm. McCollum
Reflection Lake Cabins
Orient Bay, Ont.

The Hobby House,
Red Lake, Ont.

Courtney's
Richards Landing Marina
Richards Landing, P.O., Ont.

French River Supply Post
R.R. #2
Rutter, Ont.

Esquire Sports & Toys
328 Wellington St. W.
Sault Ste. Marie, Ont.

Ontario Ministry of Natural Resources
Box 130, Airdrome Bldg.
Church St.
Sault Ste. Marie, Ont. P6A 5L5

Mr. & Mrs. E. Cruickshank
Spruce Shilling Camp
Shining Tree, Ont.

Houston Lake Camp
Shining Tree Post Office
Shining Tree, Ont.

District Forester
Ontario Ministry of Natural Resources
Box 309
Sioux Lookout, Ont.

Sioux Sport Shop
Sioux Narrows, Ont.

The Sudbury & District Chamber of Commerce
103 Elm St. W.
Sudbury, Ont.

District Manager
Ontario Ministry of Natural Resources
Swastika, Ont. P0K 1T0

Keewaydin Camps Ltd.
Temagami, Ont.

District Manager
Ontario Ministry of Natural Resources
Box 38
Temagami, Ont. P0H 2H0

Mr. P. Panarites
Peters Holiday Shop
Box 311
Temagami, Ont.

Temagami Sportsmen Services Ltd.
Temagami Outfitters
R.R. #1
Temagami, Ont.

Mr. E.J. Whitehouse
Ted's Store of Little Things
Temagami, Ont.

Northland Traders
Box 181
Temagami, Ont.

Mr. J. Cryderman
Cryderman's Esso Service
May & Miles
Thunder Bay "F", Ont.

Rutledge Stationery Ltd.
512 Victoria Ave.
Postal Station F
Thunder Bay, Ont.

J.C. Chartrand
Cornerstore
698 Riverside Dr.
Timmins, Ont.

Dumoulin Fishing Tackles
1014 Riverside Dr.
Timmins, Ont.

Milne's Sports Centre
146 Cedar St. S.
Box 686
Timmins, Ont.

The Timmins-Porcupine Chamber of Commerce
P.O. Box 985
Timmins, Ont.

Mr. R.O. Spring
Wawa Electric Hardware Ltd.
Wawa, Ont.

D.T. Summers
Michipicoten Harbour
Wawa, Ont.

Wawa & District Chamber of Commerce
P.O. Box 858
Wawa, Ont.

Mariette's Trading Post
P.O. Box 155
Wawa, Ont.

Annies Sport Shop
Box 24
White River, Ont.

Mr. K. Eisenman
Kens Freezer
White River, Ont.

Pauls W.R. Freezer
White River, Ont.

Mr. Jos. Marshall
White River
Ont.

Mr. Wilbert Woito
White Lake Lodge
P.O. Box 155
White River, Ont.

For a provincial road map and lure literature on canoe routes write:

Ministry of Tourism & Information
Queen's Park
Toronto, Ontario

For marked road route maps write:

Sun Oil Ltd.
85 Bloor St.
Toronto, Ont.

Shell Canada
505 University Ave.
Toronto, Ont.

Petrofina (Canada) Ltd.
1910 Yonge St.
Toronto, Ont.

Gulf Oil Canada
800 Bay St.
Toronto, Ont.

District Offices at the Ministry of Natural Resources (Northern Ontario)

Northwestern Region

Red Lake District
Forestry Road
Red Lake, Ont.
P0V 2M0

Kenora District
808 Robertson St.
P.O. Box 1080
Kenora, Ont.
P9N 3X7

Dryden District
P.O. Box 640
Dryden, Ont.
P8N 2Z3

Sioux Lookout District
P.O. Box 309
Sioux Lookout, Ont.
P0V 2T0

Fort Frances District
922 Scott Street
Fort Frances, Ont.
P9A 1J4

Ignace District
Highway 17
Ignace, Ont.
P0T 1T0

North Central Region

Atikokan District
Atikokan Ont.
P0T 1C0

Thunder Bay District
14 North Algoma Street
Thunder Bay "P", Ont.
P7B 5G5

Nipigon District
P.O. Box 729
Nipigon, Ont.
P0T 2J0

Geraldton District
P.O. Box 640
Geraldton, Ont.
P0T 1M0

Terrace Bay District
Terrace Bay, Ont.
P0T 2W0

White River District
200 Winnipeg Street
White River, Ont.
P0M 3G0

Northern Region

Hearst District
P.O. Box 670
Hearst, Ont.
P0L 1N0

Kapuskasing District
5 Government Road
Kapuskasing, Ont.
P5N 2W4

Moosonee District
Moosonee, Ont.
P0L 1Y0

Gogama District
Gogama, Ont.
P0M 1W0

Cochrane District
2 Third Avenue
P.O. Box 730
Cochrane, Ont.
P0L 1C0

Kirkland Lake District
Swastika, Ont.
P0K 1T0

Timmins District
896 Riverside Drive
Timmins, Ont.
P4N 3W2

Chapleau District
34 Birch Street
Chapleau, Ont.
P0M 1K0

Northeastern Region

Wawa District
P.O. Box 1160
Wawa, Ont.
P0S 1K0

Sault Ste. Marie District
Aerodrome Building
P.O. Box 130
Sault Ste. Marie, Ont.
P6A 5L5

Blind River District
62 Queen Street
P.O. Box 190
Blind River, Ont.
P0R 1B0

Espanola District
P.O. Box 1340
Espanola, Ont.
P0P 1C0

Sudbury District
174 Douglas Street West
Sudbury, Ont.
P3E 1G1

Temagami District
P.O. Box 38
Temagami, Ont.
P0H 2H0

North Bay District
P.O. Box 3070
North Bay, Ont.
P1B 8K7

Outfitters (Northern Ontario)

	canoe rental only	partial outfitting	complete outfitting	packaged canoe trips
North Bay District				
Temagami Outfitters P.O. Box 271 Temagami, Ont.			X	
Upper Ottawa Air Services Box 549 Mattawa, Ont.		X		
Timberline Saw & Marine Ltd. Trout Lake Road North Bay, Ont.		X		
Trout Lake Marine Ltd. Trout Lake Road North Bay, Ont.		X		
Headwaters P.O. Box 288 Temgami, Ont. P0H 2H0			X	
James Bay Watershed				
James Bay Outfitters P.O. Box 1866 Cochrane, Ont.			X	
James Bay Marine P.O. Box 38 Moosonee, Ont.		X		
Hearst Pioneer Saws & Canoe Rentals Hearst Ont.	X			
Rufus Lake Lodge c/o Mr. Roch Isabelle Opasatika, Ont.	X			
Wilderness Canoe Tours Box 219, Moose Factory, Ont.			X	
Chapleau District				
Pellow's Cottages P.O. Box 802 Chapleau, Ont.		X		
Coeur Du Bois R. O'Hara et al Chapleau, Ont. P0M 1K0			X	

	canoe rental only	partial outfitting	complete outfitting	packaged canoe trips
Jim Hong Sports General Delivery Chapleau, Ont.		X		
Bates' Camps Mrs. Marion Somers Biscotasing, Ont. P0M 1C0		X		
Bill Ritchies Hunts William Ritchie Box 359 Chapleau, Ont. P0M 1K0		X		

Sudbury District

	canoe rental only	partial outfitting	complete outfitting	packaged canoe trips
Sportsman's Inn Killarney, Ont.		X		
Sudbury Boat & Canoe Ramsey Lake Sudbury, Ont.	X			
Art Cox 207 Albinson St. Sudbury, Ont.	X			
Mrs. Chapman, Bell Lake Killarney, Ont.		X		

Algoma District

	canoe rental only	partial outfitting	complete outfitting	packaged canoe trips
Ranger Lake Holidays Ltd. P.O. Box 145, Sault Ste. Marie, Ont.			X	
Heyden Crafts Co. R.R. #2 Sault Ste. Marie, Ont.	X			
Duke of Windsor Sports Shop 655 Queen St. E. Sault Ste. Marie, Ont.			X	
Camp 88 Lodge Franz, Ontario Via: Chapleau, Ont.		X		
Megisan Lake Trout Camps P.O. Box 416 Sault Ste. Marie, Ont.			X	
Trading Post 1362 Great Northern Rd. Sault Ste. Marie, Ont.			X	

	canoe rental only	partial outfitting	complete outfitting	packaged canoe trips
Arctic Rivers Ltd. P.O. Box 874 Sault Ste. Marie, Ont.			X	
Keith Fletcher 143 Meadow Park Cres. Sault Ste. Marie, Ont.			X	
Elliot Lake Marina P.O. Box 157, Water Front Elliot Lake, Ont.		X		
P & J Sales & Service 27 Timber Road Elliot Lake, Ont.		X		
South Bay Park 15 Valley Cres. Elliot Lake, Ont.		X		

Nipigon District

	canoe rental only	partial outfitting	complete outfitting	packaged canoe trips
Canoes North Ogoki Outfitters Box 56, Caribou Lake Rd. Armstrong, Ont.			X	

White River District

	canoe rental only	partial outfitting	complete outfitting	packaged canoe trips
Canada North Outfitters General Delivery White River, Ont. (summer) or 98 Pageant Dr. Sault Ste. Marie, Ont. (winter)			X	

Quetico Park District

	canoe rental only	partial outfitting	complete outfitting	packaged canoe trips
Wilderness Canada Trips Inc. P.O. Box 388 Atikokan, Ont.			X	
Camp North Ontario Ltd. Box 1510 Atikokan, Ont.			X	
Voyageur Wilderness Program Box 1210 Atikokan, Ont.			X	
Adventure Canoe Trails Box 208 Atikokan, Ont.			X	

	canoe rental only	partial outfitting	complete outfitting	packaged canoe trips
Clearwater West Lodge Box 790 Atikokan, Ont.			X	
Powell Lake Resort Box 1526 Atikokan, Ont.			X	
Canadian Quetico Outfitters Box 910 Atikokan, Ont.			X	
Caribou Resort Box 1390 Atikokan, Ont.			X	
North Country Wilderness Outfitters Box 850 Atikokan, Ont.			X	
Quetico North Tourist Services Box 100 Atikokan, Ont.			X	
Canoe Canada Outfitters Box 388 Atikokan, Ont.			X	

Rainy River District

	canoe rental only	partial outfitting	complete outfitting	packaged canoe trips
Wickstrom's Camp 512 Church Street Fort Frances, Ont.			X	
Nestor Falls Canoe Outfitters Box 247 Nestor Falls, Ont.			X	
Northern Wilderness Outfitters Box 637 Fort Frances, Ont.			X	
Clearwater Pipestone Portage Box 48 Emo, Ont.			X	

Sioux Lookout District

	canoe rental only	partial outfitting	complete outfitting	packaged canoe trips
Voyageurs North Canoe Outfitters Box 507 Sioux Lookout, Ont. P0V 2T0			X	
Albany Outfitters Osnaburgh House, Ont.		X		

	canoe rental only	partial outfitting	complete outfitting	packaged canoe trips
Winisk River Camps P.O. Box 388 Geraldton, Ont.		X		
Big Trout Lake Camps c/o Department of Indian Affairs Big Trout Lake Via Central Patricia, Ont.		X		

Red Lake District

Canadian Canoe Routes c/o John McPherson Box 70 Cochenour, Ont.			X	

 Air Charter Services

Canoeists requiring airlift in Northern Ontario may contact the following commercial carriers:

Air-Dale Ltd.
Box 416
Sault Ste. Marie, Ont.

Austin Airways Ltd.
Toronto Island Airport
Toronto, Ont. M5V 1A1

Bearskin Lake Air Service Ltd.
Big Trout Lake
Central Patricia, Ont.

Batchawana Bay Air Service
Batchawana Bay, Ont.

Dogtooth Air Service
611-6th St.
Kenora, Ont.

Green Airways Ltd.
Box 331
Red Lake, Ont.

Hearst Air Service Ltd.
Box 201
Hearst, Ont.

Hooker Air Service Ltd.
Central Patricia, Ont.

Ignace Airways Ltd.
Box 244
Ignace, Ont.

Lac La Croix-Quetico Air Service Ltd.
Lac La Croix, Ont.

Luenberger Air Service Ltd.
Box 22
Nakina, Ont.

North Western Flying Service Ltd.
Box 6
Nestor Falls, Ont.

Ontario Northern Airways Ltd.
Jellicoe, Ont.

Pioneer Airways Ltd.
Box 357
Atikokan, Ont.

White River Air Service Ltd.
Box 220
White River, Ont.

Severn Enterprises Ltd.
Box 52
Station F
Thunder Bay, Ont.

Rainy Lake Airways Ltd.
Box 790
Fort Frances, Ont.

In addition to these companies and their home bases, the Ministry of Transport lists the following landing waters throughout the province. Some of them may fit into your airlift plans:

Algoma, Attapwapiskat River, Azilda, Bainsville, Bending Lake, Big Beaverhouse, Bonfield, Bruce Channel, Bull Lake, Cat Lake, Chapleau, Cliff Lake, Coboconk, Cochrane, Combermere, Constance Lake, Crystal Lake, Deep River, Deer Lake, Doghole Bay, Dogtooth Lake and Dryden.

Eagle River, Ear Falls, English River, Flame Lake, Fort Albany, Fort Frances, Fort Hope, Fort Severn, Geraldton, Gogama, Goldpines, Gore Bay, Grassy Narrows, Haliburton, Harbour Island, Hudson, Huntsville, Hurkett; International Seaplane Base, Ranier, Minn., USA.

Jumping Caribou Lake, Kapuskasing, Kashabowie, Kirkland Lake, Lake St. John, Lansdowne House, Leigh's Bay, Longpoint Lake, Mattawa, Minaki, Mississagagon Lake, Mississauga Lake, Moose Factory, Moosonee, Nezah Lake, Nipigon, Orillia, Osnaburgh House.

Ottawa, Parry Sound, Partridge Point, Pays Plat, Petawawa, Pickle Lake, Port Carling, Port Loring, Port Perry, Rainy River, Round Lake, Saganaga Lake, St. Catherines, Sandy Lake, Shebandowan, Sioux Lookout, Sioux Narrows, Smoke Lake, South Porcupine Lake, Stony Lake, Sturgeon Lake, Sudbury, Temagami, Uchi Lake, Wawa Lake, Webbwood.

West of Lake Superior and bordering on the state of Minnesota, Quetico Provincial Park is renowned for the beauty of its many fine lakes. This vast area attracts a broad range of canoeists and campers.

MANITOBA

Manitoba is the sixth largest province in the nation (approximately 250,000 square miles) and includes 39,225 square miles which are covered by water. The land levels of Manitoba rise gradually from sea leavel to 500 feet, reaching the highest point at 2,727 foot Duck Mountain in Duck Mountain Provincial Park.

The province has 400 miles of tidal coastline on the west coast of Hudson Bay, including Churchill, the only inland saltwater seaport in Canada. Due to its subarctic climate, navigation at Churchill is limited to ninety days a year. Manitoba boasts three very large freshwater lakes. Lake Winnipeg is 260 miles long and at its widest point 70 miles across, making it the seventh largest lake in North America; adjoining it to the west are Lake Winnipegosis, 180 miles long by about 15 miles wide, and Lake Manitoba, 55 miles long by 15 across. All three lakes present formidable problems for small craft, especially Lake Winnipeg. Veteran canoemen regard it as the most dangerous inland lake in Canada, the Great Lakes excepted. Rivers feed into these three inland "seas" from the south, west and east, and they are emptied by rivers flowing in a northeasterly direction to Hudson Bay. The Churchill River and its drainage basin compose a major maze of northern waterways across the top of the province from Saskatchewan to Hudson Bay.

 Fishing

Information for fishing can be gathered beforehand by writing the Department of Tourism, Recreation and Cultural Affairs, Winnipeg, Manitoba. It is possible, however to suggest here what kinds of fish are most plentiful in given areas:

Eastern (Whiteshell and Winnipeg)   northern pike, walleye, small-mouth bass, perch, goldeye, mooneye and tullibee.

Western (Dauphin and The Pas)   pike, walleye, perch, lake, rainbow and speckled trout and splake (a speckled-lake trout hybrid).

Northern   pike, lake and brook trout, walleye, whitefish and arctic grayling.
White whale (beluga), are hunted with hired Eskimo or Indian guides and gear at Port Churchill.

Angling Permits

Resident and nonresident Canadians over 16 years of age $3.00
nonresidents who are non-Canadian $10.00

Special angling licenses for Riding Mountain National Park ($2.00 for the season) must be purchased by all anglers at the park headquarters.

Previous page. Manitoba offers the canoeist a number of historic canoe routes. This particular one is situated in Whiteshell Provincial Park. Wild rice, a delicacy prized by gourmets, grows in abundance along the water's edge.

Climate

The climate of Manitoba is characterized by long severe winters and short springs which start as early as mid-April in the south, are delayed to mid-May and June in central areas and may not occur until even later in the subarctic regions. The break-up of rivers, of course, follows the pattern of the seasons. Freeze-up begins first in the northern parts of the province in September, working gradually south.

The range of normal summer weather in Manitoba is most clearly reflected by the three regions in the following table:

Manitoba	Mean temperatures In Fahrenheit (Celsius)				Rainfall In Mean Inches (Millimetres)	
	Min		Max			
Southern (Winnipeg)						
June	50.6	(10.3)	72.8	(22.7)	3.16	(80.3)
July	56.3	(13.5)	78.6	(25.9)	3.16	(80.3)
August	54.0	(12.2)	77.0	(25.0)	2.90	(73.7)
Central (Norway House)						
June	43.6	(6.4)	68.5	(20.3)	3.23	(82.0)
July	52.7	(11.5)	73.3	(22.9)	2.64	(67.1)
August	49.8	(9.9)	71.3	(21.8)	2.24	(56.9)
Northern (Churchill)						
June	34.7	(1.5)	50.5	(10.3)	1.47	(37.3)
July	45.2	(7.3)	61.7	(16.5)	1.93	(49.0)
August	46.4	(8.0)	59.3	(15.2)	2.27	(57.7)

History

Manitoba has as long a history of early European exploration and settlement as any inland region in North America. The search by Europeans for a northwest passage to the Orient was the original motive, but very soon the riches of the fur trade became the prime attraction.

The English were the first to arrive, wintering at the mouth of the Nelson River in 1612-1613, followed by the Danes at Churchill in 1619-1620. The English became aware of the potential wealth of the fur trade and in 1670 established the Hudson's Bay Company. Reaching the region by way of Hudson Bay, they built their first posts at the mouth of the Hayes River (York Factory) in 1682 and the Churchill River in 1717.

French explorers and traders, by contrast, came overland from Montreal and built rival posts in the Hayes-Nelson region, but then became more interested in following more southerly waterways across the prairie. They built posts at the mouth of the Winnipeg River, in the vicinity of today's city of Winnipeg, and at other points farther west.

After the fall of Quebec, Scottish fur traders — the North West Company — followed the southern route, building posts in the regions explored earlier by the French. The westward expansion of the North West Company took its traders across the prairie and eventually to the Pacific. The Nor'Westers quickly became strong competitors for the English traders on the Hudson Bay coast. The Bay Company, as a result, was forced to expand its operations inland to the south and west. Following the Hayes-Nelson River and the Saskatchewan, they crossed central Manitoba and pushed into the southern trading area to establish rival trading posts.

Thus it was that at an early date the explorers and fur traders established Lake Winnipeg as a key pivotal point for six major canoe routes. The Hayes and Nelson Rivers were the alternate approach routes to Hudson Bay and the northeast corner of the province, while the Winnipeg River opened the way to the Great Lakes and Lake of the Woods in the southeast corner of the province. Important inland routes from Lake Winnipeg led south by way of the Red River to the headwaters of the Mississippi River, southwest on the Souris and Assiniboine Rivers into North Dakota, and west on the Assiniboine into the plains country. The busiest of all inland routes led from the northwest corner of the great lake to the Saskatchewan River, the Athabasca fur country, the Rocky Mountains, the Arctic and the Pacific Ocean.

In 1812, Lord Selkirk brought a group of Scottish settlers to Manitoba. In and around the Winnipeg area, they became the first to establish the agricultural tradition of the Canadian west. Mennonites and Ukranians further developed agriculture, south of Winnipeg, starting in 1875. At the same time, Icelanders populated the southwest shores of Lake Winnipeg at Gimli and Riverton, bringing to the region their lake fishing skills.

Manitoba became a province after the Red River Rebellion of 1869-70. The Hudson's Bay Company had recently sold its vast holdings on the prairie (the historic Rupert's Land territory) to the government of Canada. The Métis people of the Red River Colony, fearing the end of their traditional life centred on the buffalo hunt and fur trapping, resisted the transfer of authority to the government in Ottawa and established a provisional government of their own under their leader, Louis Riel. The Rebellion was put down by the Canadian government, but the colony, a small area around present day Winnipeg, was given provincial status. Riel fled and the Métis people moved farther west, hoping to find a new home where they could continue to live according to their traditional customs. Sadly, they were overtaken once more by settlement fifteen years later.

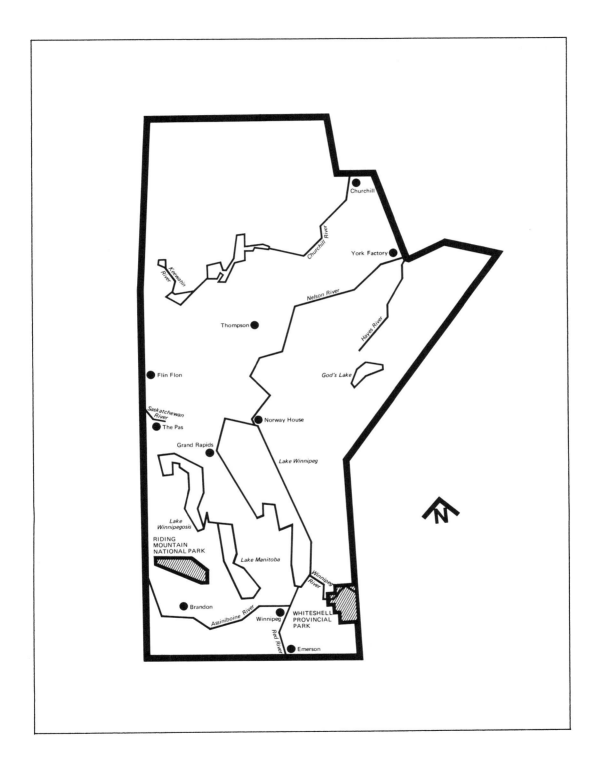

Churchill

York Factory

Churchill River

Keewatin River

Nelson River

Hayes River

Thompson

Flin Flon

God's Lake

Saskatchewan River

The Pas

Norway House

Grand Rapids

Lake Winnipeg

Lake Winnipegosis

RIDING MOUNTAIN NATIONAL PARK

Lake Manitoba

Winnipeg River

Brandon

Assiniboine River

Winnipeg

WHITESHELL PROVINCIAL PARK

Red River

Emerson

N

Manitoba Routes

Canoe routes in Manitoba are more straightforward than those found in the eastern provinces because most of them flow in and out of the large, centrally-located Lake Winnipeg. They can be easily classified into nine drainage basin patterns as follows:

(1) The *Red River* and the *Souris River*, both of which rise in North Dakota and flow north, meet the *Assiniboine River*, which flows from Saskatchewan in the west. All join to flow into the south end of Lake Winnipeg.

(2) The *Winnipeg River* flows in from Ontario in the east to enter the southeast corner of Lake Winnipeg.

(3) *Lake Winnipeg, east shore*, boasts a network of rivers; some connect with the Winnipeg River and others run parallel and north of it.

(4) *Lake Winnipeg, northwest corner,* is a drainage basin for Lake Winnipegosis and the *Saskatchewan River*, which flows into the lake at Grand Rapids and then turns north to join the

(5) *Nelson River* which flows northeast out of Cross Lake to debouch at the Hudson Bay shore.

(6) *Hayes River* flows out from the northeast corner of Lake Winnipeg in two branches,

coursing northeast. The south branch travels via Cross Lake, the Bigstone and Fox Rivers. The north branch, also travells through Cross Lake (where the Nelson River has its main feeder source), via Oxford, Knee and Swampy Lakes, becomes the Hayes River proper. In the days of the fur trade, the route was known as the "Middle Track". It empties into Hudson Bay.

(7) *The Gods River* rises inland but joins the Hayes River near the coast.

(8) *The Churchill River* flows across the top of the province and empties into Hudson Bay; it rises in the Province of Saskatchewan and is joined there by the North Saskatchewan River.

(9) *The Seal River* is a branch of the Churchill River within Manitoba but it flows separately into Hudson Bay.

Many of the above rivers are plotted in great detail on handsome, historic and graphic maps issued free by the Parks Branch, Department of Tourism, Recreation and Cultural Affairs, 409 Norquay Building, Winnipeg, Man. The Canada Topographic maps are listed with each individual route.

Winnipeg River Drainage Basin

347   WHITESHELL - CADDY LAKE

Length   105 miles (169 km)
Access   By Highway 44 in Whiteshell Provincial Park
Maps   Kenora 52E
Pointe du Bois 52L

Start at Caddy Lake and paddle north through the Canadian Pacific Railway tunnel into South Cross Lake, keeping sharp lookout for a reef 3/4 of a mile from the entrance. The lake narrows and passes through the Canadian National Railways tunnel into North Cross Lake. Paddle across, portage

to the left and paddle through onto
Sailing Lake and Mallard Lake.
Portage into Whiteshell River
and paddle 5 miles to the forks. Take the
right fork into Little Whiteshell
Lake. Portage into Crowduck Lake,
paddle through and portage around Crowduck
Falls into Boundary Lake and Eaglenest Lake.

Keep bearing left and portage around
Lamprey Falls. Continue on the
river, portage around Pointe du Bois,
paddle, then portage again at Slave Falls
Dam, between the two spillways to the left
of the powerhouse. Walk along the left path.
Paddle through to Sturgeon Falls and
portage around on the right. Then, keep
bearing left and paddle down Whiteshell
River.

You are now making a loop back on a
stretch of many rapids, falls and portages
to Betula Lake. Paddle southeast to pick
up the river again. Portage around one
rough stretch into White Lake (visit
Rainbow Falls here). Portage into
Jessica Lake and continue on the river
into Lone Island Lake and paddle
southeast to the river forks.

You have completed the loop. Bear right
and find Mallard Lake again, reversing
the trip to *finish* at the Caddy Lake take-out.

348 FRANCES LAKE
Length 22 return miles (35 km)
Approx trip time 1 day
Access By Highway 44, east of Rennie
Map Kenora 52E

Start at Frances Lake and paddle
through about 10 miles of beaver marshes and
return to starting point. There are three
portages and about twelve beaver dams to haul
over. Travel lightly for a pleasant day-long
trip.

349 WHITEMOUTH RIVER - WINNIPEG
RIVER
Length 125 miles (201 km)
Approx trip time 6 days
Access By part 1, Highway 210 SE to
Woodridge
Maps Kenora 52E
Selkirk 62 I
Winnipeg 62H

Start part one, which is only navigable
until the end of May, at Whitemouth
Lake after getting directions to it at the
village of Woodridge. Paddle past the
junction of St. Labre Creek and continue
on to *finish* at the village of Prawda.
Return to Winnipeg by Highway 1.

Start part two, after the spring
high water, at the village of Prawda;
paddle down the Whitemouth River to the
Seven Sisters hydro dam on the Winnipeg
River.

Winnipeg River (Proper)

The Manitoba Tourism Department has
published a map that clarifies the complex
network of canoe routes offered by the
Winnipeg River. The map shows four
routes:

350 WINNIPEG RIVER, KENORA
Map Pointe du Bois 52L

Start at Kenora, Ontario, via
Winnipeg River, Sand, Roughrock, Tetu
and Boundary Lakes (all in Ontario)
to join the Whiteshell-Caddy Lake route
earlier described.

351 WINNIPEG RIVER, SHOAL LAKE
Map Kenora 52E

Start at Shoal Lake, Ontario
(On the Manitoba-Ontario boundary),
via Mud Lake, Falcon, Lyons, Hunt,
West Hawk and Caddy Lakes. Both
Kenora and Shoal Lakes routes have
now joined the Whiteshell-Caddy,
anti-clockwise loop.

352 WINNIPEG RIVER, OISEAU RIVER
Map Pointe du Bois 52L

A new offshoot route on the above loop
starts at Eaglenest Lake, then
via Ryerson, Summerhill, Booster,
Tulabi and Oiseau Lakes and Oiseau
River to join the widening of the Winnipeg
River at Lac du Bonnet. This route
runs parallel but north of the Winnipeg
River.

353 WINNIPEG RIVER
Maps Pointe du Bois 52L
Selkirk 62 I

While the Winnipeg River forms
the northern half of the Whiteshell-Caddy
loop, it can also be followed to Lake
Winnipeg. Branching from the loop, the
river flows through Dorothy, Eleanor,
Sylvia and Natalie Lakes into Lac du
Bonnet, and out again, to be interrupted
by MacArthur Falls, Great Falls
and Pine Falls Generating Stations,
as it drains into Traverse Bay, Lake
Winnipeg.

Red River Drainage Basin

354 RAT RIVER (RIVIÈRE AUX RATS)
Length 140 miles (225 km)
Approx trip time 7 days
Access Off Highway 12, south of the river
crossing
Maps Winnipeg 62H
Selkirk 62 I

It's not recommended for summer travel due
to low water conditions but is navigable
until the end of May. It joins the Red
River at Otterburne. Pass St. Adolphe
and St. Norbert to *finish* at the junction
of the Red and Assiniboine Rivers in
Winnipeg.

355 SWAN LAKE, PEMBINA RIVER,
LA RIVIÈRE
Length 60 miles (97 km)
Approx trip time 4 days
Access Mariapolis Campground on Highway 23
Map Brandon 62G

This is the Pembina River canoe route.
Paddle southwest from Mariapolis
Campground on Swan Lake and the Pembina
River to La Rivière village. *Finish* on Highway
3.

356 WINNIPEG (CITY) - LAKE
WINNIPEG
Access Any accessible public river site
Maps Selkirk 62 I
Winnipeg 62N

Any number of short trips on the Red
River (north) can be taken from numerous
public access points within the city of
Winnipeg. Paddle downstream, 17 miles
to the locks at Old St. Andrews Rapids.
Lock through, paddle on and visit Lower
Fort Garry, a national historic park. It
was built in 1831-36 by the Hudson's Bay
Company, chiefly as a trans-shipment point
for northern fur brigades. Paddle on
down to Selkirk, home port of Lake
Winnipeg's commercial fishing fleet and
floatplane terminal.

Past Petersfield you enter the
Netley Marsh area of the river delta,
one of the greatest waterfowl nesting regions
in North America.

None but the most expert open lake
canoeists are advised to navigate on Lake
Winnipeg — it is a dangerous inland "sea".

357 WINNIPEG (CITY) - EMERSON
Length 70 miles (113 km)
Approx trip time 4 days
Access Any public access sites on Red River
Map Winnipeg 62H

On the Red River (south) paddle
through Morris, St. Jean Baptiste,
Letellier and *finish* at Emerson on
the Manitoba-North Dakota border
on Highway 75.

Riding Mountain National Park

The park has few suitable canoe routes
within its boundaries, most of them are on
Clear Lake and others are generally shallow,
feeder creeks and streams. Access to the
park entrance at Wasagaming is by Highway 4,
west of Portage La Prairie, then north
on Highway 10. The Riding Mountain (62K)
map covers all three of the routes within the
park.

358 CLEAR LAKE
Clear Lake offers good, open-lake canoeing and
parkside camping.

359 LAKE AUDEY - MINNEDOSA RIVER
The headwaters of the Minnedosa River are
at the south end of Lake Audey. This stream
flows south from the lake and out of the park
and meanders through an ancient glacial

valley. Camping facilities are available at
Lake Audey.

360 WHIRLPOOL CREEK - WHIRLPOOL LAKE

This route flows south from Whirlpool
Lake and out of the park. Camping facilities
are located near the lake.

Lake Winnipeg-East Shore Drainage Basin

The Whiteshell Provincial Park is a
complicated maze of waterways very clearly
described by the Manitoba Parks Department
in three graphic maps entitled "Sasaginnigak
Canoe Country", "Kautunigan Route"
and "Little Grand Rapids". All routes
finish at the Wallace Lake Provincial Recreation Area.

361 DOGSKIN RIVER - LITTLE GRAND RAPIDS

Access Highway 304 E of Bissett
Map Carroll Lake 52M

Start at Wallace Lake park, take the
creek to Siderock Lake, portage and
paddle through two unnamed lakes to Obukowin
Lake. Continue northeast and then
southwest through a small river to Carroll
Lake, northeast through Craven Lake;
cross the lake-like widening of Bloodvien
River, continually alternating between
portaging and paddling through a maze of
ponds and small lakes, coming finally to
Hobbs Lake, the Dogskin River, and the
settlement of Little Grand Rapids between
Family Lake and Fishing Lake.

362 BRUCE LAKE (ONTARIO) - LITTLE GRAND RAPIDS

Length 280 miles (451 km)
Approx trip time 14 days
Access Ontario Highway 105 (Red Lake Road)
Maps Deer Lake 53D
Carroll Lake 52M

Start at Pakwash Provincial Park,
putting in at Bruce Lake. Paddle
north on Trout Lake River, through
Woman Lake, passing Jackson Manion
Mine to Swain Lake. Portage to
Shabumini Lake, and then to Upper Goose

Lake, and Berens River. Continue on the
river, passing through Pikangikum Indian
settlement, then Barton, Stout and Family
Lakes to *finish* at Little Grand Rapids.
At this point one can fly out by charter
floatplane or continue paddling the
Dogskin route (361) in reverse to Wallace
Lake park.

A third alternative also exists. Swing
back to the Dogskin River trunk line
waterway. It trends northeasterly but from
it, trending west, north and west again, is
the maze of large, connecting rivers that
end on the lower east shore of Lake
Winnipeg: the Bloodvein, Sasaginnigak,
Leyond, Poplar, Wanipagow, Pigeon
and Berens Rivers.

Some of the above rivers flow for miles
under one name, break for a way under another
name and finish under the starting name.
Other large rivers rise in the interior and
join the named rivers.

Nelson River Drainage Basin

363 MYSTIC CREEK

Length 50 return miles (80 km)
Approx trip time 7 days
Access On Highway 10, 60 miles (97 km)
north of The Pas
Map Cormorant Lake 63K

Access to the *starting* point is on
Highway 10, about 60 miles (97 km) north
of The Pas. Mystic Creek flows between
Payuk Lake on the south of the highway,
across it (where you *start*), and north to
Neso Lake. Paddle north along the east shore
to where Mystic Creek drains it to the
northeast. Six portages around rapids bring
you to the east end of Nisto Lake to join
the creek again and, after six more rapids,
to reach Nao Lake.

From here eleven more rapids join a
series of small lakes — Niynun, Nikotwasik,
Tapukok, Uyenanao, Mitatut, Kagat,
Payukosap to Nistosap Lake. North
from the north arm of Nistosap Lake is
the large Naosap Lake; turn west on it.
Two long portages join this lake to a
pothole. Turn south, onto Alberts Lake.
You will encounter two more portages and a
pothole at the southwest corner of Alberts

Lake. A narrow unnamed lake and creek brings you to Sourdough Bay of Lake Athapapuskow. This is a big, open lake and requires good navigation and big-lake know-how as you paddle south.

Finish the trip at the south end of the lake at Baker's Narrows campsite on Highway 10.

364 WHITEFISH LAKE - WABISOK LAKE (PINEROOT CHAIN)

Access By Highway 10, 25 miles (40 km) north of Cranberry Portage

This is a canoe route used primarily by fishermen. *Start* at Whitefish Lake on North Star Mine road. Paddle Pineroot Creek, portage past two rapids, then again portage for 1/4 mile around Minakanagan Falls to Minakanagan Lake. Continue through Aimee, Animus and Wabisok Lakes. There are several portages and float-throughs on rapids connecting this lakes chain.

Walleye and northern pike are the most common fish. The shorelines are dominated by rugged cliffs.

365 CRANBERRY PORTAGE - WEKUSKO LAKE

Length 120 miles (193 km)
Approx trip time 12 days
Access By Highway 10 at Cranberry Portage
Maps Cormorant Lake 63K
Wekusko Lake 63J

Paddle east in the Grass River Provincial Park through First, Second and Third Cranberry Lakes; Elbow Lake, Grass River, Iskwasum and Loucks Lakes, Grass River and Reed Lake where the park boundary ends. Continue through Tramping Lake and *finish* at Wekusko Lake, south arm, on Highway 391.

A bus can be taken direct to The Pas or to the village of Wekusko on the Hudson Bay Railway, which goes to The Pas.

366 WEKUSKO LAKE - WABOWDEN

Length 90 miles (145 km)
Access By Highway 391 (at finish of previous route)
Map Wekusko Lake 63J

This can be considered an extension of the above or a route of its own. Cross Berry Bay to Crowduck Bay of Wekusko Lake, continue along the Grass River, past Kanisota Falls, White Forest Rapids, Skunk Rapids, Whitewood Falls, Mitishto Lake, Ferguson Creek, Grass River, Pagwa Lake and Grass River to *finish* at Setting Net Lake.

Arrange for truck transport from the commercial fish plant (trip's end) to Wabowden village and take the Hudson Bay Railway to The Pas.

367 GRASS RIVER

Approx trip time 30 days
Access At Wabowden
Map Wekusko Lake 63J

Yet another extension to the two previous routes, from Wabowden village on Setting Net Lake, is through Paint Lake and Manasan River to Thompson. Continue along the Burntwood and Odei Rivers to Split Lake and Kelsey hydro dam on the Nelson River. Continue south along the Nelson, west to Landing Lake and the settlement of Thicket Portage. Take Wintering and Grass Lakes to Paint Lake of the Paint Lake Provincial Recreation Area. *Finish* the trip at Highway 375. This route offers various combinations of access, by highway or rail, or by air to and from the city of Thompson.

Churchill River Drainage Basin

368 PUKATAWAGAN - HIGHROCK LAKE

Length 140 loop miles (225 km)
Access Canadian National Railways (Lynn Lake line)
Map Kississing 63N

Start the trip at Pukatawagan Falls on the Churchill River where the river crosses the Canadian National Railways (Lynn Lake line) and follow the downstream current to reach High Rock Lake in three to four days. Paddle another four days to the Upper Twin Falls.

This is primarily a fishing trip and is generally done with outboard-powered canoes.

For many decades Canadian bush pilots have specialized in transporting cargo by floatplane. Today, not only do these aircraft serve as cargo carriers, they also provide the canoeist with easy access to remote areas.

Hayes River Drainage Basin

369 THE PAS - YORK FACTORY (MIDDLE TRACK)

Length 570 miles (917 km)
Approx trip time 30 days downstream
Access At the junction of Highways 10, 283 and 289
Maps Grand Rapids 63G
The Pas 63F
Cross Lake 63 I
Wekusko Lake 63J
Sipiwesk 63P
Hayes River 54C
God's River 53N
Knee Lake 53M

This was the earliest, most important exploration and fur trade route in central North America, known as the Middle Track, the supply route from Hudson Bay to Athabasca fur country and beyond.

Start at the town of The Pas and paddle west on the Saskatchewan River, swing northeast at Big Bend onto a small river and into Reader Lake, portaging 2 miles into Clearwater Lake. Portage into Cormorant Lake, paddle its southwest shoreline, enter the creek and pass under the Canadian National Railways trestle bridge into Little Cormorant Lake.

Continue down Frog Creek to North Moose Lake along its southwest shore to the control dam and portage into South Moose Lake. Continue southeast then northeast along the lakeshore to enter Minago River, Hill Lake and Drunken Lake. Pass under the bridge.

Paddle northeast across Cross Lake, portage 2 miles north to the creek emptying into White Rabbit Lake, paddle east to the south end of Cotton Lake and east along the river through Bear and Bigstone Lakes.

Enter the Bigstone River, swing left into Fox River (at the junction of Sipanigo River) and continue on Fox to its second junction with Sipanigo. Continue down Fox to its junction with the Hayes River. Continue along Hayes, passing the junction of Gods River on the right and Pennycutaway River on the left. Also pass a conspicuous landmark, Brassey Hill, on the left bank, on past three islands at

tidewater mark and then a chain of smaller islands to *finish* opposite Hay Island at York Factory.

York Factory, a national historic site, was originally built in 1682 by the Hudson's Bay Company and played a role in the fur trade supply business for 250 years. Today the site has summer custodians and a two-way radio for outside communication. The peninsula where the factory is situated, at the mouths of the Hayes and Nelson Rivers, was the site of many of the earliest English explorers' and traders' bases, beginning with Sir Thomas Button's stay in 1612, eight years before the arrival of the Pilgrims at Plymouth, Massachusetts.

Upon reaching York Factory today, canoeists can return in three possible ways: by prearranged floatplant charter; by the Hayes River, the next route to be described; by a rugged route which involves hiring guides in outboard-powered canoes to run you around the mud flats estuary into the mouth of the Nelson River — paddle upriver, proceeding past the outflows of the Weir and Angling Rivers and Goose Creek to portage around Big and Little Limestone Rapids and up the Limestone River to the Hudson Bay Railway crossing (Mile 350). Entrain for The Pas.

370 YORK FACTORY - THE PAS (HAYES RIVER)

Length 685 miles (1,102 km)
Approx trip time 5 weeks (upstream)
Access York Factory (return trip)
Maps The Pas 63F
Grand Rapids 63G
Hayes River 54C
God's River 53N
Knee Lake 53M
Oxford House 53L
Island Lake 53E

Paddle upstream on the Hayes River, passing the junction with the Fox River on the right, and on through Swampy, Knee and Oxford Lakes. (It is possible to take the Carrot River out of Oxford Lake to join the outwardbound trip to York Factory at Cross Lake, but if you choose to complete the route new and interesting waterways are ahead.) Continue on the Hayes

Encampment on the Red River, June 1858. Seated second from right is Henry Youle Hind, who led this expedition, the first in Canada to use photography as a surveying tool. The Assiniboine and Saskatchewan Exploratory Expedition of 1858 was sent out to survey the geography and agricultural potential west of the Red River.

River through Logan and Robinson Lakes into the Echimamish River where the river current changes from upstream to downstream at Painted Stone portage. Swing into the east channel of the Nelson River and onto Little Playgreen Lake at Norway House.

Norway House, built by the Hudson's Bay Company in 1825, became the focal point in the company's transportation system, the centre of its administration and its Northern Council, as well as a major collection depot for goods and furs.

From Norway House, the canoeist may fly out to Winnipeg by charter floatplane, take the Lake Winnipeg passenger freight boat to Selkirk or continue paddling to The Pas. This destination comprises the remainder of the trip, and is as follows:

Paddle to Warren Landing on the north shore of Lake Winnipeg. Be warned that this lake is probably the most dangerous in Canada for small craft; it is windy, shelterless and shallow with high waves. To canoe it sensibly, experienced open-lake canoeists should skirt the northwest shore, usually at night — when the day winds are more likely to be down. Paddle to Grand Rapids, the mouth of the Saskatchewan River. Paddle northeast through Lower Cedar and Upper Cedar Lake to the delta inlet of the Saskatchewan and *finish* the trip at The Pas.

Seal River Drainage Basin

371 PUKATAWAGEN - SEAL RIVER

Length 600 miles (966 km)

Approx trip time 43 days

Access Drive to Clearwater Provincial Park by Highway 10; CNR to Pawistik (near Pukatawagen) on the Churchill River

Maps Kississing 63N
Granville Lake 64C
Ulhman Lake 64B
Big Sand Lake 64G
Tadoule Lake 64J
Shethanei Lake 64 I
Churchill 54L

Start at Pawistik on the Churchill River, continue to High Rock Lake, past Granville Lake, Barrington River mouth, Southern Indian Lake, Tadoule Lake, Negassa Lake, Shethanei Lake, Wolverine River and the Seal River to *finish* at the Hudson Bay shore.

From an individual trip report, quoted with the permission of Charles McLandress.

Map Sources

For free maps write to the Parks Branch, Department of Tourism, Recreation and Cultural Affairs, 408 Norquay Building, 401 York Avenue, Winnipeg 1, Manitoba.

Canada Mapping Office, 615 Booth Street, Ottawa, Ontario, is the chief supplier of topographical maps. Maps for the province are available from the following map dealers in Manitoba:

Baytides Publishers
P.O. Box 6
Churchill, Man.
R0B 0E0

Caribou Lodge
Cranberry Portage, Man.

Streamer's Limited
Cranberry Portage, Man.

Flin Flon Tourist Bureau
Box 806
Flin Flon, Man.

Don's Hinterland Camp
161 Maplewood Avenue
Winnipeg, Man.
R3L 1A1

Information Canada Bookshop
393 Portage Avenue
Winnipeg, Man.
R3B 2C6

The Happy Outdoorsman
433 St. Mary's Road
Winnipeg 8, Man.

Fresh Air Experience
773 Osborne Street
Winnipeg, Man.
R3L 2C5

Winnipeg Mapping
P.O. Box 185 G.P.O.
Winnipeg 1, Man.

For provincial road maps, a good lure booklet, excellent graphic canoe routes and maps of your choice write:

Tourist Branch
Department of Tourism, Recreation &
  Cultural Affairs
408 Norquay Building
401 York Avenue
Winnipeg, Manitoba

 Outfitters

The Happy Outdoorsman Limited
433 St. Marys Street
Winnipeg, Man.

Outdoor Adventures
1456 Pembina Highway
Winnipeg, Man.

Fresh Air Experience
773 Osborne Street
Winnipeg, Man.

or
869 Portage Avenue
Winnipeg, Man.

The Hudson's Bay Company provides a special U-paddle service. Motorists long conditioned to the availability of U-haul highway trailer units will understand the convenience of a similar service for canoe-campers in the wilds. The company calls it U-paddle.

The company provides a limited number of seventeen-foot Grumman canoes with a carrying yoke and three paddles. You pick up the canoe by arrangement at the inland post of your choice together with food supplies, camping and cooking equipment. Paddle to a destination post and leave the canoe and gear there.

So popular is the service that you should write months in advance to:

Hudson's Bay Company
Northern Stores Department
79 Main Street
Winnipeg, Manitoba

The company's serviced canoe routes are not located in Manitoba, but you must write to the Winnipeg headquarters for information about their services elsewhere. You can find these routes in the appropriate chapters: see Northwest Territories, Saskatchewan and Ontario.

 Air Charter Services

These are the head offices and service base addresses of companies in four geographical regions:

Eastern Manitoba
Tall Timber Fly-in,
Lac du Bonnet, Man.
Whiteshell Air,
Whiteshell, Man.

Central Manitoba
Gimli Air,
Arnes, Manitoba.
Pembina Air,
Morden, Man.

St. Andrews Air,
Selkirk and Winnipeg,
Man.
Airpark,
Lac du Bonnet, Man.
Silver Pine Air,
Pine Falls, Man.

Transair,
Winnipeg International Airport,
Winnipeg, Man.
Ilford-Riverton Air,
Hangar 4,
Winnipeg International Airport,
Winnipeg, Man.
Perimeter Aviation,
Hangar 2,
Winnipeg International Airport,
Winnipeg, Man.

Northern Manitoba
Lambair Ltd., The Pas, Grand Rapids,
Churchill, Cross Lake, Nelson House,
Oxford House, Wabowden, Ilford, Kelsey,
Missi Falls, Moose Lake, Split Lake,
Thompson, Gillam, Norway House.

Transair Ltd. Churchill, Cross Lake,
God's Narrows, God's River, Little Grand
Rapids, Oxford House, Poplar River,
Red Sucker Lake, Ste. Theresa Point,
Wabowden (all phone Winnipeg) Flin
Flon, Gillam, Lynn Lake, Norway House
(call The Pas radio), The Pas,
Thompson.

Ilford-Riverton Airways — Gillam,
Island Lake, God's River, Missi Falls,
Red Sucker Lake, Shamattawa, Split
Lake and Stevenson Lake (all phone
Winnipeg)

Calm Air — Lynn Lake, Brochet, Leaf
Rapids, Missi Falls, South Indian
Lake and Thompson (all phone Lynn
Lake)

Parsons Airways
Channing, Man.

Ilford-Riverton Airways (MTS toll station and
(Telex)
Thompson, Man.

St. Andrews Airways, (Radio CJX 351),
Island Lake, Man.

La Ronge Aviation,
Lynn Lake, Man.

Cross Lake Air Services, (MTS toll
station)
Cross Lake, Man.

T.C. Aviation,
Flin Flon, Man.

Ontario Central Aviation Ltd.,
Box 1248,
Gimli, Man.

Parsons Airways
Lynn Lake, Man.

Raylor Airways, (MTS Toll Station)
God's River, Man.

Kississing Air, (MTS Toll Station)
Sherridon, Man.

Norcan Air Service, (Phone Prince
Albert or La Ronge,)
Flin Flon, Man.

Moose Nose Lake Airways,
Illford, Man.

Western Manitoba
There are no charter floatplane services
listed for the Western region.

Canoeists planning airlift may find
useful the following list of floatplane bases
by the federal Ministry of Transport (they
are not mentioned in the regular service
bases listed above):

Berens River, Bird River, Bissett,
Channing, Cormorant Lake, Cranberry
Portage, Grace Lake, Herb Lake, Kistigan
Lake, Manitotagan, Matheson Island,
Moar Lake, Sandy Lake, Shamattawa,
Sherlett Lake, Thicket Portage, Victoria
Beach and Winnipegosis.

SASKATCHEWAN

Saskatchewan is Canada's fifth largest province (251,700 square miles). The name is an anglicized version of a Cree Indian word, Kis-is-ska-tche-wan, which means "swift flowing" and refers of course to the waterways. The province falls into three basic topographical regions: southern prairie, central forest-parklands and northern pre-cambrian shield regions.

The southern region is known as the "breadbasket of the nation", because it produces one-third of our grain. This land also overlays rich potash (fertilizer) deposits, petroleum crude and natural gas, and boasts a thriving cattle ranching industry. The forest and parklands of the central region of Saskatchewan produce lumber, pulp and paper. The northern region has many lakes and river systems, both great and small, which offer fine sport fishing. The area is also important as a centre of fur production, an industry that provides a direct link with the province's history.

 ## Fishing

Saskatchewan boasts of "fabulous" fishing, especially in the northern region. Northern pike, walleye, perch, lake trout and arctic grayling abound in the larger streams, while smaller streams produce brook, brown and rainbow trout, whitefish and the popular hybrid, splake.

 ## History

Saskatchewan provided the mainline waterways to the rich fur country around Lake Athabasca and beyond. From here six major routes radiated outward in three directions: from Lake Athabasca's western end in Alberta, two routes led westward to the Pacific Ocean and two northward to the Arctic; two more routes ran from the east end of the lake to Hudson Bay.

Henry Kelsey of the Hudson's Bay Company, was the first European explorer to reach Saskatchewan. In 1691, he was sent out with friendly Indians to scout the western interior of the continent. In 1754, another company scout, Anthony Henday, arrived. The following summer he returned to York Factory with the first canoe brigade of furs from Saskatchewan. At the same time he brought news of the trading forts established in that region by La Vérendrye at Fort St. Louis and La Corne at the forks of the Saskatchewan. The race to the fur country was on.

The Nor'Westers from Montreal built posts at Fond du Lac and Nipawin. Soon after, on the strength of reports from Kelsey and Henday, Samuel Hearne established Cumberland House for the English in 1774. The Hudson's Bay Company also penetrated into southeastern Saskatchewan by the Assiniboine, Qu'appelle, Swan, Red Deer and Carrot Rivers establishing posts at Fort Pelly (1816), Ellice (1831) and Fort Qu'appelle (1864).

Facing page. The prairie is not only a land of golden wheatfields, but in many areas of Saskatchewan is a panoramic world of lakes and forests as well. These densely forested islands are not uncommon in the lake regions of Saskatchewan.

The Royal North West Mounted Police now Royal Canadian Mounted Police force was established in 1873. Their initial task was to evict the renegade white traders from south of the border who were debauching the prairie Indians by trading in rum. In 1885, the force joined the militia to quell the North West Rebellion. Louis Riel, the Métis leader, was, as a result, hanged for treason the same year in Regina.

Saskatchewan became a province in 1905.

 ## Climate

Landlocked Saskatchewan experiences extremes of hot and cold weather. Short springs begin late in March in the south and do not arrive until late May and early June break-up on the far northern lakes and rivers. Usually warm days and chilly nights can be expected. Freeze-up in the north starts in mid-September, moving gradually southward. Summers in northern Saskatchewan are comfortable enough for three and a half months of good canoeing.

The following weather conditions are based on statistics from Canadian Atmospheric Environment Service reports on the southern, central and northern regions.

Saskatchewan	Mean temperatures in Fahrenheit (Celsius)				Rainfall In Mean Inches (Millimetres)	
	Min		Max			
Southern (Regina)						
June	47.4	(8.6)	71.6	(22.0)	3.25	(82.6)
July	52.9	(11.6)	78.1	(25.6)	2.28	(57.9)
August	50.8	(10.4)	77.7	(25.4)	1.96	(49.8)
Central (Prince Albert)						
June	45.1	(7.3)	70.5	(21.4)	2.24	(59.9)
July	51.0	(10.6)	76.5	(24.7)	2.53	(64.3)
August	48.5	(9.2)	73.9	(23.3)	2.09	(53.1)
Northern (Uranium City)						
June	45.4	(7.4)	66.1	(18.9)	1.50	(38.1)
July	51.9	(11.1)	70.4	(21.3)	1.89	(48.0)
August	50.0	(10.0)	67.9	(19.9)	1.80	(45.7)

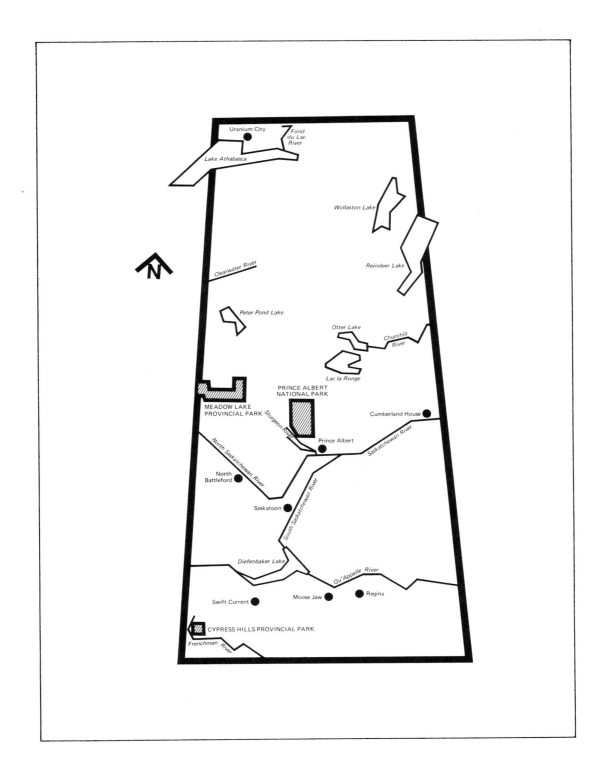

Saskatchewan Routes

Four major drainage systems shape the province's canoeing. The Saskatchewan River system is a result of the North and South Saskatchewan Rivers joining in the centre of the province. The Churchill River system flows eastward across the province and across Manitoba to drain into Hudson Bay. The Lake Athabasca system is composed of a network of small drainage rivers flowing into the east end of the lake from the south, southeast and north; chief among these is the Fond du Lac that flows northwest out of Wollaston Lake. The small Frenchman River system in the extreme southwest corner of the province flows southeast into Montana to the headwaters of the Mississippi River.

Athabasca, Saskatchewan's largest lake (3,120 square miles) dips southwestward into Alberta as well. It was a point of origin for six fur trade canoe routes: to the north, via the Slave and Mackenzie Rivers; to the west, via the Peace and Fraser Rivers; to the southwest via the Athabasca and Columbia Rivers; to the southeast (from its west end) to the Churchill River; to the northeast via Black Lake and the Dubawnt River; and the southeast via Fond du Lac River and Wollaston Lake. The second largest lake in Saskatchewan is Reindeer Lake, 2,096 square miles.

For purposes of easier geographical identification, the routes below are grouped within the following districts: Saskatchewan River; Meadow Lake (Provincial Park); Lac la Ronge; Lac la Ronge-Churchill River; Churchill River (west of Otter Lake); Churchill River; North of Churchill River; Sturgeon-Weir River (Highway 106); Clearwater River (near Careen Lake); Prince Albert National Park.

So vast is the Churchill River that various routes intermingle sometimes necessitating cross-check reference.

Saskatchewan River

372 CUMBERLAND HOUSE - THE PAS (MANITOBA)
Length 83 miles (134 km)
Approx trip time 2 - 3 days
Access By gravel road to Cumberland House, 100 miles northeast of Nipawin
Maps Pasquia Hills 63E
Cormorant Lake 63K
The Pas 63F

373 SASKATOON - BRIDGE AT NIPAWIN
Length 200 miles (322 km)
Approx trip time 5 days
Access In Saskatoon
Maps Saskatoon 73B
Melfort 73A
Prince Albert 73H

374 SQUAW RAPIDS - CUMBERLAND HOUSE
Length 70 miles (113 km)
Approx trip time 2 - 3 days
Access Department of Natural Resources Squaw Rapids campground, 47 miles northeast of Nipawin
Maps Pasquia Hills 63E
Prince Albert 73H

Meadow Lake Provincial Park

375 PIERCE LAKE - LAC DES ILES (WATERHEN RIVER)
Length 22 miles (35 km)
Approx trip time 1 - 2 days
Access Howe Bay, Pierce Lake, 15 miles from Pierceland
Map 73K Waterhen River

376 WATERHEN RIVER - BEAVER RIVER

Length 23 - 70 miles (37 - 113 km)

Approx trip time 1 to 4 days

Access Waterhen River northeast of Golden Ridge

Maps Waterhen River 73K
Green Lake 73J

Considerable wading is required on this route.

377 MALIGNE LAKE - STURGEON-WEIR RIVER

Length 53 miles (85 km)

Approx trip time 3 - 4 days

Access Maligne Lake, Mile 190, Highway 106

Map Amisk Lake 63L

Portages 4 - 5

Start from the access point, pass through Maligne Lake and along the Sturgeon-Weir River to *finish* at Amisk Lake and Denare Beach.

378 PELICAN NARROWS - STURGEON-WEIR RIVER

Length 74 miles (119 km)

Approx trip time 6 days

Access Pelican Narrows or the Department of Natural Resources campsite, Highway 135

Maps Pelican Narrows 63M
Amisk Lake 63L
For greater detail, see:
Annabel Lake 63L/16*
Birch Portage 63L/15*
Attitti Lake 63M/1W*
Pelican Narrows 63M/2E*

Start at Pelican Narrows, pass through Wunehikun Bay, Mirond, Waskwei, Attitti, Kakinagimak, Wildnest and Granite Lakes to *finish* at the Sturgeon-Weir River, Mile 190, Highway 106.

Clearwater River

379 WARNER RAPIDS, CLEARWATER RIVER (SASKATCHEWAN), FORT MCMURRAY (ALBERTA)

Length 125 miles (201 km)

Approx trip time 8 - 10 days

Access By road to Cluff Lake, if complete; check air charter from Buffalo Narrows to La Loche to Warner Rapids

Maps La Loche 74C
Waterways 74D
McMurray 74 S.W. (scale of 1:500,000 N.T.S.)

Portages 9 - 14

Prince Albert National Park

380 KINGSMERE LAKE, BAGWA LAKE, LILY LAKE, CLARE LAKE AND RETURN

Approx trip time 5 - 6 hours

Maps For this and the following park trips get maps at the park headquarters office

Portages 2

381 KINGSMERE LAKE - BLADEBONE LAKE

Approx trip time

Maps Park headquarters office

Start at Kingsmere Lake, *finish* at Bladebone Lake and return.

382 SPRUCE RIVER

Approx trip time

Access By Park road

Maps Park headquarters office

Various sections are accessible from park roads.

383 WASKESIEU RIVER

Approx trip time

Access By park road

Maps Park headquarters office

Start along the river from the park road to *finish* at Highway 2.

Lac La Ronge

384 NEMEIBEN LAKE, TROUT LAKE, CHURCHILL RIVER, OTTER LAKE

Length 63 miles (101 km)

Approx trip time 4 - 6 days

Access Department of Natural Resources Nemeiben Lake campground

Maps Lac la Ronge 73P
Otter Lake 73P/10W and E

Portages 13 - 15

Portage from the north bay of Nemeiben Lake to a small lake to a small beaver pond. From the small beaver pond, portage to a lake south of Little Crooked Lake. Continue to Little Crooked Lake, to Rachkewich Lake, and Trout Lake on through two sets of rapids. It is optional to portage between Trout and Stack Lakes. Take the second rapids to Stack Lake, to Mountney Lake. It is optional to portage between Rock Trout Portage and Mountney Lake. Continue to Dead Lake (also called Nipew Lake) to below the Great Devil Rapids, Devil Lake and Otter Lake. *Finish* at the Department of Natural Resources Missinipe campground.

385 NEMEIBEN LAKE, BESNARD LAKE, CHURCHILL RIVER, OTTER LAKE
Length 100 miles (161 km)
Approx trip time 7 - 9 days
Access Department of Natural Resources Nemeiben Lake campground
Maps Lac La Ronge 73P
Otter Lake 73P/10W and E
Portages 19 (3 more optional ones)

386 NEMEIBEN LAKE, BESNARD LAKE, CHURCHILL RIVER, TROUT LAKE, NORTH BAY NEMEIBEN LAKE
Length 103 miles (166 km)
Approx trip time 5 - 8 days
Access Department of Natural Resources Nemeiben Lake campground
Map Lac La Ronge 73P is probably sufficient
Portages 19

387 LYNX LAKE, SULPHIDE LAKE, CONTACT LAKE, KUSKAWAO LAKE
Length 13 miles (21 km)
Approx trip time 1 - 2 days
Access Lynx Lake picnic ground on Highway 2, 29 miles (47 km) north of La Ronge
Map Stanley 73P/7
Portages 7

Portage from Lynx Lake, Duck Lake to Sulphide Lake, to Mekewap Lake.

Continue to Contact Lake, Baldhead Lake and Cote Lake to *finish* at Kuskawao Lake.

388 LYNX LAKE, SULPHIDE LAKE, FREDA LAKE, FREESTONE LAKE, HEBDEN LAKE, CONTACT LAKE, SULPHIDE LAKE, LYNX LAKE
Length 33 miles (53 km)
Approx trip time 2 - 4 days
Access Lynx Lake picnic grounds, Highway 2, 29 miles (47 km) north of La Ronge
Map Stanley 73P/7
Portages 19

Lac La Ronge — Churchill River

389 OTTER LAKE, STANLEY LAKE, ISKWATIKAN LAKE, HALE LAKE, LAC LA RONGE, LA RONGE
Length 75 miles (121 km)
Approx trip time 5 days
Access Otter Lake, town of Missinipe, Highway 2, 50 miles (80 km) north of La Ronge
Maps Lac La Ronge 73P
Stanley 73P/7
Nistowiak Lake 73P/8
Otter Lake 73P/10E
Lac La Ronge hydrographic map 6821
Portages 5

Portage from Otter Lake to a small lake below Stony Mountain Portage to Mountain Lake, to Drope Lake. Continue to Nistowiak Lake, Iskwatikan Lake and Hale Lake with an outlet at Lac La Ronge. *Finish* at Bonanza Point outfitter's camp.

390 OTTER LAKE, STANLEY LAKE, ISWATIKAN LAKE, THOMAS LAKE, HUNTER BAY, LA RONGE VILLAGE
Length 90 miles (145 km)
Approx trip time 6 - 7 days
Access Missinipe on Otter Lake
Maps Same as previous route
Portages 7

391 OTTER LAKE, CHURCHILL RIVER, MOUNTAIN, HUNT AND STROUD LAKES, LAC LA RONGE, LA RONGE VILLAGE
Length 62, 70 or 78 miles (100, 113, or

This is no prairie flood. Saskatchewan boasts a remarkable variety of lakes, rivers and streams within its borders. Renowned for its excellent fishing, the province attracts a multitude of fishermen from elsewhere in Canada and the United States.

126 km) depending on which alternate
routes are chosen

Approx trip time 4 - 6 days

Access Missinipe on Otter Lake

Maps Lac la Ronge 73P. For more detail:
Stanley 73P/7
Nistowiak Lake 73P/8
Otter Lake 73P/10E and W
Lac la Ronge hydrographic map 6821

Portages 6 - 9

392   LA RONGE VILLAGE, LYNX, SULPHIDE, FREDA, OTTER LAKES

Length 57 miles (92 km)

Approx trip time 4 - 5 days

Access Department of Natural Resources
Campsite, La Ronge

Maps Lac la Ronge 73P
Stanley 73P/7
Otter Lake 73P/10E and W
Lac la Ronge hydrographic map 6821

Portages 12 (2 more optional)

393   LA RONGE VILLAGE, ISKWATIKAN LAKE, CHURCHILL RIVER, PELICAN NARROWS, DESCHAMBEAULT LAKE, MILE 146 HWY 106

Length 175 miles (282 km)

Approx trip time 8 - 10 days

Access Department of Natural Resources
Campsite, La Ronge

Maps Lac la Ronge 73P
Lac La Ronge hydrographic map 6821
Stanley 73P/7
Nistowiak Lake 73P/8
Pelican Narrows 63M
Amisk Lake 63L

Portages 13 - 14

394   LA RONGE VILLAGE, ISWATIKAN LAKE, CHURCHILL RIVER, PELICAN NARROWS, DOUPE BAY ON JAN LAKE

Length 148 miles (238 km)

Approx trip time 6 - 8 days

Access Department of Natural Resources
Campsite, La Ronge

Maps See Route 390

Portages 12

395   LA RONGE VILLAGE, ISWATIKAN LAKE, CHURCHILL RIVER, PELICAN NARROWS, MIROND LAKE, STURGEON-WEIR RIVER, MILE 190 HWY 106

Length 151 miles (243 km)

Approx trip time 7 - 10 days

Access Department of Natural Resources
Campsite, La Ronge

Maps See Route 390

Portages 15

396   WADIN BAY, HUNTER BAY, NUNN & BIG WHITEMOOSE LAKES, WHITE-MOOSE RIVER, CHURCHILL RIVER, ISWATIKAN LAKE, LAC LA RONGE, WADIN BAY

Length 126 loop miles (203 km)

Approx trip time 6 - 7 days

Access At Wadin Bay, Mile 17, Highway 2

Maps Lac La Ronge 73P
Nistowiak Lake 73P/8
Lac la Ronge hydrographic map 6821

Portages 14 (2 more optional ones)

397   LA RONGE (LAC LA RONGE), STROUD LAKE, HUNT LAKE, NISTOWIAK LAKE, ISWATIKAN LAKE, LAC LA RONGE, WADIN BAY

Length 106 miles (171 km)

Approx trip time 6 days

Access Department of Natural Resources
campground at La Ronge

Maps Lac la Ronge 73P
hydrographic maps 6821 Lac la Ronge
Stanley 73P/7
Nistowiak Lake 73P/8

Portages 7

Optional portages are from Campbell
Channel to Nut Bay, Ewan Bay to English
Bay and Wadin Bay to Pipestone Bay.
Necessary portages include: Four
Portage Bay to Leckie Lake; Leckie Lake
to Stroud Lake; Stroud Lake to Hunt
Lake; Hunt Lake to Chepakan Bay on
Mountain Lake; Mountain Lake to Drope
Lake; Nistowiak Lake to Iskwatikan
Lake; Hale Lake with the outlet of
Lac la Ronge. *Finish* here or alternately
at the Wadin Bay campsite, 17 miles (27
km) north of La Ronge on Highway 2.

398 LA RONGE VILLAGE, LYNX, SUL-PHIDE, FREDA, OTTER, STANLEY, NISTOWIAK, ISKWATIKAN LAKES, LA RONGE VILLAGE

Length 120 loop miles (193 km)

Approx trip time 8 - 10 days

Access Department of Natural Resources campground at La Ronge

Maps Lac la Ronge 73P. For more detail
Stanley 73P/7
Nistowiak Lake 73P/8
Otter Lake 73P/10E
Lac la Ronge hydrographic map 6821

Churchill River (West of Otter Lake)

399 VILLAGE OF ÎLE-À-LA-CROSSE TO OTTER LAKE

Length 240 miles (386 km)

Approx trip time 14 - 18 days

Access Village of Ile-à-la-Crosse, Highway 155

Maps Ile-à-la-Crosse 73 O
Lac La Ronge 73P
Otter Lake 73P/10E and W

Portages 13 - 19

Portages on this route include: From Shagwenaw Lake to below the rapids by portaging around Leaf Rapids, Dipper Rapids, Crooked Rapids, Knee Rapids, Snake Rapids, the rapids at the outlet of Sandfly Lake and Needle Rapids (except for Knee Rapids and those at the outlet of Sandfly Lake, the rest are optional.) Portage around Needle Falls; take the Birch Portage, Black Bear Island Lake to Trout Lake to quiet water below the rapids; between Trout and Stack Lakes (optional); quiet water below the second rapids with Stack Lake; Stack Lake with Mountney Lake; water below Rock Trout Portage with Mountney Lake (optional); Mountney Lake to Dead Lake (often referred to as Nipew Lake); Dead Lake to water below Great Devil Rapids; Great Devil Rapids to Devil Lake; Devil Lake with Otter Lake. *Finish* at Missinipe Department of Natural Resources campground.

400 ÎLE-À-LA-CROSSE TO PELICAN NARROWS

Length 340 miles (547 km)

Approx trip time 14 days

Access At Île-à-la-Crosse

Maps Lac la Ronge 73P
Stanley 73P/7
Nistowiak Lake 73P/8
Otter Lake 73P/10E and W
Pelican Narrows 63M

Pick up canoe, supplies and equipment at Île-à-la-Crosse and leave them at the destination, Pelican Narrows.

All arrangements must be made several months in advance with the Hudson's Bay Company, Northern Stores Department, 79 Main Street, Winnipeg 1, Manitoba.

Churchill River (East of Otter Lake)

401 OTTER LAKE, STANLEY LAKE, FROG PORTAGE, PELICAN NARROWS

Length 100 miles (161 km)

Approx trip time 6 - 7 days

Access Missinipe Highway 2, 50 miles (80 km) north of La Ronge

Maps Lac la Ronge 73P
Stanley 73P/7
Nistowiak Lake 73P/8
Otter Lake 73P/10E and W
Pelican Narrows 63M

Portages 13

Portages on this route include: from Otter Lake to a small lake below Robertson Falls; Stony Mountain Portage to Mountain Lake; Mountain Lake to Drope Lake; Nistowiak Lake to Drinking Lake; Brown Bay to Drinking Lake (optional); Drinking Lake via Inman Channel to Keg Lake; Keg Lake to Grand Rapids; Grand Rapids to its end; Trade Lake to Wood Lake; east of Grassy Narrows; around rapids in narrows; again; Medicine Portage to Pelican Lake. *Finish* at the Department of Natural Resources office. There is a road to the outside, radio for air charter.

402 PELICAN NARROWS, FROG PORTAGE, CHURCHILL RIVER, SANDY BAY

Length 115 miles (185 km)

Approx trip time 8 - 10 days

Access   Pelican Narrows, Highway 135, 33
miles (53 km) north of its junction
with Highway 106 (Mile 81, Hanson
Lake Road)
Map   63M Pelican Narrows
Portages   13 - 16

403   OTTER LAKE, CHURCHILL RIVER, SANDY BAY

Length   140 miles (225 km)

Approx trip time   9 - 12 days

Access   Department of Natural Resources
campground at Missinipe, Otter Lake

Maps   Churchill River sheet (From Department
of Tourism, Saskatchewan)
Lac la Ronge 73P
Pelican Narrows 63M
Nistowiak Lake 73P/8

Portages   16 - 19

404   OTTER LAKE, GRANDMOTHER BAY, FRENCH LAKE, DUCKER LAKE, RATTLER CREEK, OTTER LAKE

Length   22 miles (35 km)

Approx trip time   1 - 2 days

Access   Department of Natural Resources
campground Missinipe, Otter Lake

Maps   Otter Lake 73P/10E and W

Portages   3

Churchill River

405   BRABANT LAKE, KAKABIGISH LAKE, SETTEE LAKE, KEMP LAKE, MOUNTAIN LAKE, MISSINIPE, CHURCHILL RIVER

Length   75 miles (121 km)

Approx trip time   5 - 6 days

Access   End of road, to Brabant Lake, approximately 55 miles (88 km) north of the
Churchill River on Highway 102

Maps   Lac la Ronge 73P
Settee Lake 73P/16
Guncoat Bay 73P9
Mineral resources geology division
series: Kelly Lake area 106A
Otter Lake 73P/10E
Reindeer Lake, South 64D
Pelican Narrows 63M

Portages   14

406   MCLENNAN LAKE, DAVIS LAKE, VERSAILLES LAKE, SETTEE LAKE, GUNCOAT BAY, OTTER LAKE

Length   68 miles (109 km)

Approx trip time   5 - 6 days

Access   McLennan Lake Department of Natural
Resources campground, Highway 102,
83 (133 km) miles north of La Ronge

Maps   Lac la Ronge 73P
Settee Lake 73P/16
Churchill River sheet
Guncoat Bay 73P/9

407   BRABANT LAKE, WAPISKAU RIVER, STEEPHILL LAKE, REINDEER RIVER, CHURCHILL RIVER, SANDY BAY

Length   140 miles (225 km)

Approx trip time   10 - 14 days

Access   Brabant Lake on Highway 102,
108 miles (174 km) north of La Ronge

Maps   Reindeer Lake South 64D
Pelican Narrows 63M

Portages   21 - 25

408   PAULL LAKE, PAULL RIVER, CHURCHILL RIVER, OTTER LAKE

Length   50 miles (80 km)

Approx trip time   4 - 5 days

Access   By air to Paull Lake, 35 miles (56
km) north of Otter Lake

Maps   Foster Lake 74A
Otter Lake 73P/10W
Saskatchewan Natural Resources map,
Trout Lake 42A/E
Lac La Ronge 73P
Otter Lake 73P/10E

Portages   16 - 17

409   PAULL LAKE, PAULL RIVER, CHURCHILL RIVER, KAVANAGH LAKE, BASSETT LAKE, BARTLETT LAKE, MACKAY LAKE

Length   60 miles (97 km)

Approx trip time   5 - 6 days

Access   By air to Paull Lake, 35 miles north
of Otter Lake

Maps   Foster Lake 74A
Lac la Ronge 73P
Otter Lake 73P/10W
Stanley 73P/7
Saskatchewan Natural Resources Map,
Trout Lake 42A/E

Portages   20 - 21

410 REINDEER LAKE, REINDEER RIVER, CHURCHILL RIVER, SANDY BAY

Length 125 miles (201 km)
Approx trip time 8 - 12 days
Access Highway 102 from starting lake, 135 miles (217 km) north of La Ronge
Maps Reindeer Lake South 64D
Pelican Narrows 63M
Portages 9 - 13

North of the Churchill River

411 MCLENNAN LAKE, MCLEAN LAKE, VERSAILLES LAKE, DAVIS LAKE, MCLENNAN LAKE

Length 28 miles (45 km)
Approx trip time 2 days
Access At McLennan Lake from the Department of Natural Resources campground on Highway 102, 82 miles (134 km) north of La Ronge
Map Settee Lake 73P/16

412 BRABANT LAKE, KAKABIGISH LAKE, SETTEE LAKE, COLIN LAKE, VERSAILLES LAKE, DAVIS LAKE, MCLENNAN LAKE

Length 58 miles (93 km)
Approx trip time 4 - 5 days
Access Brabant Lake on Highway 102, 108 miles (174 km) north of La Ronge
Maps La Ronge 73P
Pelican Narrows 63M
Reindeer Lake South 64D
Settee Lake 73P/16
Dept. Mineral Resources map
Kelly Lake 106A
Portages 12

413 BRABANT LAKE, WAPISKAU LAKE, STEEPHILL LAKE, REINDEER RIVER, REINDEER LAKE SOUTH END

Length 70 miles (113 km)
Approx trip time 5 - 7 days
Access Branbant Lake on Highway 102, 108 miles (174 km) north of La Ronge
Maps Reindeer Lake South 64D
Pelican Narrows 63M
Portages 15 - 16

414 BIG SANDY LAKE, GEIKIE RIVER, HIGHWAY 105

Length 55 - 65 miles (88 - 105 km)
Approx trip time 4 - 8 days
Access By air charter from La Ronge (140 miles) (225 km) or Otter Lake (100 miles) (161 km)
Maps Geikie River 74H
Reindeer Lake North 64E
Portages 4

415 REINDEER LAKE, WOLLASTON LAKE

Length 100 miles (161 km)
Approx trip time About 18 days
Access By chartered truck from Lynn Lake, Manitoba, Highway 394, with canoes put in at Co-op Point (Kanasao) on the shore of Reindeer Lake, N.E. Saskatchewan
Map Reindeer Lake North 64E

This route is an approach to the route described next and may be treated as a single trip or as the first extension of Fond du Lac River.

Start at Kanasao, paddle southwest down Reindeer Lake to the source of Swan River. Continue to Swan Lake, along the Blondeau River, two small lakes and Middle Lake to *finish* at Wallaston Lake

416 FOND DU LAC RIVER

Length 170 miles (274 km)
Approx trip time 11 days
Access By chartered floatplane to Wollaston Lake
Maps Wollaston Lake 64L
Pasfield Lake 74 I
Stony Rapids 74P

Fond du Lac River, first documented in 1796, begins at the northwest corner of Wollaston Lake. It is a remote, challenging river for expert whitewater canoeists. There is good grayling fishing.

417 BLACK LAKE (SASKATCHEWAN), CHIPMAN LAKE, BOMPAS LAKE, SELWYN LAKE, FLETT LAKE (NORTHWEST TERRITORIES)

Length 105 miles (169 km)
Approx trip time 7 - 11 days
Access By air charter to Stony Rapids and a short road from there to Black Lake

Maps Stony Rapids 74P
Wholdaia Lake 75A
Portages 12

Start down the Fond du Lac River
to Hatchet Lake, Corson Lake, Crooked
Lake, Otter Lake, Thompson Rapids,
Manitou Falls and Brassy Rapids.

Continue through North Rapids,
Perching Lake, Perch Rapids, Burr
Falls and Black Lake. It is advisable
to *finish* at this point at the settlement
of Black Lake.

Hire ground transportation to the settlement of Stony Rapids. Connect there with
scheduled aircraft to La Ronge and Prince
Albert, Saskatchewan.

Sturgeon-Weir River (Highway 106)

**418   MILE 146, HIGHWAY 106;
DESCHAMBEAULT LAKE, PELICAN
NARROWS, MIROND LAKE,
STURGEON-WEIR RIVER; MILE 190,
HIGHWAY 106; MALIGNE LAKE**

Length 94 miles (151 km)
Approx trip time 5 - 6 days
Access Ballantyne Bay on Deschambeault
Lake; Hanson Lake Road (Highway
106), passes close to the lake at
Mile 146
Maps Amisk Lake 63L
Pelican Narrows 63M
Portages 4 - 5

Portages on this route include: from
Deschambeault Lake to South Arm, Pelican
Lake; the first portage of a double-portage
is from Deschambeault Lake to a small
pond, then to South Arm, Pelican Lake;
Mirond Lake to Corneille Lake;
Corneille Lake with Sturgeon-Weir
River; around Birch Rapids.

 Map Sources

Canada Mapping Office, 615 Booth Street, Ottawa, Ontario is the chief supplier of
topographical maps. In addition, Saskatchewan's Department of Tourism and Renew-
able Resources, has produced a very helpful canoe routes series. There are five maps,
four inches to one mile in scale, covering the Churchill and Sturgeon-Weir Rivers
system and the southern half of Reindeer Lake. Also available are two maps of the La
Ronge area at a scale of one inch to one mile. Purchase these from the department at
2340 Albert Street, Regina, Saskatchewan.

Canada Mapping Office does not list any dealers in Saskatchewan. For a provincial road map and a good lure booklet that contains a lot of information write:

Tourist Development Branch
Department Industry & Commerce
Power Building
Regina, Saskatchewan

Outfitters

Amisk Lake - Angell's Lakeview Motel & Marina
Box 342
Flin Flon, Manitoba

Anglin Lake - Jacobsen Bay Outfitters
Box 4
Christopher Lake, Sask. S0J 0N0
Winter
1707 Park Avenue
Saskatoon, Sask. S7H 2P4

Buffalo Narrows - Lloyd Lake Lodge
Box 86
Buffalo Narrows, Sask.
S0M 0J0

Christopher Lake - McIntosh Point
Summer Resort
R.R. 1, Box 4
Christopher Lake, Sask.
S0J 0N0

Brabant Lake - Brabant Lake Fishing
& Hunting Camp
Box 605
La Ronge, Sask.

East Trout Lake - Bay Resort
Box 1862
Saskatoon, Sask

Jan Lake - Jan Lake Lodge
Box 62
Flin Flon, Manitoba
(winter)
3418 Broadway Avenue
Saskatoon, Sask. S7J 0Y9

La Ronge - Bernard Lake Lodge
Box 295
La Ronge, Sask.

McLennan Lake - Mickey's Camp
Box 413
La Ronge, Sask.

Otter Lake (Missinipe) - Churchill River
Canoe Outfitters
Box 26
La Ronge, Sask.
S0J 1L0
Winter
509 Douglas Park
Crescent East
Regina, Sask.

Pelican Narrows - Mista Nosayew Outfitters
Pelican Narrows, Sask.

Wakaw Lake - Wakaw Lake Lodge
Box 340
Wakaw, Sask.
Winter
1037 Knox Place
Prince Albert, Sask.

Waterhen Lake - Tawaw Cabins
Box 59
Dorintosh, Sask. S0M 0T0

Wathaman Lake - Wathaman Lake Outfitters
Watham Lake, Sask.

There is a Hudson's Bay Company U-Paddle service from Île à la Crosse to La Ronge. Make arrangements well in advance with the Northern Stores Department, 79 Main Street, Winnipeg 1, Manitoba. See page 155 for a description of the service.

Parsons Airways
Box 759
Flin Flon, Man.

Three Lake Air Service
Box 296
Flin Flon, Man.

Nipawin Air Service
Jan Lake, Sask.
Missinipe, Sask.
Pelican Narrows, Sask.

Norcanair
Buffalo Narrows, Sask.
La Ronge, Sask.
Uranium City, Sask.
Stony Rapids, Sask.

Pacific Western Air Lines
Uranium City, Sask.

Gateway Aviation
Uranium City, Sask.

Canoeists planning airlift may find useful the following list of floatplane bases, (in addition to the service bases listed above) as compiled by the federal Ministry of Transport: Amisk, Big River, Black Lake, Camsell Portage, Cumberland House, Dillon, Emma Lake, Fond du Lac, Jan Lake, Montreal Lake, Otter Lake, Pelican Narrows, Regina Beach, Uranium City and Waskesiu Lake.

 Air Charter Services

Canoeists requiring airlift services in Saskatchewan will be concerned with those companies based in the central and northern regions. The southern, prairie region operators, who would not be involved, are not listed.

Central - Atabasca Airways
Prince Albert, Sask.

Norcanair
Prince Albert, Sask.

McPhaill Air Service
North Battleford, Sask.

Nipawin Air Service
Box 1540
Nipawin, Sask.

Carrot River Airways
Box 131
Carrot River, Sask.

Northern - Athabasca Airways
Buffalo Narrows, Sask. and
La Ronge, Sask.

C & M Airways
Box 86
Buffalo Narrows, Sask.

Miksoo Aviation
Meadow Lake, Sask.

La Ronge Aviation
Box 320
La Ronge, Sask.

ALBERTA

Alberta is Canada's fourth largest province in land mass size (255,285 square miles) and displays the greatest variety of geographical features in the nation. The magnificent Rocky Mountain chain forms its western boundary. The foothills region fans out eastward from the mountains, stretching out onto the plains and, in the northeast, to the precambrian shield. Important to the canoeist is the fact that Alberta's four geographical regions also determine its three major canoeing river systems.

With three exceptions, Alberta is not a province either of large lakes or of great mazes of interconnecting smaller lakes as are the other provinces which lie upon the precambrian shield. The exceptions are: Lake Athabasca, of which about one third of the 3,120 square miles of water falls within the borders of Alberta; Lake Claire, adjoining and slightly smaller in area (545 sq. mi.); Lesser Slave Lake, located in the Peace River country and of about equal size (461 sq. m.).

Farming and ranching predominate in the south; oil and natural gas fields are near the capital city, Edmonton; burgeoning tar and oil sands fields lie along 100 miles of the Athabasca River; great reserves of coking coal are found in the southwest; and farming occurs on the Peace River plateau in the north. Alberta is one of the most energetic provinces in the development and exploitation of its natural resources, and as a result is one of the wealthiest.

 ## Fishing

The popular sportfishing species in Alberta are rainbow, cutthroat, brook, brown, lake and Dolly Varden trout; kokanee; northern pike; mountain and lake whitefish; perch; walleye; goldeye and arctic grayling. Coho salmon have been introduced into Cold Lake.

Look for trout in mountain streams of the western region; northern pike, walleye and perch in many of the lakes; arctic grayling in the Peace and Athabasca drainage systems; trout in many lakes and streams across the province. Goldeye and mountain whitefish abound in the major rivers.

Alberta maintains a vigorous restocking program of the most popular species in small lakes, reservoirs and beaver ponds. It's a sport fisherman's country.

Angling Permits - resident & nonresident Canadians $4.00
Non-resident, non-Canadian $3.00
Special trophy lake license for some lakes that produce unusual-size fish $5.00
Children under 15 and Alberta residents over 65 years of age   free

Facing page. One of the most popular and memorable tourist spots in Canada, Lake Louise is fed by the magnificent Victoria Glacier. Facilities for almost any outdoor activity you can imagine are only a few minutes away. The lake is situated in Banff National Park, justly renowned as Canada's oldest and perhaps most famous national park.

Climate

Alberta is a landlocked province strongly influenced by the proximity of the Rocky Mountains on its western boundary. The weather in summer is dry and pleasantly warm. It moderates somewhat to the east, away from the mountains. The canoeist's weather chart shows that summer climate is quite similar regardless of the topographical differences between prairie, parkland, rock and forest.

Alberta	Mean temperatures In Fahrenheit (Celsius)				Rainfall In Mean Inches (Millimetres)	
	Min		*Max*			
Southern (Lethbridge)						
June	37.5	(3.1)	70.2	(21.2)	3.52	(89.4)
July	52.1	(11.2)	79.6	(26.4)	1.77	(45.0)
August	50.0	(10.0)	77.3	(25.2)	1.55	(39.4)
Central (Grand Prairie)						
June	45.3	(7.4)	68.0	(20.0)	2.54	(64.5)
July	49.1	(9.5)	72.5	(22.5)	2.38	(60.5)
August	46.7	(8.2)	70.5	(21.4)	2.07	(52.6)
Northern (Fort Vermillion)						
June	44.5	(6.9)	70.4	(21.3)	1.62	(41.2)
July	49.3	(9.6)	74.3	(23.5)	2.43	(61.7)
August	46.0	(7.8)	70.8	(21.6)	1.82	(46.2)

History

Exploration and the accompanying fur trade came, understandably, later to Alberta than to the east, but not by much. Rivalry between the North West Company and the Hudson's Bay Company was intense in the 1780's as the Saskatchewan, Peace and Athabasca Rivers systems became the main "highways" of the fur trade.

The Nor'Westers led the way when Alexander Mackenzie established Fort Chipewyan, in 1788, at the southwest corner of Lake Athabasca. The following year he pushed northward 2,635 miles on the Mackenzie River to its mouth. The irascible fur trader, Peter Pond, ruled the fur kingdom of the Athabasca. The company also pressed westward, and in 1808 established Fort Vermillion in the Peace River country.

Meanwhile, the Hudson's Bay Company forged up the Athabasca River, founded Fort Edmonton in 1795 and Rocky Mountain House (Jasper) in 1799. Next to be established were Fort Wedderburn in 1815 and Fort Pitt in 1835. Both companies built rival posts on the Athabasca River, at Fort McMurray, during this intense era.

The fledgling Royal North West Mounted Police (later RCMP), in 1874, marched 600 miles from Winnipeg to Alberta's Fort Pitt, driving out the whiskey traders who were debauching the plains Indians. Missionary priest, Father Albert Lacombe, came to the province in 1880 and helped to pacify the western Indians, preventing them from engaging with the eastern Indians and Métis during the Northwest Rebellion in Saskatchewan in 1885.

During these "troubles", the building of the Canadian Pacific Railway was underway — it was in fact partly responsible for them — and trade goods for the north were unloaded at Calgary into carts and driven down the Athabasca Trail to the "landing" on the river. From there, goods were floated "down north" by York boat, scow and the first steamer-tug in service, in 1887. In the years 1897 and 1898, the same waterway became one of the important gateways to the Klondike (in the Yukon) during the famous gold rush.

Alberta became a province in 1905. It takes second place to no other province in Canada when it comes to intense, hectic and colorful beginnings.

Lining a canoe on the Brazeau River. This technique is useful on Alberta's many mountain rivers. A tributary of the great North Saskatchewan, the Brazeau flows into Jasper National Park.

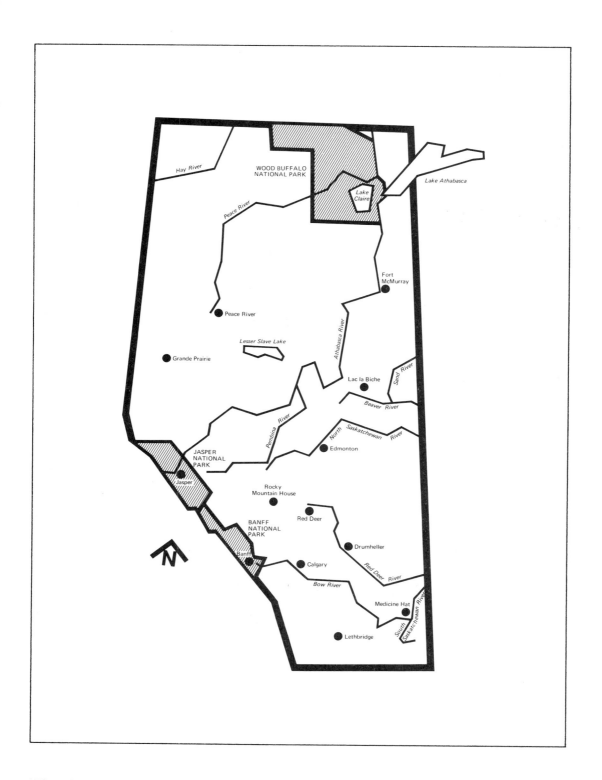

Alberta Routes

Alberta offers perhaps a greater variety of canoeing terrain than any other province in Canada, including mountains, foothills, plains and precambrian shield country. The systems are potentially confusing, but to help correct this situation provincial planners have neatly divided the province into five south-north sections: South One, South Two, Central, North One, and North Two. I have followed the same method of classification. There could be a third area of confusion to the stranger unless it is pointed out to him at the outset that, while the North Saskatchewan River and South Saskatchewan River both rise in, and flow across, the Province of Alberta, they continue across the Province of Saskatchewan as well, where they join to become the Saskatchewan River.

South One

419 SOUTH SASKATCHEWAN RIVER

Length 174 miles (280 km)
Approx trip time 7 - 10 days
Access Grand Forks, 6 miles north, 1/4 mile east of Grassy Lake
Maps Foremost 72E
Medicine Hat 72L
Prelate 72K
Grassy Lake 72E/13
Bow Island 72E/14
Suffield 72L/3W and E
Medicine Hat 72L/2E
Watching Hill 72L/7E
Hilda 72L/8W
Middle Sand Hills 72L/9W and E
Bindloss 72L/16E
Leader 72N/13W

Start at Grand Forks and *finish* at Estuary Ferry, Saskatchewan.

420 BOW RIVER, UPPER BOW

Length 5 miles (8 km)
Approx trip time 2 - 3 hours

Access By the Highway 1 bridge, north of Lake Louise
Maps Scale 1:190,080 series, Banff National Park, available at Park Headquarters. Lake Louise 82N/8W&E

Start at the Highway 1 bridge and *finish* at Highway 1A, 3-1/2 miles southeast of Lake Louise (north shore).

421 BOW RIVER

Length 42 miles (68 km)
Approx trip time 1-1/2 days
Access By the Lake Louise-Bow River bridge
Maps scale 1:190,080 series Banff National Park, available at Park headquarters. Lake Louise 82N/8W and E
Mount Eisenhower 82 O/SW
Banff 82 O/4W and E

Start from Lake Louise and *finish* at the Banff boathouse.

422 BOW RIVER (BANFF TO CALGARY)

Length 100 miles (161 km)
Approx trip time 3 - 4 days
Access By a "viewpoint" below Bow Falls, next to the mouth of Spray River
Maps Calgary 82C
Banff 82 O/4E
Canmore 82 O/3W and E
Jumpingpound Creek 82 O/2
Calgary 82 O/1W

Start from Banff and *finish* at Prince Island, downtown Calgary.

423 BOW RIVER (CALGARY TO GRAND FORKS)

Length 217 miles (349 km)
Approx trip time 6 - 7 days
Access By Calgary Cushing Street bridge.
Maps Calgary 82 O
Gleichen 82 I
Medicine Hat 72L

Foremost 72E
Calgary 82 O/1W and E
Dalemead 82 I/13W and E
Gleichen 82 I/14W and E
Cluny 82 I/13W and E
Queenstown 82 I/10
Cassils 82 I/9
Scandia 82 I/1E
Vauxhall 82 I/1E
Hays 72L/4W and E
Grassy Lake 72/E13

Start from Calgary and *finish* at either Grand Forks (junction of the Bow and Oldman Rivers or at the Bow Island bridge (15 miles downstream from Grand Forks).

424 GHOST RIVER

Length   13 miles (21 km)
Approx trip time   1/2 day
Access   Kangenios Lake Road
Maps   Calgary 82 O
Wildcat Hills 82 O/7W and E*
Lake Minnewanka 82 O/6E*

Start from the bridge on the road to Kangienos Lake and *finish* at the bridge on Highway 1A, at Ghost Reservoir.

425 KANANASKIS RIVER

Length   13 miles (21 km)
Approx trip time   1/2 day
Access   By a bridge on the Snow Ridge Road, 8 miles (13 km) south of the Eau Claire Trailer Campsite
Maps   Kananaskis Lakes 82J
Calgary 82 O
Kananaskis Lakes 82J/11*
Evans-Thomas Creek 82J/14W and E*
Canmore 82 O/3*

Start from the access point to *finish* at the bridge adjacent to a provincial campsite near Ranger Station.

426 KANANASKIS RIVER

Length   17 miles (27 km)
Approx trip time   1/2 day
Access   By a bridge adjacent to the provincial campsite near the Ranger Station
Maps   Kananaskis Lakes 82J
Calgary 82 O
Kananaskis Lakes 82J/11W and E*
Evans-Thomas Creek 82J/14W and E*
Canmore 82 O/3E*

Start from the access point to *finish* at the Seebe Dam.

427 ELBOW RIVER

Length   28 miles (45 km)
Approx trip time   1 day
Access   By the Bragg Creek bridge
Maps   Kananaskis Lakes 82J
Calgary 82 O
Bragg Creek 82J/15
Calgary 82 O/1W

Start from the town of Bragg Creek and *finish* at the boathouse, Glenmore Reservoir.

428 HIGHWOOD RIVER (TO SENTINEL RANGER STATION)

Length   4 miles (6 km)
Approx trip time   2 hours
Access   By a provincial campsite north of the junction of Highway 541 and Forestry Trunk Road
Maps   Kananaskis Lake 82J
Mount Rae 82J/10W
Mount Head 82J/7W and E

429 HIGHWOOD RIVER (TO HIGHWAY 541)

Length   16 miles (26 km)
Approx trip time   4 hours
Access   By the junction of Highway 541 and the Forestry Trunk Road
Maps   Kananaskis Lakes 82J
Mount Head 82J/7E and W

Start from the access point and *finish* at the provincial campsite on Highway 541.

430 HIGHWOOD RIVER (TO HIGHWAY 2)

Length   33 miles (53 km)
Approx trip time   2 days
Access   By the provincial campsite on Highway 541
Maps   Kananaskis Lakes 82J
Gleichen 82 I
Stimson Creek 82J/8E and W
Mount Head 82J/7E
Turner Valley 82J/9E and W
High River 82 I/12W
Dalemead 82 I/13W

Start at the provincial campsite on Highway 541 and *finish* at the Highway 2 bridge.

431 OLDMAN RIVER (TO HIGHWAY 2)

Length 84 miles (135 km)
Approx trip time 3 days
Access By the Oldman River recreation area
Maps Fernie 82G
Lethbridge 82H
Fording River 82J/2E
Maycroft 82G/16
Blairmore 82G/9
Brocket 82H/12W and E
Fort Mcleod 82H/11W
Monarch 82H/14W

Start from the access point and *finish* at the campsite on Highway 2, 2 miles (3 km) west of Fort Macleod.

432 OLDMAN RIVER (TO GRAND FORKS)

Length 168 miles (270 km)
Approx trip time 4 - 5 days
Access By the campsite, Highway 2, 2 miles (3 km) west of Fort Macleod
Maps Lethbridge 82H
Foremost 72E
Fort Macleod 82H/11W
Monarch 82H/14W and E
Picture Butte 82H/15
Lethbridge 82H/10
Taber 82H/16
Grassy Lake 72E/13

Start at Fort Macleod and *finish* either at Grand Forks (the junction of the Oldman and Bow Rivers) or at the Bow Island bridge, 12 miles down the river from Grand Forks.

433 WATERTON RIVER

Length 54 miles (87 km)
Approx trip time 2 days
Access At the Waterton National Park gate
Maps Lethbridge 82H
Waterton Lakes 82H/4W
Glenwoodville 82H/5E
Brocket 82H/12E
Fort Mcleod 82H/11W and E
Pincher Creek 82H/5

Start from the access point and *finish* at the provincial campsite on Highway 2.

South Two

434 RED DEER RIVER (MOUNTAIN AIRE LODGE TO COALCAMP)

Length 25 miles (40 km)
Approx trip time 1 day
Access Before the Forestry Trunk Road bridge crossing the Red Deer River.
Maps Calgary 82 O
Burnt Timber Creek 82 O/11W and E
Fallentimber 82 O/10W

Start from the Mountain Aire Lodge and *finish* along the road cut, just above the old town of Coalcamp, which is about 25 miles (40 km) west of Sundre.

435 RED DEER RIVER (COALCAMP TO SUNDRE)

Length 13 miles (21 km)
Approx trip time 1/2 day
Access By a road cut above Coalcamp, west of Sundre 25 miles (40 km)
Maps Calgary 82 O
Fallen Timber 82 O/10W and E
Bearberry 82 O/15E and W

Start from the access point and *finish* at the left bank, below the highway bridge in Sundre.

436 RED DEER RIVER (SUNDRE TO RED DEER)

Length 74 miles (119 km)
Approx trip time 3 days
Access Below the Sundre highway bridge
Maps Calgary 82 O
Rocky Mountain House 83B
Red Deer 83A
Bearberry 82 O/15E
Olds 82 O/16W
Markerville 83B/1W and E
Innisfail 83A/4W
Red Deer 83A/5W

Start at the access point and *finish* at Lion's Campground, just east of Highway 2.

437 RED DEER RIVER (RED DEER TO DRUMHELLER)

Length 127 miles (204 km)
Approx trip time 4 days
Access By Lion's campsite, east of Highway 2
Maps Red Deer 83A
Drumheller 82P

Start from the access point and *finish* at the campsite above Drumheller's highway bridge.

438 RED DEER RIVER (DRUMHELLER TO ESTUARY, SASKATCHEWAN)

Length 194 miles (312 km)
Approx trip time 4 days
Access By a campsite on the left bank of Red Deer River, above the bridge
Maps Drumheller 82P
Medicine Hat 72L
Oyen 72M
Prelate 72K
Drumheller 82P/7
Dorothy 82P/8
Finnegan 82P/1
Wardlow 72L/13W and E
Halsbury 72L/14W and E
Buffalo 72L/15E and W
Blindloss 72L/16W and E
Leader 72K/13W and E

Start from the access point and *finish* at the ferry across the river at Estuary, Saskatchewan.

439 PANTHER RIVER

Length 5 miles (8 km)
Approx trip time 1/2 day
Access 8 miles (13 km) up the Panther access on the Forestry Road, at the junction with the ford (West from Mountain Aire Lodge.)
Maps Calgary 82 O
Burnt Timber Creek 82 O/11W

Start from the access point and *finish* at the Red Deer River Crossing (Mountain Aire Lodge).

440 BLINDMAN RIVER

Length 45 miles (72 km)
Approx trip time 1 - 2 days
Access By the bridge on Highway 12, north-west of Rimbey
Maps Red Deer 83A
Sylvan Lake 83B/8E
Rimbey 83B/9W and E
Red Deer 83A/5W

Start from the access point and *finish* at the Highway 2A bridge, north at Red Deer.

441 NORTH SASKATCHEWAN RIVER (ALEXANDRA RIVER TO BIGHORN DAM)

Length 32 miles (51 km)
Approx trip time 1-1/2 days
Access By a "viewpoint" along the Banff-Jasper Highway, below Junction of the Alexandra and North Saskatchewan Rivers
Maps Brazeau 83C
Rocky Mountain House 83B
Golden 82N
Cline River 83C/2W
Nordegg 83C/8
Mistaya Lake 82N/15W and E
Siffleur River 82N/16W
Whiterabbit Creek 83C/1W
Scale 1:190,080
Banff National Park, available at Park Headquarters

Start from the access point and *finish* at the Bighorn Dam, Spillway Channel, on the north (left) side of the river. Pull out where the old David Thompson meets the water.

442 NORTH SASKATCHEWAN RIVER (NORDEGG BRIDGE TO ROCKY MOUNTAIN HOUSE)

Length 65 miles (105 km)
Approx trip time 2 days
Access By the bridge on the Forestry Trunk Road, south of Nordegg
Maps Brazeau 83C
Rocky Mountain House 83B
Nordegg 83C/8
Saunders 83B/5W and E
Crimson Lake 83B/6W and E
Rocky Mountain House 83B/7W and E

Start from the access point and *finish* at a bridge on the North Saskatchewan, Highway 11, just northwest of Rocky Mountain House.

443 NORTH SASKATCHEWAN RIVER (ROCKY MOUNTAIN HOUSE TO DRAYTON VALLEY

Length 81 miles (130 km)
Approx trip time 1-1/2 days
Access By the east bank above the new Highway 11 bridge, just northwest of Rocky Mountain House
Maps Rocky Mountain House 83B
Wabamun Lake 83G

Start from the access point and *finish* downstream, on the west bank of the highway bridge, east of Drayton Valley.

444 NORTH SASKATCHEWAN RIVER (DRAYTON VALLEY TO EDMONTON)

Length 100 miles (161 km)
Approx trip time   2 - 3 days
Access   By a highway bridge, east of Drayton Valley
Maps   Rocky Mountain House 83B
Edmonton 83H

Start from the access point and *finish* at any one of the many bridges in Edmonton. Mileage was taken to the Great Road Bridge at Emily Murphy Park.

445 CLEARWATER RIVER (TIMBER CREEK TO SEVEN MILE CAMPGROUND)

Length   35 miles (56 km)
Approx trip time   1 day
Access   Take the first left turn after Seven-Mile Campground, about 2 miles (3 km) down the forestry trunk road. Follow this road west across the Clearwater, up the river and Cut-Off Creek. Keep right and after about 16 miles (26 km), you should reach an old logging camp. From here, it is a 3/4 mile hike west to the river.
Maps   Calgary 82 O
Rocky Mountain House 83B
Scalp Creek 82 O/13W and E
Burnt Timber Creek 82 O/11
Limestone Mountain 82 O/14
Tay River 83B/3E

Start from the access point and *finish* at the west end of Seven Mile Flat campground.

446 CLEARWATER RIVER (SEVEN MILE CAMPGROUND TO RICINUS BRIDGE)

Length   25 miles (40 km)
Approx trip time   1 day
Access   Seven Mile Flat Campground
Maps   Calgary 82 O
Rocky Mountain House 83B
Limestone Mountain 82 O/14
Tay River 82B/3E
Caroline 83B/2W

Start from the access point and *finish* at the Ricinus Bridge, west of Caroline, Highway 54.

447 CLEARWATER RIVER (RICINUS BRIDGE TO ROCKY MOUNTAIN HOUSE)

Length   30 miles (48 km)
Approx trip time   1 day
Access   By the Ricinus bridge, Highway 54, west of Caroline
Maps   Rocky Mountain House 83B
Caroline 83B/2W
Rocky Mountain House 83B/7

Start from the access point and *finish* at the new Highway 11 bridge, northwest of Rocky Mountain House.

448 BRAZEAU RIVER

Length   60 miles (97 km)
Approx trip time   2 - 3 days
Access   By the Forestry Trunk Road bridge over the Brazeau River
Maps   Brazeau 83C
Rocky Mountain House 83B
Grave Flats 83C/15W
Pembina Forks 83C/15E
Brown Creek 83C/16W and E
Nordegg River 83B/13W and E

Start from the Brazeau Recreation Area and *finish* at the Brazeau Dam.

449 WOLF LAKE, WOLF RIVER AND SAND RIVER

Length   53 miles (85 km)
Approx trip time   3 days
Access   By the Wolf Lake campsite
Maps   Sand River 73L
Wolf River 73L/15E and W
Touchwood Lake 73L/14E
Pinehurst Lake 73L/11E
Bonnyville 73L/7W

Start from the access point and *finish* at the Road Allowance, one half mile above the mouth of the Sand River.

450 BEAVER RIVER

Length   104 miles (167 km)
Access   By a bridge at mouth of Amisk River
Maps   Tawatinaw 83 I
Sand River 73L

Start from the access point and *finish* at Cold Lake Highway 28 — Beaver Crossing.

North One

451 HAY RIVER
Access At Hobay (near Chateh)
Maps Zama Lake 84L
Steen River 84N
Tathlina Lake 85C

Start at Hay Lake and *finish* at Great Slave Lake, N.W.T.

452 PEACE AND SLAVE RIVERS
Length 140 miles (225 km)
Approx trip time 6 - 10 days
Access Peace Point or Carlson's Landing
Maps Fort Chipewyan 74L
Fitzgerald 74M

Start from Peace Point on the Peace River and *finish* at Fitzgerald on the Slave River.

453 RIVIÈRE DES ROCHERS AND SLAVE RIVER
Length 102 miles (164 km)
Access At Fort Chipewyan
Maps Fitzgerald 74M
Also, if available, the Canadian Hydrographic Chart 6301, Slave-Athabasca, from the Canadian Hydrographic Services, Department of Mines and Technical Surveys, Ottawa, Ontario

Start from Fort Chipewyan and *finish* at Fitzgerald.

454 PEACE RIVER (DUNVEGAN BRIDGE TO FORT VERMILLION)
Length 316 miles (508 km)
Approx trip time 10 - 12 days
Access At Dunvegan campsite
Maps Grande Prairie 83M
Winagami 83N
Peace River 84C
Bison Lake 84F
Mount Watt 84K
Vermillion Chute 84J

Start from the access point and *finish* at Fort Vermillion ferry.

455 PEACE RIVER (FORT VERMILION TO PEACE POINT)
Length 192 miles (309 km)
Approx trip time 7 - 8 days
Access By the Fort Vermilion ferry
Maps Vermilion Chutes 84J
Lake Claire 84 I
Peace Point 84P

Start from the access point and *finish* at Peace Point.

456 SMOKY RIVER
Length 270 miles (434 km)
Approx trip time 7 - 8 days
Access By the Grande Cache bridge
Maps Mount Robson 83E
Wapiti 83L
Grande Prairie 83M
Winagami 83N
Peace River 84C

Start from Grande Cache and *finish* at the town of Peace River boat landing.

457 LITTLE SMOKY RIVER
Length 142 miles (229 km)
Access By the Little Smoky campsite, Highway 43
Maps Iosegun Lake 83K
Winagami 83N

Start from the access point and *finish* at the Watino bridge, on the Smoky River.

458 WABASCA RIVER (NORTH WABASCA LAKE TO WABASCA BRIDGE)
Length 217 miles (349 km)
Approx trip time 5 - 15 days
Access Either by the outlet of North Wabasca Lake or the provincial campsite on North Wabasca Lake
Maps Algar Lake 84A
Peerless Lake 84B
Wadlin Lake 84G

Start from either access point and *finish* at the Wabasca Forestry Road bridge.

459 WABASCA RIVER (WABASCA BRIDGE TO MOUTH AT PEACE RIVER)
Length 66 miles (106 km)
Approx trip time 2 - 4 days

Nestled in the Valley of the Ten Peaks, Moraine Lake and the splendor of its environs are comparable only to the nearby Lake Louise—and more secluded.

Access By the Wabasca bridge
Map Vermilion Chutes 84J

Start from the access point and *finish* at Fort Vermilion or the Jean D'Or Indian Reserve.

North Two

460 ATHABASCA RIVER (ABOVE THE ATHABASCA FALLS)

Length 8 miles (13 km)
Approx trip time 1/4 day
Access At the first joining of the river and road below Sunwapta Falls, about 28 miles (45 km) above the junction of Highway 93 and 16
Maps scale 1:190,080 series Jasper National Park, South, available at the Park Information Booth.
Brazeau 83C

Start from the access point and *finish* along Highway 93, about 1 mile above the turn-off for the falls.

461 ATHABASCA RIVER (ATHABASCA FALLS TO THE OLD FORT POINT BRIDGE)

Length 18 miles (29 km)
Approx trip time 1/2 day
Access 1/4 mile down Highway 92A from Athabasca Falls, a trail turns right off the road and leads down to the big pool at the canyon outlet.
Maps scale 1:190,080 series, Jasper National Park, South
Brazeau 83C
Edson 83F

Start from the access point and *finish* on the right bank below the bridge, south of Jasper Park Lodge.

462 ATHABASCA RIVER (JASPER TO HINTON)

Length 50 miles (80 km)
Approx trip time 2 days
Access By the Old Fort Point bridge
Maps Edson 83F
scale 1:190,080 series, Jasper National Park North, available at the Park Information Booth.

Start from the access point and *finish* at the Hinton bridge or Old Entrance.

463 ATHABACA RIVER (HINTON TO ATHABASCA)

Length 320 miles (515 km)
Approx trip time 7 - 9 days
Access By the Hinton bridge
Maps Edson 83F
Iosegun Lake 83K
Whitecourt 83J
Lesser Slave Lake 83 O
Tawatinaw 83 I

Start from the access point and *finish* at the Athabasca campsite, at the east end of town, one half mile above the highway bridge on the right bank.

464 ATHABASCA RIVER (ATHABASCA TO FORT MCMURRAY)

Length 231 miles (372 km)
Approx trip time 8 - 12 days
Access By the Athabasca provincial campsite at the east end of town on the right bank.
Maps Tawatinaw 83 I
Pelican 83P
Algar Lake 84A
Waterways 74D

Start from the access point and *finish* at the Fort McMurray Bridge, Highway 63.

465 ATHABASCA RIVER (FORT MCMURRAY TO FORT CHIPEWYAN)

Length 190 miles (306 km)
Access At Fort McMurray
Maps Waterways 74D
Bitumont 74E
Fort Chipewyan 74L

Start from Fort McMurray and *finish* at Fort Chipewyan. (There is no means of returning south except by aircraft.)

466 MIETTE RIVER (GEIKIE TO OLD FORT POINT BRIDGE)

Length 10 miles (16 km)
Approx trip time 1/2 day
Access Follow the access road to Christine and Dorothy Lakes Trail, till it ends at the old Canadian National Railway siding of Geikie. Cross the tracks and follow the trail 100 yards down to the river.
Maps scale 1:190,080 series, Jasper National Park South, available at the Park Information Booth
Canoe River 83D

Start from Geikie and *finish* at the Old Fort Point bridge on the Athabasca River, west of the Jasper Park Lodge on the right bank, below the bridge.

467 MALIGNE RIVER
Length 10 miles (16 km)
Approx trip time 1/2 day
Access At the mouth of Maligne River at Maligne Lake, just past the Lodge
Maps Scale 1:190,080 Jasper National Park South, available at the Park Information Booth
Brazeau 83C

Start from Maligne Lake and *finish* on the east shore of Medicine Lake, next to the highway, just after the river enters the lake.

468 MALIGNE RIVER - MALIGNE CANYON
Length 8 miles (13 km)
Approx trip time 1/2 day
Access Along the road to Medicine Lake, where enough water is present for paddling
Maps scale 1:190,080 series, Jasper National Park, South, available at the Park Information
Brazeau 83C

Start from the access point and *finish* behind the Maligne Canyon Youth Hostel, about 1/2 mile above the canyon.

469 MALIGNE RIVER (FIFTH TO SIXTH BRIDGE, MALIGNE CANYON)
Length 1.7 miles (2.7 km)
Approx trip time 8 - 10 minutes
Access At the fifth bridge over Maligne River (follow signs on the Maligne Lake Road)
Maps scale 1:190,080 series, Jasper National Park, South, available at the Park Information Booth
Brazeau 83C

Start from the fifth bridge and *finish* at the sixth. Follow signs to the old fish hatchery, then take the first left turn down to the picnic site.

470 MCLEOD RIVER - EMBARRAS RIVER
Length 47 miles (76 km)
Approx trip time 2 days
Access By a provincial campsite on the Forestry Trunk Road, 18 miles (29 km) south of the highway

Maps Edson 83F
Pedly 83F/6
Dalehurst 83F/11E
Bickerdike 83F/10W and E
Erith 83F/7

Start from the McLeod Recreation Area provincial campsite and *finish* at Highway 47, the Embarras River bridge.

471 MCLEOD RIVER - WHITECOURT
Length 116 miles (187 km)
Approx trip time 3 - 4 days
Access By the Highway 47 bridge on McLeod River at the junction of Embarras River, 8 miles (13 km) south of Highway 16.
Maps Edson 83F
Wabamun Lake 83G
Whitecourt 83J
Erith 83F/7E
Bickerdike 83F/10E
Edson 83F/9W and E
Carrot Creek 83G/12W
Hattonford 83G/13W
Whitecourt 83J/4W and E

Start from the access point and *finish* at the Highway 43 bridge, west of Whitecourt.

472 CLEARWATER RIVER
Length 103 miles (166 km)
Approx trip time 7 - 9 days
Access By La Loche on Lac La Loche at the end of Highway 115 in Saskatchewan
Maps La Loche 74C
Waterways 74D
Canadian Geological Survey Report of Progress of 1882-84 by Dr. Bell (indicates portages).
Planimetric Map 74D/3: Alberta Department of Lands and Forests (indicates rapids).

Start from LaLoche and *finish* at Fort McMurray.

473 WILDHAY RIVER - GRANDE CACHE
Length 19 miles (31 km)
Approx trip time 1 day
Access At Rock Lake
Maps Mount Robson 83E
Edson 83F
Rock Lake 83E/8E
Moberly Creek 83E/9
Entrance 83F/5

Start from Rock Lake and *finish* at the Grande Cache Highway 40 bridge.

474 WILDHAY RIVER - GREGG LAKE ROAD

Length 43 miles (69 km)
Approx trip time 2 days
Access By Highway 40 bridge
Maps Edson 83F
Gregg Lake 83F/12W and E
Hightower 83F/13E

Start from Grande Cache Highway 40 and *finish* at the Pinto Creek bridge at the end of Gregg Lake Road.

475 WILDHAY AND BERLAND RIVERS

Length 56 miles (90 km)
Approx trip time 2 days
Access At the mouth of Pinto Creek
Maps Edson 83F
Iosegun Lake 83K
Hightower Creek 83F/13W and E
Oldman Creek 83F/14W and E
Donald Flats 83E/16W and E
Moberly Creek 83E/9
Marsh Head Creek 83K/2W
Berland River 83K/3W and E

Start from the mouth of Pinto Creek, continue to the mouth of the Wildhay River and *finish* at the Hudson's Bay Oil and Gas Co. campsite on the west bank of the Athabasca just north of the highway bridge.

476 JARVIS CREEK

Length 15 miles (24 km)
Approx trip time 1 day
Access From the Jarvis Lake campground
Map Edson 83F

Start from Jarvis Lake and *finish* at the Gregg Lake campground.

The Bow River, which winds its way through the mountains of Banff National Park, is ideal for the canoeist. Trips can be made up the Bow, on one of its tributaries, Echo Creek, and into Willow Creek and the Vermillion Lakes. Canoes can be hired at the Banff River Boathouse in the town of Banff.

Map Sources

Canada Mapping Office, 615 Booth Street, Ottawa, Ontario is the chief supplier of topographical maps. These maps are available from the following agents in Alberta:

Banff Book & Art Den Co. Ltd.
108 Banff Avenue
Box 1420
Banff, Alta.

Canadian Mountain Holidays
132 Banff Avenue
P.O. Box 1660
Banff, Alta.

Dave Siggelkow
Waybest Tower
Burdett, Alta.

Barotto Sports Ltd.
605 - 7th St. S.W.,
Calgary 2, Alta.

Carter Mapping Ltd.
510 5th St. S.W.
Calgary 1, Alta.
T2P 1V6

Foothills Distributors Ltd.
642 16th Ave. N.W.,
Calgary, Alta.

Institute of Sedimentary
& Petroleum Geology
3303 33rd St. N.W.
Calgary, Alta.

Nickle Map Service
330 9th Ave. S.W.
Calgary, Alta.

The Hostel Shop
1414 Kensington Rd. N.W.
Calgary 41, Alta.

Information Canada Bookstore
c/o Carmen Moore Books Ltd.
Library, University of Calgary
Calgary, Alta.
T2N 1N4

Alberta Department of Lands & Forests
Director of Technical Division
Natural Resources Building
Room 325
Edmonton, Alta.

Alberta & Northwest Chamber of Mines
 Oils & Resources
10009 105 St.
Edmonton, Alta.

The Mountain Shop
10918 88 Ave.
Edmonton 61, Alta.

Uncle Ben's Sporting Goods
10138 101st St.
Edmonton, Alta.

Wildcat Guns Limited
10726 101 St.
Edmonton 17, Alta.

Kiyooka Mingei Limited
Box 2066
Hinton, Alta.

Manning Drug Store
Manning, Alta.

Jackson Bros. Hardware
P.O. Box 730
Pincher Creek, Alta.

Great Bear Trophy Lodge Ltd.
Box 9000
Ponoka, Alta.

Grable's Sports & Hobbie Centre
4934 51st St
Red Deer, Alta.

Rex Logan, Guide & Outfitters
Mackenzie Mountain Dist. N.W.T.
Box 484
Sundre, Alta.

For a provincial road map and a good lure booklet containing a lot of information, write:

Government Travel Bureau
1629 Centennial Building
Edmonton, Alberta

 ## Outfitters

Travel Alberta (Department of Tourism) advises that it has no listing of outfitters for canoeists but gives a list of canoe club addresses which may, directly or through their members, provide such services. The clubs might welcome your membership and therefore enable you to avail yourself of their scheduled safaris. Here they are:

Northwest Voyageurs
10918 88 Avenue
Edmonton, Alta.

Calgary Canoe Club,
2619 63 Avenue S.W.
Calgary, Alta.

Medicine Hat Canoe Club
c/o Medicine Hat Tourist Centre
Box 605
607 - 4th Street S.E.
Medicine Hat, Alta.

Red Deer Canoe & Kayak Club
3901 47 Street
Red Deer, Alta.

East Calgary Canoe Club
2201 38 Street S.E.
Calgary, Alta.

Sundre Canoe Club
Sundre, Alta.

Associations - Canadian Canoe Association
Alberta Division, Percy Page Centre
31 Mission Avenue, Box 205
St. Albert, Alta.

Alberta Recreational Canoe Association
(same address as above)

Alberta Whitewater Canoe Association
6508 109 B Avenue
Edmonton, Alta.

 ## Air Charter Services

Floatplane services for canoeists in Alberta are confined to the northern half of the province and the companies listed below have main bases as well as several bush bases which they will list for you.

Contact Airways Ltd.
Box 75,
Fort McMurray, Alta. T0A 1K0

Gateway Aviation Ltd.
#13 Hangar
International Airport
Edmonton, Alta.

Northward Airlines Ltd.,
10240 124th Street
Edmonton, Alta.

Noralta Flights Limited,
Box 365,
Fort Chipewyan, Alta.

Bayview Air Services Ltd.
Box 480
Slave Lake, Alta. T0G 2A0

The following floatplane bases are listed by the Canada Ministry of Transport:
Athabasca, Calling Lake, Cold Lake, Cooking Lake, Embarras, Footner Lake, Fort Fitzgerald, Fort McKay, Fort Vermilion, Lac la Biche and Peace River. Some Alberta river raft operators are:

Athabasca, Brazeau, Red Deer Rivers
North West Expeditions Ltd.
Box 1551
Edmonton, Alta. T5J 2N7

Bow, Athabasca Rivers
Rocky Mountain Raft Tours
Box 1771
Banff, Alta.

BRITISH COLUMBIA

The Province of British Columbia has the most diverse and spectacular geography of any province in Canada. It ranges from towering mountain ranges down to alpine meadows, pleasant lowlands, interior plains and deep-cut river valleys. The province is the nation's third largest in land area (366,255 square miles), about 400 miles across and 760 miles from south to north. It is in the Cordilleran region of North America.

The cordillera comprises three distinct systems of mountain ranges, the eastern, interior and western systems. In the east, the most famous range is the Rockies, in which the highest peak is Mount Robson (12,872 feet). In the western system, the most prominent range is the Coast Mountains, in which the highest peaks are Mount Waddington (13,260 feet) and Mount Fairweather (15,300 feet). Between these two systems lies a plateau studded with older, lower mountain ranges; in the south are the Columbia, Selkirk, Purcell, Cariboo and Cascade Ranges and in the north-central area are the Hazelton, Skeena, Ominica, Cassairs and St. Elias ranges.

The eastern border of British Columbia is formed by the continental watershed in the southern part of the province, but in the north, it follows a straight line that cuts across a corner of the interior plain, or prairies, of North America. Across this plain runs the Peace, Fort Nelson and Liard Rivers to the great Mackenzie River that empties into the Arctic Ocean.

Among the spectacular rivers which flow to the Pacific through the mountain passes are: the Fraser, Thompson, Chilcoten, Columbia, Kootenay, Akeena and Stikine Rivers. The larger lakes in British Columbia are: Atlin, Babine, Kootenay, Stuart, Okanagan, Shuswap, Takla, Quesnel and Williston Lakes.

In addition to some 250 provincial parks, there are seven national parks in British Columbia: Kootenay, Glacier, Fort Langley, Yoho, Mount Revelstoke, Pacific Rim and Fort Rod Hill.

The city of Victoria on Vancouver Island, is the provincial capital, with a population of over 50,000. Vancouver, located on the mainland in the lower Fraser Valley, has a population approaching one million.

The mineral output of British Columbia is fourth in the nation and includes copper, molybdenum, gold, iron ore, smelted aluminum, asbestos and sulphur. The forests contain one-quarter of the timber cover of North America; 118 million acres are marketable, supporting lumber, pulp, newsprint and plywood operations.

The province leads all others in commercial fish production. It is followed closely by Nova Scotia. The most important fish is Pacific salmon, of which there are five species caught: sockeye, pink, coho, chum and chinook. Ten per cent of the provincial land area is used for agriculture and grazing: dairy, poultry and fruit predominate in the Fraser Valley; fruit in the Okanagan and Kootenay Valleys; cattle ranching in the central interior plateau. Combined, wild fur and ranch fur production approach six million dollars annually in value. Hydro-electric power output is immense. Manufacturing is confined pretty well to the lower mainland and Vancouver Island.

Facing page. The Similkameen River runs through the Keremeos region of British Columbia here. The fruit production of this river valley rivals that of the more famous Okanagan valley. In the area rockhounds will find good specimens of rhodonite and dark red jasper.

Climate

British Columbia's summer climate varies considerably from one region of the province to another. On the coast, the level of precipitation is rather high, averaging from forty inches to sixty inches of rain annually. Certain areas receive as much as 100 inches of rain annually, and at Henderson Lake, Vancouver Island, an incredible 262 inches of rain has been recorded.

In the interior, on the other hand, a dry climate predominates. It is safe to expect only ten to fifteen inches of rain each year. Approaching the Rockies in the east, the level of precipitation picks up to a level of thirty inches per year.

The province is broken down into three basic climatic regions, as follows:

British Columbia	Mean Temperatures In Fahrenheit (Celsius)				Rainfall In Mean Inches (Millimetres)	
	Min		Max			
North Coastal (Atlin)						
June	40.1	(4.5)	60.0	(15.6)	0.84	(21.3)
July	44.7	(7.1)	64.4	(18.0)	0.80	(20.3)
August	43.8	(6.6)	62.0	(16.7)	1.26	(32.0)
South Coastal (Squamish)						
June	49.0	(9.4)	67.1	(19.5)	2.71	(68.8)
July	52.6	(11.4)	72.0	(22.2)	2.13	(54.1)
August	52.4	(11.3)	70.8	(21.6)	2.09	(53.1)
North Interior (Cassair)						
June	35.9	(2.2)	60.0	(15.6)	1.62	(41.2)
July	40.5	(4.7)	63.4	(17.4)	2.14	(54.4)
August	38.5	(3.6)	59.9	(15.5)	2.61	(66.3)
South Interior (Kimberly)						
June	43.6	(6.4)	71.2	(21.8)	2.04	(51.8)
July	46.8	(8.2)	80.9	(27.2)	0.83	(21.1)
August	45.5	(7.5)	78.6	(25.9)	1.24	(31.5)
North Rocky Mountains			not given			
South Rocky Mountains (Golden)						
June	44.5	(6.9)	74.0	(23.3)	1.57	(39.9)
July	48.0	(8.9)	80.8	(27.1)	1.37	(34.8)
August	46.2	(7.9)	77.2	(25.1)	1.42	(36.1)

Northern Interior Plains (Fort Nelson)							
June	46.5	(8.1)	69.6	(20.9)		2.53	(64.3)
July	50.7	(10.4)	73.4	(23.0)		2.94	(74.7)
August	47.2	(8.4)	70.2	(21.2)		2.19	(55.6)
South Interior Plains (Dawson Creek)							
June	43.1	(6.2)	67.9	(19.9)		2.25	(57.2)
July	46.5	(8.1)	72.5	(22.5)		1.89	(48.0)
August	44.4	(6.9)	70.7	(21.5)		1.47	(37.3)

Fishing

Canoeists in British Columbia will find the most recent listing of species, regions and the license structure helpful:

Trout

Steelhead	Vancouver Island, lower mainland, southern interior, Prince Rupert, Queen Charlotte Island, Coastal (Bella Coola).
Kamloops	The Kootenays and Okanagan, Kamloops, Quesnel-Chilcotin, Burns Lake, Vancouver Island, upper and lower coast.
Brown	East coast of Vancouver Island
Coastal cutthroat	Lower mainland, upper coast, Queen Charlotte Islands, Vancouver Island
Yellowstone cutthroat	Southeastern region of province
Kokanee	Most larger lakes on mainland and on Vancouver Island.

Char

Lake trout	Adams, Lac la Hache-Quesnel, Fraser River, Stuart, Francois, Babine and Morrison Lakes.
Dolly Varden	Throughout many lakes and streams of British Columbia, except the Okanagan drainageway.
Eastern brook	Vancouver Island, southeastern region of the province, Princeton, lower Okanagan.

Salmon

The coastal waters support five species of salmon: chinook, coho, pink, sockeye and chum. Of these, only two species, chinook and coho, may be taken by sport fishermen in non-tidal waters.

Warm Water Fish

Smallmouth bass   southern Vancouver Island, north of Nanaimo and in the Cranbrook region.
Largemouth bass   The Columbia River drainage system.
Yellow perch   Lakes of the southern Okanagan drainage pattern.

Licences required and fees applicable are as follows:
Resident of B.C. (16 years and over) $5.00
Canadian resident (not B.C.) (16 years and over) $5.00
Resident of B.C. (Canadian citizen, 65 years or over) $1.00
Nonresident (3-day) angling licence (16 years or over) $6.00
Nonresident angling licence (annual) (16 years or over) $15.00
B.C. resident, steelhead angling licence (16 years or over) $3.00
Canadian resident/nonresident, Steelhead angling licence (16 years or over) $10.00
Nonresident, "special lakes" angling licence (16 years or over) $15.00
Nonresident, "special rivers" angling licence (16 years or over) $25.00

For fishing and hunting information write to:

Fish and Wildlife Branch
Department of Recreation and Conservation
Parliament Buildings
Victoria, British Columbia

 History

British Columbia's history reaches far into the past. It is believed that man came overland from Asia at least 10,000 years ago; the Eskimo made his way along the northern coasts of Alaska, Yukon and the Northwest Territories, and the Indian came through mountain passes, down the British Columbia coast, inland through the deep-cut river valleys, to the plains and eastward.

The first European discoverers found 25,000 native people inhabiting the mountains just east of the Coast Mountains as well as areas along the coast. It is only speculation that Sir Francis Drake sighted Vancouver Island in 1579. The first non-native to make a landfall was an European, Vitus Bering, of Imperial Russia (1741). Thirty-five years later, Juan Perez and Bodega y Quadra of Spain explored portions of the coast. In 1778, Captain James Cook of England claimed the coast for the Crown. Captain John Meares of the East India Company established a trading post at Nootka in 1788; he was followed the next year by the Spaniards at the same location.

Captain George Vancouver surveyed the Pacific Coast from San Francisco to the Bering Sea in 1792-94. Alexander Mackenzie and a party from the North West Company, in 1793, became the first white men to reach the Pacific overland from the east. Mackenzie and his ten men walked the last fifteen days from the Fraser River to Bella Coola. The breadth of Canada had finally been paddled, and portaged. David

Thompson, also of the North West Company, came to the northern interior of British Columbia in 1807. He discovered the route through Howse Pass (Columbia River) and went on to explore the region.

The following year, 1808, Simon Fraser of the Hudson's Bay Company travelled with his party by canoe down the length of what is now the Fraser River to the Pacific coast.

The merger of the two great rival fur trading companies in 1821 gave the Hudson's Bay Company a trading monopoly west of the Rockies and the right to establish trading posts as it saw fit. The first was Vancouver, in 1825; Victoria followed in 1843. Vancouver Island became a Crown Colony in 1849 with Victoria as its capital. Nine years later, a mainland Crown Colony was established with New Westminster as the capital. The two colonies united in 1861.

In the Cariboo district, 1860 was the year of the gold rush. It drew world-wide attention to British Columbia and may have had a bearing on its decision to join the Confederation of Canada in 1871, earlier than it might have done.

The Canadian Pacific Railway was completed to the coast from the east in 1885. Today the Alaska Highway extends 673 miles through British Columbia and across the Yukon Territory to Fairbanks, Alaska — a total of 1,523 miles.

Skidegate Indian Village, Queen Charlotte Islands, British Columbia, July 26, 1878. The Haida Indians of the west coast built and used dugout canoes for ocean fishing. Able to withstand the rigors of the sea, these canoes were far sturdier than the birchbark canoes common among the Indians of the central and eastern woodlands.

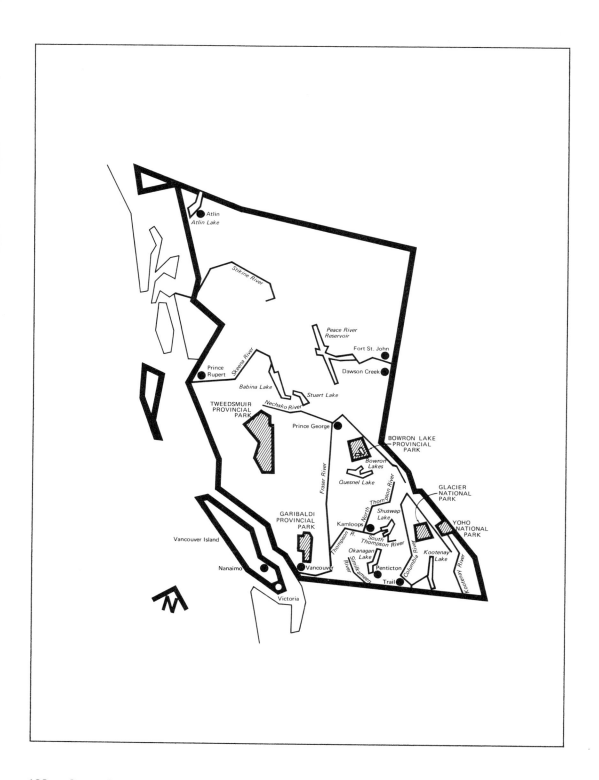

Atlin
Atlin Lake

Stikine River

Peace River
Reservoir

Fort St. John

Prince
Rupert

Skeena River

Dawson Creek

Babina Lake

Stuart Lake

TWEEDSMUIR
PROVINCIAL
PARK

Nechako River

Prince George

BOWRON LAKE
PROVINCIAL
PARK

Fraser River

Bowron
Lakes

Quesnel Lake

GLACIER
NATIONAL
PARK

Thompson River

GARIBALDI
PROVINCIAL
PARK

North

Shuswap
Lake

YOHO
NATIONAL
PARK

Vancouver Island

Kamloops

South
Thompson River

Thompson R.

Okanagan
Lake

Nanaimo

Vancouver

Similkameen River

Penticton

Kootenay
Lake

Columbia River

Kootenay River

Victoria

Trail

British Columbia Routes

Canoeing in mountainous British Columbia, as in its neighbouring province, Alberta, offers violent whitewater rivers of immense size and danger; medium waterways of moderate difficulty for the canoeist with some experience; placid lakes and connecting rivers systems for the enjoyment of the whole family.

Data for the routes in British Columbia has been derived from *British Columbia Canoe Routes*, prepared under the auspices of Canoe British Columbia. The most recent edition of this valuable book contains in-depth descriptions of all the routes and can be obtained from Nunaga Publications, P.O. Box 157, New Westminster, British Columbia, or from retail booksellers. Also available from the same source is an excellent book of maps, *British Columbia Recreational Atlas*.

Fraser River

477 FRASER RIVER (YELLOWHEAD LAKE TO REARGUARD)
Length 46 miles (74 km)
Approx trip time 2 days
Access Yellowhead Pass divide
Maps Canoe River 83D
Mount Robson 83E

478 FRASER RIVER (REARGUARD TO PRINCE GEORGE)
Length 280 miles (451 km)
Approx trip time 7 days
Access Rearguard
Maps Carrot River 83SW
McBride 93SE
McBride 93NE
These maps are to a scale of 1″ = 500,000″

479 FRASER RIVER (PRINCE GEORGE TO QUESNEL)
Length 70 miles (113 km)
Approx trip time 2 days
Access Hudson's Bay Slough, Prince George

Maps Prince George 93G
Quesnel 93B for details of last 2 miles

480 FRASER RIVER (QUESNEL TO SODA CREEK)
Length 53 miles (85 km)
Approx trip time 1 day
Access Fraser River bridge in Quesnel
Map Soda Creek 93B/8W

481 FRASER RIVER (SODA CREEK TO GANG RANCH BRIDGE)
Length 65 miles (105 km)
Approx trip time 2 days
Access Soda Creek
Map Soda Creek 93B/8W

482 FRASER RIVER (GANG RANCH BRIDGE TO BIG BAR CREEK FERRY)
Length 28 miles (45 km)
Approx trip time 1 day
Access Gang Ranch Bridge
Map Taseko Lakes 92 O

483 FRASER RIVER (LILLOOET TO LYTTON)
Length 37 miles (60 km)
Approx trip time 2 days
Access Cayoosh Provincial Park at Lillooet
Map Ashcroft 92 I

484 FRASER RIVER (LYTTON TO NORTH BEND AERIAL FERRY)
Length 27 miles (43 km)
Approx trip time 1 day
Access By a trail from Highway 12 to the beach at the confluence of the Thompson and Fraser Rivers or at Ferry landing, 3/4 of a mile up the Fraser from the confluence
Maps Lytton 92 I/4E
Scuzzy Mountain 92H/13E
Boston Bar 92H/14W

485 FRASER RIVER (NORTH BEND AERIAL FERRY TO ALEXANDRA BRIDGE)

Length 13-1/2 miles (22 km)
Approx trip time 1 day
Access By trail from the west terminal of the North Bend Aerial Ferry which leads to a beach on the west shore.
Maps Boston Bar 92H/14W
Spuzzum 92H/11W

486 FRASER RIVER (ALEXANDRA BRIDGE TO YALE)

Length 12-1/4 miles (20 km)
Approx trip time 1/2 day
Access By Highway 1, north of Spuzzum; the launching area is at Alexandra Bridge
Map Spuzzum 92H/11W
Hope 92H/6

487 FRASER RIVER (YALE TO HOPE)

Length 14 miles (23 km)
Approx trip time 3 - 4 hours
Access By Highway 1 at Yale
Maps Spuzzum 92H/11W
Hope 92H/6

488 FRASER RIVER (AGASSIZ TO GEORGIA STRAIT)

Length 80 miles (129 km)
Approx trip time 2 - 3 days
Access At many excellent launching points including the Rosedale-Agassiz bridge (left bank upstream a little), Harrison Mills, Dewdney, Mission, Albion, Fort Langley, Annacis Island and Point Grey (U.B.C.)
Maps Dominion Map Ltd., map of the Lower Fraser Valley or
Vancouver South 92G/3
Vancouver North 92G/6

489 FRASER RIVER (HOPE TO ENGLISH BAY)

Length 108 miles (174 km)
Approx trip time 3 days
Access Municipal park in Hope (follow the North Arm from New Westminster)
Maps Hope 92H/6W
Harrison Lake 92H/5E

Chilliwack 92H/4E and W
Sumas 92G/1E and W
New Westminster 92G/2E and W
Vancouver South 92G/3E and W
Vancouver North 92G/6E

Thompson River

490 THOMPSON RIVER (CLEARWATER TO KAMLOOPS)

Length 88 miles (142 km)
Approx trip time 2 - 3 days
Access Clearwater
Maps Seymour Arm 82M
Bonaparte Lake 92P
Ashcroft 92 I

491 THOMPSON RIVER (KAMLOOPS LAKE)

Length 26 miles (42 km)
Approx trip time 1 day
Access Kamloops Municipal Park
Map Ashcroft 92 I

492 THOMPSON RIVER (SAVONA TO ASHCROFT)

Length 24 miles (39 km)
Approx trip time 4 to 8 hours
Access Savona
Maps Tranquille River 92 I/15W
Cache Creek 92 I/14E
Ashcroft 92 I/11W

Camping is not organized. Try one mile upstream from Ashcroft on the left bank.

It is an exciting trip in dry country. The river is strong and swift, and wide enough so that alternative courses may be selected at most rapids. However, this trip should be taken only in groups of at least three canoes since mid-stream rescues will probably be necessary.

Strong head winds occur after noon. Be cautious at all bridges.

Distances are measured starting at Savona Bridge and then between rapids. *Start* at the Provincial Government campsite at Savona or at the mouth of the river as it leaves Kamloops Lake. Access is from the left bank just upstream from the bridge or downstream (there may be a parking charge).

Finish just before Ashcroft or the left bank, upstream from the mobile home park.

Distance of rapids:

First bridge rapids   3 miles (scout)
Slough Rapids   2 miles
Second Bridge rapids   3 miles - keep right
Anglesey rapids   3 miles - keep right
Mauvais Roche (Bad Rock rapids)   1 mile
Semlin Rapids   1 mile
Maharg rapids   4 miles

493   THOMPSON RIVER (ASHCROFT TO SPENCES BRIDGE)

Length   22 miles (35 km)
Approx trip time   4 - 8 hours
Access   Ashcroft Bridge
Maps   Ashcroft 92 I/11W
Spences Bridge 92 I/6W
Camping   Unorganized

This section of the Thompson is decidedly more difficult than above Ashcroft.

Rapids distances are measured from Ashcroft Bridge and then between rapids:

Tunnel rapids   2 miles (scout)
Cheetsum rapids   miles (scout)
Black Canyon   1/2 mile

Rapids every 1/2 mile to

Oregon Jack rapids   3 miles
Martel rapids   3 miles
Orchard rapids   1 mile
Nicola River   4 miles
Spences Bridge   1 mile

It's an exciting trip in dry country. The river is strong and swift, and wide enough so that alternative courses may be selected at most rapids. However, this trip should be taken only in groups of at least three canoes since mid-stream rescues will probably be necessary.
Start one mile above Ashcroft Bridge on the left bank or at Ashcroft Bridge.
Finish at Spences Bridge.

494   THOMPSON RIVER (SPENCES BRIDGE TO GOLDPAN, OR ON TO THE NICOAMEN RIVER)

Length   7 miles (11 km) to Goldpan
6 additional miles (10 km) to Nicoamen River

Approx trip time   2 hours to Goldpan; 2 hours further to Nicoamen River
Access   Spences Bridge
Map   Spences Bridge 92 I/6W
Camping   Goldpan Government campsite

Strong head winds occur after noon. Be cautious at all bridges. Distances are measured from Spences Bridge and then between rapids:

Dryrock rapid   1 mile
Graveyard rapids   2 miles (scout)
Nicoamen River   3 miles

All parties must stop at this point. There are grade 4 and 5 rapids immediately below. *Start* anywhere in Spences Bridge.
To *finish*, keep to the left and take out just below the outlet of the Nicoamen River. Extreme caution is necessary because to capsize would be serious.

495   THOMPSON RIVER - NICOAMEN RIVER TO LYTTON

Length   10 miles (16 km)
Approx trip time   2 hours
Access   By railway overpass at Nicoamen
Map   92 I Ashcroft

Vancouver Island

496   CITY OF VICTORIA

Length   11 miles (18 km) (approximately)
Approx trip time   1/2 - 1 day
Access   In Victoria
Maps   City of Victoria and Victoria 92B

497   THETIS LAKE

Length   1-1/2 miles (2.4 km)
Approx trip time   1/2 day
Access   Drive north of Victoria on the Island Highway and turn right a few hundred yards north of the Colwood overpass
Map   Sooke 92B/5E

498   SAN JUAN RIVER

Length   12 miles (19 km)
Approx trip time   1 day from Victoria and return
Access   San Juan River bridge
Maps   SGS No. 1 Vancouver Island or San Juan 92C/9W and E

499   NANAIMO LAKES

Length   6 miles (10 km)
Approx trip time   1 day

Access Turn west 1/4 mile (.4 km) north of the Cassidy Hotel. Drive 10 miles (16 km) and turn left just before the gate.
Map Alberni 92F/1E*

500 NANAIMO RIVER
Length 21 miles (34 km)
Approx trip time 1 day
Access Nanaimo
Maps Nanaimo 92G/4W
Nanaimo Lakes 92F/1E

501 COWICHAN LAKE
Length 24 miles (39 km)
Approx trip time 2 days
Access Cowichan Lake village
Map Haslam Lake 92F/16E and W

502 COWICHAN RIVER
Length 21 miles (34 km)
Approx trip time 1 - 2 days
Access Off Highway 16
Maps Cowichan 92C/16E
Duncan 92B/13W and E

Camping Limited at Skutz Falls; otherwise un-organized

This trip is a difficult one for open canoes and should only be attempted by teams of expert paddlers. For closed boats the canyon offers a challenge.

All Vancouver Island rivers are flash rivers. Cowichan River can be easy in summer but the canyon does have its cascades. Winter rains often swell the river to the point where the canyon will be very heavy going, even for closed boats. As there is a trail alongside much of this, scouting can be done. There is much wildlife and the area is very beautiful.

Cowichan Lake to Skutz Falls is 6 miles. *Start* at the Park in the middle of the town and just before the bridge. There is a mixture of slow and swift sections. Watch for log jams. Slow run-off in summer makes it necessary to walk a canoe in some riffles. Portage around Skutz Falls.

Marie Canyon is 3 miles. First fall rains will begin to swell the river quickly, making the canyon hazardous. Rapids to the

suspension bridge could be impassible. The slow sections are easy, but three cascades might have to be portaged: one is before the Canadian National Railway trestle; two are just past the trestle. *There are dangerous back rollers at low water even for kayaks.*

Marie Canyon to Duncan is 12 miles. The terrain spreads out again but there are some tricky spots which make it interesting going. Watch for log jams. *Finish* at the first bridge, which is close to Duncan.

Directions — Turn west from Duncan on Highway 16. For a shorter, easy run, take River Bottom Road to the river. Otherwise, take either the Skutz Falls road or Cowichan Lake itself.

503 NITINAT TRIANGLE (HOBITON-TSUSIAT-SQUALICUM WATERSHED)
Length Hobiton Lake - 4 miles (6 km)
Tsusiat Lake - 4 miles (6 km)
Squalicum Lake - 2-1/2 miles (4 km)
Approx trip time 3 - 5 days
Access Knob Point picnic site on Nitinat Lake
Alberni
Maps Carmanah 92C/10W
Nitinat 92C/15E

504 GREAT CENTRAL LAKE
Length 20 miles (32 km)
Approx trip time 3-5 days
Access At the end of the main road from Alberni
Maps Provincial Government Horne Lake 92F/7 W*
Great Central 92F/6E and W
Bedwell 92F/5 E (if you are including Della Falls)

505 BAMFIELD INLET
Length 4 miles (6 km)
Approx trip time 1/2 day
Access Inquire locally
Maps Victoria 92B
Cape Flatlery 92C

506 COMOX LAKE
Length 10 miles (16 km)
Approx trip time 1 day
Access Kin Park, 3 miles (5 km) past Cumberland

Map Forbidden Plateau 92F/11E

507 COMOX LITTLE LAKES - WILLEMAR AND FORBUSH
Length 4 miles (6 km)
Approx trip time 1 day
Access By Crown Zellerbach Road at Comox Lake
Maps Forbidden Plateau 92F/11 E

508 CHEMAINUS RIVER MOUTH AND SHOAL ISLANDS
Length 5 miles (8 km)
Approx trip time 1/2-1 day
Access By Chemainus River Bridge
Map Victoria 92B

509 KENNEDY LAKE, KENNEDY RIVER, TOFINO INLET
Length 16 miles (26 km)
Approx trip time 1 day
Access By Kennedy Lake
Maps S.G.S. No. 1 Vancouver Island
Tofino 92F/4 E
Canadian Hydrographic Chart No. 3649
Pacific Coast Tide Tables Volume 6

Immediate Vancouver Area

510 CAPILANO RIVER
Length 3½ miles (5.6 km)
Approx trip time 1/2 day
Access In North Vancouver, below the Capilano Dam at Capilano Canyon Park
Maps Howe Sound/Burrard Inlet, B.C. Dept. of Lands, # Special 5 B South or Vancouver 92G/6E

511 SEYMOUR RIVER
Length 2 miles (3 km)
Approx trip time 45 minutes
Access At the top of Riverside Drive
Maps Howe Sound/Burrard Inlet, B.C. Dept. of Lands, # Special 5 B South or Vancouver 92G/6E

512 DEER LAKE
Length 5/8 mile (1 km)
Approx trip time 2 hours

Access 1/4 mile south of Canada Way on Sperling Avenue
Map Dominion Map Ltd. road map of the Lower Fraser Valley or New Westminster 92G/2W

513 BURNABY LAKE
Length 2½ miles (4 km)
Approx trip time 1/2 day
Access At the south foot of Piper Avenue, city of Burnaby
Map Burnaby Municipality map or New Westminster 92G/2 W

514 BUNTZEN LAKE
Length 3 miles (5 km)
Approx trip time 1 day
Access Drive through Port Moody to Ioco. Turn right and take the Anmore Road
Map Howe Sound/Burrard Inlet, B.C. Dept. of Lands, # Special 5 B South or Coquitlam 92G/7 W

515 SERPENTINE AND NICOMEKL RIVERS
Length 20 and 16 miles respectively (32 and 26 km)
Approx trip time 1 day each
Access From Port Kells (Serpentine); from Latimer Road (Nicomekl)
Map Dominion Map Ltd. map of the Lower Fraser Valley or New Westminster 92G/2W and E

Squamish

516 SQUAMISH RIVER
Length 20 miles (32 km)
Approx trip time 1 day
Access Cheekye
Maps Cheakamus River 92G/14E and W

517 CHEAKAMUS RIVER
Length 6 miles (10 km)
Approx trip time 1/2-1 day
Access Cheekye
Map Cheakamus River 92G/14 E

518 RIVER OF GOLDEN DREAMS (ALTA RIVER)
Length 4 miles (6 km)

Approx trip time 3 hours
Access Alta Lake off Highway 99
Map Pemberton 92J

South Coast

519 RUBY LAKE, SAKINAW LAKE AND AGAMEMNON CHANNEL
Length 3 miles (5 km)
Approx trip time 2 days
Access Earls Cove
Map Marine chart #3589
or Sechelt Inlet 92G/12 W
Texada Island 92F/9

520 NELSON ISLAND, WEST LAKE
Approx trip time 2 days from Vancouver
Access Earls Cove, the northern ferry terminal
on the Sunshine Coast
Map Marine chart #3589 or
Texada Island 92F/9

Lower Fraser Valley

521 CHILLIWACK RIVER (CHILLIWACK LAKE TO VEDDER CROSSING)
Length 30 miles (48 km)
Approx trip time 3 days
Access Take Sardis-Vedder Crossing, turn off
from Trans-Canada Highway. Turn left
at Vedder Crossing at the Chilliwack
River. Paved road gives way to gravel
road beyond the Tamihi Creek bridge.
Map Hope 92H/6

522 CHILLIWACK RIVER CANYON
Length 6 miles (10 km)
Approx trip time 1/2 day
Access About 20 miles (32 km) upstream from
Vedder Crossing
Map Hope 92H/6

523 CHILLIWACK RIVER (SLESSE CREEK TO PONTA VISTA COFFEE SHOP)
Length 10 miles (16 km)
Approx trip time 1/2 day
Access Drive to Vedder Crossing, then 16
miles (26 km) upstream to Slesse
Creek.
Map Hope 92H/6

524 COQUIHALLA RIVER
Length 20 miles (32 km)
Approx trip time 1 day
Access Hope-Princeton Highway to the turn-
off for Kawkawa Lake. From there
the timber company will provide
information.
Map Hope 92H

525 SKAGIT RIVER
Length 10 miles (16 km)
Approx trip time 1 day
Access Skagit River bridge
Map Chilliwack Lake 92H/4 W

526 SUMAS RIVER
Length Up to 10 miles (16 km)
Approx trip time Any time you wish
Access Jack MacDonald Park
Map Dominion Map Ltd. map of the Lower
Fraser Valley or
Sumas 92G/1E

527 PITT LAKE
Length 17 miles (27 km)
Approx trip time 2 days
Access By Lougheed Highway
Map Vancouver 92G

528 WIDGEON CREEK
Length 50 to 100 feet - delta, many inter-
connecting channels
Approx trip time 1/2 - 1 day
Access South end of Pitt Lake
Map Vancouver 92G

529 HAYWARD LAKE
Length 3 miles (5 km)
Approx trip time 1/2 day
Access Stave Falls at the north end of the lake
Map Sumas 92G/1

530 NICOMEN SLOUGH
Length 8 miles (13 km)
Approx trip time 1/2 day
Access 3 miles (5 km) east of Deroche on
Highway 7, turn south on Malcolm Road
Road and put in where the slough
is dammed.
Map Dominion Map Ltd. map of the Lower
Fraser Valley or Sumas 92G/1 E

531 WEAVER LAKE
Length 2 miles (3 km)
Approx trip time 1 day

Both in its history and physical features, the Fraser is one of Canada's most spectacular and truly remarkable rivers.

Access By Lougheed Highway
Map Harrison Lake 92H/5 W

532 ALOUETTE LAKE
Length 10 miles (16 km)
Approx trip time 1-2 days
Access By a sign posted from Haney or make local enquiries
Map Stave Lake 92G/8 W

533 NORTH ALOUETTE RIVER
Length 4 miles (6 km)
Approx trip time 2 hours
Access By Haney, where the road crosses the North Alouette (2nd bridge)
Maps New Westminster 92G/2 E
Coquitlam 92G/7 E
Dominion Map Ltd. road map of the Lower Fraser Valley

534 STAVE LAKE
Length 20 miles (32 km)
Approx trip time 2 days
Access Stave Falls
Map 92G Vancouver

535 HARRISON LAKE
Length 40 miles (64 km)
Approx trip time Plenty of time and be prepared to stay out for a night, or even two, if on a day trip.
Access By the public beach at Harrison Hot Springs or the Greenpoint Provincial Park picnic site, 4 miles north on the east side
Maps Harrison Lake 92H/5 W for south end
Hope 92H and
Vancouver 92G, cover the whole lake

536 HARRISON RIVER
Length 10 miles (16 km)
Approx trip time 6 hours
Access By the public beach at Harrison Hot Springs
Map Harrison Lake 92H/5 W

Similkameen

537 SIMILKAMEEN RIVER, PRINCETON TO KEREMEOS
Length 48 miles (77 km)
Approx trip time 1-2 days

Access By the right bank of the river just east of Princeton, at the road bridge
Maps Princeton 92H/7
Hedley 92H/8
Camping Government campsites at Bromley and Stemwinder

This is a typical interior river valley with scattered deciduous trees along the river banks, replaced by scattered evergreens in the narrow parts of the valley. The road parallels the river and can usually be reached easily.

Rapids at the Bromley campsite continue for 2 miles. There are more rapids just below the Stemwinder campsite. The dam at Hedley may be portaged, the water level falls rapidly and the river is almost dry in August.

Depending on the water level, parts are suitable for experienced white water canoeists only. Otherwise, the river is suitable for open canoes but full precautions for dumping must be observed. Life jackets and rescue lines are essential.

Take the Hope-Princeton Highway 3 to Princeton. Access at the beginning is on the right bank of river just east of Princeton, at the road bridge. Access at the end is on the north bank of the river, just east of Keremeos.

538 KETTLE RIVER
Length 15 miles (24 km)
Approx trip time 1 day
Access Rock Creek, Kelowna Highway, Zamora Mill Site
Map Penticton 82E

539 PENTICTON TO OLIVER (SKAHA AND VASEUX LAKES ARE CONNECTED BY THE OKANAGAN RIVER)
Length 30 miles (48 km)
Approx trip time 1 or more days
Access Penticton
Maps Penticton 82E/5 E
Keremeos 82E/4 E

540 SHUSWAP RIVER
Length 40 miles (64 km)
Approx trip time 2 - 3 days
Access Highway 6 at Cherryville or at the dam at Sugar Lake

541 SHUSWAP RIVER TO SOUTH THOMPSON RIVER

Length   110 miles (177 km)
Approx trip time 5 days
Access   Enderby, by paved road to the bridge over the Shuswap River for the put-in
Map   Ashcroft 92I

South Columbia

542 ARROW LAKES - COLUMBIA RIVER (REVELSTOKE TO HIGH ARROW DAM)

Length   Approximately 200 miles (322 km)
Approx trip time 5 - 10 days
Access   Revelstoke
Maps   A tourist map from the B.C. Provincial Government is probably good enough. Most economical, detailed maps (shore lines only) are on the Columbia River Basin M.S. series. Write:

Map Distribution Office
Department of Mines & Technical Surveys
Ottawa, Ontario.

Ask for maps 15 through 22 and map 24 (25 cents each). Ask for a copy of the Index Sheet. The entire series consists of 97 maps.
or Vernon 92L

543 WHATSHAN RIVER

Length   2 miles (3 km)
Approx trip time 1 hour
Access   Fauquier
Maps   Edgewood 82E/16 E (Edition 1, printed in 1968, does not show relocations of Highway 6)

544 INONOAKLIN CREEK

Length   8-1/2 miles (14 km)
Approx trip time 2 - 4 hours
Access   One mile down the Edgewood turn-off and take the first road to the right. Drive to the wooden bridge over the creek and put in.
Map   Edgewood 82E/16 E

Kootenays

545 KOOTENAY RIVER (CANAL FLATS TO FORT STEELE)

Length   42 miles (68 km)

Approx trip time 3 days
Access   From Highway 95, north of Cranbrook
Maps   Kananaskis Lakes 82J
Fernie 82G
Camping   Along the route, a government camp-site at Wasa and Fort Steel. There is also one at Canal Flats, overlooking Columbia Lake.

For the canal flats to Skookumchuk segment *start* from the south end of the Highway 95 bridge on the downstream side. The river has a mixture of swift sections and slow moving pools. The gravel and mud beds make the rapids straightforward, mostly wide and shallow. Hazards include deadheads, sweepers, overhanging branches and debris jams. Be especially careful in rapids that include sharp turns against rock face which generate strong whirlpools. Most of these can be portaged if seen in time.

The first section is set in wilderness inhabited by all manner of wildlife. This environment is broken only occasionally by the railway on the west side. *Finish* at the bridge at Skookumchuk or continue to the Wasa Bridge.

The second section of this trip, from Skookumchuk to Wasa, passes through well timbered flatland and farmland. Swift sections and slow pools are the dominant features. Expect to encounter a considerable amount of debris, overhanging branches, fallen trees, etc. coming from the rapid eating away of the high muddy banks. Lots of wildlife, ranging from deer to ducks, make for an interesting paddle. The mile above the Wasa Bridge is very slow with mud banks and very typical of the section from Wasa to Fort Steele.

This is a relatively uninteresting, very slow moving stretch. The mile above Wasa Bridge is typical and can be easily viewed from the road. Well timbered farmland, on high mud banks, prevents all but fleeting views of the Rocky Mountains.

Beware of getting stuck on the shallow sand bars.

There is plenty of birdlife, but due to the high banks you are unlikely to spot game. Cows are often about.

The Fort Steele Rapids are an easy grade 2 to 3, depending on the water level. You can easily avoid them by portaging on the east bank along the railroad. The rapids are overlooked by Fort Steele itself.

There is plenty of warning for the rapids. A long straight stretch precedes them. Do not portage on the west bank as the entry of the St. Mary's River will cut you off.

546 WHITESWAN LAKE
Length 3 miles (5 km)
Approx trip time 1 day
Access Whiteswan is sign-posted on Highway 95, about 8 miles (13 km) south of Canal Flats.
Map Kananaskis Lakes 82J

547 WASA LAKE
Length 1-1/2 miles (2.4 km)
Approx trip time 1 hour
Access By Highway 95, 22 miles (35 km) north of Cranbrook
Map Fernie 82G

548 MOYIE LAKE
Length 8 miles (13 km)
Approx trip time 1 day
Access 13 miles (21 km) south of Cranbrook on Highway 95
Map Fernie 82G

549 JIM SMITH LAKE
Length 1/2 mile (.8 km)
Approx trip time 1/2 day
Access 1/2 mile south of Cranbrook
Map Fernie 82G

550 ST MARY LAKE
Length 2 miles (3 km)
Approx trip time 1 day
Access Take the first turn on the left, travelling towards Kimberley from Marysville. It's a good gravel road.
Map Nelson 82F

551 PREMIER LAKE
Length 2-1/2 miles (4 km)
Approx trip time 1 day
Access North of Skookumchuk. Ask the locals for directions.
Map Fernie 82G

Lilloet

552 LILLOOET LAKE
Length 21 miles (34 km)
Approx trip time 3 days from Vancouver
Access From Pemberton proceed to Mount Currie. From Mount Currie proceed east on the south side of the Birkenhead River
Map Pemberton 92J

553 LOWER LILLOOET RIVER (LILLOOET LAKE TO HARRISON LAKE)
Length Approximately 40 miles (64 km)
Approx trip time 2 - 3 days, plus time to get out of Harrison Lake
Access 40 miles (64 km) paddling from Pemberton to the south end of Lilloet Lake or a 4-wheel drive truck ride
Maps Vancouver 92G
Pemberton 92J

554 NAHATLATCH LAKE
Length 8 miles (13 km)
Approx trip time 1 day and some
Access North Bend
Maps Ashcroft 92 I
Hope 92H

North Columbia

555 BIG BEND OF COLUMBIA RIVER (DONALD TO OUTLET OF KINBASKET LAKE)
Length 60-1/2 miles (97.3 km)
Approx trip time 2 1/2 days
Access Donald
Maps M.S. 40, 39, 38, 37, 35, 34, 33 Columbia River Basin and Golden 82N Recently dammed, consult B.C. authorities.

556 BIG BEND OF COLUMBIA RIVER (OUTLET OF KINBASKET LAKE TO MICA CREEK DAM SITE)
Length 28-1/2 miles (45.8 km)
Approx trip time 1 day
Access By a logging skid road that leads to the shore immediately northeast of Kinbasket Lake outlet, from Big Bend Highway
Maps M.S. 33, 32, 31 Columbia River Basin and Golden 82N

Canoe River 83D
Seymour Arm 82M

557 COLUMBIA RIVER BIG BEND (MICA CREEK DAM SITE TO REVELSTOKE)
Length 87 miles (140 km)
Approx trip time 2 days
Access By a construction access road that leads to the dam site from the Big Bend Highway
Maps M.S. 31, 30, 29, 28, 27, 26, 25, 24
Columbia River Basin and
Seymour Arm 82M
Vernon 82L

South Cariboo

558 HORSEFLY RIVER (BLACK CREEK TO HORSEFLY)
Length 20 miles (32 km) approximately
Approx trip time 1/2 - 1 day
Access Black Creek. Enquire locally
Map Quesnel Lake 93A

Bowron Lake Provincial Park

Bowron Lake Provincial Park, located about ninety miles southeast of Prince George in the Cariboo Mountains, is a magnificent wilderness of more than 297,000 acres. It is roughly rectangular in shape and characterized by a system of six major lakes and connecting waterways. The park, which was established in 1961, is named for Bowron Lake, the namesake of a pioneer settler and early Gold Commissioner of nearby Barkerville.

The northwest corner of the park is easily accessible from Quesnel by a seventy mile road that passes through Wells and near Barkerville Historic Park.

Rugged mountains, averaging about 7,000 feet in elevation, form a majestically scenic backdrop for a challenging wilderness adventure. The Park's unique and justly famous water circuit, some seventy-three miles in length, consists of Bowron, Indianpoint, Isaac, Lanezi, Sandy and Spectacle Lakes, a number of smaller lakes and streams and the Bowron and Cariboo Rivers, together with several portages and a canal. The Bowron River drains the west and north sides of the circuit and flows north to enter the Fraser River near Prince George. The Cariboo River drains the east and south sides of the circuit and flows south to join the Quesnel River which is another tributary of the Fraser.

Bowron Lake Park is a wildlife sanctuary and as such is closed to hunting. Visitors can observe and sometimes take big game with their cameras. Moose frequently feed along the waterway and -- although seldom seen — deer are present near the western borders of the park. The high remote country is home to caribou, mountain goat and grizzly bear. In the autumn these bears feed on spawning sockeye salmon on the upper reaches of the Bowron River. Waterfowl share the streams and marshes with that diligent hydraulic engineer, the beaver.

Kamloops trout inhabit all the lakes and streams with Indianpoint and Isaac Lakes usually providing the best fishing. Dolly Varden, lake trout, Rocky Mountain whitefish and kokanee are also present. Do not count on catching fish though — the fishing can vary from poor to excellent depending on the season.

Forest cover is mainly white spruce and alpine fir. Lodge-pole pine grows along the western perimeter and western hemlock and western red cedar thrive on the slopes around Isaac and Lanezi Lakes.

Most visitors to Bowron Lake Provincial Park come to travel the water circuit. For those who do not wish to make the complete loop or who do not have the time to complete it, there is abundant beauty on Bowron Lake and as far as the head of Spectacle Lake; this is an easy journey with no portages.

Accommodation and Camping
Two privately owned lodges are located on the northwest shore of Bowron Lake near the park entrance. These lodges can supply accommodation, meals, canoes, boats and guides. All these facilities depend upon previously concluded arrangements.

Refer to the map for the location of camping areas and shelters. The camping areas have two or three cleared tent spaces, fireplace rings and some have a latrine or pit toilet. The shelters are log cabins —

most in poor condition — with a minimum of equipment.

The shelters are intended for emergency use or to give a party an opportunity to dry out. Do not count on staying in the shelters instead of camping. The shelters may be occupied by others.

An undeveloped campground is situated at park headquarters about a mile from the park entrance on the north shore of Bowron Lake. Vehicles may be parked here. It is intended to develop a campground in the future, but at present all that is available is a parking area, an open field for camping, a few picnic tables and fireplaces and a canoe launching ramp.

Canoes and Safety

The park is good canoe country. A canoe or kayak allows a noiseless approach to photograph moose, beaver and other wildlife. Paddling quietly through these beautiful waterways is a most satisfying experience. Power boats and motors are prohibited in the park except on Bowron Lake and the west side of the circuit as far as the head of Spectacle Lake.

Inexperienced canoeists are well advised to do some practicing and conditioning before leaving home. Learn the "J" stroke for good control and ease of paddling. All travellers should be water wise and observe proper safety procedures. Never overload or stand up in a canoe. Tie gear to the thwarts and gunnels in case of an upset. Stay close to shore on the big lakes and be watchful for sudden squalls. All the major lakes are subject to dangerous winds.

Equipment

Equipment should include a light sixteen foot two-man canoe, three paddles, about 10 feet of 1/2 inch rope — preferably nylon — for lining the canoe, lifejackets (for novices get a type that can be worn at all times while on the water; even experts should wear lifejackets when negotiating rivers), and perhaps a sail if it can be handled. Also needed is a warm sleeping bag and a waterproof tent with a mosquito bar. Waterproof footwear and outer garments are well worth carrying since the park lies in the Interior Wet Belt and has

frequent rainy spells. Sneakers (highcut) should be worn while paddling and as protection against cold water a pair of light hip waders can be most useful. Waders will be particularly useful on Three Mile Creek where the canoe must be lined and pulled over many beaver dams. Tarpaulins and plastic sheets will keep gear dry. An absolute MUST is a canvas, burlap or heavy plastic trash bag to carry your refuse for dumping at the end of the circuit.

559 BOWRON RIVER

Length 72 miles (116 km)
Approx trip time 3 days - minimum
Access Bowron Provincial Park
Maps Indian Point 93H/6 W
Stony Lake 93H/5 E
Narrow Lake 93H/12 E & W
Hutton 93H/13E and W

560 BOWRON LAKES CHAIN

Length 73 miles (117 km)
Approx trip time 7 - 10 days
Access Bowron Lake Provincial Park
Maps McBride 93H

This trip is taken from the Parks Board brochure which also has its own map. Write to:

Department of Travel Industry
Parliament Buildings
Victoria, British Columbia

Anyone contemplating taking the circuit trip should come to the park well prepared and well equipped. While it is true that many canoeists with only limited experience have successfully completed the circuit, good physical condition and good equipment are essential. Since Bowron Lake Provincial Park is essentially an undeveloped wilderness, users of the waterway can expect to experience conditions similar to the hazards and hardships of pioneer travel. At least a week, and preferably 10 days, should be allocated to make the trip. It is quite common to be storm bound for several days.

There are seven portages around the circuit. All the portage trails are in good condition with the exception of the seldom used one along the lower portion of the Isaac River.

The first one, between Bowron and Kibbee Lakes, is 2 miles long and the second, between Kibbee and Indianpoint Lakes is 1-1/4 miles in length. Most canoeists run the navigable portion of the Isaac River but if this is not possible there is a 1-1/4 mile portage of which the last half is quite rough. Canoes have capsized in the fast waters of both the Isaac and Cariboo Rivers.

The posted park information and regulations are there for the benefit of visitors and should be read and understood before travelling into the wilderness. Registration is required for the visitor's own protection.

The Circuit

The circuit can be made anytime through June to the end of October. Many beaches are inundated by high water in June. Flies can be bad in July but the worse of the biting insects is usually over by mid August. Some people prefer September when the deciduous trees along the lakeshores are displaying their fall colours.

Bowron Lake to Isaac Lake

Circumnavigation is made easier by travelling with the water flow (clockwise). The trip begins with the hardest work of the entire journey — a 2 mile portage from Bowron Lake Campground to the beaver dam on Kibbee Creek where the canoe is wetted for the first time. The creek leads into beautiful little Kibbee Lake which is soon crossed to the start of a 1-1/4 mile portage to Indianpoint Lake.

The east end of Indianpoint Lake is marshy but there is a channel marked which leads to a slough with the portage trail at its head. From here the portage to Isaac Lake is less than a mile of fairly easy going. Launch into the small pond and enter Isaac Lake through the canoe slides.

Most people prefer to follow the outer perimeter of Isaac Lake where the camping areas are located. This is the safest and most interesting way to travel.

Isaac River

Near the south end of Isaac Lake, land at the portage marked sign and carefully study the chute on the Isaac River. It has a sharp jog which requires a quick right turn. Depending upon experience a decision must be made whether to portage around the chute or to run it.

Gear should be well wrapped since water is often shipped while negotiating this chute. Lifejackets should be worn. This part of the Issac River is navigable for only about 1/4 mile; the first stretch ends in a large pool at the head of foaming cascades. At the pool there is a large sign indicating a left turn. Land on the left bank and portage past the riotous waters.

At the foot of the cascade there is a choice of either continuing on the portage or taking to the river again. If the choice is to paddle — and most people make this choice — then depending on one's skill, canoes may be launched above or below the chute at this point. If the decision is to launch, study the water in the chute thoroughly before proceeding. Downstream it is a mildly thrilling paddle to a log jam above Isaac River Falls. The short portage to McLeary Lake starts on the right bank of the river above the log jam.

For a worthwhile side trip, take the trail up the east bank of the Isaac River to the falls where the river plunges 35 feet over a ledge.

McLeary Lake to Unna Lake

Speed, well in excess of the current, is a safety factor that assures steerageway on the swift silt-laden Cariboo River between McLeary and Lanezi Lakes. Sweepers — tree trunks in the river usually extending out from the bank across the current — occasionally encountered on the tight curves are the main hazard. If the river is low, as it often is in late summer or autumn, there may not be enough water to float a canoe over some of the wide riffles. In such situations it may be necessary for both bowman and sternman to jump out to lighten the canoe. The lining rope — which should be secured to the stern — will assist in keeping the canoe under control.

There are few places to land along the shore of Lanezi Lake so it is inadvisable to travel if the wind is threatening. The inside perimeter of the lake is the favoured route. Shallows and dead-heads in the narrows between Lanezi and Sandy Lakes demand careful reading of the opaque water.

On the south shore of beautiful Sandy Lake there is a short trail that ascends to Hunter Lake where the fly fishing can be very good. Keen fishermen consider it worthwhile to portage their canoes up to this lake. There are difficult shallows at the outlet of Sandy Lake but a channel can often be found towards the north side.

Below Sandy Lake the Cariboo River flows slack; but the 80 foot high Caribou Falls makes it folly to run beyond Unna Lake. Watch carefully for the narrow entrance to this perfect gem of clear water and sandy shores. The roar of Caribou Falls entices most visitors to walk to the viewpoint by the trail that starts on the southwest shore of Unna Lake.

Unna Lake to Bowron Lake

To continue the circuit from Unna Lake, backtrack about 1/4 mile to the big bend of the Cariboo River where a sign indicates the mouth of Three Mile Creek. This shallow little stream cannot be paddled but there is generally sufficient water in most places to float a canoe. The simplest way to make this passage is to walk the mid-channel, lining the canoe. An occasional shove on the stern when the keel touches the gravel is usually all that is needed. Deeper water is found above the numerous beaver dams on the upper reaches. Try not to disturb the dams when hauling the canoe across them.

The two short portages between Babock and Skoi Lakes and between Skoi and Spectacle Lakes are easily made. There is also a canal between Skoi and Spectacle Lakes.

Once afloat on Spectacle Lake it is all downstream paddling. This is fascinating canoe water, quite different in character from the more truly mountain lakes on the eastern and southern sections of the circuit. There are shallows and sand beaches where the water may be warm enough in midsummer for swimming. The passage is navigable on either side of the islands in Swan Lake but keep close to the west side to find the outlet stream to the Bowron River. As the channel is marked and the current is slack there is little difficulty in reaching the river. The current in the Bowron River is also slack as it meanders through a magnificent marsh where moose and waterfowl may very likely be seen.

It is difficult to land in many places along the shore of Bowron Lake because the prevailing high water has undermined the trees. No camping areas are available. The landing point for Bowron Lake Campground is in Kibbee Creek.

Circuit Mileages

Portage:	Bowron Lake to Kibbee Creek	2	miles
Paddle:	Kibbee Lake	1-1/2	miles
Portage:	Kibbee Lake to Indianpoint Lake	1-1/4	miles
Paddle:	Indianpoint Lake	4	miles
Portage:	Indianpoint Lake - slough at east end - to Isaac Lake	1	mile
Paddle:	Isaac Lake - west arm	4-1/4	miles
Paddle:	Isaac Lake - main lake	19-1/2	miles
Portage and paddle:	Isaac River - Isaac Lake to McLeary Lake (about 1 mile can be paddled)	1-3/4	miles
Paddle:	McLeary Lake	3/4	mile
Paddle:	Cariboo River - McLeary Lake to Lanezi Lake	3-1/4	miles
Paddle:	Lanezi Lake	9-1/4	miles
Paddle:	Cariboo River - Lanezi Lake to Sandy Lake	3/4	mile
Paddle:	Sandy Lake	3	miles
Paddle:	Cariboo River - Sandy Lake to Three Mile Creek	2-1/4	miles
Lining:	Three Mile Creek - Cariboo River to Babcock Lake	3/4	mile
Paddle:	Babcock Lake	1-3/4	miles
Portage:	Babcock Lake to Skoi Lake	1/2	mile
Portage or canal:	Skoi Lake to Spectacle Lake	1/4	mile
Paddle:	Spectacle Lakes - including Swan Lake	7-3/4	miles

Paddle:	Swan Lake outlet - Spectacle Lake to Bowron River	1/4 mile
Paddle:	Bowron River - Swan Lake outlet to Bowron Lake	2-1/2 miles
Paddle:	Bowron Lake	4-1/2 miles

Circuit Mileage Totals

Portages	5 or 6-1/2
Canal	1/2
Lining	3/4
River paddling	10 or 9††
Lake paddling	56-3/4
TOTAL	73 miles (117 km)

†† If Isaac River cannot be run.

The following addresses will be helpful in providing information about the Bowron Lake Provincial Park:

Provincial Parks
Parks Branch
Department of Recreation and Conservation
Parliament Buildings
Victoria, British Columbia

Fish and Wildlife
Fish and Wildlife Branch
Department of Recreation and Conservation
Parliament Buildings
Victoria, British Columbia

Travel, Tourism and Accommodation
Department of Travel Industry
Parliament Buildings
Victoria, British Columbia

A contoured map of Bowron Lake Park at a scale of 1 inch to 1 mile, can be obtained by writing to:
Director,
Surveys and Mapping Branch
Geographic Division
Department of Lands, Forests
  and Water Resources
Parliament Buildings
Victoria, British Columbia

There is a charge of 60¢ for the map and applicants are requested to enclose the correct payment with their orders, as Government publications must be paid in advance. Orders to points within Canada may be sent C.O.D. upon request. For orders to be delivered within the Province the 5% social services

tax must be added. Cheques or money orders should be made payable to the Minister of Finance for the Province of British Columbia. In addition, there is a 25¢ handling charge on all orders. Addresses of lodge and store owners are Bowron Lake Park are:

R. Becker
Bowron-Cariboo Lodge
Box 129
Wells, British Columbia

R. McKitrick
Bowron Lake Lodge
Box 265
Wells, British Columbia

Mrs. J. DeVaul
The Wilderness Store
Wells
British Columbia

Nechako

561 NECHAKO RIVER (KENNY DAM TO FORT FRASER)

Length Approximately 40 miles (64 km)
Approx trip time 2 days
Access Vanderhoof
Maps Nechako River 93F
Fort Fraser 93K

Take the road from Vanderhoof to Kenny Dam. Cross the dam; immediately after the dam is a small road to the right. Drive or portage 5 miles (8 km) to Cheslatta Falls. The trip *starts* here at the confluence of the Cheslatta and Nechako Rivers. The Nechako cannot be run above this point because there is no water. There are three moderate rapids in the upper 10 miles. These should be reconnoitered before running.

It is really worthwhile to explore the bottom of the Nechako Canyon near the end of the portage. You will see a huge pothole 20 feet wide and 30 feet deep, stone bridges and unusual architecture.

Fishing is excellent all along the river.

The trip may be terminated at Fort Fraser or may be continued on to Prince

A glacier feeding into the Stikine River. During the Klondike gold rush the Stikine provided an important access route to the Yukon. Today it is a transportation route to Alaska. During summer riverboats make weekly trips to and from the northern state, but the river retains much of its wilderness beauty.

George. For further information see Mr. Reedland at the hardware store in Fort Fraser.

562 STEWART RIVER - NECHAKO RIVER (FORT ST. JAMES TO PRINCE GEORGE)

Length Approximately 100 miles (161 km)
Approx trip time 2 - 4 days
Access Fort St. James
Maps Fort Fraser 93K
McLeod Lake 93J
Prince George 93G

563 CROOKED RIVER - CONTINENTAL DIVIDE (SUMMIT LAKE TO MCLEOD LAKE)

Length 50 to 70 miles total (80 - 113 km), but the trip can be divided into many smaller trips as Highway 97 is never far from the river.

Approx trip time 1 - 2 days
Access Highway 97 to put-in at the Summit Lake public landing
Maps Summit Lake 93J/7E
Tacheeda Lakes 93J/10E
McLeod Lake 93J/15E and W

Coastal

564 PRINCE RUPERT TO KLOIYA BAY
Length 14 miles (23 km)
Approx trip time Half day
Access New Flats in Prince Rupert
Maps Charts #3735 and #3705
Prince Rupert 103J

Stellako River

565 STELLAKO RIVER

The short, 5 miles (8 km) river empties Francis Lake into Fraser Lake. It is a shallow, rocky little river which is very fast and not really suitable for canoes unless they are decked.

The river is great for liferafts. There is a small waterfall about 6 feet high, about 2/3 to 3/4 of the way down. Although some canoeists have run it, a portage is recommended.

See Mr. Reedland at the hardware store in Fort Fraser for details and/or liferafts.

 ## Map Sources

Canada Mapping Office, 615 Booth Street, Ottawa, Ontario is the chief supplier of topographical maps. Maps for the Province are also available from the following map dealers in British Columbia:

Agassiz Hardware
Box 37
7054 Pioneer St.
Agassiz, B.C.

Cliff Kopas Store
Bella Coola Supply Co. Ltd.
Bella Coola, B.C.

Gleig Bros Ltd.
Sporting Goods
52 Yale Road E.
Chilliwack, B.C.

J. L. Parker
1130 Fitzgerald St.
Courtenay, B.C.

Dutchie's Sport Shop Ltd.
P.O. Box 481
Golden, B.C.

E & D Sports Shop Ltd.
22344 Lougheed Highway
Haney, B.C.

Frontier Sporting Goods
P.O. Box 757
Hope, B.C.

Graphic Supply & Service Centre
254 Seymour St.
Kamloops, B.C.

K.T. Sporting Goods Ltd.
266 City Centre
Kitimat, B.C.

Reliable Cycle & Sport Shop
20478 Fraser Highway
P.O. Box 55
Langley, B.C.

R. Selbie
P.O. Box 844
Mission City, B.C.

Skips Sporting Goods Ltd.
Box 1386
Mission City, B.C.

Nanaimo News Stand
8 Church St.,
Nanaimo, B.C.

Nixons Book Store Ltd.,
635 Clarkson St.
New Westminster, B.C.

Osoyoos Sport & Camera Shop
189 Main St.
Box 507
Osoyoos, B.C.

Relaine's Sport Shop
2669 Shaughnessy St.
Port Coquitlam, B.C.

Kamsport Marine
1514 Lorne St.,
Kamloops, B.C.

Western Mapping Ltd.
P.O. Box 590
Kamloops, B.C.

Treadgold Sporting Goods
1615 Pandosy St.
Kelowna, B.C.

Golden Eagle Trading Post
Box 174
Radium Hot Springs, B.C.

Cloverdale Sporting Goods Ltd.
5783 Pacific Highway
Surrey, B.C.

Robert E.A. Ball
Guide & Outfitter
Telegraph Creek, B.C.

A.B.C. of Canada
1822 West 4th Ave.
Vancouver 9, B.C.

Arlberg Ski Hut
Sporting Goods
2401 Cambie St.
Vancouver, B.C.

Dominion Map Ltd.
571 Howe St.
Vancouver 1, B.C.

I.B. Guest Ltd.,
345 George St.,
Prince George, B.C.

Evergreen Supply Ltd.
Box 585
Princeton, B.C.

Graham Island Gift Shop
Box 111
Queen Charlotte City, B.C.

Information Canada Centre
800 Granville St.
Vancouver, B.C.

Map Distribution Office
Geological Survey
100 West Pender St.
Vancouver 2, B.C.

Picadilly Enterprises Ltd.,
2215 Birch St.
Vancouver, B.C.

Department of Lands & Forests
Map & Photo Sales
Map Production Division
Victoria, B.C.

Island Blue Print & Map Co. Ltd.
1124 Blanchard St.
Victoria, B.C.

For a provincial road map and a good lure booklet containing a lot of information write:

Department of Travel Industry
Parliament Buildings
Victoria, B.C.

For Bowron Lakes, Wells Gray, Mount Robson, Strathcona and Tweedsmuir Provincial Parks, write:

Parks Branch
Department Recreation & Conservation
Victoria, B.C.

 Outfitters

Vancouver Area

A to Z Rental Centre
4311 Buchanan
Burnaby, B.C.
 (Canoes)

Ambleside Boat Rentals & Marina
1352 Argyle Ave.
West Vancouver, B.C.
 (Canoes)

The Jib Set Sailing School Ltd.
1010 Beach Ave.
Vancouver 5, B.C.
 (Canoes)

Richmond Rentals
665 Buswell St.
Vancouver, B.C.
 (Canoes)

B & D Outdoor Equipment
5566 Mavis
Burnaby, B.C.
 (Canoe Rental)

Portaging a dugout canoe at Murchison's Rapids along the North Thompson River, November 1871. These men were part of an expedition sent out by the Geological Survey of Canada to determine the best route for the Pacific railway.

Flare Craft Marine
2155 Rosser
Burnaby, B.C.
  (Canoes)

Tepee Sporting Goods Ltd.
1601 West 5th Avenue
Vancouver, B.C.
  (Canoes and equipment)

Port Coquitlam

Alouette Boat Sales and Rentals
1780 Fremont
Port Coquitlam, B.C.
  (Canoes, Canoe Safaris)

Cariboo

Mr. Roy McKitrick
Bowron Lake Lodge & Resorts Ltd.
740 Naughton St.
Quesnel, B.C.
or
Chain of Lakes Canoe Outfitters
  and Lakeshore Campsite
Quesnel, B.C.
  (Canoe outfitters)

Lowry's Lodges Ltd.
Cariboo Island Boat Supply
Hunting and Fishing Lodge
Box 40
Horsefly, B.C.
Radio-Phone via Williams Lake
  (Canoes)

Four Lakes Resorts Ltd.
Big Lake Ranch P.O., B.C.
  (Canoes)

J Bar T Guest Ranch
Box 65
70 Mile House, B.C.
  (Canoes)

Canim Lake Resort
Box 96
Canim Lake. B.C.
  (Canoes)

North Country Lodge
Box 100
Horsefly, B.C.
  (Canoes)

Air Charter Services

Canoeists requiring airlift may contact in the planning stages the following commercial carriers:

Airwest Airlines Ltd.
468 Cowley Cres.
Vancouver, B.C.

Alert Bay Air Service Ltd.
Box 317
Campbell River, B.C.

Columbia Airlines Ltd.
Box 1565
Prince George, B.C.

Harrison Airways Ltd.
479 Bell-Irving St.
Vancouver, B.C.

Island Airlines Ltd.
Box 1510
Campbell River, B.C.

North Coast Air Service Ltd.
Box 610
Prince River, B.C.

Northern Thunderbird Airlines Ltd.
Box 1510
Prince George, B.C.

Wilderness Airlines Ltd.
Box 1659
Williams Lake, B.C.

In addition to these companies and their home bases, the Ministry of Transport lists the following floatplane bases:

Alert Bay, Atla Lake, Atlin, Bedwell Harbour, Bella Bella, Bella Coola, Bull Harbour, Cariboo Canim Ranch, Comox, Burns Lake, Co-op Bay, Dawson Creek, Dease Lake, Eddontenajon, Ethelda Bay, Fort Langley, Fort Nelson, Fort St. James, Fort St. John, Fort Ware.

Kelsey Bay, Kinaskan Lake, Kugami Lake, Masset, Mansons Landing, Mayne Island, Moyie Lake, Nakusp, Nanaimo, Nelson Forks, Nimpoh, Ocean Falls, Penticton, Pitt Meadows, Port Alberni, Port Washington, Powell Lake, Prince Rupert, Queen Charlotte City, Quesnel, Sechelt, Shawnigan Lake, Sproat Lake, Stewart, Sullivan Bay.

Summit Lake, Tabor Lake, Tahsis, Takla Landing, Tchesinkut Lake, Terrace, Tofino, Tyhee Lake, Ucleulet, Vernon, Victoria, Watson Lake, Whaletown, Zeballos.

The following companies provide river raft trips:

Canadian River Expeditions Ltd.
1412 Sandhurst Place
West Vancouver, B.C.
Chilcotin and Fraser Rivers

Cascade River Holidays Ltd
Box 46441
Vancouver, B.C.
*Chilcotin, Fraser, Similkameen and
Thompson Rivers*

Kechika River Tours
c/o No. 302
1155 Beach Ave.
Vancouver, B.C.
Kechika River

Rocky Mountain Raft Tours
Box 1771
Banff, Alta.
Kootenay River, B.C.

Facing page. Mush Lake, in Kluane National Park, is typical of the many lakes in the Yukon which offer solitude, fresh air and clear, clean water. The surrounding park includes Canada's highest mountains and most spectacular icefields. As well, it is one of the few remaining locations of major populations of grizzly bears and curly-horned Dall sheep. Other animals to be found in the park include moose and caribou, wolves and wolverines, and large numbers of golden eagles and ptarmigans.

YUKON
TERRITORY

The Yukon Territory (207,076 square miles) is a land of mighty mountains and rivers. Mountain chains wrinkle the interior and form the territory's natural boundaries; to the south-southwest are the Campbell Range and the St. Elias Mountains, dividing the Yukon from British Columbia and Alaska. The Ogilvie and British Mountains separate the Yukon from Alaska on the west. The Richardson, Selwyn and Logan Mountains form the eastern boundary with the Northwest Territories. There are twenty mountain peaks towering to at least 10,000 feet; Mount Logan, at 19,850 feet, is the highest in Canada. The Arctic Ocean coastline stretches for 200 miles.

In the mountain passes run the great rivers. More than 560 miles of the Yukon River (1,979 miles in total) runs northwest through the territory, gathering in its tributaries — the Salmon, Teslin, White, Hess, Stewart, McQuesten, Macmillan and Pelly Rivers. The Porcupine River, rising in the territory, joins the Yukon River in Alaska. The Liard River swings southeast into British Columbia and then east to join the Mackenzie River. The Ogilvie-Peel Rivers, with their tributaries the Blackstone, Hare, Wind, Bonnet Plume and Snake, also flow to the Mackenzie, northeastward. And these are only the larger rivers.

The Alaska Highway, which runs for 1,523 miles from Dawson Creek, British Columbia to Fairbanks, Alaska, crosses 600 miles of southern Yukon and connects at strategic points with a web of eleven territorial highways. The Canol Road connects Yukon with the Northwest Territories.

The 110 mile White Pass & Yukon Railway connects the territorial capital, Whitehorse, with the Pacific Ocean at Skagway, Alaska; it was one of the first lines in the world to establish a water-rail-highway service. Adequate scheduled and charter airline services complete the versatile transportation system of the territory.

Whitehorse, with a population of 10,000, is home to half the people of the territory. That figure doubled during the Klondike gold rush in the early 1900's and again during World War II.

The mountains give the Yukon its primary resources: gold, silver, base metals and asbestos. Recent exploration has revealed iron deposits and exploration for petroleum and natural gas is now taking place off the Arctic coast. Fur trapping, commercial fishing, some lumbering and tourism all contribute to the economy.

The territory's only national Park is Kluane, in the southwestern corner. It is a region of mountains, glaciers and unspoiled nature.

 Climate

The climate of the Yukon is moderate in comparison to that of the Northwest Territories, softened by the prevailing winds from the Pacific and relatively dry. Daylight hours in summer are long and conducive to lush growth. The following summer climate table for the territory's two regions allows the visiting canoeist to prepare to meet conditions adequately:

Yukon Territory	Mean temperatures In Fahrenheit (Celsius)				Rainfall In Mean Inches (Millimetres)	
	Min		Max			
Southern (Whitehorse)						
June	42.7	(5.9)	65.7	(18.7)	1.13	(28.7)
July	46.5	(8.1)	68.1	(20.1)	1.31	(33.3)
August	43.9	(6.6)	64.5	(18.1)	1.42	(36.1)
Central (Dawson)						
June	44.1	(6.7)	69.8	(21.0)	1.45	(36.8)
July	47.9	(8.8)	71.9	(22.2)	2.09	(53.1)
August	43.4	(6.3)	66.2	(19.0)	1.99	(50.6)
Northern (Old Crow)						
June	34	(1.1)	83	(28.3)	0.25	(6.4)
July	32	(0.0)	82	(27.8)	1.26	(32.0)
August	34	(1.1)	74	(23.3)	1.05	(26.7)

Fishing

Territorial sport fish are found in abundance in even the most accessible regions, which is a boon for tourism. Somewhat untypically, Yukon lists species which may be caught along its main highways (this suggests that off the highways anglers might have even better success). In addition to the grayling, northern pike and lake trout found in all regions, the following additional species are to be found in specific areas:

Alaska Highway   - Dolly Varden, salmon, rainbow, inconnu
Haines Road   - salmon, Dolly Varden
Mayo-Dawson Roads   - inconnu, salmon, cisco
Carcross area   - cisco
Watson Lake - Carmacks Road - rainbow trout

History

Explorer-fur traders entered the Yukon Territory almost half a century after the discovery of the Mackenzie River in 1789 by Alexander Mackenzie. Thomas Simpson of the Hudson's Bay Company travelled westward along the territorial coast to Point Barrow, Alaska, in 1837, and fellow trader Robert Campbell located the headwaters of the Stikine River one year later, and the Pelly River in 1840.

In 1842, trader Alexander Hunter Murray travelled overland and established Fort Yukon in Russian Alaska, while Campbell extended his exploration of the interior.

Then came the dormant years until prospectors started drifting inland via the Mackenzie and Liard Rivers, finding some gold in the Yukon River valley. But the discovery of gold on the Klondike River in 1898 sparked one of the most famous gold rushes in history.

Adventurers came overland from the east and by river from the Pacific. Swelling tent cities became, almost overnight, communities of more than 40,000 people. Poet Robert W. Service and novelist Jack London eulogized it all. As of 1966, frontier recovery methods and modern extraction plants had produced $300 million worth of gold. Restored vintage buildings and sternwheel steamboats at Dawson are the greatest tourist attraction of the territory. A World War II "invasion" of Canadian and U.S. troops created another great, short-term population explosion during the building of the Alaska Highway and the Canol Road.

The federal government created the Northwest Territories in 1895. In 1898, the Yukon was made a separate territory with local government, administered today by a commissioner, two deputy commissioners and seven elected council members.

The Yukon first captured the imagination of adventuring spirits in the days of the Klondike gold rush. Once the home of the miner, hunter, trapper and explorer, in recent years the territory has attracted both the naturalist and the sportsman. The Yukon is renowned for the magnificence of its mountain scenery and wilderness life.

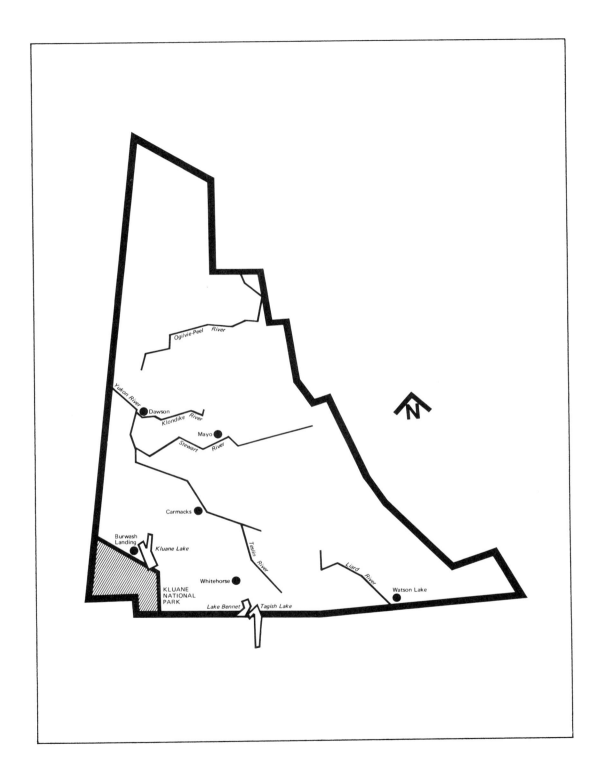

Ogilvie-Peel River

Yukon River

Dawson

Klondike River

Mayo

Stewart River

Carmacks

Burwash
Landing

Kluane Lake

KLUANE
NATIONAL
PARK

Whitehorse

Teslin River

Lake Bennet

Tagish Lake

Liard River

Watson Lake

N

Yukon Territory Routes

While the Yukon Territory is large, and relatively distant for most of us, it is readily accessible by rail, road and air.

The three main rivers — the Yukon, Teslin and Stewart Rivers — require the normal degree of canoeing skill and caution. Fourteen other important rivers, however, should be attempted only by very expert canoeists. They are the Big Salmon, Klondike, North Klondike, Ogilvie, Peel, MacMillan, Ross, Nisultin, Bell, Porcupine, Pelly, Sixty Mile, White and Firth Rivers. The above, together with four large interconnecting lakes — Bennett, Tagish, Atlin and Marsh — are described below in some detail.

The lesser travelled rivers of the Yukon — Tatdonak, Forty Mile, Blackstone, Blow, Yusezyu, Thomas, Anderson, Liard and Francis Rivers — are not detailed in this book.

All canoeists not resident in the Yukon are required to report to the Royal Canadian Mounted Police at Whitehorse, Carmacks, Dawson City and at any other detachments on the canoeist's route of travel, the names of everyone in their party and the estimated times of arrival at planned travel points. These precautions are for the welfare of the traveller.

Most Travelled Rivers

566 YUKON RIVER
Length   530 miles (853 km)
Access   At Alaska Highway dam, (Milepost 890, 1,432 km) access to Lewes River Clinton Creek, Yukon Territory
Maps   Whitehorse 105D
Laberge 105E
Glenlyon 105L
Carmacks 115 I
Snag 115J
Stewart River 115O
Dawson 116B,C

From its source, the Lewes River Tributary at Marsh Lake, to its mouth at the Yukon-Alaska Boundary, the Yukon River is 530 miles long. Its mainstream is joined by several branches that are important rivers in their own rights.

Start at Milepost 890, Alaska Highway, down the Lewes River, Miles Canyon, Schwatka Lake, Whitehorse (city), passing the junction of the Takhini River, down Lake Laberge to Thirty Mile Stretch.

Continue from Hootalinqua village at the junction of Teslin River, the junctions of Big Salmon and Little Salmon Rivers, Carmacks village, Five Finger Rapids, Rink Rapids, Fort Selkirk at the junction of Pelly River, pass the junction of White River, Stewart River and the village of Dawson City at the junction of the Klondike River to *finish* at the Alaska Boundary or to continue along for another 175 miles (282 km) and the Arctic Circle.

567 TESLIN RIVER
Length   260 miles (418 km)
Approx trip time   13 days
Access   At Teslin town (Mile 804, Alaska Highway)
Maps   Teslin 105C
Whitehorse 105D
Laberge 105E
Glenlyon 105L
Carmacks 115 I

Start from Teslin and finish at the village of Hootalinqua.

568 STEWART RIVER
Length   360 miles (579 km)
Approx trip time   14 days
Access   At the junction of Beaver River 14 miles upstream from the abandoned village of Lansing
Maps   Nadaleen River 106C
Lansing 105N

Mayo 105M
McQuesten 115P
Stewart River 115 O

Start from the access point and **finish** at Dawson City. Pass the Keno-Ladue River junction, Seven Mile Canyon, Lansing River, Lansing, the junction of Hess River, Horseshoe Slough, Five Mile Rapids, Three Mile Rapids, Fraser Falls, Gordon Landing, Mayo, Stewart Crossing, McQuesten Airstrip, Stewart River (an abandoned village) to join the main Yukon River and **finish** at Dawson City.

Four Interconnecting Lakes

569 BENNETT, TAGISH, ATLIN AND MARSH LAKES

Access   At Bennett, British Columbia
Maps   Atlin 104N
Skagway 104M
Whitehorse 105D

This conglomerate of intermingling lakes and fjordlike arms weaves from northern British Columbia into Yukon Territory and back again. The tangle is accessible from many points by rail and highways. It may suit both the placid and more active canoeist.

570 TAGISH LAKE - ATLIN

Access   Bennett, B.C.
Maps   Same as previous route

Swing south from the centre of Tagish Lake, down its Tako Arm to Graham Inlet, B.C. east to Atlin village on Atlin road.

571 TAGISH LAKE - BEN-MY-CHREE

Access   Bennet, B.C.
Maps   Same as route 569

Start as in route 570, continue south past Graham Inlet to the abandoned settlements of Hale, Kirtland, Engineer and Ben-My-Chree.

572 TAGISH LAKE - TUTSHI LAKE

Access   Bennett, B.C.
Maps   Same as route 569

Follow route 571 and continue to **finish** in Tutshi Lake.

573 WHITE RIVER

Length   180 miles (290 km)
Approx trip time   8 days
Access   At Snag
Maps   Snag 115J,K
Stewart River 115 O, N

Start 15 miles upstream from Snag, pass the junction of the Donjek River, join mainstream Yukon River at the settlement of Stewart River and paddle north to **finish** at Dawson City.

574 BELL AND PORCUPINE RIVERS

Length   508 miles (181 km)
Approx trip time   18 days
Access   From Summit Lake on the Yukon/ Northwest Territories boundary
Maps   Bell River 116P   Old Crow 116 O, N
U.S. Army Map Service
Corps of Engineers Series Q501
Coleen, Alaska NQ7, 8 - 1
Black River, Alaska NQ7, 8-5
Fort Yukon, Alaska NQ5, 6 - 8

Start at Summit Lake, continue down the Little Bell River, onto the Bell River past the Lapierre House trading post and a junction with the mainstream Porcupine River. Paddle north and west, pass the junctions of Berry and Rat Indian Creeks, Driftwood River, Lord Creek, and the settlement of Old Crow. Pass Caribou Bar Creek, Ramparts House (abandoned), cross the Yukon-Alaska boundary at the junction of Sunaghun Creek.
Continue along the Upper Ramparts section of Porcupine River, pass the junction of Salmon Trout River at Old Ramparts House (abandoned), Red Gate, Canyon Village, the Lower Ramparts section of the Porcupine River and Joe Ward Camp (abandoned). **Finish** at Fort Yukon, two miles above the junction of the Porcupine and the Yukon Rivers.

575 OGLIVIE AND PEEL RIVERS

Length   430 miles (692 km)
Approx trip time   3 weeks
Access   At the Ogilvie River bridge, Yukon Territory
Maps   Ogilvie River 116F,G
Wind River 106E
Martin House 106K

Fort McPherson 106M
Hart River 116H
Snake River 106F
Trail River 106L

Start where the bridge crosses the Ogilvie River at Mile 123 on the Dempster Highway, to the junction of the Ogilvie with the Blackstone River which then becomes Peel River.

"Mileages" established on the 1971 rivers survey mark the part of the route that is *extremely* hazardous with rapids, falls and portages on the Peel River.

The route follows past the junction of Hart River, Aberdeen Falls, past the junctions of Wind River, Mountain Creek, Bonnet Plume, Snake, Caribou, Trail, Road, Satah Rivers, Fort McPherson, Mackenzie River, East Channel of Mackenzie Delta. *Finish* at the town of Inuvik in the N.W.T.

576 BIG SALMON RIVER

Length   247 miles (397 km)
Approx trip time   10 days
Access   At Quiet Lake
Maps   Quiet Lake 105F
Laberge 105E
Carmacks 115 I

Start at Quiet Lake, continue through Sandy Lake, Big Salmon Lake, Big Salmon River, past the South Big Salmon River and North Big Salmon River junctions. Where the Big Salmon River joins the main Yukon River, the trip extends a further 77 miles to the village of Carmacks.

577 NORTH KLONDIKE AND KLONDIKE RIVERS

Access   By Dempster Highway
Map   Dawson 116B,C

These two famous rivers of the spectacular Gold Rush of 1897-98 join at right angles, 30 miles upstream from Dawson City, which is situated at the confluence with the mainstream Yukon River at Dawson.

The North Klondike parallels Dempster Highway, which gives access to it. Paddling down it to the Klondike proper and swinging west, the canoeist parallels the Klondike Highway into Dawson. This section is a one day paddle.

578 MACMILLAN RIVER

Length   145 miles (233 km)
Approx trip time   6 days
Access   At Russell Creek tributary mouth
Maps   Tay River 105K
Lansing 105N
Mayo 105M
Glenlyon 105L

There are three alternative means of access: by paddling upstream from Pelly Crossing on the Pelly River, 160 miles; by charter aircraft (expensive and landing area doubtful); road access by the Canol Road which crosses the upper reaches of the South MacMillan River (branch).

From Russel Creek the MacMillan flows west, past its South Fork junction and those of the Moose, Kalzas and Pelly Rivers to Pelly Crossing on the Klondike Highway.

579 PELLY RIVER

Length   249 miles (401 km)
Approx trip time   8 days
Access   At Ross River settlement
Maps   Quiet Lake 105F
Tay River 105K
Glenlyon 105L
Carmacks 115 I

Start from Ross River settlement and continue to Fort Selkirk on the Yukon River. From the Faro Bridge Crossing, pass the junctions of Anvil Creek, Glenlyon River, Harvey Creek, MacMillan River, Granite Canyon, Pelly Crossing (over Klondike Highway) and Bradens Canyon to the junction of the Pelly and Yukon Rivers. *Finish* at Fort Selkirk (abandoned).

580 ROSS RIVER

Length   150 miles (241 km)
Approx trip time   7 days
Access   By Canol Road or charter aircraft to John Lake
Maps   Sheldon Lake 105J
Tay River 105K

Take the Ross River to a deep canyon through Sheldon, Field and Lewis Lakes, past the Prevost River junction, Prevost Canyon, Skookum Rapids, Otter Creek Canyon and Ross Canyon to *finish* at the settlement of Ross River on the Canol Road.

581 NISUTLIN RIVER

Length   110 miles (177 km)
Approx trip time   9 days
Access   Mile 42 Canol Road
Maps   Quiet Lake 105F
Teslin 105C

Start where the Nisutlin River crosses
Canol Road, pass the junctions of Thirty
Mile Creek and Wolf River and *finish*
at the mouth of Nisutlin River and Teslin
Lake at the settlement of Teslin or at
Johnsons Crossing on the Alaska Highway
at the mouth of Teslin Lake.

582 SIXTY MILE RIVER

Length   About 110 miles (177 km)
Approx trip time   6 days
Access   At the mouth of Glacier Creek
Maps   Dawson 116C,B
Stewart River 115N,O

Start at the abandoned settlement of
Glacier Creek at the creek mouth and Sixty
Mile River, pass the junctions of California,
Enchantment, Fifty Mile, and Matson Creeks
to junction with the mainstream Yukon River
at the abandoned settlement of Ogilvie and
paddle north to *finish* at Dawson City.

583 FIRTH RIVER

Maps   Davidson Mountains 117B
Herschel Island 117D
Demarcation Point 117C

The last 70 miles were surveyed:
The Firth River rises in Alaska,
flows 90 miles (145 km) through the British
Mountains in Yukon, lowland tundra and Arctic
Coastal plain. Inuvik, Northwest Territories,
lies 160 miles east of the river basin; Old
Crow, Yukon Territory, is 60 miles to the
south. Firth is a canoe route that is more
remote, isolated and vulnerable to weather
than any other in Canada.
It is for very experienced canoeists,
who should preview the proposed route from
the air and, while tripping, carry a portable
communications radio set. It is only for
kayak, covered canoe and top wilderness
experts.
The above segment was surveyed by chartered floatplane from Mackenzie River settlements to the only landing, Margaret Lake, 72
miles from river mouth, and *start.*
Finish on the Arctic Coastal plain
near an unnamed lake adjoining Kugaryuk
Creek. Portage three miles over hummocky tundra from the river to await pick-up by charter floatplane to Inuvik.

 Map Sources

Canada Mapping Office, 615 Booth Street, Ottawa, Ontario is the chief supplier of
topographical maps. Maps for the Yukon are available from the following agents:

Mining Recorder
Department of Indian Affairs and
  Northern Development
Dawson, Yukon Territory and
Watson Lake, Yukon Territory

Resident Geologist
Box 1767
Whitehorse, Yukon Territory

For a provincial road map and good lure
booklets that contain a lot of information
write:

Department of Travel and Information
Box 2703
Whitehorse, Yukon Territory

Outfitters

Canoe Rentals

Yukon Canoe Rental
507 Alexander Street
Whitehorse, Yukon

Karl's Outdoor Living
Box 4643
Whitehorse, Yukon

River Outfitters

Mr. Paul Licier
507 Alexander Street
Whitehorse, Yukon

Yukon Expeditions
P.O. Box 23
Dawson City, Yukon
Canada, Y0B 1G0

Mr. John Lammers
Box 4126
Whitehorse, Yukon

Dawson Trail Services
Jack and Ruth Small
Box 20, Mackenzie, R.R. #1
Whitehorse, Yukon

Yukon Outdoor Adventures Ltd.
Box 4164
Whitehorse, Yukon

 Air Charter Services

Canoeists requiring air lift may contact during planning stages the following commercial carriers:

B.C. Yukon Air Service Ltd.
Box 68
Watson Lake, Yukon

Terr-Air Ltd.
Ross River, Yukon

Watson Lake Flying Services
Box 7
Watson Lake, Yukon

Dalziel Hunting Ltd.
Watson Lake, Yukon

Trans North Turbo Air
Box 4338
Whitehorse, Yukon

Yukon Airways Ltd.
Box 4428
Whitehorse, Yukon

In addition to the above bases, the Ministry of Transport lists the following landing lakes in the event some of them fit into air-lift plans: Carcross, Clarence Lagoon, Dawson and Mayo.

River raft trip operators can be contacted at:

Yukon River Expedition
Box 23
Whitehorse, Y.T. Y0B 1G0

NORTHWEST TERRITORIES

The Northwest Territories encompass one-third of the land-water mass of Canada (1,305,903 square miles), an area five times the size of Texas. The territories are bounded on the west by the Mackenzie Mountain Range, which also reaches into the Yukon Territory; on the north, by the Arctic Ocean; on the east, by Hudson Bay and the North Atlantic Ocean; and on the south, by the provinces below — Alberta, Saskatchewan and Manitoba. Canoeing country within this vast area is generally confined to the mainland (755,650 square miles).

The mainland territories contain two large freshwater lakes, Great Bear Lake (12,275 square miles) and Great Slave Lake (11,269 square miles). At 2,635 miles, the Mackenzie River is the longest in North America.

The economy of the Northwest Territories comes from the mining of gold and base metals, from the exploration and discovery of petroleum and natural gas on the northern coast, on the islands, and from commercial fishing on Great Slave Lake. Tourism and fur trapping are of less importance, though not to be ignored.

The capital, Yellowknife, has a population of about 8,000 people. It is situated on Great Slave Lake and is the seat of the territorial government.

The mainline transportation route is the Mackenzie River, which flows "down north" from the town of Hay River at the southwest end of Great Slave Lake to the river delta at the Arctic coast. The vast spread of the territories is served by a web of charter and scheduled airline services. A total of 800 miles of gravel highways serve the southern Mackenzie region. Free ferrys cross the Mackenzie and Liard Rivers. Fort Simpson is the farthest down river crossing by road on the Mackenzie.

 Climate

Only a small band in the southwestern region of the Mackenzie district of the Northwest Territories has frost-free weather and soil in summer. The remainder of the mainland is subarctic, shaped by the prevailing northwest winds that form a "boundary edge" treeline that runs diagonally northwest to southeast from the delta of the Mackenzie River to Hudson Bay. About one-quarter of the mainland lies above the Arctic Circle. Weather on the Queen Elizabeth Islands archipelago is polar.

Preceding page. The strange and almost surrealistic beauty of this bay is undoubtedly the inspiration for its name, Conjurer Bay. Situated in the Northwest Territories, it exemplifies the rugged magnificence of this last great frontier of North America.

Visiting canoeists will be concerned with the mainland weather at three points:

Northwest Territories	Mean Temperatures In Fahrenheit (Celsius)				Rainfall In Mean Inches (Millimetres)	
	Min		Max			
Southern (Hay River)						
June	42.7	(5.9)	62.2	(16.8)	1.03	(26.2)
July	51.0	(10.6)	69.1	(20.6)	1.88	(47.8)
August	48.7	(9.3)	67.1	(19.5)	1.34	(34.0)
Northeast-central (Baker Lake)						
June	31.3	(-0.4)	44.2	(6.8)	0.63	(16.0)
July	42.1	(5.6)	60.3	(15.7)	1.40	(35.6)
August	42.1	(5.6)	57.3	(14.1)	1.36	(34.5)
Northern (Inuvik)						
June	38.6	(3.7)	60.8	(16.0)	0.51	(13.0)
July	45.3	(7.4)	66.5	(19.2)	1.35	(34.3)
August	41.0	(5.0)	59.9	(15.5)	1.82	(46.2)

Depending on whether spring is early or late, navigation on the Mackenzie River from Hay River to Inuvik is generally possible from June 15 to September 30.

The southern canoeist will perhaps find it difficult at first to adapt himself to the long daylight hours on the mainland of the territories. During the summer equinox in June, there is an average of twenty hours of light in the Great Slave and Upper Mackenzie Valley; and twenty-four hours of light on June 21, as one advances to the coastlines of the Mackenzie delta and the Keewatin regions.

 Fishing

Regardless of a mean density population on the Northwest Territories mainland of twenty native and non-native persons to the mile, and the annual one million dollar-plus lake trout and whitefish commercial fishing industry at Great Slave Lake, there are sport fish aplenty for everyone, as one would expect in the "land of the last frontier".

So avid is the taking of giant trophy lake trout at Great Bear Lake fishing resorts that the territorial government has banned barbed hook lures. This restriction would hardly affect the travelling canoe tripper who is only interested in a meal at the end of a long day of paddling.

One can expect a range of species from lake trout to grayling, walleye, northern pike, arctic char and inconnu.

The angling licenses for the Northwest Territories, available in most communities in the territory, are:

Resident (Canadian) $3.00
Nonresident -   season $10.00
            -   short term (3 days) $3.50
            -   under 16 years   nil

Catch & possession limits	Daily Maximum	Maximum Possession
Lake trout	3	5
Grayling	5	10
Walleye	5	10
Northern pike	5	10
Humpback & broad whitefish	10	20
Dolly Varden	4	7
Brook trout	5	10
Inconnu	5	10
Goldeye	5	10
All ciscoes	50	50
Arctic char	4	7

 History

The remoteness and harshness of the land brought exploration and the fur trade later to the Northwest Territories than to other regions of Canada. The Hudson's Bay Company gave first impetus when it sent Samuel Hearne overland from Fort Churchill to explore the interior. He was the first white man on the Barren Grounds (1770) and the first to reach the Arctic Ocean (at the mouth of the Coppermine River, 1771).

Following this achievement, the North West Company established a trading post on Great Slave Lake and Alexander Mackenzie came on the scene. Living by the canoe, in 1789 he mapped the Mackenzie River (longest river on the continent, 2,625 miles) and found some of the richest fur country in the world. Little wonder, then, that the great river, a mountain range, and a district bear his name.

The rival fur trading companies joined in 1821 and the region came under the visiting scrutiny (1820-1824) of the Governor-in-chief of the Hudson's Bay Company, Sir George Simpson, who urged further northern exploration by the company. Bay men such as Ross, Back, Richardson, Thomas Simpson, Peter Warren Dease and John Rae explored the mainland coast of the territories from Point Barrow, Alaska to the west, to Boothia Peninsula on the east.

The British Admiralty also took an interest in the territory. Idle ships and men between the Napoleonic and Crimean wars turned to searching for the Northwest Passage. At first, land expeditions were equipped by the navy, often based at Hudson's

Paddling through candle ice at Faber Lake, Northwest Territories. In this latitude winter's ice lingers until July. The northern summer is short but intense, encompassing within a few weeks all the phases that are spread over several months in southern Canada.

Bay Company posts and sent northward to the Arctic coast to explore, make observations and recommendations for an assault on the Passage by naval force "through the ice".

The most publicized expeditioner, Sir John Franklin, made two land trips in 1819 and 1824 to the Arctic coast before the Admiralty sent him with two ships to "find the Passage" in 1845. He failed, indeed, disappeared with ships and 139 officers and men. The search for them continued for eleven years at huge cost and was then abandoned.

Lost, too, in that harsh land were many employees of the fur trade. On the treacherous Liard River alone 14 fur trader-canoeists were lost up to the year 1851. Such statistics serve as a warning to all present day canoeists that they must be expert to travel in the wake of the traders' craft.

Tuktoyaktuk

Inuvik

Norman
Wells

Great Bear
Lake

Coppermine

Coppermine
River

Nahanni
River

Mackenzie River

South Nahanni R.

Fort
Simpson

Liard River

Yellowknife

Great Slave
Lake

Snare
River

Hay
River

Hay
River

Slave
River

Hanbury
River

Thelon
River

Dubawnt River

Dubawnt
Lake

Baker
Lake

Back River

Baker Lake

Kazan

River

Baffin Island

AUYUITTUG
NATIONAL
PARK

Pangnir-
tung

Frobisher Bay

Cape
Dorset

Northwest Territories Routes

Of all Canada's canoeing regions, none has greater appeal than the Northwest Territories. Much of the appeal is based on the colorful journals of the explorers, myths that grow out of popular reporting and the mystique of far-off, wilderness places. In reality, none but very experienced canoeists should actually tackle the waterways of this land. Such experts must possess great stamina, high courage to keep moving at all physical costs, and a spirit of determination to win.

No trips in this land are cut and dried. "The most detailed trip notes must be taken with a grain of salt by future expeditions", says one seasoned canoeist. "Notes must never be adhered to blindly . . . However, fully marked map notes are an integral part of each trip's equipment. Notes help to find portages, foretell the nature of rapids, the general territory and the locations of campsites". These warnings are confirmed by my own trip logs that contain such notes as: "maps corrected to 1973 show the position of this very poorly; it is actually farther south than shown."

The canoeist travels through the territories during the short season of total daylight. Exposure in the extremely cold waters can only be endured up to five minutes in case of accident before loss of consciousness and death. All equipment must be the best available, from special tents to prepared foods and scuba wet suits. There is no second guessing after a start is made and very often there are slim chances of rescue in the event of emergencies. Only the best canoeist will consider travel in the Northwest Territories and it would be irresponsible to suggest otherwise.

So vast is the region I have divided it into the following geographical districts:

The Mackenzie District (waters flowing into the Arctic Ocean): Coppermine, South Redstone, Snare River, Camsell Lake-Great Slave Lake, Natla and Keele Rivers, Hare Indian River, Back River, the Mountain River and the Mackenzie River, South Nahanni River (Nahanni National Park).

The Keewatin District (where rivers flow generally northeasterly across the Barren Grounds into Hudson Bay): the Hanbury, Thelon, Kazan and Dubawnt Rivers.

Baffin District: the Lower Goose River on Auyuittuq National Park (formerly Baffin Island National Park).

Special arrangements can be made for the Hudson's Bay Company U-paddle services. See page 240 for details.

Mackenzie River District

584 COPPERMINE RIVER
Length 266 miles (428 km)
Approx trip time 18 days
Maps Winter Lake 86A
Point Lake 86H
Redrock Lake 86G
Hepburn Lake 86J
Sloan River 86K
Dismal Lakes 86N
Coppermine 86 O

The Coppermine River is 400 miles long from its headwaters in Lac de Gras, (N. Lat 64°, W. Long 110° 30') to Coronation Gulf on the Arctic Ocean.

The survey crew warns that the Coppermine River can be extremely dangerous. Only very experienced wilderness canoeists should attempt it. The region is isolated, the water is fast and the ice cold. It could be fatal in upsets.

There are many points of access by charter floatplane from Yellowknife, Northwest Territories, but for the above trip *start* at the south end of Point Lake at Obstruction Rapids. Paddle through Redrock Lake, Rocknest Lake, past the junction of the

Napatolik River and Fairy Lake River, then the Hook and Kendall Rivers and Stony Creek.

Continue through Muskox Rapids and Sandstone Rapids and portage around Bloody Falls (historic) to *finish* at the settlement of Coppermine. Radio for charter floatplane pick-up or await regular schedule calls at the settlement. Return to Yellowknife.

585   SOUTH REDSTONE RIVER
Length   170 miles (274 km)
Approx trip time   21 leisurely days
Maps   Wrigley Lake 95M
　　　　　Fort Norman 96C
　　　　　Dahadinni River 95N
South Redstone River, a major west bank tributary of the Mackenzie River, rises in the Backbone Range of the Mackenzie Mountains, 100 air miles (161 km) west of Wrigley, Northwest Territories. The river flows northeast and enters the Mackenzie River 60 miles south of Fort Norman.

From Wrigley, travel by charter floatplane to *start* at Little Dal Lake by covered canoe or kayak. Expect a large number of rapids from the June melt and generally heavy rains at this season. After completing the length of the South Redstone, paddle two days from the confluence with Mackenzie River to *finish* at Fort Norman. Await biweekly air service.

This route is dangerous for even very experienced whitewater canoeists. There is spectacular scenery, wildlife, hiking and rock climbing in the river valley and mountains.

586   SNARE RIVER
Length   140 miles (225 km)
Approx trip time   14 days
Maps   Yellowknife 85J
　　　　　Rae 85K
　　　　　Wecho 85 O
　　　　　Marian River 85N
　　　　　Indin Lake 86B
　　　　　Winter Lake 86A

Located northeast of Great Slave Lake, Snare River trends southwest for 232 miles in a river-lakes pattern. It empties into Marian Lake, north of the north arm of Great Slave Lake at the settlement of Rae. The river's

headwaters rise just northwest of Jolly Lake (116° 5' lat.; 112° 14' long.), 100 miles from Yellowknife, Northwest Territories.

Fly by charter floatplane from Yellowknife to Winter Lake to *start*. Paddle through Roundrock, Snare, Indin, Kwejinne and Bigspruce Lakes to the dam site. Continue again down Snare River and Marian Lake to *finish* at the Rae settlement. Fly out to Yellowknife by prearranged chartered floatplane.

587   CAMSELL LAKE - GREAT SLAVE LAKE
Length   270 miles (434 km)
Approx trip time   25 days
Maps   Lac de Gras 76D
　　　　　Alymer Lake 76C
　　　　　Walmsley Lake 75N
　　　　　Fort Reliance 75K
The description of this route comes from a trip by five American canoeists in two canoes and one kayak, in July, 1967. They and their gear were flown from Yellowknife by chartered floatplane, 130 miles northeast to *start* at Camsell Lake. This route meanders generally east, south, then southwest to Fort Reliance on the northeast corner of Great Slave Lake.

They began in late June pack ice, paddled through MacKay Lake, down Lockhart River, Aylmer Lake, a string of small lakes 55 miles long to *finish* at Fort Reliance. The party then flew by prearranged charter floatplane to Yellowknife.

588   NATLA AND KEELE RIVERS
Length   70 miles and 180 miles respectively (113 and 290 km)
Approx trip time   20 days
Maps   Sekwi Mountain 105P
　　　　　Wrigley Lake 95M
　　　　　Mount Eduni 106A
　　　　　Nahanni 105 I
　　　　　Carcajou Canyon 96D
　　　　　Fort Norman 96C

Natla River, 70 miles long, rises in the Mackenzie Mountains, 125 miles northeast of Ross River settlement, Yukon Territory. It is an exciting, dangerous river with rapids for most of its length, through wide mountain valleys. It joins the Keele River — which flows 180 miles from its junction with the Natla River — to its mouth at the mainstream Mackenzie River through mountain valleys to lowlands.

Access to the Natla River by charter floatplane is possible from a number of Mackenzie River settlements. *Start* at O'Grady Lake when it is free of ice (about the end of June). Paddle to the Keele River junction and paddle 180 miles through mountain valleys and lowlands to the mainstream MacKenzie River, then 60 miles downstream to *finish* at Fort Norman.

Fly out north or south by chartered floatplane.

589 HARE INDIAN RIVER

Length   160 miles (257 km)
Maps   Lac des Bois 96K
Fort Good Hope 106 I
Lac Belot 96L

Hare Indian River, a major east bank tributary of the Mackenzie River, rises in the first of the two lakes located six miles west of the Smith Arm of Great Bear Lake. Access by charter floatplane is usually from Yellowknife, Northwest Territories, to Lac des Bois.

This route was not paddled by a government surveys team but described by them (it is presumed by study from the air).

The first source lake mentioned above is joined by the river to a second lake to the west and the balance of the route is all river travel. The river empties into the mainstream Mackenzie River at Fort Good Hope.

Prearranged charter planes will fly either north or south.

590 BACK RIVER

Length   600 miles (966 km)
Approx trip time   41 days
Maps   Many aerial photos used.
These maps are to a scale of 1:1,000,000
Lockhart River 2113
Thelon River 2080

In the remote northeast corner of the mainland Northwest Territories rises the little known Back River, historically important but little travelled during modern times.

The river was named after Capt. George Back, RN, of England, the first non-native to travel it, in 1834. He was searching for the survivors of the Sir John Franklin expedition. The next traveller was James Anderson of the Hudson's Bay Company.

This report is culled from the log of an American canoe party in 1962. There have been few, if any, trips since, so remote is the region. Without inhabitants, it seems to be challenged "because it is there".

The four highly experienced American canoeists flew in a chartered floatplane from Yellowknife, Northwest Territories, 300 miles northeast, landing to *start* at Aylmer Lake, the beginning of the 600 mile trip. From the Aylmer Lake outlet, the party entered the mainstream Back River, Beechey Lake, the Cascades, junction of Baillie River, Hawk Rapids, McKinley River.

They continued through Pelly Lake, Garry Lake, Rock Rapids, Franklin Lake, Franklin Rapids and Falls to *finish* at a government nursing station at the head of tidewater Chantrey Inlet on the Arctic Ocean.

The party flew back to Yellowknife by prearranged chartered floatplane.

591 MOUNTAIN RIVER (TO FORT GOOD HOPE)

Length   210 miles (338 km)
Approx trip time   14 days
Maps   Mount Eduni 106A
Sans Sault Rapids 106H

The Mountain River rises in the Mackenzie Mountains (130° 45' longitude, 60° 6' latitude) approximately ten miles east of the Northwest Territories and Yukon Territory boundary. The river flows north, then northeast, entering the Mackenzie River above Sans Sault Rapids (128° 5' longitude, 65° 42' latitude).

592 MOUNTAIN RIVER (TO NORMAN WELLS)

Length   224 miles (360 km)
Approx trip time   14 days
Maps   Same as previous route

Follow the preceding route until the junction. Paddle 64 miles upstream to *finish* at Norman Wells. Await a chartered floatplane.

Fly by charter floatplane from the Mackenzie River settlement to a landing lake 145 air miles west. Portage 5 miles from the landing lake to the Mountain River to *start*.

Paddle downstream through many connecting, unnamed lakes, continuing through or portaging around four major river canyons on 100 miles of the route through the Mackenzie Mountains.

Next, a 60 mile paddle through lowlands offers one river canyon, flat, tree-covered banks and negligible current to a junction with the mainstream Mackenzie River.

Paddle 50 miles downstream from the junction to *finish* at Fort Good Hope. Await a chartered floatplane.

593 MACKENZIE RIVER (FORT PROVIDENCE TO DELTA)

Length 1070 miles (1,728 km)
Access Fort Providence
Maps List of required charts is available from the Canada Map Office

From Fort Providence at the outlet of Great Slave Lake, the Mackenzie River flows northwest for 1,070 miles to discharge in its huge, meandering delta into the Beaufort Sea. It is navigable along its entire length including sections of fast water. It is joined by numerous large rivers and streams. The river is generally travelled by large power vessels and barges although it is occasionally attempted by individuals in outboard-powdered freight canoes rather than small paddled pleasure canoes.

So large is the Mackenzie River that it is controlled (as are all major waterways) by the Ministry of Transport, which covers the entire system — including Great Slave Lake and a distance of the Beaufort Sea coast — with numerous and necessary navigation charts.

A free list of required charts can be obtained from Canada Map Office, 615 Booth Street, Ottawa, Ontario. A large book on Sailing Directions is available from Information Canada bookstores in major cities.

Nahanni National Park

594 SOUTH NAHANNI RIVER

Length 240 miles (386 km), a dangerous, remote river

Access There are no roads into the park. Access by air and river boat to Fort Simpson, Northwest Territories and Watson Lake, Yukon Territory and beyond these points by local air charter to start at headwaters.

Maps Nahanni 105 I
Glacier Lake 95L
Flat River 95E
Virginia Falls 95F
Sibbeston Lake 95G
Fort Simpson 95H
(Index No. 7 - corrected to May, 1973 - shows position of the South Nahanni River very poorly; it is actually farther south)

Nahanni Butte 95G/3*
The Twisted Mountain 95G/4*
Matou River 95G/8*
First Canyon 95F/8*
Second Canyon 95F/7*

High water on the South Nahanni River usually occurs in mid-June. Summer rainstorms can cause river levels to rise 3-5 feet overnight; prolonged rain can make travel impossible. River hazards are difficult to describe; they change throughout the season. Some of the major rapids are: Rabbitkettle River — Virginia Falls; Virginia Falls — Five Mile Rapids; Figure Eight Rapids (Hell's Gate); the Gate; George's Riffle (Cache Rapids); Lafferty Riffle; Unnamed Riffle; The Splits; Flat River (Cascade of the Thirteen Steps).

Finish at Fort Simpson where the South Nahanni joins the Mackenzie River. Leave Fort Simpson by air or boat charter.

A fishing license is required from the Federal Fisheries Service. Information about carrying firearms can be obtained from Travel Arctic. Both agencies are located in Yellowknife.

Keewatin District

595 HANBURY AND THELON RIVERS

Length 471 miles (758 km)
Approx trip time 5 weeks
Maps Artillery Lake 75 O
Aberdeen Lake 66B
Tammarvi River 66D
Beverly Lake 66C

Clarke River 65M
Hanbury 75P
Schultz Lake 66A

The headwaters of the Hanbury River rise in Campbell Lake some 250 air miles east-northeast of Yellowknife, Northwest Territories. The river flows generally southeast through the Barren Grounds to join the Thelon River, then east through Thelon Game Sanctuary to Baker Lake settlement at the head of Chesterfield Inlet on the west coast of Hudson Bay.

A permit must be obtained from the Territorial Wildlife Service to travel through this river system.

A popular five week trip starts at Hanbury Portage out of Artillery-Sifton Lakes, or, a start may be made at Steele Lake, east of Ford Falls. The above trip was made by *starting* from Sifton Lake, 35 miles downstream from Campbell Lake on the Hanbury River. Paddle through Hanbury and Hoare Lakes, portage around MacDonald Falls and Dickson Canyon (2 miles long, unnavigable for open canoes) to the mouth of the Hanbury River, where it joins the Thelon River.

Paddle down the Thelon River, pass John Hornby's Cabin (historic), Beverly Lake, the mouth of the Dubawnt River, Aberdeen Lake (50 miles long), Schultz Lake and the Thelon River again to *finish* at the settlement of Baker Lake.

Radio here, or await regular landplane air schedule to Churchill, Manitoba. Then travel by rail or air to Winnipeg and beyond.

596 KAZAN RIVER

Length 640 miles (1,030 km)

Approx trip time 33 days

Maps Purchase 4 mile to inch topo maps of the region from Map Distribution Office, Ottawa, Ontario. See previous route.

The Kazan River rises in Snowbird Lake, Northwest Territories, approximately 103° west longitude and 60° north latitude, near the tree line. It flows chiefly northeast across the Barren Grounds, finishing at Baker Lake, a westward extension of Chesterfield Inlet at the northeast corner of Hudson Bay.

Access to the route from Lynn Lake, (Manitoba) town railhead is 2-1/2 hours by charter floatplane. *Start* at Snowbird Lake, Northwest Territories.

Paddle through Obre, Atzinging, Bourassa, Kasba to the beginning of the Kazan River. Continue through Tabane, Ennadai, Dimma, Angikuni and Yathkyed Lakes.

Pass the mouth of the Kunwak River, through Thirty Mile Lake and Kazan River again to *finish* at the settlement of Baker Lake. Radio from here for regular schedule land plane pick-up to Churchill. From there, travel by rail or air to Winnipeg and beyond. Ship out canoes and excess gear by sea vessel to Montreal and beyond.

Coffin's Notes: Very remote wilderness region to be attempted by very experienced whitewater trippers familiar with Barren Ground living conditions.

From individual trip reports (printed with permission) Stewart T. Coffin

597 DUBAWNT RIVER

Length 1,150 miles (1,851 km)

Approx trip time 45 days

Maps These maps are to a scale of 1:1,000,000
Clearwater River 2141
Lockhart River 2113
Dubawnt River 2112
Thelon River 2080

The Dubawnt River (as does the Back River) flows across the Barren Grounds northeast from the Height of Land to the settlement of Baker Lake. However, an American foursome in two canoes in 1966, started their epic trip from Stony Rapids settlement on Lake Athabasca. Theirs was the first trip attempted since 1955, when another American expedition ended in tragedy. Before that year no non-native trip had been made since that of the Canadian geologist brothers J.B. and J.W. Tyrell, in 1893.

The following trip started at Uranium City on Lake Athabasca, continued to Fond du Lac River, Black Lake, Chipman River, crossing the Arctic Divide to the junction of Thelon River, to the settlement of Baker Lake. The party paddled another 200 miles east to *finish* at the settlement of Chesterfield Inlet on Hudson Bay. The party was evacuated by regular schedule plane to Churchill, Manitoba.

From individual trip reports (printed with permission) Lincoln Canoe Library

598 HANBURY-THELON RIVERS (YELLOWKNIFE-BAKER LAKE)
Length 507 miles (805 km)
Approx trip time 5 weeks (return by air charter)

Start at Campbell Lake.

599 LAC DE GRAS (YELLOWKNIFE-COPPERMINE)
Length 400 miles (644 km)
Approx trip time 2 weeks (return by air charter)

600 MACKENZIE RIVER (FORT PROVIDENCE-INUVIK)
Length 1,070 miles (1,722 km)
Approx trip time 4 - 6 weeks (return by air charter or boat)

Auyuittuq National Park (formerly Baffin Island National Park)

601 LOWER GOOSE RIVER
Length 20 miles (32 km) return
Map Clearwater Fiord 26J

Lower Goose River as a canoe route is mentioned here as a "novelty" trip; it is for visitors to the park who would take the trouble and expense to fly in their own kayaks and to boast that they had made the trip.

The park is developed for summer mountaineers, glaciologists, flora and fauna watch-ers. Sea trips by Eskimo outboard-powered freight canoes may be arranged for sightseeing purposes.

Auyuittuq National Park (pronounced O-wee-it-TUK "where the ice never melts") is 1,500 air miles northeast of Montreal to Frobisher, then another 180 miles beyond by smaller charter plane to the park headquarters at the village of Pangnirtung. Full information should be requested about the park from the superintendent well in advance of the trip. It is the world's only Arctic park.

Start above the falls at the river mouth (adjacent to southeastern Kekertelung Island). Continue to the Badlands junction of the river, turn around and *finish* at the river mouth.

Hudson's Bay Company U-paddle Services
The Hudson's Bay Company offers its unique U-paddle services for three routes in the Northwest Territories. These are all accessible by road or air to starting points where canoes, supplies and equipment may be picked up and left at destinations.

The company will probably assist with information about air service connections. Direct all inquiries well in advance of take-off to:

Hudson's Bay Company
Northern Stores Department
79 Main Street
Winnipeg 1, Manitoba

 Map Sources

Canada Mapping Office, 615 Booth Street, Ottawa, Ontario, is the chief supplier of topographical maps. Maps for the Northwest Territories are available from the following local dealers:

Charts Unlimited
P.O. Box 8
Hay River, N.W.T.
X0E 1G0

Regional Treasury Office
Government of the Northwest
Territories
Inuvik, N.W.T.

Mack Travel
P.O. Box 1589
Inuvik, N.W.T.

Tuk Traders Limited
Box 1129
Inuvik, N.W.T.

Department of Indian Affairs
and Northern Development
Resident Geologist
Box 1500
Room 203, Bromley Building
Yellowknife, N.W.T.
X0E 1H0

For a provincial road map and good lure booklet write:

TravelArctic
Yellowknife
Northwest Territories

 ## Outfitters

There are a few outfitters listed by TravelArctic (tourism) in Yellowknife. These are:

The Sportsman (NWT) Limited
Box 162
Yellowknife, N.W.T. X0E 1H0

Marlene Waugh
Yellowknife River
Yellowknife, N.W.T.

The Hudson's Bay Company U-paddle service provides complete outfitting for the three routes previously mentioned. A full description of the service is given on p 000.

 ## Air Charter Services

Canoeists who plan to fly into some starting point within the mainland Northwest Territories or to be flown out at the trip's end can make advance arrangements with the following companies:

Aero Arctic
Box 1496
Yellowknife, N.W.T.

Aklavik Flying Service
Box 1158
Inuvik, N.W.T.

Associated Helicopters Ltd.
Box 1895
Inuvik, N.W.T.

Buffalo Airways
Box 168
Fort Smith, N.W.T.

Cooper & Sons Aviation Ltd.
Box 222
Fort Smith, N.W.T.

International Jet Air
Box 1056
Inuvik, N.W.T.

Mackenzie Air Ltd.
Box 1295
Hay River, N.W.T.

Northward Airlines
Box 356
Yellowknife, N.W.T.

Northwest Territorial
Airways Ltd.
Box 100
Yellowknife, N.W.T.

Pacific Western Airlines Ltd.
Industrial Airport
Edmonton, Alta.

Reindeer Air Services Ltd.
Box 1068
Inuvik, N.W.T.

Air Providence
Fort Providence, N.W.T.

Arctic Air Ltd.
Box 90
Fort Simpson, N.W.T.

Bo Helicopters Ltd.
Box 1581
Inuvik, N.W.T.

Carter Air Service
Box 510
Hay River, N.W.T.

Gateway Aviation Ltd.
Box 880
Yellowknife, N.W.T.

Klondike Helicopters
#3 Hangar, McCall Field
Calgary, Alta.

Nahanni Air Services
— Norman Wells — Tel: 3288
— Fort Franklin — Tel: 2431
— Yellowknife, Box 2277

Northward Airlines
Box 1099
Inuvik, N.W.T.

Okanagan Helicopters
Box 1492
Inuvik, N.W.T.

Ptarmigan Airways Ltd.
Box 66
Yellowknife, N.W.T.

Transair Ltd.
Winnipeg International Airport
Winnipeg 12, Man.

Wardair Canada Ltd.
Box 610
Yellowknife, N.W.T.
or
Wardair Canada Ltd.
Box 2096
Inuvik, N.W.T.

For further use of canoe trip planners the federal Ministry of Transport lists the following floatplane bases in the Northwest Territories:

Acadie Cove, Aklavik, Aylmer Lake, Baker Lake, Bathurst Inlet, Bernard Harbour, Big Lake, Boffa Lake, Cameron Bay, Chesterfield Inlet, Conwoyto Lake, Coppermine, Eskimo Point, Fort Franklin, Fort Good Hope.

Fort Liard, Fort McPherson, Fort Norman, Fort Rae, Fort Reliance, Fort Resolution, Norman Wells, Rocher River, Wrigley, Port Radium and Sawmill Bay.

River raft operators offer trips on the Coppermine and South Nahanni Rivers. Write:

North West Expeditions Ltd.
Box 1551
Edmonton, Alta. T5J 2N7

MAPS AND HOW TO USE THEM

Most of us regularly use road maps. However, road maps are useful to the canoeist only insofar as they can guide him to the waterways. Fortunately for the canoeist and all serious outdoorsmen, topographical maps covering every part of Canada are readily available. These maps are invaluable as a guide to the topographical features the canoeist can expect to encounter along a particular route and as a tool for plotting canoe routes.

In Canada, topographical maps can be obtained from the central map office in Ottawa or from its dealers across the country. Maps are also available in several United States cities and abroad. These are listed below.

Not only is the Canada Map Office useful for its maps, the canoeist can also benefit from the expertise of its officials. As a result, my own visits to the office have been very productive. The office customarily handles roughly 500 map requests per day. Naturally, map orders are filled more quickly when the office is not swamped with orders. To avoid any delays due to heavy spring ordering, place your order well beforehand.

This book attempts to provide you with the most appropriate maps possible, wherever possible. From the information in the data block - name and number - order the maps you need. Addresses for the Canada Map Office and its dealers are listed at the end of each chapter.

How To Order A Topographic Map

For the canoeist who wishes to order his own topographic maps from the Canada Map Office instead of using the map numbers given for each route listed in this book, there is a very simple method.

The master index for the 1:50,000 map of Canada shown on page 244 is divided into areas numbered 1 to 17A and for each area there is a regional map index. These indices are for maps at scales of 1:50,000 and 1:63,360. All available maps at these scales are named and numbered on the indices. Order the numbered regional map index for the maps at the scales most suitable to your needs and that cover the particular area in which you are interested.

Suppose you want a 1:50,000 scale map of some area in Newfoundland or New Brunswick. Write for regional map scale index no. 1. The map indices are free from the Canada Map Office.

Read the instructions on the bottom of your regional map index when you receive it. These instructions will show you how to identify the maps you want and will enable the Canada Map Office to fill your order quickly and accurately.

The scale of a topographical map in Canada is expressed by a figure such as 1:50,000 or 1:250,000, the relationship between a distance on the map and actual distance on the ground. The following table gives approximate equivalents for miles-per-inch for some of the commonly used maps scale:

1:	25,000	= approx.	2-1/2	inches (6.3 cm) to 1 mile (1.6 km)
1:	50,000	= approx.	1-1/4	inches (3.1 cm) to 1 mile (1.6 km)
1:	125,000	= approx.	1	inch (2.5 cm) to 2 miles (3.2 km)
1:	250,000	= approx.	1	inch (2.5 cm) to 4 miles (6.4 km)
1:	500,000	= approx.	1	inch (2.5 cm) to 8 miles (12.8 km)
1:1,000,000		= approx.	1	inch (2.5 cm) to 16 miles (25.7 km)

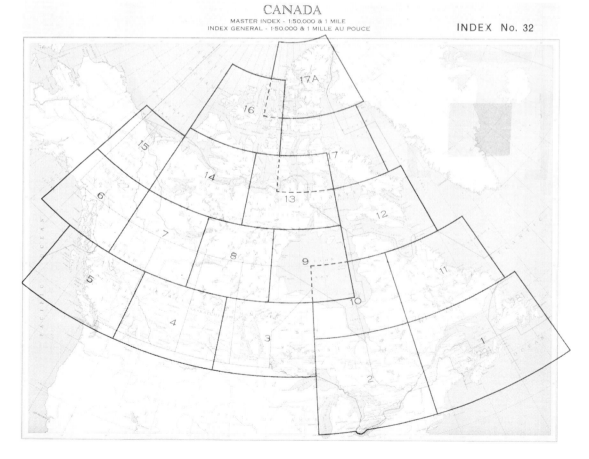

CANADA

MASTER INDEX - 1:50,000 & 1 MILE
INDEX GENERAL - 1:50,000 & 1 MILLE AU POUCE

INDEX No. 32

In the data blocks, the names and numbers of the relevant topographic maps are provided. From these names and numbers you can determine what the scale of each map is. In this book, the maps are mostly of three scales:

    1:50,000
    1:125,000
    1:250,000

The following example illustrates how each scale has a different kind of map number:

Duck Mountain 62N is a 1:250,000 map

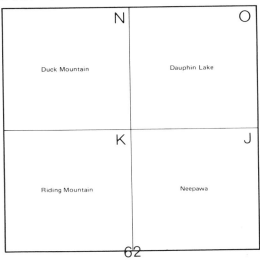

1:250,000 scale
These maps cover a large area and have been published for all of Canada

Kamsack 62N/NW is a 1:125,000 map

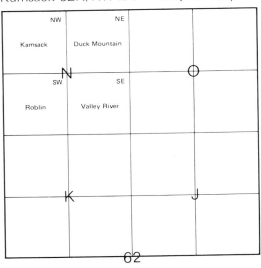

1:125,000 scale
These maps cover a smaller area in greater detail.

Arran 62N/13W is a 1:50,000 map

13 Arran	14 Durban	15 Pine River	16 Sagemace Bay		
12 Kamsack	11 Child's Lake	10 Singuish Lake	9 Garland		
5 Togo	6 Angling Lakes	7 Baldy Mountain	8 Sifton		
4 Calder	3 Roblin	2 Grand-view	1 Dauphin		

N   O

K   J

62

1:50,000 scale
These maps cover the smallest area in the greatest detail.

Each map number indicates the specific map coordinates you require. As you can see, the 1:250,000 map provides the least detail (62N), the 1:125,000 map somewhat more detail (62N/NW) and the 1:50,000 map (62N/13W) the greatest detail.

The 1:250,000 maps exist for every part of Canada. The two other series are not as complete. However, when these small scale maps are available, it is a good idea to obtain them. The areas you are interested in will be shown in far greater detail and as a result, will be that much more helpful.

The accompanying illustrations clearly show how these map numbers and names are derived.

How To Use A Topographic Map

You can read map references quickly and accurately. To find the map reference of ± on the "map" above proceed as follows:

1. Find the number of grid line west of ± (91). Ascertain the number of tenths ± is east of (91). This is observed to be 6. Set it down thus, 916. This is known as *easting.*

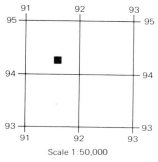

Scale 1:50,000

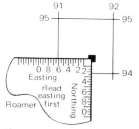

If you use a roamer use it this way
This example is not drawn to scale

2. Find number of grid line south of ± (94). Ascertain number of tenths ± is north of (94). This is observed to be 4. Set it down thus, 944. This is known as *northing.*

The map reference of ± is therefore 916944. *Always measure over to the east and then up to the north. In other words find the easting, then the northing.*

Note - when using a reference on the 1:250,000 map give the letters of the large square concerned.

The map reference above on 1:250,000 scale is NT9393.

This example is not drawn to scale

A map is oriented when it is made to correspond with the ground it represents. North is the top of the map.

Four Ways To Set A Map

By Compass

With a protractor draw a magnetic north line anywhere on your map. The declination diagram in the margin of the map will give you the direction and the size of the angle between grid north and magnetic north. (Note — don't use the margin diagram itself as the angles are often exaggerated by the cartographer so that the numerical value of the angle can be inserted.) Place the compass on the magnetic north line and turn the map and compass together slowly until the needle points to magnetic north on the map.

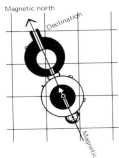

The compass points to magnetic north which may not be the same as grid north. It depends on your locality.

If you live close to the line that runs near Thunder Bay, Savant Lake, Churchill, you're in luck. Here your compass north is approximately the same as grid north. But if you live east of this line, your compass points off to the west, while west of that line it points off to the east. The reason is that the magnetic north pole, which attracts the compass needle, is situated on Bathurst Island, about 970 miles south of the true north pole.

Compasses are made in many forms. The simplest is the common needle compass which consists of a magnetic needle held free to rotate over a compass card. Remember, the needle comes to rest pointing at magnetic north. Turn the compass case gently under the needle until North on the card lies under the north end of the needle. Magnetic directions are then indicated by the card. (More expensive compasses, such as prismatic compasses and orienteering compasses, have additional features which facilitate the reading of directions. Instructional booklets for these compasses may be obtained free from the dealer.)

Finding Compass Bearings and Grid Bearings

To find grid bearings you must know how much off grid north the compass points in your locality. Look in the margin of your topographic map for the compass declination. The rhyme is:

Declination East - Magnetic least (i.e., magnetic less than grid); Declination West - Magnetic best.

As an example, in Ottawa the compass points off to the west (declination west) about 15°. So according to the rhyme magnetic is greater than grid north.

Following a Compass Bearing

With your compass oriented (i.e., with North on the card under the north end of the needle) look along the compass bearing you want to follow. Pick a landmark in this direction. Paddle forward to this landmark, then sight with the compass to the next landmark along the route. Continue to the destination.

By Objects

When the observer knows his position on the map and can identify the position of some distant object, he turns the map so that it corresponds with the ground.

By Watch and Sun

(for northern hemisphere): If Daylight Saving Time is in effect, first set your watch back on Standard Time. Place watch flat with the hour hand pointing to the sun. True South is midway between the hour hand and XII. True North is directly opposite. This method is only a crude indicator.

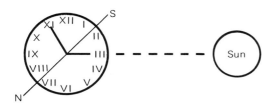

By The Stars

In latitudes below 60° N the bearing of Polaris is never more than 2-1/4° from True North. These constellations revolve counterclockwise around the Pole.

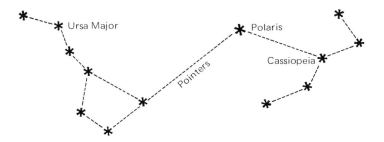

Make Your Own Map Case

You can make your own waterproof map case for use in the field. Purchase two 8-1/2 by 11 inch heavy plastic report covers (containing three perforations). Fold your large map flat to 8 by 10 inches, showing your immediate route section uppermost. Insert your folded map between the plastic covers and close edges and perforations with strong transparent sticky tape (take a roll with you). You may outline your route detail on the map face, or on the outside of the plastic covering to save defacing the original map. Elsewhere write lots of marginal notes and corrections for your own future reference or for friends who may follow, or officials.

How Many Paces In A Portage?

Land maps are plotted by land surveyors, drawn by cartographers and used by people in many disciplines. The casual map user, such as the canoeist, can be justifiably confused by the map makers' jargon. Units of measurement can be expressed in feet, yards, paces, chains, rods, miles and, soon to come to North America, metres. We have the following foot equivalents:

1 yard	=	3 feet
1 pace	=	about 4 double-stepped feet (see below)
1 chain	=	66 feet
1 rod	=	16-1/2 feet
1 metre	=	about 3-1/4 feet
1 mile	=	5,280 feet

Upon beaching his canoe at the head of a strange portage, you can hardly blame the normal canoeist for his confusion as he studies his map marked in any of the above measurements. He might better establish his personal pace measure before leaving home by measuring off his normal walking pace between posted 1/4-mile highway markers. A pace is a normal double step counted off each time one puts down his left (or right) foot. The pace count between 1/4-mile markers multiplied by 4 gives one's personal pace-per-mile count. The 1/4-mile count should work out to about 330 paces between markers, or 1,320 feet.

But perhaps you just don't care to be precise about the length of a portage in any unit of measurement and who can blame you. Should you find the portage criss-crossed with deadfalls, rising up ridge and down through muskeg, it will be twice as long as the map says it is, anyway. Of course it will, for surveyors calculate all portage measurements by level line of sighting.

Provincial & Territorial Road Maps & Canoe Routes Books

The following tourist offices supply free detailed maps of their jurisdictions. Most road maps include a wealth of material such as fishing and hunting dates, location of park campsites, fees and facilities. Some provinces provide lure booklets as well. Always ask for one and, of course, ask for any free canoe routes booklets or maps in the areas of interest from all offices.

Yukon Department of Travel & Information
P.O. Box 2703
Whitehorse, Yukon

Tourist Development Section
TravelArctic
Yellowknife, Northwest Territories

British Columbia Travel Bureau
Dept. of Travel Industry
Parliament Buildings
Victoria, British Columbia

Alberta Government Travel Bureau
1629 Centennial Building
Edmonton 15, Alberta

Saskatchewan Tourist Development Branch
Dept. Industry & Commerce
Power Building
Regina, Saskatchewan

Manitoba Tourist Branch
Dept. of Tourism, Recreation and Cultural
   Affairs
408 Norquay Bldg., 401 York Ave.
Winnipeg 1, Manitoba

Ontario Ministry of Tourism & Information
Queens Park
Toronto, Ontario

Tourism Branch
Dept. Tourism, Fish & Game
Place de la Capitale
150 St. Cyrille Blvd. E.
15th Floor
St. Foy, Quebec

New Brunswick Promotion & Development
   Branch
Department of Tourism
P.O. Box 1030
Fredericton, New Brunswick

Prince Edward Island
   Travel Bureau
Dept. of Tourist Development
P.O. Box 940
Charlottetown, P.E.I.

Nova Scotial Travel Bureau
Department of Tourism
5670 Spring Garden Road
Halifax, Nova Scotia

Newfoundland & Labrador Tourist
   Development Office
Elizabeth Towers
St. John's, Newfoundland

United States

Alaska

McCauley's Reprographics and
Mapping
721 Airport Road
Fairbanks, Alaska 99701

California

Lucas College Book Co. Inc.,
2430 Bancroft Way
Berkeley 4, Calif.

Ski Hut,
Expedition Outfitters
1615 University Ave.
Berkeley, Calif. 94703

Map Library University Library
University of Southern California
University Park
Los Angeles, Calif.

The Map Shop
1634 Westwood Boulevard
Los Angeles, Calif. 90024

Mountain Travel
6201 Medau Place
Oakland, Calif. 94611

The H.M. Gousha Co.
2001 The Alameda
San Jose, Calif.

Illinois

Rand McNally Map Store
124 W Monroe St.
Chicago 3, Ill.

Elliot Flying Service, Inc.,
Quad City Airport,
Box 31,
Moline, Ill.

Maine

The Action Agency, Realtors,
P.O. Box 302
Machias, Maine, 04654

The Outdoorsman
Turner Ridge Rd.
Palermo, Maine

Maryland

Hudson Bay Outfitters Ltd.
10560 Metropolitan Ave.
Kensington, Maryland 20795

Massachusetts

Attn. Mr. C.F. Belcher
Executive Director
Appalachian Mountain Club
5 Joy St.
Boston, 8, Mass.

R.C. Ralys
265 West River St.
Orange, Mass.

Minnesota

Burger Brothers Inc.
4402-1/2 France Ave. South
Edina, Minn. 55410

Canoe Country Outfitters
629 E. Shevidan St.
Ely, Minn. 55731

Trygg Land Office
Box 628
Ely, Minn. 55731

Benson Brothers
Midway Service Station
Grand Marais, Minn.

Riley's Sporting Goods Co., (Fishing)
343 Third St.
International Falls, Minn.

Iltis Drug Store
International Falls,
Minn.

ACE Stores
Erickson Hardware
International Falls, Minn.

Mr. E.L. Anderson
City Drug Store
International Falls, Minn.

Einarson Bros.
Rogers Rt. Box 1
International Falls, Minn.

Hoigaard's Inc.
3550 So. Highway 100
Minneapolis, Minn. 55416

Hudson Map Co.
1506 Henn
Minneapolis, Minn. 55403

Mr. Don Trompeter
Northland Sportsmen's Service Agency
Box 45
Ranier, Minn.

Remer Oil Co. Inc.
Box 147
421 N. Lakeview Ave.
Remer, Minn. 56672

F.R. Engelhardt Realty
274 Mainzer St.
West St. Paul, Minn. 55118

Mr. W.A. Fisher
W.A. Fisher Co.
123-125 Chestnut St.
Virginia, Minn. 55792

New Hampshire

Mr. Mert Cotton, Trader,
Opechee Trading Post
13 Opechee St.
Laconia, N.H.

Keewaydin Camps Ltd.
Hanover, N.H.
Attn. Mr. H.P. Chivers

New Jersey

Mr. S.J. Eckerson
Gen. Drafting Co. Inc.
Convent Station, N.J.
Attn. Mr. A.F. Talbot, Sen. Editor

C.S. Hammond & Co.
515 Valley St.
Maplewood, N.J.
Attn: Mr. A.F. Talbot,
        Sen. Editor

International Map Co.
595 Broad Ave.
Ridgefield, N.J. 07657

The Bass "N" Quail
Post Office Box 1095
Tom River, N.J. 087553

New York

Thousand Island Bait Store
Mr. Ellis R. Lake
Alexandria Bay, N.Y.

Hevener Map Co.
350 Ellicott St.
Buffalo, N.Y., 14203

Attn: Mr. J.M. Benson
Benson, Jessup & Knapp, Inc.
809 Pennsylvania Ave.
Elmira, N.Y.

Mr. V.R. Landi
Sportsman's Map Co. Ltd.
3 East 76th St.
New York, N.Y., 10022

Rand McNally & Co.
405 Park Ave.
New York 22, N.Y.

Ohio

Camping and Education Foundation
Camp Kooch-i-ching
7930 Indian Hill Road
Cincinnati, Ohio, 45243

The Standard Oil Co.
Sohio Aviation Services
Sohio Hangar
Cleveland Hopkins Int'l. Airport
Cleveland, Ohio 44135

Ohio Canoe Adventures Inc.
1528 Colorado Ave.
P.O. Box 2092
Sheffield Lake, Ohio
Attn: Mr. L.E. Barnum

Crow Incorporated
Route # 4
Swanton, Ohio

Oregon

Mr. Clint Needy
Hillsboro Aviation
Municipal Airport
Hillsboro, Oregon

Pennsylvania

Clay Book Store
R.D. 1
Ephrata, Penna. 17522

Yoas Services, Inc.
P.O. Box 1025
Williamsport, P.A. 17701

Vermont

Kaywaydin Camps Corp.
Salisbury, Vermont 05769

Kenette's,
Restaurant & Motor Court
Star Route
Newport, Vt.

Washington

Belairco Aviation Inc.
1485 Bakerview Rd.
Bellingham, Wash.

Kenmore Air Harbour, Inc.
Box 64
Kenmore, Wash.
Attn: Mr. Dave Trygg

Cardinal Book Store
2405 College Way
Mount Vernon, Wash. 98273

Captains Nautical Supplies
1324 Second Ave.
Seattle, Wash. 98101

Recreational Equipment Inc.
1525 - 11th Ave.
Seattle, Wash. 98122

Wisconsin

Milwaukee Map Service
4519 W. North Ave.
Milwaukee, Wisc. 53208

Other Countries

Bermuda

The Bermuda Book Stores
Bermuda Islands

England

Edward Stanford Ltd.
12-14 Long Acre
Attn: Mr. K. Winch
London, W.C. 2, England

Holland

Saint Lucas Society
Rapenburg 83
Box 49
Leiden, Holland

Japan

Naigai Trading Co. Ltd.
P.O. Box 38

Akasaka, Tokyo 107
Japan

West Germany

Geo Center
7000 Stullgart 80 (Vaihingen)
Honigwiesenstrabe 25
Postfach 80-08-30
W. Germany

Gleumes & Co.
5000 Kolna Rh
Hohenstauienring, W. Germany

Wild River Book Series

The Parks Branch (Parks Canada, Department of Indian & Northern Affairs, Ottawa) has compiled from its canoeing surveys reports, ten detailed books. Summaries of these routes are contained in this book. The Wild Rivers series began to appear for sale in 1975 at Information Canada bookstores in Halifax, Montreal, Ottawa, Toronto, Winnipeg and Vancouver.

Wild Rivers: Saskatchewan (R62-82/1974-1) } on sale 1975
Wild Rivers: Alberta (R62-82/1974-2)
Wild Rivers: Central British Columbia (R62-82/1974-3)
Wild Rivers: Northwest Mountains (R62-82/1974-4)
Wild Rivers: Yukon Territory (R62-82/1974-5)
Wild Rivers: The Barrenlands (R62-82/1974-6)
Wild Rivers: The James Bay/Hudson Bay Region (R62-82/1974-7)
Wild Rivers: Southwestern Quebec and Eastern Ontario (R62-82/1974-8)
Wild Rivers: Quebec North Shore (R62-82/1974-9)
Wild Rivers: Labrador and Newfoundland (R62-82/1974-10)

A Canoe Routes Data Service

Perhaps I can short-circuit some of your research time by supplying information about the specific canoe route of your choice, from my files on hundreds of detailed routes from which this and former books have been compiled. Because some routes are straight forward and others intricate, I will advise you of my fee for preparing your route report. Drop me a line.

Nick Nickels
Lakefield, Ontario K0L 2H0

CANOES AND CANOE TECHNIQUES

Today's canoe-camper wants to buy a safe and practical canoe that he can use on vacations over many future seasons. As there are many canoe models to choose from, it is important for the canoeist to know which type of craft will best suit his own particular needs. Is the canoe often going to be used for running whitewater or primarily for lake travel — or both?

Each of the four basic types of canoe — cedar, fiberglass, aluminum and birchbark — display different characteristics. The descriptions which follow should help you to begin selecting the proper type of canoe for your purposes:

The *fine cedar strip canoe* is really for "drifting and dreaming". This type is usually judged for its appearance. Most owners of these canoes take great pains to ensure that the canoes are kept in perfect condition. Both the interior and exterior of the canoe are carefully protected from rubbing and scraping and the hull is never left exposed to sunlight when not in use. The cedar strip canoe is also a joy to handle because the hull seems to "give" when paddling. But essentially it is an expensive showpiece that is impractical for serious use.

The *canvas covered cedar plank canoe* is also beautiful in appearance and a delight to paddle. But this canoe does not bear well under rough canoeing conditions and requires frequent minor repairs. The lightness of the canoe (65 pounds) makes for easier portaging. This is partially offset by a further disadvantage: the need for careful off-season storage and maintenance. A more recently developed variation of this canoe is the *fiberglass covered cedar plank canoe*. It is a heavier canoe but will wear well under rough conditions.

Fiberglass canoe hulls with wood or metal gunwales, thwarts, seats and decks do not need regular maintenance. They come in a variety of models, some of which are well-designed while others are very poorly made. There are a number of things that I always immediately look for when considering this type of canoe. Low profile lines give the wind less surface to work on. Seats should be set at least thirteen inches from the floor so that you are able to double the feet under without being cramped when paddling in the proper kneeling position. Seats should be sprung almost level with the gunwale so that the paddler does not have to reach over the gunwale to paddle. Look for a rigid craft, strongly supported by thwarts and seats so that it doesn't wobble.

Fiberglass canoes are widely used, very practical and, being mass produced, are an economical buy. The canoe does not absorb water and at 65-70 pounds is a light craft to portage.

The aluminum canoe is as practical as the fiberglass canoe. It requires no maintenance and can be repaired in the wilderness, even when severely bashed. Most out-

Four types of canoe (clockwise from top left): *the elegant cedar strip is impractical for the serious canoe tripper, but a joy to own and paddle; the light canvas covered craft is easy to portage and a delight to paddle, but it is easily damaged and requires regular maintenance care; the fiberglass variety is very practical and an economic buy; the aluminum canoe is perhaps the most practical of all, although a little heavier than the fiberglass.*

fitters in North American stock aluminum canoes for hire season after season. At 75 pounds, the standard seventeen foot model is light to portage.

The final type of canoe is of course the *Indian birch bark canoe*. All other canoes are based upon this original model. Today, the birchbark canoe no longer serves as a vehicle for transportation but remains a fascinating crafted object. People avidly watch birchbark canoes being made at sportsmen's shows or on Indian reservations. The canoe is made with oak ribs, cedar plank sheathing and woven babiche seats. The birchbark bag is sewn together with watape (white spruce rootlets) and sealed with white spruce gum and fat. It makes for a good show, but of course it is impractical for use. The birchbark canoe should be purchased only as an expensive curio to be hung from the rafters of the summer lodge or cottage.

Whatever your choice of modern canoe, be sure to consider the type of keel. The single centre keel offers advantages for quiet water travel but it manoeuvres slowly in whitewater. The double keel on the other hand manoeuvres quickly in whitewater but is not as good in quiet water.

A canoe should be no shorter than sixteen feet in length. When loaded down and paddling, this is very important. There are a great many short canoes on the market and some are so short that they are dangerous even in quiet water. Short craft were originally designed for trappers to manoeuvre very easily in marshland areas. Modern manufacturers perhaps expect the consumer will want a canoe that is easier to load onto his car rack and to portage. For the canoeist to select a short canoe for these reasons would be foolishness.

It is advisable to buy certain accessories from your canoe dealer:

1. Two 1/4 inch nylon or dacron bow and stern ropes, each ten feet long. Make sure that the canoe rope eye rings are solidly attached to the decks.

2. A fifty foot piece of the same kind of rope. This may be needed for roping canoes down tricky rapids from shorelines and for a variety of rigging uses around camps.

3. Enough canvas material to make a splash cover to keep the canoe load dry from rain and whitewater. The cover should include bow and stern cockpit holes for the paddlers. The portholes should *not* fit so snugly that you won't be able to wriggle out quickly in the event of upset. The finished cover should be secured with harness straps to a tight line under the outside gunwale. This accessory has been praised time and again by experienced canoe trippers.

4. Be prepared to pay a substantial sum for government approved life jackets. This is not a purchase on which to cut corners.

5. It is recommended that the canoeist paddle from a kneeling position, and if he does, pieces of foam cushion material to kneel on will make the method work much better for him.

Canoe Repair Kits

If you are travelling in any wilderness area, you should take along with your first aid kit simple canoe repair material suited to the type of canoe you have.

For the aluminum canoe: Bring a small container of roofing cement to seal small breaks in the canoe skin, pulled rivets and other leaks. It can also be used to hold down fiberglass cloth pieces on the inside of the skin. Heavy polyethylene or plastic tape of strong adhesive quality can be applied to the dried outside of the skin breaks as an alternative method and material.

For the fiberglass canoe: Bring a prepared kit of fiberglass patching pieces and epoxy bonding mixture. Applied to the outside of the hull, epoxy bonds more strongly to cured fiberglass than to the original polyester itself.

The Paddle

It is almost as important to buy a satisfactory paddle as it is to choose the proper canoe. After all, the paddle is an extension of your arm that provides your locomotion for hours, days and weeks at a time. Paddlers generally belong to two distinct schools: wide bladers and narrow bladers.

How long should the paddle be? Should it be long enough to reach the chin, the nose or the forehead? It depends on what you're most comfortable with. A blade that is too long is clumsy. I recommend one that is long enough to reach the nose.

Proponents of the wide blade claim that it pushes more water per stroke and requires less strokes. Proponents of the narrow blade hold the opposite view.

I prefer the narrow blade myself. My own paddles were made by Alvin Avery of Whitney. Roughed out from a hard maple billet, then onto a shaping machine and hand finished, the paddle is five feet seven inches in length. A thin-edged blade measures 5-1/2 inches across with a 3/4 inch fist taper above the blade and a pear-shaped handle that nicely fits the palm. The paddle weighs 2 lbs. and has no wax or varnish.

This paddles is heavier than others but springy. I can swing it automatically for long periods without undue tiring of muscles. Now that I have to buy paddles from the store, I buy spruce and have it trimmed to similar dimensions. Spruce is soft, brittle and frays quickly; but it is the only wood in which one-piece paddles are sold. The painted and stained paddles sold in bargain basements and surplus supply stores should be avoided. Such finishes hide knots, filled cracks and cranky grain.

How long should the paddle be? Should it be long enough to reach the chin, the nose or the forehead? This depends on what you're comfortable with. Certainly a blade that is too long is clumsy.

Paddle blades come in all shapes. Many have names of Indian origin. For example, your outfitter may recommend the Ojibwa shape of my own paddle. Be sure when buying or renting paddles to check for straightness. Much new stock is already warped. When your paddle is not being used, hang it up. Don't stand it in the corner for all paddles warp quickly.

On every trip, carry one extra paddle with each canoe. A paddle can break or float away in fast water. It is a long, difficult chore to paddle back to base with a makeshift branch or piece of driftwood.

Paddle Repair Material

Use fiberglass or epoxy. Face a cracked blade with a single layer of material. For a new paddle, apply it overall. Paddles are so expensive that it's worth it. An old method of repair used to be to hand-drill a series of eyelet holes with an awl along both sides of a crack. These were closed with a lacing of soft copper or brass wire. You can still buy these at wilderness posts.

While on a trip, a cracked paddle should be repaired immediately. This should prevent a broken blade at a time when you don't need such a handicap.

Outboard Motors

Most canoe-campers should really have little need for outboard motors. But older or partially disabled people may find the motor a necessity.

Most manufacturers of popular makes produce a two-horse outboard motor which they recommend for powering a standard 16 foot canoe. Its specifications are:

Full throttle range from 4200 to 4800 rpm

Speeds from slow troll (2 mph) to full cruising at 9 mph

Two-cycle cylinder

Built-in gas tank which holds two quarts of fuel mix

Motor weighs 24 lbs.

The manufacturers claim that a normal day's travel at trolling speed uses about one tankful of gas.

In addition to the motor, the tripper must have a metal outrigger motor mount bracket that attaches to the left hand side of the canoe near the stern. It's recommended over the homemade wooden bracket. Gas containers will add considerably to your portaging weight. But if your trip logistics are accurate, you may find marine facilities for refilling along chosen routes.

Optional accessories include a J-shaped metal bracket (to ease the carrying of the motor on the shoulder blades) and a winter motor storage case. Musts are a simple tool kit and a couple of spark plugs.

By Road

All vehicle owners should have the foresight to houseclean car trunks of junk and unseasonal baggage, for they will need every inch of stowage space they can create.

The family tripping unit will use one vehicle while a larger group will require a fleet arrangement and the suitable distribution of passengers and gear. Some groups will load a flatbed snowmobile trailer with canoes and some gear. Others will resort to rooftop car carriers. This method requires very cautious and knowledgeable know-how.

First, you will have made sure your carrier bars are wide enough to extend beyond the beam of the canoe, or if two canoes are carried instead, wider still. In either case, stout wooden extension bars bolted to the metal carrier bars are needed.

Tighten the carrier tie-downs and, if necessary, replace frayed ones. Lift the single canoe onto the carrier, turn it over and centre it back, front and sideways. Starting at the stern, thread a coil of 1/4 inch nylon rope over the hull and through the top of the stern seat, crisscrossing the ends to tie to left and right ends respectively of the rear bumper.

At the bow end, pull the canoe forward tightly to snug the stern bindings. Fashion a second crisscross "harness" making sure it is positioned on the hull back of the bow, pull the ends of rope tightly forward, down and tie to the ends of front bumper. Secure the canoe amidships with tight lengths of shock cord spaced over the hull and hooked to carrier gutters.

Never use the single bow painter (rope) to secure the front of the canoe to the centre of the bumper. The rope can fray if it's not sufficiently tight, which could result in your canoe flying off the roof to cause undetermined accidents to your own and other cars on highspeed highways. Some regions in the United States will soon legislate safe methods of transporting canoes, I believe, and none too soon.

Before reaching your launching site you should advise police, forestry officials or other responsible authorities of the names and addresses of your party members, your proposed route and trip time. This is a most necessary procedure.

At The Launching Site

Trippers who have planned a loop canoe route or who will travel to launch site and be picked up at journey's end by charter air support, have only the chore of parking and securing their road vehicles. But the choice of downstream routes brings up the problem of vehicle logistics. If yours is a two car operation, unload both cars at the launch site and drive both cars to the finish point. Leave one car and return to the launching site with the other. The U-route presents yet another problem, starts and finishes at different road endings. Arrange with a co-operative service station to ferry cars back to the station from the launch site, store them and ferry them to the agreed finish point on agreed dates.

Loading & Launching the Canoe

Unload the canoe from its carrier and float it parallel to shore if the water is calm and deep enough, or at right angles to shore if the water is rough and shallow, with the stern at shore. Here is where you will first get your feet wet, wading to load the canoe. Lay poles on canoe bottom to keep the load dry from bilge water.

Load two heavy packsacks amidships, side by side or end to end and the third pack ahead of the sternman. Stow tents and sleeping bag rolls, grub box and haversacks

beside, back of or in front of packsacks, always mindful of weight trim. Small pieces can be stowed ahead of the bowman. The bow must ride slightly higher than the stern. Allow a six inch free-board i.e., the waterline should come no higher than a six inch mark below the gunwales. Be sure the whole load floats sideways level at all times.

Some last-minute adjustments to make are to have the route map section folded in the map case and secured with compass to the top of that dunnage that is within reach of the sternman. Also have the handle of the extra paddle stowed and handy to sternman who is the captain, steersman and navigator. If it is raining at take-off cover the load with tent fly or a plastic sheet brought along for the purpose.

While the sternman steadies the loaded canoe the bowman takes his place in a kneeling position; the sternman may have to shove off by wading into the water until the canoe floats, all the while holding onto the tops of the gunwales ahead of his paddling position. He steps lightly into the canoe onto the keel and kneels gingerly to his paddling position. As both canoeists become more adept at balancing in a floating canoe such movements will become smooth and automatic. After making the necessary last-minute load and balance adjustments only then can you strike off.

Paddling the Guide Stroke

After many years of canoeing, I found when I began teaching a group of women that the "J stroke or hook stroke" which they were interested in learning, was the same stroke that fishing guides had taught me when I was a child. The stroke looks very energetic but is not, for my guide-tutors were not energetic men. It was the easiest method on their muscles and it became automatic to them in a very short time.

- Kneel on the bottom of the canoe with some padding under the knees, which should be spread outward to the curved sides of the hull to give the paddler a gripping, steady balance.
- Do not sit on the seat but rest the rump on the forward edge of the seat with feet doubled under the seat and crossed, soles uppermost. This is why I recommend a canoe with a seat 13 inches above the floor, to allow for easy untangling of crossed feet in the event of upset. Go in soft footwear or sock feet to prevent cramp in the foot arch.
- Bowman and steerman paddle on opposite sides at all times.

Top left: *the food and cooking equipment before being packed in a wooden grub box. Eliminate as many boxes, cans and other excess wrappings as possible. Nesting pots and a stove can be packed in a previously soiled packsack.* **Top right**: *personal gear is kept separate from the food. It can be contained in one large packsack (see also below).* **Centre left**: *to board correctly, place both hands on the gunwales and step into the centre of the canoe. The correct paddling position is kneeling.* **Centre right**: *it is important to load the canoe properly with the packs and grub box amidships. The weight should be distributed so that when fully loaded the bow is slightly higher than the stern (see also below).* **Lower left**: *the canoe is properly loaded and the paddlers ready for take-off, with paddles held low and outspread. The bowman does not paddle with a hook or "J" stroke but instead uses a plain, water-pulling stroke.* **Lower right**: *the canoe here exhibits proper weight distribution but the paddlers in my opinion are holding their paddles raised too high. In this position the paddles are too close to the canoe and the stroke will have to be deep, digging and tiresome, rather than more shallow and easy to maintain for long periods.*

Top left: *the sternman's "hook" or "J" stroke. All strokes are short — from knee to waist. The stroke begins with the paddle off the gunwale. As the paddle is brought back, it is also brought in to* **just** *touch the gunwale. Then, simultaneously, the blade is slightly twisted and the stroke continues in a short, sharp hook away from the gunwale. The paddle handle should never be higher than the shoulder. Keep the knees spread to gain the best support and the strongest thrust. Allow the torso to twist into the stroke. The canoe can be ferried sideways by either a zig-zag sculling of the paddle, pulling toward the hull (**top right**), or a digging, prying, leverage stroke, using the gunwale as a fulcrum (**lower left**). The former technique will move the canoe in the direction of the side being paddled and is useful inshore for approaching the shore or a dock. The latter technique will move the canoe in the direction opposite the side being paddled and is useful offshore.* **Lower right:** *to turn, while the sternman paddles forward on the opposite side with strong, outward sweeping strokes.*

- Grasp the paddle with one hand hooked over the top, the other grasped around the shaft of the blade but below the outside gunwale. Lower the angle of attack by lowering the top hand to chest level. This pushes the blade outward, almost parallel to the water.
- The sternman with the top hand at chest height dips his paddle in the water at knee point, pulls back on the blade and, at the seat point, rests the shaft quickly on the gunwale, twists both wrists outward while the blade makes a flat, continuous, oval motion. This is the J, or hook or guide stroke. The more twist-fulcrum pressure applied by the sternman the more he controls the bow of the canoe, to swing in the direction he wants it to point. The trick is to exert just enough pressure to direct the bow as straight as possible toward a given landmark. If the canoe is well balanced and loaded with the bowman stroking at the same speed, the sternman will take several strokes without pressure-hooking and only apply it when needed.
- The short quick strokes should reach a tempo of 30 to the minute. This can easily be achieved and maintained after back and forearm muscles become limbered up. The bowman never uses the hook stroke. Paddlers should change sides every ten minutes or so to rest tired muscles.
- Smooth tandem paddling takes considerable practice. It can start early in the season near home, perhaps, and by trip time you will understand in watching floundering novices why they are not getting anywhere and are wearing themselves out in the attempt.

Reading the Weather

Important to canoeing is the ability to read weather. Canoeists can benefit from the experience of such professional outdoorsmen as farmers, fishermen, sailors, prospectors, lumbermen, pilots and native people who automatically read weather as a part of their vocations. Most of them have reduced forecasting to simple cues that are remarkably accurate:

A red sky at morning is a sailor's warning; a red sky at night is a sailor's delight.

When a north wind veers clockwise to east and then west, clear weather can be expected; when a north wind backs into northwest and then west, worsening conditions will follow.

In deteriorating weather smoke flows down to the ground; in fair weather smoke rises.

Dew in the morning foretells fine weather; a dewless night and morning do not. Sudden storms are generally of short duration while storms with a sustained buildup are long lasting.

Mountainous thunderheads, with flattened anvil tops, accompanied by lightning flashes and rumbling can warn you how far away the storm is. Divide the number of seconds between the flash and the thunder by five. So if there is a lapse of twenty seconds, the storm is about four miles away. Head for shore and stay put until the weather clears.

Don't be deceived by calm shoreline water at the campsite: offshore wind and high waves could be just ahead. You can only hope your destination is down wind. Never paddle beyond the point of easy return on expansive stretches of strange lakes.

In regions with prevailing winds, the winds will usually begin building up after 10 A.M. and decreasing towards evening. Fair weather usually precedes and follows this period. Experienced canoeists have found under such conditions, that it is wise to break camp and start paddling shortly after daylight. During midday and afternoon, it is often wise to hole up and camp for a while.

Running Whitewater

It is almost presumptuous to attempt to explain moving water. The canoeist can only learn from his own experience. However, an understanding of certain principles is essential to safe whitewater canoeing.

Canoeists should not run whitewater alone but in a group. Only an experienced woodsman who has spent his life on rivers is knowledgeable enough to attempt river-running alone. A minimum of three canoes or teams is advisable. Such numbers ensure a sensible interdependence.

A river is always strange to a group even if it has been travelled in the past. Water conditions always change, whether it be due to recent rains, late run-off or drought. Nothing is constant about moving water but change. The group must always assess a river in terms of the immediate conditions.

It is the nature of lake chains that as water funnels from one to the next that a drop in elevation occurs through narrowing water channels. Canoeists are continually faced with the problem of accurately appraising the whitewater channels ahead. Three choices are open to canoeists: run the water; line the canoe down by ropes from the shoreline; portage around the entire whitewater section.

To run whitewater it is best for the group to begin by landing ashore above the water. The members of the group should then walk around and study the conditions so as to adopt the proper strategy for running the rapids. The two most experienced canoeists should be well spaced apart. The lead canoe must never be passed by another nor must the last canoe ever pass another.

I will not attempt to explain the basic techniques of canoeing in whitewater, for I am not expert at it. But young, athletic canoeists are continually learning under the supervision of expert club guidance. There are also a number of excellent books on the subject which explain the basic techniques. While no substitute from the real thing, these manuals are an excellent preparation for it. Commendably, these books emphasize the seriousness of whitewater canoeing and the need for constant practice and upgrading.

The following chart presents a number of different canoeing positions. This should indicate to the novice team the various canoeing positions open to them in various whitewater situations. The expert instructor can teach you how to assume these positions and why they are necessary.

Each team keeps the team behind it in sight, waiting if it's necessary to do so. The group leader must be a very knowledgeable and responsible person. He knows that the river always wins and the only way to meet its challenge is through paddling skills. Once a decision is reached, it must be executed quickly with no hesitations.

A few of the basic precautions the group leader should see to before the drop begins:

The 1/4 inch nylon tracking lines in each canoe should be fastened loosely between the bow and stern seat outside the gunwale on each side. (Grab lines in the event of upset).

The tie strings of each member's life preserver should be loosened so that if he is upset into vertical counter currents he can slip out of the jacket (which might otherwise trap him under the water) and grab for the loose safety lines under the gunwales.

The spare paddle in each canoe should be tied loosely to the top of the load so that it can be jerked free quickly in the event that a paddle is lost or broken during the drop. Tie packs and haversacks to thwarts.

Reading A River

Landing above a whitewater section ahead, the canoeing group assesses the difficulties ahead but does not finalize strategy until some members have walked ahead along the stream banks to study each difficulty to be overcome. In this following diagram the manoeuvering pattern of the lead canoe only is shown:

Avoid the first midstream boulder by changing course well ahead of it to the right. If you change course too late, the canoe will drift sideways against the rock, fill with water, capsize and probably damage the canoe.

Drift sideways with the current before straightening the canoe into the centre of the main current.

Paddle straight through past the rocks on the right. Then, allowing for the current to drift the canoe sideways around the sharp bend, drift stern first into the eddy at right.

Drift down the fast current that follows the left bank and slip bow first into the slack water behind the midstream boulder. Half pivot the canoe to the right into the main current that has now shifted course towards the right bank.

The paddlers hear falls ahead, see rising spray and ferry right across the current to land above the falls on the left bank. Carry the canoe and luggage across the portage to the smooth water below the obstruction, reload and push off.

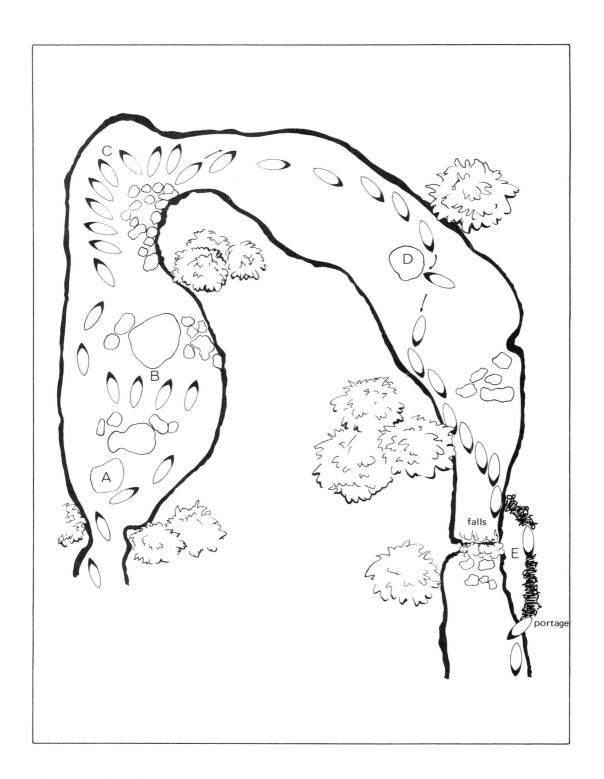

Portaging

Whether you follow the English pronounciation of pōr'tij or the French pōr tāj' (as in mirage), you will find that the bull work of carrying the canoe and gear is necessary on the shortest of canoe trips.

Although your maps may indicate the approximate whereabouts of rapids, you must keep your ears attuned to the tumbling sound of rough water ahead and your eyes peeled for shore signs of the used portage carrying place. (These days unfortunately, portages are often marked by the trail of litter.) Land, assess the situation and pace it out. If in doubt about your ability to run the fast water, portage.

Canoe carrying may be simplified if the centre thwart is a built-in yoke. If not, lash a pair of paddle blades foremost to the back seat and centre thwart, leaving head room between them. Use a life preserver or rolled clothing for shoulder pads.

Grasp the near gunwale of the upright canoe at the bow seat with both hands and pull the canoe onto your forelegs above the knee. With your left hand grasping the near gunwale, reach over and grasp the far gunwale with your right hand. You should be facing the stern of the canoe, with the stern on the ground.

Swing the canoe above your head while twisting your body towards the bow end. Move backwards to the paddles notch, or yoke, until the stern end lifts from the

The strongest of the team does the heavy portaging work. He rolls and twists the canoe from the front of his upper legs, raises it and then drops its weight onto his shoulders. The paddles have previously been tied in a V-shape to the thwarts so that they can come to rest on the shoulders. He completes the carry with as many rests as he feels necessary.

ground. Shift position until the canoe balances, keeping the bow raised slightly to see where you are walking. To settle the canoe to the ground after the carry, carefully reverse the exercise.

The canoe toter generally fits loose objects into a light packsack before hoisting the craft to his shoulders. It is a common sight to see an experienced canoeman crossing a gentle portage with the camp axe in one free hand and the tea pail in the other.

But wrasslin' the packsack to the back also has a knack. Kneeling, lift the pack to the right knee, straps facing you. Poke your right arm through the right strap, heave and swing the pack backwards onto your back. When the pack is settled into place, reach back with the left arm and fit it into the loose left strap. (I don't recommend the popular tubular back frames beloved by backpackers. They are awkward to fit snugly into the bottom of the canoe, the pack material is not as tough and the overall pack is smaller than its canvas counterpart.)

With the main pack in position, you can carefully reach down and swing up sleeping bags, rolls and other light bulky gear to ride on top. Perhaps your canoe toter will help you get into your pack harness and send you along the portage ahead of him so that he can watch for fallen articles.

Your soft muscles will soon harden up to this bull work and, since you are on holiday, you can rest frequently and set a leisurely pace.

CAMPING

A wood campfire affords one of the great pleasures of canoe camping. But it is sometimes a luxury, for well-used campsites have often been stripped bare of fuel for considerable distances. Also, be sure to check for forestry signs prohibiting fires in areas with hazardously dry conditions.

For gathering wood, canoeists have something of an advantage over other campers. During the day, canoeists can keep their eyes open for suitable burning materials — dried twigs and branches, the frayed outer layers of birchbark and occasional pieces of dry stumps. Be sure to take along a garbage bag for stowing fuel materials. Suggested for gathering wood are a 1-1/2 lb. hand axe (not a hatchet) and a 15 inch folding Swede saw.

For cooking over wood fires a folding wire grill is a great help. Preferrably take a mini-barbecue stand and charcoal. White gas fuel, propane or butane stoves force you to load up with extra fuel that has to be toted over portages. Bring along four nested aluminum cooking pots, round or square. Heavy foil can be used for making utensils, wrapping food and as a reflector surface for baking biscuits, cookies or bannock. A paperback book on foil cookery is well worth studying. Experiment at home with meals and take the book along with you for ready reference.

Useful as well are an oven mitt, a long-handled fork, spoon and flipper; an iron fry pan with a long extension handle; a strong five inch blade hunting knife and sheath. Keep the knife sharp. A good knife is a tripping and camping tool of 100 uses.

Plastic coated paper plates don't get soggy and should be burned after use. Bring heavy plastic cups and a good supply of metal or plastic knives, forks and spoons.

Heavy polyethelene disposal bags are a must. Burn all trash that is flammable, including soft plastics. All foil, metals, tins and glass should be taken to disposal areas — not buried in the camp latrine. Take another heavy polyethelene bag to hold all sooty campfire gear. This will keep it from fouling other things and helps avoid pot scrubbing after every meal.

Sleeping bags vary considerably in price and quality. Bags can be down filled or quilted in cotton. All have outer nylon shells and strong zippers. For the individual, a mummy-shaped bag is good, while for small children who can double up, a smaller square bag is suitable. Also as good are flannelette sheet liners that keep bags both warm and clean inside. In fair weather, bags can and should be aired out regularly, and especially after rain or dunking.

A foam pad of at least 3 inches thickness is very popular as an outdoors mattress. Cut it from large pieces of material to fit the user from shoulders to hips. Also cut out kneeling pads for padding from the same material. Air them as well. For adults with small children, a four-man tent may be the best. But adults by themselves are best off with a two-man tent.

There are good tents in either lightweight woven cotton or nylon. A good tent should have a low profile, a sewn floor, netting doorway and ventilation windows. An

Left: *a warm sleeping bag in place before dark and the tent pre-sprayed against insects, ensures a good night's rest, in spite of strange wildlife sounds.* **Right:** *keeping campfires under control should be one of the canoe tripper's chief concerns. When breaking camp, drown the fire thoroughly and "paddle" the ashes with a stick to ensure that it is completely extinguished.*

overlapping fly sheet to drain off heavy rain, provide insulation space and lessen the tent's strain in spells of excessive wind is desirable. Include telescoping aluminum poles and plastic tent pegs. Use a 50 foot length of 1/4 inch nylon rope. You could use the extended aluminum tent poles on the bottom of the canoe to keep your packs from lying in the bilge created from rain or wave slop. My preference would be to cut and carry at all times stout sapling poles for that purpose. The poles can be used to advantage around campsites, too.

An army surplus store folding shovel is a handy camp tool for digging the latrine and trenching around the tent perimeter to run off heavy rain that would form in puddles under the woven tent floor. An obvious warning: do not pitch tent on a ground hollow.

Food

Thank goodness the bacon-bean-flapjack era of camping has vanished forever. It has been replaced by instant-powdered, dehydrated, freeze-dried foods that are nourishing and have elevated the woman canoeist from the squaw role in preparing foods. Back-yard barbecue cooking has come to involve all members of the family as cooks. May they continue it at campside.

Do as much of your food shopping at home as possible to avoid the high mark-up of wilderness outfitters. You may however have to replenish staples at outpost stores. If you wish, complete packaged meals are available. Just add lake water and stir. But it is far more economical to buy piecemeal instead, using as a yardstick 3,500 calories per person per day. The buying of dry staples, spices, soaps, toilet paper, drugs and so forth will not change from the norm.

The campfire meal, perhaps the canoe tripper's greatest reward.

When choosing one-dish, freeze dried stews and casseroles avoid chicken-styled or beef-flavoured brands that list the vegetables bases first. Deal at store management level if you have to and don't be put off with "not available" or "just-as-good" substitutes. You can choose from cake, muffin and pastry mixes; dried fruit juice substitutes, instant rice and potatoes. Consider buying rich fruit cake in bulk as an energy substitute for chocolate bars that tend to heighten thirst.

When assembling food supplies at home, do away with as many dry food containers, jars, tins, plastic bottles as possible (not disposing of box top instructions and brand names). Repack where possible in sturdy plastic bags; seal with sticky tape. You must eliminate all extra weight in this manner, for you have to carry your food, shelter and tools over portage trails.

You should experiment at home with strange packaged foods that may intrigue you at the time of purchase. My young canoeing relatives have come to detest a scrambled egg-mushroom mixture, for instance. You may wean the family away from home fare by taking along for the first day on the water left-over, perishable foods from the fridge. Such food will thaw without spoilage during that short period, providing you judge just the right amount of perishables and use them up quickly.

Personal Gear

Begin with clothing. Layers of light, warm clothing that can be peeled off and layered back on again are warmer and more convenient than heavy outside jackets and parkas. An overall nylon shell is the sensible substitute. Consider long johns, warm-suits and rubber scuba suits for use on icy subarctic routes. Disposable panties for men and women will eliminate some laundry problems. Burn soiled garments with other burnable trash on post-meal fires.

Running shoes, stout leather moccasins and heavy wool socks are recommended footwear. These will dry out eventually, but wet feet are always the price of canoe-tripping. I belong to the old school that argues against the wearing of heavy bush boots in a canoe. They're dangerous when upsets occur. One-piece wool mitts rather than wool gloves are a great comfort at times. Wet mitts are warm for some reason, as all maritime commercial fishermen will tell you. A poncho, rather than a two-piece rain suit or long raincoat, is the sensible rain garment. It can double for a load splash cover or a sail before a following wind. Masting can be fashioned from your tent poles. Take a stiff wide-brimmed hat for rain and to support a mosquito net.

The emergency kit should be packed in its own bright colored haversack, secured to the canoe load at all times. All members of the party should be familiar with its contents and their use. One person should be responsible for guarding it afloat and ashore.

You may want to include additional items to the kit, but basically it should contain the following items that have been stripped of bulky store packaging and compressed into a flat survival package:

Aspirin tablets; bouillon cubes; band aids; tubes of antiseptic ointment; squares of unsweetened chocolate; compressed roll of heavy aluminum foil; twenty-five feet of nylon fishing line and twelve small fish hooks; twenty-five feet of nylon string to weave a brush shelter together; water purifying tablets or a small phial of Javex (two drops to the cup;) a small bundle of waxed kitchen matches in a waterproof plastic container; small piece of yellow laundry soap; small plastic container of baking soda. First Aid Manual.

The same haversack can hold camera and film in strong polyethelene, sealed bags; binnoculars; unused route maps; canoe repair kits; sunglasses when not in use; spare eyeglasses and so forth.

Choosing the right packsack is an especially important decision. Three packs for two people per canoe load is the general rule. Picking a suitable packsack, bushmen say, is "as chancy as choosing a wife." The basic rule to follow is to choose the pack that feels most comfortable on your body and suits your carry capacity. I prefer the heavy khaki duck pack measuring 25 by 21 by 8-inch wall with strong leather shoulder straps and the added accessory, the leather tumpline.

Canoe trippers keen on backpacking and cross-country skiing will argue that the light nylon packsack with metal frame is best. I feel that for the rough and tumble, the wetting, the tugging and pulling, the heavy canvas has the longest life.

Perhaps clever packers can eliminate one of the three packsacks with a grub box — homemade, 18 by 24 by 14 inch deep, plywood, with rope handles and hinged lid. Experienced trippers swear by them. Fiberglass grub boxes are also being made. Styrofoam cooler chests are brittle and should not be considered at all, nor should metal chests that will sink during an upset.

Those Damn Bugs

Canada's summer scourge of blackflies and mosquitoes is legendary. Seventy-four species of mosquitoes, 120 species of blackflies, and innumerable types of horseflies, sand flies and ticks are a nuisance that every outdoorsman knows well and must cope with.

Blackflies are a serious nuisance in August in some parts of the Arctic north of the tree line and in southern Baffin Island. In such areas, the Queen Elizabeth Islands or tiny Sable Island, southwest of the Nova Scotia mainland, there are no blackflies but also no canoeing.

Mosquitoes on the other hand are just about everywhere. As their peak breeding periods do not coincide with that of the blackflies, the bug season spreads out even longer. The accompanying map and table indicate the length of the season for blackflies and mosquitoes in different parts of the country as well as their periods of peak abundance. This information has been supplied by Dr. Monty Wood, Biosystematics Research Institute, Agriculture Canada, Ottawa.

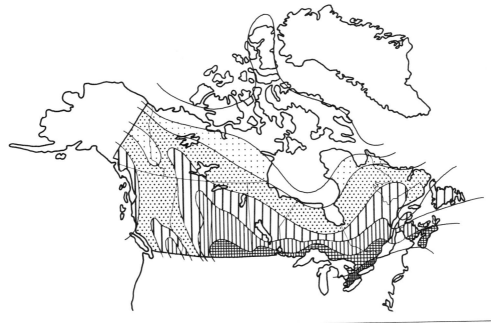

TOTAL SEASONAL PREVALENCE OF MOSQUITOES and BLACK FLIES		PEAK ABUNDANCE	
		Blackflies	Mosquitoes
	1 July - 10 Aug	nil	June 25 - July 30
	21 June - 20 Aug	Aug 1 - 15	June 25 - July 30
	11 June - 31 Aug	July	June 15 - July 30
	1 June - 10 Sept	July	June 10 - July 30
	21 May - 20 Sept	early June - mid July	June 1 - Aug. 10
	11 May - 30 Sept	June	May 24 - Aug 1
	1 May - 10 Oct	mid-May/mid-June nil/southern Ont	May 24 - Aug 1*
			several peaks * possible, depending on rains

In Southern Ontario, blackflies precede or accompany mosquitoes whereas in the far north, they lag behind. Generally, in the more southern regions of Canada, the rivers warm up more quickly so that larvae are ready to pop out in early or mid May. But in the Yukon, for example, the rivers are frigid all summer long while tiny, shallow mosquito pools warm up each day in the sun. Every ten degrees fahrenheit upward or downward doubles or halves the rate of breeding. The millions of miles of streams and rivers and innumerable puddles, make it impossible to control the blackfly and mosquito populations in the north.

Blackflies

Wear light colored clothing — a white shirt if practical and a white or light colored kerchief. Blackflies love dark blue, purple and black. Blue jeans may help draw them away from your head, but check for holes.

Blackflies like to crawl into clothing before biting. So, button your sleeves, use elastic bands if necessary and keep your shirt tucked in at all times. Wear tightly laced, high shoes: blackflies easily gain access to rubber boots and crawl down into the sock cuffs if they are not tight. Completely cover your hair with a white kerchief or hat.

Always have a head net in your kit in case pests appear in unbearable hordes as they often do quite unexpectedly, especially in the evenings. It is easy to make a very satisfactory head net. Simply tie a sleeve of nylon netting around the hat band or close it over the hair with an elastic closure on top and with the bottom tucked in below the shirt collar.

For materials, purchase a rectangle of netting approximately 1-1/2 by 2 feet. Look through the netting for transparency before buying it, because the duller it is the less light it will allow to reflect into your eyes. The holes should be about 1/16 inch in diameter.

You can also try repellant, but don't rely on it. Some species of blackflies seem unaffected or possibly even stimulated by it. But before you get all wrapped up, check to see if the flies are really biting. Often they are just flying in close and may not start biting until later in the day. "There is no use buttoning up for nothing," says the very experienced Dr. Wood.

Mosquitoes

The first thing mosquitoes do after hatching is mate. The male dies within a week and the female goes after a blood meal — the action of biting — and flies off to some dense bush cover for four days to give the blood a chance to nourish her eggs. She does not need to mate again to lay another batch of eggs. All she needs is another blood meal. The number of hatches of eggs depends on the number of meals — or bites.

Nobody knows why some people are more susceptible to being bitten than others. The female mosquito zooms in on your body scent and the scent of your expelled carbon dioxide. She opens up a hole in your skin, slips in two tubes to pump in her saliva and pump it out again mixed with your blood. It takes about a minute. The most aggressive and persistent female mosquitoes leave the most progeny. Personal protection, says Dr. Wood, is the only solution for canoe-campers. Which is really not a difficult matter except in very hot weather.

Diethyl toluamide ("deet") in liquid form is indispensable. One leading brand now has nearly 50 per cent toluamide and another is still stronger at 70 per cent. One small bottle can last a month. Avoid products with lower percentages; they have to be applied more liberally and more often. Leave the spray can at home if either weight or space presents a problem. The convenience of the can is more than offset by its very low percentage of toluamide.

A head net against mosquitoes is a useful addition to your kit. It is a must in July in the subarctic forest or barren grounds regions. If it's not too hot, a second shirt will help prevent mosquitoes biting through. All clothing should be of tightly woven cotton; knitted fabrics are as porous to a mosquito's mouth parts as cheesecloth.

It's not as vital to seal up sleeves and pant legs as it is against blackflies, unless one is sitting still. Repellant around wrists and ankles is sufficient, for mosquitoes do not crawl into clothing as do blackflies. Pant legs will certainly protect your ankles. Colour of clothing doesn't seem to matter for mosquitoes.

Sand Flies

It is difficult to know how to deal with sand flies, except to keep moving slowly. The flies are very poor flyers and sometimes to move only a few hundred feet will be enough for a person to get away from them. Unfortunately for canoeists, sand flies seem most abundant near river waters. Standard mosquito netting does not seem to keep them out and it is almost impossible to purchase a netting that will be effective. Fortunately, sand flies are intolerably abundant only in the boreal forest regions of Eastern Canada. For canoeists in this region a completely sealed tent is a must which, on warm evenings, can be unbearable.

Horse and Deer Flies

These pests are abundant, too, especially in the Hudson Bay lowlands. Their noise alone is a nuisance. Only wearing a head net can stop them completely, although a hat helps to keep deer flies out of one's hair. No scientific work seems to have been done on their color preferences. Repellant seems to discourage horse and deer flies from biting but does not drive them away. Except on hot days, neither species is really a problem.

Dr. Wood advises that the Canadian Armed Forces are developing an open mesh, parka-like shirt that has been impregnated with toluamide. If they're safe and effective, he predicts that such garments may soon be commercially available.

Ticks

Ticks are wingless parasites which depend on blood for existence. They are found in open areas on trails, clearings and forest edges, but rarely in dense growth.

Of the many species of ticks found in Canadian national parks, you may draw slight comfort that only two species bite humans:

| American dog tick | - found in Kejimkujik National Park, Nova Scotia and Riding Mountain National Park, Manitoba, from April to mid-July. |
| Rocky Mountain Wood Tick | - found at Kootenay, Glacier and Yoho National Parks, all in B.C., and Elk Island, Banff and Jasper National Parks, all in Alberta; from March to mid-May in B.C. and from April until late June in Alberta. |

Remove a tick from the skin by holding the front part of it and pull slowly; a sudden pull may result in its mouth parts remaining in the skin. If this happens, remove the insect as you would an ordinary splinter and treat with antiseptic.

You may have heard that the Rocky Mountain Wood Ticks are carriers of such diseases as Rocky Mountain Spotted Fever, Colorado Tick Fever, Tularaemia and tick paralysis. Very few cases of such tick-related diseases have been reported in Canada. Prompt removal of the insect will minimize the possibility of such illnesses. For instance, a Rocky Mountain Wood Tick would have to be attached to the skin from four to six days before any symptoms of tick paralysis became apparent, and then the symptoms would disappear quickly once the tick was removed.

Survival

The "Be Prepared" watchword of Boy Scout and Girl Guide memory is no corny catch phrase. An injury, broken or lost gear, sickness, starvation or straying from a charted waterway are all very real emergencies, indeed, when they occur miles from communication centres. A serious canoeist should have one or more good books on survival practices in his home library and study them thoroughly before starting out. From these a novice can pickup hints on how to put together simple survival equipment whose applications on the spot are limited only by his ingenuity.

I have laid out a personal basic survival kit in an earlier section that should help deal with emergencies encountered in the bush. Here are some applications:

Poison Ivy

First learn to spot this poisonous three-leafed plant and, if possible, avoid walking through it. The poison smears on the skin from the oily surfaces of the leaves. It can be transmitted by brushing the hands against footwear after walking through it. Rub affected parts with yellow laundry soap from the kit and let dry. It relieves the itch. Some lucky people are not allergic to the plant.

Bee and Wasp Stings

Include the necessary medication in your first-aid kit if you are allergic to these poisons. Otherwise, apply a mud pack of water or spittle and organic soil. A water and baking soda paste is also effective.

Snake Bites

Check with the wildlife departments for information on venomous snakes in the region